Consumer Behavior
MKTG 351

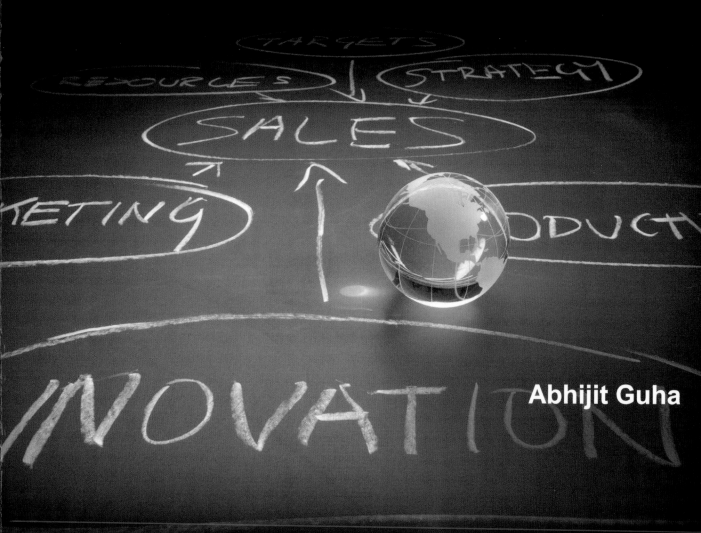

Abhijit Guha

UNIVERSITY OF SOUTH CAROLINA

MARKETING DEPARTMENT

Course   Consumer Behavior
MKTG 351

Abhijit Guha

UNIVERSITY OF SOUTH CAROLINA

MARKETING DEPARTMENT

http://create.mheducation.com

ISBN-10: 1308541104   ISBN-13: 9781308541105

Contents

Credits

Utility Maximization

CHAPTER **7**

Utility Maximization

Learning Objectives

LO7.1 Define and explain the relationship between total utility, marginal utility, and the law of diminishing marginal utility.

LO7.2 Describe how rational consumers maximize utility by comparing the marginal utility-to-price ratios of all the products they could possibly purchase.

LO7.3 Explain how a demand curve can be derived by observing the outcomes of price changes in the utility-maximization model.

LO7.4 Discuss how the utility-maximization model helps highlight the income and substitution effects of a price change.

LO7.5 Give examples of several real-world phenomena that can be explained by applying the theory of consumer behavior.

LO7.6 (Appendix) Relate how the indifference curve model of consumer behavior derives demand curves from budget lines, indifference curves, and utility maximization.

If you were to compare the shopping carts of almost any two consumers, you would observe striking differences. Why does Paula have potatoes, peaches, and Pepsi in her cart, while Sam has sugar, saltines, and 7-Up in his? Why didn't Paula also buy pasta and plums? Why didn't Sam have soup and spaghetti on his grocery list?

In this chapter, you will see how individual consumers allocate their incomes among the various goods and services available to them. Given a certain budget, how does a consumer decide which goods and services to buy? This chapter will develop a model to answer this question.

Law of Diminishing Marginal Utility

LO7.1 Define and explain the relationship between total utility, marginal utility, and the law of diminishing marginal utility.

The simplest theory of consumer behavior rests squarely on the **law of diminishing marginal utility.** This principle, first discussed in Chapter 3, is that added satisfaction declines as a consumer acquires additional units of a given product. Although consumer wants in general may be insatiable, wants for particular items can be satisfied. In a specific span of time over which consumers' tastes remain unchanged, consumers can obtain as much of a particular good or service as they can afford. But the more of that product they obtain, the less they want still more of it.

Consider durable goods, for example. A consumer's desire for an automobile, when he or she has none, may be very strong. But the desire for a second car is less intense; and for a third or fourth, weaker and weaker. Unless they are collectors, even the wealthiest families rarely have more than a half-dozen cars, although their incomes would allow them to purchase a whole fleet of vehicles.

Terminology

Evidence indicates that consumers can fulfill specific wants with succeeding units of a product but that each added unit provides less utility than the last unit purchased. Recall that a consumer derives utility from a product if it can satisfy a want: **Utility** is want-satisfying power. The utility of a good or service is the satisfaction or pleasure one gets from consuming it. Keep in mind three characteristics of this concept:

- "Utility" and "usefulness" are not synonymous. Paintings by Picasso may offer great utility to art connoisseurs but are useless functionally (other than for hiding a crack on a wall).

- Utility is subjective. The utility of a specific product may vary widely from person to person. A lifted pickup truck may have great utility to someone who drives off-road but little utility to someone unable or unwilling to climb into the rig. Eyeglasses have tremendous utility to someone who has poor eyesight but no utility to a person with 20-20 vision.

- Utility is difficult to quantify. But for purposes of illustration we assume that people can measure satisfaction with units called *utils* (units of utility). For example, a particular consumer may get 100 utils of satisfaction from a smoothie, 10 utils of

satisfaction from a candy bar, and 1 util of satisfaction from a stick of gum. These imaginary units of satisfaction are convenient for quantifying consumer behavior for explanatory purposes.

Total Utility and Marginal Utility

Total utility and marginal utility are related, but different, ideas. **Total utility** is the total amount of satisfaction or pleasure a person derives from consuming some specific quantity—for example, 10 units—of a good or service. **Marginal utility** is the *extra* satisfaction a consumer realizes from an additional unit of that product—for example, from the eleventh unit. Alternatively, marginal utility is the change in total utility that results from the consumption of 1 more unit of a product.

Figure 7.1(Key Graph) and the accompanying table demonstrate the relation between total utility and marginal utility. The curves reflect the data in the table. Column 2 shows the total utility associated with each level of consumption of tacos. Column 3 shows the marginal utility—the change in total utility— that results from the con-

ORIGIN OF THE IDEA

07.1
Diminishing marginal utility

sumption of each successive taco. Starting at the origin in Figure 7.1a, observe that each of the first five units increases total utility (TU), but by a diminishing amount. Total utility reaches a maximum with the addition of the sixth unit and then declines.

So in Figure 7.1b marginal utility (MU) remains positive but diminishes through the first five units (because total utility increases at a declining rate). Marginal utility is zero for the sixth unit (because that unit doesn't change total utility). Marginal utility then becomes negative with the seventh unit and beyond (because total utility is falling). Figure 7.1b and table column 3 reveal that each successive taco yields less extra utility, meaning fewer utils, than the preceding taco.[1] That is, the table and graph illustrate the law of diminishing marginal utility.

Marginal Utility and Demand

The law of diminishing marginal utility explains why the demand curve for a given product slopes downward. If

---
[1]Technical footnote: In Figure 7.1b we graphed marginal utility at half-units. For example, we graphed the marginal utility of 4 utils at $3\frac{1}{2}$ units because "4 utils" refers neither to the third nor the fourth unit per se but to the *addition* or *subtraction* of the fourth unit.

KEY GRAPH

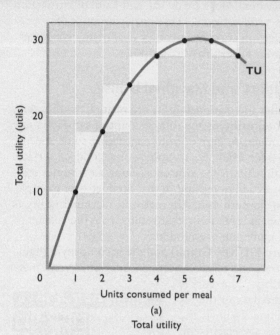

(a)
Total utility

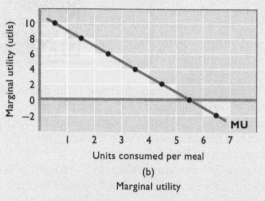

(b)
Marginal utility

FIGURE 7.1 Total and marginal utility. Curves TU and MU are graphed from the data in the table. (a) As more of a product is consumed, total utility increases at a diminishing rate, reaches a maximum, and then declines. (b) Marginal utility, by definition, reflects the changes in total utility. Thus marginal utility diminishes with increased consumption, becomes zero when total utility is at a maximum, and is negative when total utility declines. As shown by the shaded rectangles in (a) and (b), marginal utility is the change in total utility associated with each additional taco. Or, alternatively, each new level of total utility is found by adding marginal utility to the preceding level of total utility.

(1) Tacos Consumed per Meal	(2) Total Utility, Utils	(3) Marginal Utility, Utils
0	0	
1	10	10
2	18	8
3	24	6
4	28	4
5	30	2
6	30	0
7	28	−2

QUICK QUIZ FOR FIGURE 7.1

1. Marginal utility:
   a. is the extra output a firm obtains when it adds another unit of labor.
   b. explains why product supply curves slope upward.
   c. typically rises as successive units of a good are consumed.
   d. is the extra satisfaction from the consumption of 1 more unit of some good or service.

2. Marginal utility in Figure 7.1b is positive, but declining, when total utility in Figure 7.1a is positive and:
   a. rising at an increasing rate.
   b. falling at an increasing rate.
   c. rising at a decreasing rate.
   d. falling at a decreasing rate.

3. When marginal utility is zero in graph (b), total utility in graph (a) is:
   a. also zero.
   b. neither rising nor falling.
   c. negative.
   d. rising, but at a declining rate.

4. Suppose the person represented by these graphs experienced a diminished taste for tacos. As a result the:
   a. TU curve would get steeper.
   b. MU curve would get flatter.
   c. TU and MU curves would shift downward.
   d. MU curve, but not the TU curve, would collapse to the horizontal axis.

Answers: 1. d; 2. c; 3. b; 4. c

CONSIDER THIS . . .

Vending Machines and Marginal Utility

Newspaper dispensing devices and soft-drink vending machines are similar in their basic operations. Both enable consumers to buy a product by inserting coins. But there is an important difference in the two devices. The newspaper dispenser opens to the full stack of papers and seemingly "trusts" the customer to take only a single copy, whereas the vending machine displays no such "trust," requiring the consumer to buy one can at a time. Why the difference?

The idea of diminishing marginal utility is key to solving this puzzle. Most consumers take only single copies from the newspaper box because the marginal utility of a second newspaper is nearly zero. They could grab a few extra papers and try to sell them on the street, but the revenue obtained would be small relative to their time and effort. So, in selling their product, newspaper publishers rely on "zero marginal utility of the second unit," not on "consumer honesty." Also, newspapers have little "shelf life"; they are obsolete the next day. In contrast, soft-drink sellers do not allow buyers to make a single payment and then take as many cans as they want. If they did, consumers would clean out the machine because the marginal utility of successive cans of soda diminishes slowly and buyers could take extra sodas and consume them later. Soft-drink firms thus vend their products on a pay-per-can basis.

In summary, newspaper publishers and soft-drink firms use alternative vending techniques because of the highly different rates of decline in marginal utility for their products. The newspaper seller uses inexpensive dispensers that open to the full stack of papers. The soft-drink seller uses expensive vending machines that limit the consumer to a single can at a time. Each vending technique is optimal under the particular economic circumstance.

successive units of a good yield smaller and smaller amounts of marginal, or extra, utility, then the consumer will buy additional units of a product only if its price falls. The consumer for whom Figure 7.1 is relevant may buy two tacos at a price of $1 each. But because he or she obtains less marginal utility from additional tacos, the consumer will choose not to buy more at that price. The consumer would rather spend additional dollars on products that provide more utility, not less utility. Therefore,

additional tacos with less utility are not worth buying unless the price declines. (When marginal utility becomes negative, Taco Bell would have to pay you to consume another taco!) Thus, diminishing marginal utility supports the idea that price must decrease in order for quantity demanded to increase. In other words, consumers behave in ways that make demand curves downsloping.

QUICK REVIEW 7.1

- Utility is the benefit or satisfaction a person receives from consuming a good or a service.
- The law of diminishing marginal utility indicates that gains in satisfaction become smaller as successive units of a specific product are consumed.
- Diminishing marginal utility provides a simple rationale for the law of demand.

Theory of Consumer Behavior

LO7.2 Describe how rational consumers maximize utility by comparing the marginal utility-to-price ratios of all the products they could possibly purchase.

In addition to explaining the law of demand, the idea of diminishing marginal utility explains how consumers allocate their money incomes among the many goods and services available for purchase.

Consumer Choice and the Budget Constraint

For simplicity, we will assume that the situation for the typical consumer has the following dimensions.

- *Rational behavior* The consumer is a rational person, who tries to use his or her money income to derive the greatest amount of satisfaction, or utility, from it. Consumers want to get "the most for their money" or, technically, to maximize their total utility. They engage in **rational behavior.**

- *Preferences* Each consumer has clear-cut preferences for certain of the goods and services that are available in the market. Buyers also have a good idea of how much marginal utility they will get from successive units of the various products they might purchase.

- *Budget constraint* At any point in time the consumer has a fixed, limited amount of money income. Since each consumer supplies a finite amount of human and property resources to society, he or she earns only limited income. Thus, as noted in Chapter 1, every consumer faces a **budget constraint,** even consumers who earn millions of dollars a year. Of course, this budget limitation is more severe for a consumer with an average income than for a consumer with an extraordinarily high income.

- *Prices* Goods are scarce relative to the demand for them, so every good carries a price tag. We assume that the price of each good is unaffected by the amount of it that is bought by any particular person. After all, each person's purchase is a tiny part of total demand. Also, because the consumer has a limited number of dollars, he or she cannot buy everything wanted. This point drives home the reality of scarcity to each consumer.

So the consumer must compromise; he or she must choose the most personally satisfying mix of goods and services. Different individuals will choose different mixes.

Utility-Maximizing Rule

Of all the different combinations of goods and services a consumer can obtain within his or her budget, which specific combination will yield the maximum utility or satisfaction? *To maximize satisfaction, the consumer should allocate his or her money income so that the last dollar spent on each product yields the same amount of extra (marginal) utility.* We call this the **utility-maximizing rule.** When the consumer has "balanced his margins" using this rule, he has achieved **consumer equilibrium** and has no incentive to alter his expenditure pattern. In fact, any person who has achieved consumer equilibrium would be worse off—total utility would decline—if there were any alteration in the bundle of goods purchased, providing there is no change in taste, income, products, or prices.

Numerical Example

An illustration will help explain the utility-maximizing rule. For simplicity we limit our example to two products, but the analysis also applies if there are more. Suppose consumer Holly is analyzing which combination of two products she should purchase with her fixed daily income of $10. Let's suppose these products are apples and oranges.

Holly's preferences for apples and oranges and their prices are the basic data determining the combination that will maximize her satisfaction. Table 7.1 summarizes those data, with column 2a showing the amounts of marginal utility she will derive from each successive unit of A (apples) and with column 3a showing the same thing for product B (oranges). Both columns reflect the law of diminishing

TABLE 7.1   The Utility-Maximizing Combination of Apples and Oranges Obtainable with an Income of $10*

(1) Unit of Product	(2) Apple (Product A): Price = $1		(3) Orange (Product B): Price = $2	
	(a) Marginal Utility, Utils	(b) Marginal Utility per Dollar (MU/Price)	(a) Marginal Utility, Utils	(b) Marginal Utility per Dollar (MU/Price)
First	10	10	24	12
Second	8	8	20	10
Third	7	7	18	9
Fourth	6	6	16	8
Fifth	5	5	12	6
Sixth	4	4	6	3
Seventh	3	3	4	2

*It is assumed in this table that the amount of marginal utility received from additional units of each of the two products is independent of the quantity of the other product. For example, the marginal-utility schedule for apples is independent of the number of oranges obtained by the consumer.

marginal utility, which, in this example, is assumed to begin with the second unit of each product purchased.

Marginal Utility per Dollar To see how the utility-maximizing rule works, we must put the marginal-utility information in columns 2a and 3a on a per-dollar-spent basis. A consumer's choices are influenced not only by the extra utility that successive apples will yield but also by how many dollars (and therefore how many oranges) she must give up to obtain additional apples.

The rational consumer must compare the extra utility from each product with its added cost (that is, its price). Switching examples for a moment, suppose that you prefer a pizza whose marginal utility is, say, 36 utils to a movie whose marginal utility is 24 utils. But if the pizza's price is $12 and the movie costs only $6, you would choose the movie rather than the pizza! Why? Because the marginal utility per dollar spent would be 4 utils for the movie (= 24 utils/$6) compared to only 3 utils for the pizza (= 36 utils/$12). You could see two movies for $12 and, assuming that the marginal utility of the second movie is, say, 16 utils, your total utility would be 40 utils. Clearly, 40 units of satisfaction (= 24 utils + 16 utils) from two movies are superior to 36 utils from the same $12 expenditure on one pizza.

To make the amounts of extra utility derived from differently priced goods comparable, marginal utilities must be put on a per-dollar-spent basis. We do this in columns 2b and 3b by dividing the marginal-utility data of columns 2a and 3a by the prices of apples and oranges—$1 and $2, respectively.

TABLE 7.2 Sequence of Purchases to Achieve Consumer Equilibrium, Given the Data in Table 7.1

Choice Number	Potential Choices	Marginal Utility per Dollar	Purchase Decision	Income Remaining
1	First apple	10	First orange for $2	$8 = $10 − $2
	First orange	12		
2	First apple	10	First apple for $1	$5 = $8 − $3
	Second orange	10	and second orange for $2	
3	Second apple	8	Third orange for $2	$3 = $5 − $2
	Third orange	9		
4	Second apple	8	Second apple for $1	$0 = $3 − $3
	Fourth orange	8	and fourth orange for $2	

Decision-Making Process Table 7.1 shows Holly's preferences on a unit basis and a per-dollar basis as well as the price tags of apples and oranges. With $10 to spend, in what order should Holly allocate her dollars on units of apples and oranges to achieve the highest amount of utility within the $10 limit imposed by her income? And what specific combination of the two products will she have obtained at the time she uses up her $10?

Concentrating on columns 2b and 3b in Table 7.1, we find that Holly should first spend $2 on the first orange because its marginal utility per dollar of 12 utils is higher than the first apple's 10 utils. But now Holly finds herself indifferent about whether to buy a second orange or the first apple because the marginal utility per dollar of both is 10 utils per dollar. So she buys both of them. Holly now has 1 apple and 2 oranges. Also, the last dollar she spent on each good yielded the same marginal utility per dollar (10). But this combination of apples and oranges does not represent the maximum amount of utility that Holly can obtain. It cost her only $5 [= (1 × $1) + (2 × $2)], so she has $5 remaining, which she can spend to achieve a still higher level of total utility.

Examining columns 2b and 3b again, we find that Holly should spend the next $2 on a third orange because marginal utility per dollar for the third orange is 9 compared with 8 for the second apple. But now, with 1 apple and 3 oranges, she is again indifferent between a second apple and a fourth orange because both provide 8 utils per dollar. So Holly purchases 1 more of each. Now the last dollar spent on each product provides the same marginal utility per dollar (8), and Holly's money income of $10 is exhausted.

The utility-maximizing combination of goods attainable by Holly is 2 apples and 4 oranges. By summing marginal-utility information from columns 2a and 3a, we find that Holly is obtaining 18 (= 10 + 8) utils of satisfaction from the 2 apples and 78 (= 24 + 20 + 18 + 16) utils of satisfaction from the 4 oranges. Her $10, optimally spent, yields 96 (= 18 + 78) utils of satisfaction.

Table 7.2 summarizes our step-by-step process for maximizing Holly's utility. Note that we have implicitly assumed that Holly spends her entire income. She neither borrows nor saves. However, saving can be regarded as a "commodity" that yields utility and can be incorporated into our analysis. In fact, we treat it that way in problem 4 at the end of this chapter.

Inferior Options Holly can obtain other combinations of apples and oranges with $10, but none will yield as great a total utility as do 2 apples and 4 oranges. As an example, she can obtain 4 apples and 3 oranges for $10. But this combination yields only 93 utils, clearly inferior to the 96 utils provided by 2 apples and 4 oranges. True, there are other combinations of apples and oranges (such as 4 apples and 5 oranges or 1 apple and 2 oranges) in which the marginal utility of the last dollar spent is the same for both goods. But all such combinations either are unobtainable with Holly's limited money income (as 4 apples and 5 oranges) or do not exhaust her money income (as 1 apple and 2 oranges) and therefore do not yield the maximum utility attainable.

WORKED PROBLEMS

W7.1 Consumer choice

Algebraic Generalization

Economists generalize the utility-maximizing rule by saying that a consumer will maximize her satisfaction when she allocates her money income so that the last dollar spent on product A, the last on product B, and so forth, yield equal amounts of additional, or marginal, utility. The marginal utility per dollar spent on A is indicated by the MU of product A divided by the price of A (column 2b in Table 7.1), and the marginal utility per dollar spent on B by the MU of product B divided by the price of B (column 3b in Table 7.1). Our utility-maximizing rule merely requires that these ratios be equal for the last dollar spent on A and the last dollar spent on B. Algebraically,

$$\frac{\text{MU of product A}}{\text{Price of A}} = \frac{\text{MU of product B}}{\text{Price of B}}$$

And, of course, the consumer must exhaust her available income. Table 7.1 shows us that the combination of 2 units of A (apples) and 4 of B (oranges) fulfills these conditions in that

$$\frac{8 \text{ utils}}{\$1} = \frac{16 \text{ utils}}{\$2}$$

and the consumer's $10 income is all spent.

If the equation is not fulfilled, then some reallocation of the consumer's expenditures between A and B (from the low to the high marginal-utility-per-dollar product) will increase the consumer's total utility. For example, if the consumer spent $10 on 4 of A (apples) and 3 of B (oranges), we would find that

$$\frac{\text{MU of A of 6 utils}}{\text{Price of A of \$1}} < \frac{\text{MU of B of 18 utils}}{\text{Price of B of \$2}}$$

Here the last dollar spent on A provides only 6 utils of satisfaction, while the last dollar spent on B provides 9 (= 18/$2). So the consumer can increase total satisfaction by purchasing more of B and less of A. As dollars are reallocated from A to B, the marginal utility per dollar of A will increase while the marginal utility per dollar of B will decrease. At some new combination of A and B the two will be equal and consumer equilibrium will be achieved. Here that combination is 2 of A (apples) and 4 of B (oranges).

Utility Maximization and the Demand Curve

LO7.3 Explain how a demand curve can be derived by observing the outcomes of price changes in the utility-maximization model.

Once you understand the utility-maximizing rule, you can easily see why product price and quantity demanded are inversely related. Recall that the basic determinants of an individual's demand for a specific product are (1) preferences or tastes, (2) money income, and (3) the prices of other goods. The utility data in Table 7.1 reflect our consumer's preferences. We continue to suppose that her money income is $10. And, concentrating on the construction of an individual demand curve for oranges, we assume that the price of apples, now representing all "other goods," is still $1.

Deriving the Demand Schedule and Curve

We can derive a single consumer's demand schedule for oranges by considering alternative prices at which oranges might be sold and then determining the quantity the consumer will purchase. We already know one such price-quantity combination in the utility-maximizing example: Given tastes, income, and the prices of other goods, Holly will purchase 4 oranges at $2.

Now let's assume the price of oranges falls to $1. The marginal-utility-per-dollar data of column 3b in Table 7.1 will double because the price of oranges has been halved; the new data for column 3b are (by coincidence) identical to the data in column 3a. The doubling of the MU per dollar for each successive orange means that the purchase of 2 apples and 4 oranges is no longer an equilibrium combination. By applying the same reasoning we used previously, we now find that Holly's utility-maximizing combination is 4 apples and 6 oranges. As summarized in the table in Figure 7.2,

FIGURE 7.2 Deriving an individual demand curve. The consumer represented by the data in the table maximizes utility by purchasing 4 oranges at a price of $2. The decline in the price of oranges to $1 disrupts the consumer's initial utility-maximizing equilibrium. The consumer restores equilibrium by purchasing 6 rather than 4 oranges. Thus, a simple price-quantity schedule emerges, which locates two points on a downsloping demand curve.

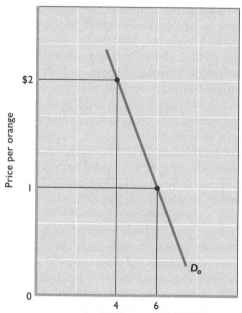

Price per Orange	Quantity Demanded
$2	4
1	6

Holly will purchase 6 oranges when the price of oranges is $1. Using the data in this table, we can sketch the downward-sloping demand curve for oranges, D_0, shown in Figure 7.2. This exercise, then, clearly links the utility-maximizing behavior of a consumer and that person's downsloping demand curve for a particular product.

Income and Substitution Effects

LO7.4 Discuss how the utility-maximization model helps highlight the income and substitution effects of a price change.

Recall from Chapter 3 that the **income effect** is the impact that a change in the price of a product has on a consumer's real income and consequently on the quantity demanded of that good. In contrast, the **substitution effect** is the impact that a change in a product's price has on its relative expensiveness and consequently on the quantity demanded. Both effects help explain why a demand curve such as that in Figure 7.2 is downsloping.

Let's first look at the substitution effect. Recall that before the price of oranges declined, Holly was in equilibrium when purchasing 2 apples and 4 oranges because

$$\frac{\text{MU of apples of 8}}{\text{Price of apples of \$1}} = \frac{\text{MU of oranges of 16}}{\text{Price of oranges of \$2}}$$

But after the price of oranges declines from $2 to $1,

$$\frac{\text{MU of apples of 8}}{\text{Price of apples of \$1}} < \frac{\text{MU of oranges of 16}}{\text{Price of oranges of \$1}}$$

Clearly, the last dollar spent on oranges now yields greater utility (16 utils) than does the last dollar spent on apples (8 utils). This will lead Holly to switch, or substitute, purchases away from apples and toward oranges so as to restore consumer equilibrium. This substitution effect contributes to the inverse relationship between price and quantity that is found along her demand curve for oranges: When the price of oranges declines, the substitution effect causes Holly to buy more oranges.

What about the income effect? The decline in the price of oranges from $2 to $1 increases Holly's real income. Before the price decline, she maximized her utility and achieved consumer equilibrium by selecting 2 apples and 4 oranges. But at the lower $1 price for oranges, Holly would have to spend only $6 rather than $10 to buy that particular combination of goods. That means that the lower price of oranges has freed up $4 that can be spent on buying more apples, more oranges, or more of both. How many more of each fruit she ends up buying will be determined by applying the utility-maximizing rule to the new situation. But it is quite likely that the increase in real in-

come caused by the reduction in the price of oranges will cause Holly to end up buying more oranges than before the price reduction. Any such increase in orange purchases is referred to as the income effect of the reduction in the price of oranges and it, too, helps to explain why demand curves are downward sloping: When the price of oranges falls, the income effect causes Holly to buy more oranges.

> ### QUICK REVIEW 7.2
>
> - The theory of consumer behavior assumes that, with limited income and a set of product prices, consumers make rational choices on the basis of well-defined preferences.
> - A consumer maximizes utility by allocating income so that the marginal utility per dollar spent is the same for every good purchased.
> - A downsloping demand curve can be derived by changing the price of one product in the consumer-behavior model and noting the change in the utility-maximizing quantity of that product demanded.
> - By providing insights on the income effect and substitution effect of a price decline, the utility-maximization model helps explain why demand curves are downsloping.

Applications and Extensions

LO7.5 Give examples of several real-world phenomena that can be explained by applying the theory of consumer behavior.

Many real-world phenomena can be explained by applying the theory of consumer behavior.

iPads

Every so often a new product totally captures consumers' imaginations. One such product is Apple's iPad, which debuted in April 2010. Less than three years later, Apple sold its 100-millionth unit.

The swift ascendancy of the iPad resulted mainly from a leapfrog in technology. It was the first touchscreen tablet computer and became a hit because it was much better for the consumption of digital media—music, pictures, videos, and many games—than existing laptop or desktop computers. Those larger machines still held the advantage if a consumer wanted to create content or edit documents, but for consuming digital content the iPad was far superior in the eyes of millions of consumers.

In the language of our analysis, Apple's introduction of the iPad severely disrupted consumer equilibrium. Consumers en masse concluded that iPads had a higher marginal-utility-to-price ratio ($= MU/P$) than the ratios for alternative products. They therefore shifted spending away from those other products and toward iPads as a way to increase total utility. Of course, for most people the marginal utility of a second or third iPad relative to price is quite low, so most consumers purchased only a single iPad. But Apple continued to enhance the iPad, enticing some of the buyers of older models to buy new models.

This example demonstrates a simple but important point: New products succeed by enhancing consumers' total utility. This "delivery of value" generates a revenue stream. If revenues exceed production costs, substantial profits can result—as they have for Apple.

The Diamond-Water Paradox

Early economists such as Adam Smith were puzzled by the fact that some "essential" goods had much lower prices than some "unimportant" goods. Why would water, essential to life, be priced below diamonds, which have much less usefulness? The paradox is resolved when we acknowledge that water is in great supply relative to demand and thus has a very low price per gallon. Diamonds, in contrast, are rare. Their supply is small relative to demand and, as a result, they have a very high price per carat.

Moreover, the marginal utility of the last unit of water consumed is very low. The reason follows from our utility-maximizing rule. Consumers (and producers) respond to the very low price of water by using a great deal of it—for generating electricity, irrigating crops, heating buildings, watering lawns, quenching thirst, and so on. Consumption is expanded until marginal utility, which declines as more water is consumed, equals its low price. On the other hand, relatively few diamonds are purchased because of their prohibitively high price, meaning that their marginal utility remains high. In equilibrium:

$$\frac{\text{MU of water (low)}}{\text{Price of water (low)}} = \frac{\text{MU of diamonds (high)}}{\text{Price of diamonds (high)}}$$

Although the marginal utility of the last unit of water consumed is low and the marginal utility of the last diamond purchased is high, the total utility of water is very high and the total utility of diamonds quite low. The total utility derived from the consumption of water is large because of the enormous amounts of water consumed. Total utility is the sum of the marginal utilities of all the gallons of water consumed, including the trillions of gallons that have far higher marginal utilities than the last unit consumed. In contrast, the total utility derived from diamonds is low since their high price means that relatively few of them are bought. Thus the water-diamond "paradox" is solved: Water has much more total utility (roughly, usefulness) than diamonds even though the price of diamonds greatly exceeds the price of water. These relative prices relate to marginal utility, not total utility.

ORIGIN OF THE IDEA

O7.3
Diamond-water paradox

Opportunity Cost and the Value of Time

The theory of consumer behavior has been generalized to account for the economic value of *time*. Both consumption and production take time. Time is a valuable economic commodity; by using an hour in productive work a person can earn $6, $10, $50, or more, depending on her or his education and skills. By using that hour for leisure or in consumption activities, the individual incurs the opportunity cost of forgone income; she or he sacrifices the $6, $10, or $50 that could have been earned by working.

Imagine a self-employed consumer named Linden who is considering buying a round of golf, on the one hand, and a concert, on the other. The market price of the golf game is $30 and that of the concert is $40. But the golf game takes more time than the concert. Suppose Linden spends 4 hours on the golf course but only 2 hours at the concert. If her time is worth $10 per hour, as evidenced by the $10 wage she can obtain by working, then the "full price" of the golf game is $70 (the $30 market price plus $40 worth of time). Similarly, the full price of the concert is $60 (the $40 market price plus $20 worth of time). We find that, contrary to what market prices alone indicate, the full price of the concert is really less than the full price of the golf game.

If we now assume that the marginal utilities derived from successive golf games and concerts are identical, traditional theory would indicate that Linden should consume more golf games than concerts because the market price of the former ($30) is lower than that of the latter ($40). But when time is taken into account, the situation is reversed and golf games ($70) are more expensive than concerts ($60). So it is rational for Linden to consume more concerts than golf games.

By accounting for the opportunity cost of a consumer's time, we can explain certain phenomena that are otherwise quite puzzling. It may be rational for the unskilled worker

LAST WORD

Criminal Behavior

Although Economic Analysis Is Not Particularly Relevant in Explaining Some Crimes of Passion and Violence (for Example, Murder and Rape), It Does Provide Interesting Insights on Such Property Crimes as Robbery, Burglary, and Auto Theft.

The theory of rational consumer behavior can be extended to provide some useful insights on criminal behavior. Both the lawful consumer and the criminal try to maximize their total utility (or net benefit). For example, you can remove a textbook from the campus bookstore by either purchasing it or stealing it. If you *buy* the book, your action is legal; you have fully compensated the bookstore for the product. (The bookstore would rather have your money than the book.) If you *steal* the book, you have broken the law. Theft is outlawed because it imposes uncompensated costs on others. In this case, your action reduces the bookstore's revenue and profit and also may impose costs on other buyers who now must pay higher prices for their textbooks.

Why might someone engage in a criminal activity such as stealing? Just like the consumer who compares the marginal utility of a good with its price, the potential criminal compares the marginal benefit from his or her action with the "price" or cost. If the marginal benefit (to the criminal) exceeds the price or marginal cost (also to the criminal), the individual undertakes the criminal activity.

Most people, however, do not engage in theft, burglary, or fraud. Why not? The answer is that they perceive the personal price of engaging in these illegal activities to be too high relative to the marginal benefit. The price or marginal cost to the potential criminal has several facets. First, there are the "guilt costs," which for many people are substantial. Such individuals would not steal from others even if there were no penalties for doing so. Their moral sense of right and wrong would entail too great a guilt cost relative to the benefit from the stolen good. Other types of costs include the direct cost of the criminal activity (supplies and tools) and the forgone income from legitimate activities (the opportunity cost to the criminal).

Unfortunately, guilt costs, direct costs, and forgone income are not sufficient to deter some people from stealing. So society imposes other costs, mainly fines and imprisonment, on lawbreakers. The potential of being fined increases the marginal cost to the criminal. The potential of being imprisoned boosts marginal cost still further. Most people highly value their personal freedom and lose considerable legitimate earnings while incarcerated.

Given these types of costs, the potential criminal estimates the marginal cost and benefit of committing the crime. As a simple example, suppose that the direct cost and the opportunity cost of stealing an $80 textbook are both zero. The probability of

getting caught is 10 percent and, if apprehended, there will be a $500 fine. The potential criminal will estimate the marginal cost of stealing the book as $50 (= $500 fine × .10 chance of apprehension). Someone who has a guilt cost of zero will choose to steal the book because the marginal benefit of $80 would exceed the marginal cost of $50. In contrast, someone having a guilt cost of, say, $40 will not steal the book. The marginal benefit of $80 will not be as great as the marginal cost of $90 (= $50 of penalty cost + $40 of guilt cost).

This perspective on illegal behavior has some interesting implications. For example, other things equal, crime will rise (more of it will be "bought") when its price falls. This explains, for instance, why some people who do not steal from stores under normal circumstances participate in looting stores during riots, when the marginal cost of being apprehended has substantially declined.

Another implication is that society can reduce unlawful behavior by increasing the "price of crime." It can nourish and increase guilt costs through family, educational, and religious efforts. It can increase the direct cost of crime by using more sophisticated security systems (locks, alarms, video surveillance) so that criminals will have to buy and use more sophisticated tools. It can undertake education and training initiatives to enhance the legitimate earnings of people who might otherwise engage in illegal activity. It can increase policing to raise the probability of being apprehended for crime. And it can impose greater penalties for those who are caught and convicted.

or retiree whose time has little market value to ride a bus from Chicago to Pittsburgh. But the corporate executive, whose time is very valuable, will find it cheaper to fly, even though bus fare is only a fraction of plane fare. It is sensible for the retiree, living on a modest company pension and a Social Security check, to spend many hours shopping for bargains at the mall or taking long trips in a motor home. It is equally intelligent for the highly paid physician, working 55 hours per week, to buy a new personal computer over the Internet and take short vacations at expensive resorts.

People in other nations often feel affluent Americans are "wasteful" of food and other material goods but "overly economical" in their use of time. Americans who visit developing countries find that time is used casually or "squandered," while material goods are very highly prized and carefully used. These differences are not a paradox or a case of radically different temperaments. The differences are primarily a rational reflection of the fact that the high productivity of labor in an industrially advanced society gives time a high market value, whereas the opposite is true in a low-income, developing country.

Medical Care Purchases

The method of payment for certain goods and services affects their prices at the time we buy them and significantly changes the amount purchased. Let's go back to Table 7.1. Suppose the $1 price for apples is its "true" value or opportunity cost. But now, for some reason, its price is only, say, $0.20. A rational consumer clearly would buy more apples at the $0.20 price than at the $1 price.

That is what happens with medical care. People in the United States who have health insurance pay a fixed premium once a month that covers, say, 80 percent of all incurred health care costs. This means that when they actually need health care, its price to them will be only 20 percent of the actual market price. How would you act in such a situation? When you are ill, you would likely purchase a great deal more medical care than you would if you were confronted with the full price. As a result, financing health care through insurance is an important factor in explaining today's high expenditures on health care and the historical growth of such spending as a percentage of domestic output.

Similar reasoning applies to purchases of buffet meals. If you buy a meal at an all-you-can-eat buffet, you will tend to eat more than if you purchased it item by item. Why not eat that second dessert? Its marginal utility is positive and its "price" is zero!

Cash and Noncash Gifts

Marginal-utility analysis also helps us understand why people generally prefer cash gifts to noncash gifts costing the same amount. The reason is simply that the noncash gifts may not match the recipient's preferences and thus may not add as much as cash to total utility. Thought of differently, consumers know their own preferences better than the gift giver does, and the $100 cash gift provides more choices.

Look back at Table 7.1. Suppose Holly has zero earned income but is given the choice of a $2 cash gift or a noncash gift of 2 apples. Because 2 apples can be bought with $2, these two gifts are of equal monetary value. But by spending the $2 cash gift on the first orange, Holly could obtain 24 utils. The noncash gift of the first 2 apples would yield only 18 (= 10 + 8) units of utility. Conclusion: The noncash gift yields less utility to the beneficiary than does the cash gift.

Since giving noncash gifts is common, a considerable value of those gifts is potentially lost because they do not match their recipients' tastes. For example, Uncle Fred may have paid $15 for the Frank Sinatra CD he gave you for the holidays, but you would pay only $7.50 for it. Thus, a $7.50, or 50 percent, value loss is involved. Multiplied by billions of gifts a year, the total potential loss of value is huge.

But some of that loss is avoided by the creative ways individuals handle the problem. For example, newlyweds set up gift registries for their weddings to help match up their wants to the noncash gifts received. Also, people obtain cash refunds or exchanges for gifts so they can buy goods that provide more utility. And people have even been known to "recycle gifts" by giving them to someone else at a later time. All three actions support the proposition that individuals take actions to maximize their total utility.

SUMMARY

LO7.1 Define and explain the relationship between total utility, marginal utility, and the law of diminishing marginal utility.

The law of diminishing marginal utility states that beyond a certain quantity, additional units of a specific good will yield declining amounts of extra satisfaction to a consumer.

LO7.2 Describe how rational consumers maximize utility by comparing the marginal utility-to-price ratios of all the products they could possibly purchase.

The utility-maximization model assumes that the typical consumer is rational and acts on the basis of well-defined preferences. Because income is limited and goods have prices, the consumer cannot purchase all the goods and services he or she might want. The consumer therefore selects the attainable combination of goods that maximizes his or her utility or satisfaction.

A consumer's utility is maximized when income is allocated so that the last dollar spent on each product purchased yields the same amount of extra satisfaction. Algebraically, the utility-maximizing rule is fulfilled when

$$\frac{\text{MU of product A}}{\text{Price of A}} = \frac{\text{MU of product B}}{\text{Price of B}}$$

and the consumer's total income is spent.

LO7.3 Explain how a demand curve can be derived by observing the outcomes of price changes in the utility-maximization model.

The utility-maximizing rule and the demand curve are logically consistent. Because marginal utility declines, a lower price is needed to induce the consumer to buy more of a particular product.

LO7.4 Discuss how the utility-maximization model helps highlight the income and substitution effects of a price change.

The utility-maximization model illuminates the income and substitution effects of a price change. The income effect implies that a decline in the price of a product increases the consumer's real income and enables the consumer to buy more of that product with a fixed money income. The substitution effect implies that a lower price makes a product relatively more attractive and therefore increases the consumer's willingness to substitute it for other products.

LO7.5 Give examples of several real-world phenomena that can be explained by applying the theory of consumer behavior.

The theory of consumer behavior can explain many real world phenomena, including the rapid adoption of popular consumer goods like the iPad that feature disruptive technologies, the over-consumption of products like health care that have artificially low prices, and why people often prefer gifts of cash to receiving particular items or objects of the same monetary value as gifts.

TERMS AND CONCEPTS

law of diminishing marginal utility

utility

total utility

marginal utility

rational behavior

budget constraint

utility-maximizing rule

consumer equilibrium

income effect

substitution effect

The following and additional problems can be found in connect
ECONOMICS

DISCUSSION QUESTIONS

1. Complete the following table and answer the questions below: **LO7.1**

Units Consumed	Total Utility	Marginal Utility
0	0	
1	10	10
2	—	8
3	25	—
4	30	—
5	—	3
6	34	—

a. At which rate is total utility increasing: a constant rate, a decreasing rate, or an increasing rate? How do you know?

b. "A rational consumer will purchase only 1 unit of the product represented by these data, since that amount maximizes marginal utility." Do you agree? Explain why or why not.

c. "It is possible that a rational consumer will not purchase any units of the product represented by these data." Do you agree? Explain why or why not.

2. Mrs. Simpson buys loaves of bread and quarts of milk each week at prices of $1 and 80 cents, respectively. At present she is buying these products in amounts such that the marginal utilities from the last units purchased of the two products are 80 and 70 utils, respectively. Is she buying the utility-maximizing combination of bread and milk? If not, how should she reallocate her expenditures between the two goods? **LO7.2**

3. How can time be incorporated into the theory of consumer behavior? Explain the following comment: "Want to make millions of dollars? Devise a product that saves Americans lots of time." **LO7.2**

4. Explain: **LO7.2**

a. Before economic growth, there were too few goods; after growth, there is too little time.

b. It is irrational for an individual to take the time to be completely rational in economic decision making.
c. Telling your spouse where you would like to go out to eat for your birthday makes sense in terms of utility maximization.

5. In the last decade or so, there has been a dramatic expansion of small retail convenience stores (such as 7-Eleven, Kwik Shop, and Circle K), although their prices are generally much higher than prices in large supermarkets. What explains the success of the convenience stores? **LO7.2**

6. Many apartment-complex owners are installing water meters for each apartment and billing the occupants according to the amount of water they use. This is in contrast to the former procedure of having a central meter for the entire complex and dividing up the collective water expense as part of the rent. Where individual meters have been installed, water usage has declined 10 to 40 percent. Explain that drop, referring to price and marginal utility. **LO7.3**

7. Using the utility-maximization rule as your point of reference, explain the income and substitution effects of an increase in the price of product B, with no change in the price of product A. **LO7.4**

8. **ADVANCED ANALYSIS** A "mathematically fair bet" is one in which the amount won will on average equal the amount bet, for example, when a gambler bets, say, $100 for a 10 percent chance to win $1,000 ($100 = 0.10 × $1,000). Assuming diminishing marginal utility of dollars, explain why this is *not* a fair bet in terms of utility. Why is it even a less fair bet when the "house" takes a cut of each dollar bet? So is gambling irrational? **LO7.4**

9. **LAST WORD** In what way is criminal behavior similar to consumer behavior? Why do most people obtain goods via legal behavior as opposed to illegal behavior? What are society's main options for reducing illegal behavior?

REVIEW QUESTIONS

1. True or false. The law of diminishing marginal utility predicts the consumption behavior of addicts quite well. **LO7.1**

2. Frank spends $75 on 10 magazines and 25 newspapers. The magazines cost $5 each and the newspapers cost $2.50 each. Suppose that his MU from the final magazine is 10 utils while his MU from the final newspaper is also 10 utils. According to the utility-maximizing rule, Frank should: **LO7.2**
   a. Reallocate spending from magazines to newspapers.
   b. Reallocate spending from newspapers to magazines.
   c. Be satisfied because he is already maximizing his total utility.
   d. None of the above.

3. Demand curves slope downward because, other things held equal, **LO7.3**
   a. An increase in a product's price lowers MU.
   b. A decrease in a product's price lowers MU.
   c. A decrease in a product's price raises MU per dollar and makes consumers wish to purchase more units.

   d. An increase in a product's price raises MU per dollar and makes consumers wish to purchase more units.

4. Jermaine spends his money on cucumbers and lettuce. If the price of cucumbers falls, the MU per dollar of cucumbers will _____ and Jermaine will _____ cucumbers for lettuce. **LO7.4**
   a. Fall; substitute
   b. Rise; substitute
   c. Fall; supply
   d. Rise; demand

5. Tammy spends her money on lemonade and iced tea. If the price of lemonade falls, it is as though her income _____. **LO7.4**
   a. Increases.
   b. Decreases.
   c. Stays the same.

PROBLEMS

1. Mylie's total utility from singing the same song over and over is 50 utils after one repetition, 90 utils after two repetitions, 70 utils after three repetitions, 20 utils after four repetitions, −50 utils after five repetitions, and −200 utils after six repetitions. Write down her marginal utility for each repetition. Once Mylie's total utility begins to decrease, does each additional singing of the song hurt more than the previous one or less than the previous one? **LO7.1**

2. John likes Coca-Cola. After consuming one Coke, John has a total utility of 10 utils. After two Cokes, he has a total utility of 25 utils. After three Cokes, he has a total utility of 50 utils. Does John show diminishing marginal utility for Coke, or does he show increasing marginal utility for Coke?

Suppose that John has $3 in his pocket. If Cokes cost $1 each and John is willing to spend one of his dollars on purchasing a first can of Coke, would he spend his second dollar on a Coke, too? What about the third dollar? If John's marginal utility for Coke keeps on increasing no matter how many Cokes he drinks, would it be fair to say that he is addicted to Coke? **LO7.1**

3. Suppose that Omar's marginal utility for cups of coffee is constant at 1.5 utils per cup no matter how many cups he drinks. On the other hand, his marginal utility per doughnut is 10 for the first doughnut he eats, 9 for the second he eats, 8 for the third he eats, and so on (that is, declining by 1 util per additional doughnut). In addition, suppose

Column 1		Column 2		Column 3		Column 4		Column 5	
Units of A	MU	Units of B	MU	Units of C	MU	Units of D	MU	Number of Dollars Saved	MU
1	72	1	24	1	15	1	36	1	5
2	54	2	15	2	12	2	30	2	4
3	45	3	12	3	8	3	24	3	3
4	36	4	9	4	7	4	18	4	2
5	27	5	7	5	5	5	13	5	1
6	18	6	5	6	4	6	7	6	$\frac{1}{2}$
7	15	7	2	7	$3\frac{1}{2}$	7	4	7	$\frac{1}{4}$
8	12	8	1	8	3	8	2	8	$\frac{1}{8}$

that coffee costs $1 per cup, doughnuts cost $1 each, and Omar has a budget that he can spend only on doughnuts, coffee, or both. How big would that budget have to be before he would spend a dollar buying a first cup of coffee? **LO7.2**

4. Columns 1 through 4 in the table at the top of the page show the marginal utility, measured in utils, that Ricardo would get by purchasing various amounts of products A, B, C, and D. Column 5 shows the marginal utility Ricardo gets from saving. Assume that the prices of A, B, C, and D are, respectively, $18, $6, $4, and $24 and that Ricardo has an income of $106. **LO7.2**

   a. What quantities of A, B, C, and D will Ricardo purchase in maximizing his utility?

   b. How many dollars will Ricardo choose to save?

   c. Check your answers by substituting them into the algebraic statement of the utility-maximizing rule.

5. You are choosing between two goods, X and Y, and your marginal utility from each is as shown in the table to the right. If your income is $9 and the prices of X and Y are $2 and $1, respectively, what quantities of each will you purchase to maximize utility? What total utility will you realize? Assume that, other things remaining unchanged, the price of X falls to $1. What quantities of X and Y will you now purchase? Using the two prices and quantities for X, derive a demand schedule (a table showing prices and quantities demanded) for X. **LO7.3**

Units of X	MU_x	Units of Y	MU_y
1	10	1	8
2	8	2	7
3	6	3	6
4	4	4	5
5	3	5	4
6	2	6	3

6. **ADVANCED ANALYSIS** Let $MU_A = z = 10 - x$ and $MU_B = z = 21 - 2y$, where z is marginal utility per dollar measured in utils, x is the amount spent on product A, and y is the amount spent on product B. Assume that the consumer has $10 to spend on A and B—that is, $x + y = 10$. How is the $10 best allocated between A and B? How much utility will the marginal dollar yield? **LO7.3**

7. Suppose that with a budget of $100, Deborah spends $60 on sushi and $40 on bagels when sushi costs $2 per piece and bagels cost $2 per bagel. But then, after the price of bagels falls to $1 per bagel, she spends $50 on sushi and $50 on bagels. How many pieces of sushi and how many bagels did Deborah consume before the price change? At the new prices, how much money would it have cost Deborah to buy those same quantities (the ones that she consumed before the price change)? Given that it used to take Deborah's entire $100 to buy those quantities, how big is the income effect caused by the reduction in the price of bagels? **LO7.4**

FURTHER TEST YOUR KNOWLEDGE AT www.mcconnell20e.com

Practice quizzes, student PowerPoints, worked problems, Web-based questions, and additional materials are available at the text's Online Learning Center (OLC), **www.mcconnell20e.com**, or scan here. Need a barcode reader? Try ScanLife, available in your app store.

Indifference Curve Analysis

LO7.6 Relate how the indifference curve model of consumer behavior derives demand curves from budget lines, indifference curves, and utility maximization.

The utility-maximization rule previously discussed requires individuals to measure and compare utility, much as a business would measure and compare costs or revenues. Such *cardinal utility* is measured in units such as 1, 2, 3, and 4 and can be added, subtracted, multiplied, and divided, just like the cardinal numbers in mathematics. More importantly, cardinal utility allows precise quantification of the marginal utilities upon which the utility-maximizing rule depends. In fact, the marginal-utility theory of consumer demand that we explained in the body of this chapter rests squarely on the assumption that economists be able to measure cardinal utility. The reality, however, is that measuring cardinal utility is highly difficult, at best. (Can you, for instance, state exactly how many utils you are getting from reading this book right now or how many utils you would get from watching a sunset?)

To avoid this measurement problem, economists have developed an alternative explanation of consumer behavior and equilibrium in which cardinal measurement is not required. In this more-advanced analysis, the consumer must simply *rank* various combinations of goods in terms of preference. For instance, Sally can simply report that she *prefers* 4 units of A to 6 units of B without having to put number values on how much she likes either option. The model of consumer behavior that is based upon such *ordinal utility* rankings is called

indifference curve analysis. It has two main elements: budget lines and indifference curves.

The Budget Line: What Is Attainable

We know from Chapter 1 that a **budget line** (or, more technically, a *budget constraint*) is a schedule or curve showing various combinations of two products a consumer can purchase with a specific money income. If the price of product A is $1.50 and the price of product B is $1, a consumer could purchase all the combinations of A and B shown in the table in Figure 1 with $12 of money income. At one extreme, the consumer might spend all of his or her income on 8 units of A and have nothing left to spend on B. Or, by giving up 2 units of A and thereby "freeing" $3, the consumer could have 6 units of A and 3 of B. And so on to the other extreme, at which the consumer could buy 12 units of B at $1 each, spending his or her entire money income on B with nothing left to spend on A.

Figure 1 also shows the budget line graphically. Note that the graph is not restricted to whole units of A and B as is the table. Every point on the graph represents a possible combination of A and B, including fractional quantities. The slope of the graphed budget line measures the ratio of the price of B to the price of A; more precisely, the absolute value of the slope is $P_B/P_A = \$1.00/\$1.50 = \frac{2}{3}$. This is the mathematical way of saying that the consumer must forgo 2 units of

---

FIGURE 1 A consumer's budget line. The budget line shows all the combinations of any two products that someone can purchase, given the prices of the products and the person's money income.

Units of A (Price = $1.50)	Units of B (Price = $1)	Total Expenditure
8	0	$12 (= $12 + $0)
6	3	$12 (= $9 + $3)
4	6	$12 (= $6 + $6)
2	9	$12 (= $3 + $9)
0	12	$12 (= $0 + $12)

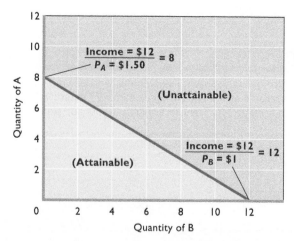

A (measured on the vertical axis) to buy 3 units of B (measured on the horizontal axis). In moving down the budget or price line, 2 units of A (at $1.50 each) must be given up to obtain 3 more units of B (at $1 each). This yields a slope of $\frac{2}{3}$.

Note that all combinations of A and B that lie on or inside the budget line are attainable from the consumer's $12 of money income. He can afford to buy not only the combinations of A and B that lie along the budget line itself but also those that lie below it. He could, for instance, afford to buy 2 units of A and 4 units of B, thereby using up only $7 (= $3 spent on 2 units of A at a price of $1.50 each + $4 spent on 4 units of B at a price of $1 each). That combination is clearly attainable because it would use up only half of the consumer's $12 budget. But to achieve maximum utility, the consumer will want to spend the full $12. The budget line shows all combinations that cost exactly the full $12.

The budget line has two other significant characteristics:

- **Income changes** The location of the budget line varies with money income. An increase in money income shifts the budget line to the right; a decrease in money income shifts it to the left. To verify this, recalculate the table in Figure 1, assuming that money income is (a) $24 and (b) $6, and plot the new budget lines in Figure 1.

- **Price changes** A change in product prices also shifts the budget line. A decline in the prices of both products—the equivalent of an increase in real income—shifts the curve to the right. (You can verify this by recalculating the table in Figure 1 and replotting Figure 1 assuming that P_A = $0.75 and P_B = $0.50.) Conversely, an increase in the prices of A and B shifts the curve to the left. (Assume P_A = $3 and P_B = $2, and rework the table and Figure 1 to substantiate this statement.)

Note what happens if P_B changes while P_A and money income remain constant. In particular, if P_B drops, say, from $1 to $0.50, the lower end of the budget line fans outward to the right. Conversely, if P_B increases, say, from $1 to $1.50, the lower end of the line fans inward to the left. In both instances the line remains "anchored" at 8 units on the vertical axis because P_A has not changed.

Indifference Curves: What Is Preferred

Budget lines reflect "objective" market data, specifically income and prices. They reveal combinations of products A and B that can be purchased, given current money income and prices.

Indifference curves, on the other hand, reflect "subjective" information about consumer preferences for A and B. An **indifference curve** shows all the combinations of two products A and B that will yield the same total satisfaction or total utility to a consumer. The table and graph in Figure 2 present a hypothetical indifference curve for products A and B. The consumer's subjective preferences are such that he or she will realize the same total utility from each combination of A and B shown in the table or on the curve. So the consumer will be indifferent (will not care) as to which combination is actually obtained.

Indifference curves have several important characteristics.

> **ORIGIN OF THE IDEA**
>
> **07.4**
> Indifference curves

FIGURE 2　A consumer's indifference curve. Every point on indifference curve *I* represents some combination of products A and B, and all those combinations are equally satisfactory to the consumer. That is, each combination of A and B on the curve yields the same total utility.

Combination	Units of A	Units of B
j	12	2
k	6	4
l	4	6
m	3	8

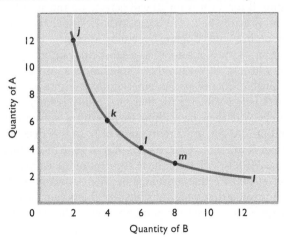

Indifference Curves Are Downsloping

An indifference curve slopes downward because more of one product means less of the other if total utility is to remain unchanged. Suppose the consumer moves from one combination of A and B to another, say, from j to k in Figure 2. In so doing, the consumer obtains more of product B, increasing his or her total utility. But because total utility is the same everywhere on the curve, the consumer must give up some of the other product, A, to reduce total utility by a precisely offsetting amount. Thus "more of B" necessitates "less of A," and the quantities of A and B are inversely related. A curve that reflects inversely related variables is downsloping.

Indifference Curves Are Convex to the Origin

Recall from the appendix to Chapter 1 that the slope of a curve at a particular point is measured by drawing a straight line that is tangent to that point and then measuring the "rise over run" of the straight line. If you drew such straight lines for several points on the curve in Figure 2, you would find that their slopes decline (in absolute terms) as you move down the curve. An indifference curve is therefore convex (bowed inward) to the origin of the graph. Its slope diminishes or becomes flatter as we move down the curve from j to k to l, and so on. Technically, the slope of an indifference curve at each point measures the **marginal rate of substitution (MRS)** of the combination of two goods represented by that point. The slope or MRS shows the rate at which the consumer who possesses the combination must substitute one good for the other (say, B for A) to remain equally satisfied. The diminishing slope of the indifference curve means that the willingness to substitute B for A diminishes as more of B is obtained.

The rationale for this convexity—that is, for a diminishing MRS—is that a consumer's subjective willingness to substitute B for A (or A for B) will depend on the amounts of B and A he or she has to begin with. Consider the table and graph in Figure 2 again, beginning at point j. Here, in relative terms, the consumer has a substantial amount of A and very little of B. Within this combination, a unit of B is very valuable (that is, its marginal utility is high), while a unit of A is less valuable (its marginal utility is low). The consumer will then be willing to give up a substantial amount of A to get, say, 2 more units of B. In this case, the consumer is willing to forgo 6 units of A to get 2 more units of B; the MRS is $\frac{6}{2}$, or 3, for the jk segment of the curve.

But at point k the consumer has less A and more B. Here A is somewhat more valuable, and B less valuable, "at the margin." In a move from point k to point l, the consumer

is willing to give up only 2 units of A to get 2 more units of B, so the MRS is only $\frac{2}{2}$, or 1. Having still less of A and more of B at point l, the consumer is willing to give up only 1 unit of A in return for 2 more units of B and the MRS falls to $\frac{1}{2}$ between l and m.[1]

In general, as the amount of B *increases*, the marginal utility of additional units of B *decreases*. Similarly, as the quantity of A *decreases*, its marginal utility *increases*. In Figure 2 we see that in moving down the curve, the consumer will be willing to give up smaller and smaller amounts of A to offset acquiring each additional unit of B. The result is a curve with a diminishing slope, a curve that is convex to the origin. The MRS declines as one moves southeast along the indifference curve.

The Indifference Map

The single indifference curve of Figure 2 reflects some constant (but unspecified) level of total utility or satisfaction. It is possible and useful to sketch a whole series of indifference curves or an **indifference map,** as shown in Figure 3. Each curve reflects a different level of total utility and therefore never crosses another indifference curve. Specifically, each curve to the right of our original curve (labeled I_3 in

FIGURE 3 An indifference map. An indifference map is a set of indifference curves. Curves farther from the origin indicate higher levels of total utility. Thus any combination of products A and B represented by a point on I_4 has greater total utility than any combination of A and B represented by a point on I_3, I_2, or I_1.

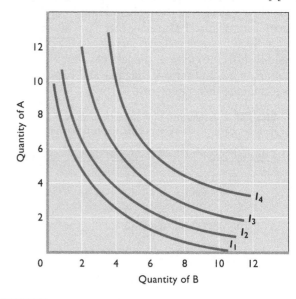

---

[1] MRS declines continuously between j and k, k and l, and l and m. Our numerical values for MRS relate to the curve segments between points and are not the actual values of the MRS at each point. For example, the MRS *at* point l is $\frac{2}{3}$.

Figure 3) reflects combinations of A and B that yield more utility than I_3. Each curve to the left of I_3 reflects less total utility than I_3. As we move out from the origin, each successive indifference curve represents a higher level of utility. To demonstrate this fact, draw a line in a northeasterly direction from the origin; note that its points of intersection with successive curves entail larger amounts of both A and B and therefore higher levels of total utility.

Equilibrium at Tangency

Since the axes in Figures 1 and 3 are identical, we can superimpose a budget line on the consumer's indifference map, as shown in Figure 4. By definition, the budget line indicates all the combinations of A and B that the consumer can attain with his or her money income, given the prices of A and B. Of these attainable combinations, the consumer will prefer the combination that yields the greatest satisfaction or utility. Specifically, the utility-maximizing combination will be the combination lying on the highest attainable indifference curve. It is called the consumer's **equilibrium position.**

In Figure 4 the consumer's equilibrium position is at point X, where the budget line is *tangent* to I_3. Why not point Y? Because Y is on a lower indifference curve, I_2. By moving "down" the budget line—by shifting dollars from purchases of A to purchases of B—the consumer can attain an indifference curve farther from the origin and thereby increase the total utility derived from the same income. Why not point Z? For the same reason: Point Z is on a lower

indifference curve, I_1. By moving "up" the budget line—by reallocating dollars from B to A—the consumer can get on higher indifference curve I_3 and increase total utility.

How about point W on indifference curve I_4? While it is true that W would yield a greater total utility than X, point W is beyond (outside) the budget line and hence is *not* attainable by the consumer. Point X represents the optimal *attainable* combination of products A and B. Note that at the equilibrium position, X, the definition of tangency implies that the slope of the highest attainable indifference curve equals the slope of the budget line. Because the slope of the indifference curve reflects the MRS (marginal rate of substitution) and the slope of the budget line is P_B/P_A, the consumer's optimal or equilibrium position is the point where

$$\text{MRS} = \frac{P_B}{P_A}$$

(You may benefit by trying Appendix Discussion Question 3 at this time.)

Equivalency at Equilibrium

As indicated at the beginning of this appendix, an important difference exists between the marginal-utility theory of consumer demand and the indifference curve theory. The marginal-utility theory assumes that utility is *numerically* measurable, that is, that the consumer can say how much extra utility he or she derives from each extra unit of A or B. The consumer needs that information to determine the utility-maximizing (equilibrium) position, which is defined by

$$\frac{\text{Marginal utility of A}}{\text{Price of A}} = \frac{\text{Marginal utility of B}}{\text{Price of B}}$$

The indifference curve approach imposes a less stringent requirement on the consumer. He or she need only specify whether a particular combination of A and B will yield more than, less than, or the same amount of utility as some other combination of A and B will yield. The consumer need only say, for example, that 6 of A and 7 of B will yield more (or less) satisfaction than will 4 of A and 9 of B. Indifference curve theory does not require that the consumer specify *how much* more (or less) satisfaction will be realized.

That being said, it is a remarkable mathematical fact that both models of consumer behavior will, in any given situation, point to exactly the same consumer equilibrium and, consequently, exactly the same demand behavior. This fact allows us to combine the separate pieces of information that each theory gives us about equilibrium in order to deduce an interesting property about marginal utilities that must also hold true in equilibrium. To see this, note that when we

FIGURE 4 The consumer's equilibrium position. The consumer's equilibrium position is represented by point X, where the black budget line is tangent to indifference curve I_3. The consumer buys 4 units of A at $1.50 per unit and 6 of B at $1 per unit with a $12 money income. Points Z and Y represent attainable combinations of A and B but yield less total utility, as is evidenced by the fact that they are on lower indifference curves. Point W would entail more utility than X, but it requires a greater income than the $12 represented by the budget line.

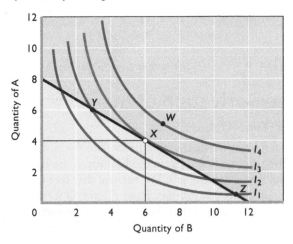

CONSIDER THIS . . .

Indifference Maps and Topographical Maps

The familiar topographical map may help you understand the idea of indifference curves and indifference maps. Each line on a topographical map represents a particular elevation above sea level, such as 500 feet. Similarly, an indifference curve represents a particular level of total utility. When you move from one point on a specific elevation line to another, the elevation remains the same. So it is with an indifference curve. A move from one position to another on the curve leaves total utility unchanged. Neither elevation lines nor indifference curves can intersect. If they did, the meaning of each line or curve would be violated. An elevation line is "an equal-elevation line"; an indifference curve is "an equal-total-utility curve."

Like the topographical map, an indifference map contains not just one line but a series of lines. That is, the topographical map may have elevation lines representing successively higher elevations of 100, 200, 300, 400, and 500 feet. Similarly, the indifference curves on the indifference map represent successively higher levels of total utility. The climber whose goal is to maximize elevation wants to get to the highest attainable elevation line; the consumer desiring to maximize total utility wants to get to the highest attainable indifference curve.

Finally, both topographical maps and indifference maps show only a few of the many such lines that could be drawn. The topographical map, for example, leaves out the elevation lines for 501 feet, 502, 503, and so on. The indifference map leaves out all the indifference curves that could be drawn between those that are displayed.

FIGURE 5 **Deriving the demand curve.** (a) When the price of product B is increased from \$1 to \$1.50, the equilibrium position moves from X to X', decreasing the quantity demanded of product B from 6 to 3 units. (b) The demand curve for product B is determined by plotting the \$1–6-unit and the \$1.50–3-unit price-quantity combinations for product B.

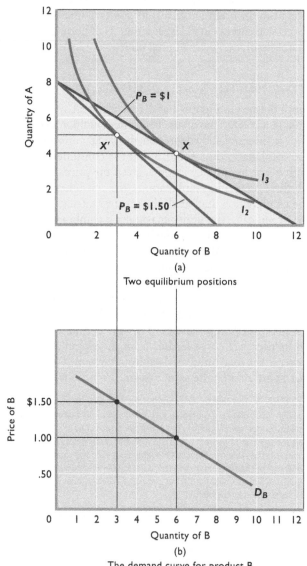

compare the equilibrium situations in the two theories, we find that in the indifference curve analysis the MRS equals P_B/P_A at equilibrium; however, in the marginal-utility approach the ratio of marginal utilities equals P_B/P_A. We therefore deduce that at equilibrium the MRS is equivalent in the marginal-utility approach to the ratio of the marginal utilities of the last purchased units of the two products.[2]

---

[2]Technical footnote: If we begin with the utility-maximizing rule, $MU_A/P_A = MU_B/P_B$, and then multiply through by P_B and divide through by MU_A, we obtain $P_B/P_A = MU_B/MU_A$. In indifference curve analysis we know that at the equilibrium position MRS = P_B/P_A. Hence, at equilibrium, MRS also equals MU_B/MU_A.

The Derivation of the Demand Curve

We noted earlier that with a fixed price for A, an increase in the price of B will cause the bottom of the budget line to fan inward to the left. We can use that fact to derive a demand curve for product B. In Figure 5a we reproduce the part of Figure 4 that shows our initial consumer equilibrium at point X. The budget line determining this equilibrium position assumes that money income is $12 and that $P_A = \$1.50$ and $P_B = \$1$. Let's see what happens to the equilibrium position when we increase P_B to $1.50 and hold both money income and the price of A constant. The result is shown in Figure 5a. The budget line fans to the left, yielding a new equilibrium point X' where it is tangent to lower indifference curve I_2. At X' the consumer buys 3 units of B and 5 of A, compared with 4 of A and 6 of B at X. Our interest is in B, and we now have sufficient information to locate two points on the demand curve for product B. We know that at equilibrium point X the price of B is $1 and 6 units are purchased; at equilibrium point X' the price of B is $1.50 and 3 units are purchased.

These data are shown graphically in Figure 5b as points on the consumer's demand curve for B. Note that the horizontal axes of Figures 5a and 5b are identical; both measure the quantity demanded of B. We can therefore drop

vertical reference lines from Figure 5a down to the horizontal axis of Figure 5b. On the vertical axis of Figure 5b we locate the two chosen prices of B. Knowing that these prices yield the relevant quantities demanded, we locate two points on the demand curve for B. By simple manipulation of the price of B in an indifference curve–budget line context, we have obtained a downward-sloping demand curve for B. We have thus again derived the law of demand assuming "other things equal," since only the price of B was changed (the price of A and the consumer's money income and tastes remained constant). But, in this case, we have derived the demand curve without resorting to the questionable assumption that consumers can measure utility in units called "utils." In this indifference curve approach, consumers simply compare combinations of products A and B and determine which combination they prefer, given their incomes and the prices of the two products.

APPENDIX SUMMARY

LO7.6 Relate how the indifference curve model of consumer behavior derives demand curves from budget lines, indifference curves, and utility maximization.

The indifference curve approach to consumer behavior is based on the consumer's budget line and indifference curves.

The budget line shows all combinations of two products that the consumer can purchase, given product prices and his or her money income. A change in either product prices or money income moves the budget line.

An indifference curve shows all combinations of two products that will yield the same total utility to a consumer. Indifference curves are downsloping and convex to the origin.

An indifference map consists of a number of indifference curves; the farther from the origin, the higher the total utility associated with a curve.

The consumer is in equilibrium (utility is maximized) at the point on the budget line that lies on the highest attainable indifference curve. At that point the budget line and indifference curve are tangent.

Changing the price of one product shifts the budget line and determines a new equilibrium point. A downsloping demand curve can be determined by plotting the price-quantity combinations associated with two or more equilibrium points.

APPENDIX TERMS AND CONCEPTS

budget line

indifference curve

marginal rate of substitution (MRS)

indifference map

equilibrium position

The following and additional problems can be found in **connect**
| ECONOMICS

APPENDIX DISCUSSION QUESTIONS

1. What information is embodied in a budget line? What shifts occur in the budget line when money income (*a*) increases and (*b*) decreases? What shifts occur in the budget line when the price of the product shown on the vertical axis (*c*) increases and (*d*) decreases? **LO7.6**

2. What information is contained in an indifference curve? Why are such curves (*a*) downsloping and (*b*) convex to the origin? Why does total utility increase as the consumer moves to indifference curves farther from the origin? Why can't indifference curves intersect? **LO7.6**

3. Using Figure 4, explain why the point of tangency of the budget line with an indifference curve is the consumer's equilibrium position. Explain why any point where the budget line intersects an indifference curve is not equilibrium. Explain: "The consumer is in equilibrium where $MRS = P_B/P_A$." **LO7.6**

APPENDIX REVIEW QUESTIONS

1. Consider two bundles of coffee and chocolate and how Ted feels about them. The first bundle consists of two cups of coffee and two chocolate bars. The second bundle consists of one cup of coffee and three chocolate bars. If the first bundle gives Ted a total utility of 18 utils while the second bundle gives Ted a total utility of 19 bundles, could the two bundles be on the same indifference curve? Answer yes or no. **LO7.6**

2. Bill spends his money on flowers and cookies so as to maximize his total utility. Both flowers and cookies start off costing $2 each. At that price, Bill buys three flowers and two cookies. When the price of flowers is lowered to $1, Bill buys eight flowers and one cookie. Which of the following statements about Bill's reaction to the price change is **not** true? **LO7.6**

   a. Bill's budget line shifted outward when the price of flowers fell.

   b. Bill moved to a higher indifference curve after the price of flowers fell.

   c. Bill's demand curve for flowers shifted to the right.

   d. Bill's attainable set was smaller before the price of flowers fell.

APPENDIX PROBLEMS

1. Assume that the data in the accompanying table give an indifference curve for Mr. Chen. Graph this curve, putting A on the vertical axis and B on the horizontal axis. Assuming that the prices of A and B are $1.50 and $1, respectively, and that Mr. Chen has $24 to spend, add his budget line to your graph. What combination of A and B will Mr. Chen purchase? Does your answer meet the $MRS = P_B/P_A$ rule for equilibrium? **LO7.6**

Units of A	Units of B
16	6
12	8
8	12
4	24

2. Explain graphically how indifference analysis can be used to derive a demand curve. **LO7.6**

3. **ADVANCED ANALYSIS**   First, graphically illustrate a doubling of income without price changes in the indifference curve model. Next, on the same graph, show a situation in which the person whose indifference curves you are drawing buys considerably more of good B than good A after the income increase. What can you conclude about the relative coefficients of the income elasticity of demand for goods A and B (Chapter 6)? **LO7.6**

CHAPTER 8

Behavioral Economics

Learning Objectives

LO8.1 Define behavioral economics and explain how it contrasts with neoclassical economics.

LO8.2 Discuss the evidence for the brain being modular, computationally restricted, reliant on heuristics, and prone to various forms of cognitive error.

LO8.3 Relate how prospect theory helps to explain many consumer behaviors, including framing effects, mental accounting, anchoring, loss aversion, and the endowment effect.

LO8.4 Describe how time inconsistency and myopia cause people to make suboptimal long-run decisions.

LO8.5 Define fairness and give examples of how it affects behavior in the economy and in the dictator and ultimatum games.

Scientific theories are judged by the accuracy of their predictions. As an example, nobody would take physics seriously if it weren't possible to use the equations taught in college physics classes to predict the best trajectory for putting a satellite into orbit or the best radio frequency to penetrate buildings and provide good indoor cellular service.

Conventional **neoclassical economics** makes many accurate predictions about human choice behavior, especially when it comes to financial incentives and how consumers and businesses respond to changing prices. On the other hand, a number of neoclassical predictions fail quite dramatically. These include predictions about how people deal with risk and uncertainty; choices that require willpower or commitment; and decisions that involve fairness, reciprocity, or trust.

Behavioral economics attempts to make better predictions about human choice behavior by combining insights from economics, psychology, and biology. This chapter introduces you to behavioral economics and the areas in which it has most dramatically increased our understanding of economic behavior. Among the highlights is prospect theory, which was such a large advance on our understanding of how people deal with risk and uncertainty that its inventor, Daniel Kahneman, received the Nobel Prize in economics.

Systematic Errors and the Origin of Behavioral Economics

LO8.1 Define behavioral economics and explain how it contrasts with neoclassical economics.

We tend to think of ourselves as being very good at making decisions. While we may make a few mistakes here and there, we generally proceed through life with confidence, believing firmly that we will react sensibly and make good choices whenever decisions have to be made. In terms of economic terminology, we feel that our decisions are **rational,** meaning that they maximize our chances of achieving what we want.

Unfortunately, scientists have amassed overwhelming evidence to the contrary. People constantly make decision errors that reduce—rather than enhance—the likelihood of getting what they want. In addition, many errors are **systematic errors,** meaning that people tend to repeat them over and over, no matter how many times they encounter a similar situation.

Behavioral economics developed as a separate field of study because neoclassical economics could not explain why people make so many systematic errors. The underlying problem for neoclassical economics is that it assumes that people are fundamentally rational. Under that worldview, people might make some initial mistakes when encountering a new situation. But as they gain experience, they should learn and adapt to the situation. As a result, decision errors should be rare—and definitely not systematic or regularly repeated.

When evidence began to pile up in the late 20th century that even highly experienced people made systematic errors, neoclassical economists assumed that people were just ignorant of what was in their best interests. They assumed that a little education would fix everything. But people often persisted in making the same error even after they were informed that they were behaving against their own interests.

As a result, several researchers realized that it would be necessary to drop the neoclassical assumption that people are fundamentally rational. With that assumption relaxed, economists could develop alternative theories that could make more accurate predictions about human behavior—including the tendency people have toward making systematic errors in certain situations. The result of those efforts is what we today refer to as behavioral economics. Its distinguishing feature is that it is based upon people's actual behavior—which is in many cases substantially irrational, prone to systematic errors, and difficult to modify.

Comparing Behavioral Economics with Neoclassical Economics

While rationality is the most fundamental point of disagreement between behavioral economics and neoclassical economics, it is not the only one. Behavioral economics also contends that neoclassical economics makes a number of highly unrealistic assumptions about human capabilities and motivations, including

- People have stable preferences that aren't affected by context.
- People are eager and accurate calculating machines.
- People are good planners who possess plenty of willpower.
- People are almost entirely selfish and self-interested.

Neoclassical economics made these "simplifying assumptions" for two main reasons. First, they render neoclassical models of human behavior both mathematically elegant and easy enough to solve. Second, they enable neoclassical models to generate very precise predictions about human behavior.

Unfortunately, precision is not the same thing as accuracy. As noted behavioral economist Richard Thaler has written, "Would you rather be elegant and precisely wrong—or messy and vaguely right?"

Behavioral economists err on the side of being messy and vaguely right. As a result, behavioral economics replaces the simplifying assumptions made by neoclassical economics with much more realistic and complex models of human capabilities, motivations, and mental processes.

TABLE 8.1 Major Differences between Behavioral Economics and Conventional Neoclassical Economics

Topic	Neoclassical Economics	Behavioral Economics
Rationality	People are fundamentally rational and will adjust their choices and behaviors to best achieve their goals. Consequently, they will not make systematic errors.	People are irrational and make many errors that reduce their chances of achieving their goals. Some errors are regularly repeated systematic errors.
Stability of preferences	People's preferences are completely stable and unaffected by context.	People's preferences are unstable and often inconsistent because they depend on context (framing effects).
Capability for making mental calculations	People are eager and accurate calculators.	People are bad at math and avoid difficult computations if possible.
Ability to assess future options and possibilities	People are just as good at assessing future options as current options.	People place insufficient weight on future events and outcomes.
Strength of willpower	People have no trouble resisting temptation.	People lack sufficient willpower and often fall prey to temptation.
Degree of selfishness	People are almost entirely self-interested and self-centered.	People are often selfless and generous.
Fairness	People do not care about fairness and only treat others well if doing so will get them something they want.	Many people care deeply about fairness and will often give to others even when doing so will yield no personal benefits.

Table 8.1 summarizes how the two approaches differ in several areas.

Focusing on the Mental Processes behind Decisions

Another major difference between behavioral economics and neoclassical economics is in the amount of weight and importance that they attach to predicting decisions on the one hand and in understanding the mental processes used to reach those decisions on the other. While neoclassical economics focuses almost entirely on predicting behavior, behavioral economics puts significant emphasis on the mental processes driving behavior.

Neoclassical economics focuses its attention on prediction because its assumption that people are rational allows it to fully separate what people do from how they do it. In particular, perfectly rational people will always choose the course of action that will maximize the likelihood of getting what they want. How they actually come to those optimal decisions might be interesting—but you don't need to know anything about that process to predict a perfectly rational person's behavior. He will simply end up doing whatever it is that will best advance his interests. Consequently, neoclassical economists have felt free to ignore the underlying mental processes by which people make decisions.

Behavioral economists disagree sharply with the neoclassical neglect of mental processes. To them, the fact that people are not perfectly rational implies two important reasons for understanding the underlying mental processes that determine decisions:

- It should allow us to make better predictions about behavior.

- It should provide guidance about how to get people to make better decisions.

Improving Outcomes by Improving Decision-Making

Neoclassical economics and behavioral economics differ on how to improve human welfare. Neoclassical economics focuses its attention on providing people with more options. That's because a fully rational person can be trusted to select from any set of options the one that will make him best off. As a result, the only way to make him even happier would be to provide an additional option that is even better.

By contrast, the existence of irrationality leads behavioral economists to conclude that it may be possible to make people better off without providing additional options. In particular, improvements in utility and happiness may be possible simply by getting people to make better selections from the set of options that is already available to them.

This focus on improving outcomes by improving decisions is one of the distinguishing characteristics of behavioral economics. This chapter's Last Word reviews several instances where substantial benefits arise from helping people to make better choices from among the options that they already have.

Viewing Behavioral Economics and Neoclassical Economics as Complements

It would be hasty to view behavioral economics and neoclassical economics as fundamentally opposed or mutually exclusive. Instead, many economists prefer to think of them as complementary approaches that can be used in conjunction to help improve our understanding of human behavior.

As an example of their complementary nature, consider how using the two approaches in tandem can help us achieve a better understanding of how customers behave at a local supermarket.

Neoclassical Economics at the Supermarket The major neoclassical contribution to our understanding of the customers' shopping behavior can be summarized by the phrase "incentives matter." In particular, the customers will care a great deal about prices. When prices go up, they buy less. When prices go down, they buy more.

That insight goes a long way toward explaining how customers behave. But there are other shopping behaviors that neoclassical economics cannot explain with its emphasis on people reacting rationally to incentives and prices. In those cases, behavioral economics may be able to help us figure out what people are up to.

Behavioral Economics at the Supermarket A good example of a shopping behavior that neoclassical economics can't explain very well is that people tend to buy what they happen to see. This behavior is called *impulse buying* and it contradicts the neoclassical assumption that consumers carefully calculate marginal utilities and compare prices before making their purchases. On the other hand, it is a very common behavior that is regularly exploited by retailers.

For instance, nearly all supermarkets attempt to take advantage of impulse buying by placing staple products like milk and eggs against the back walls of their stores. Placing those products at the rear increases impulse buying by forcing customers to walk past hundreds of other items on the way to the milk and eggs. A few of those items will catch their eyes and thereby increase sales as customers end up purchasing products that they had no intention of buying when they first entered the store.

Marketers also know that impulse purchases are highest for items that are stacked on shelves at eye level. So, believe it or not, food manufacturers actively bid against each other and pay supermarkets for the privilege of having their brands stacked at eye level. In cereal aisles, the most expensive shelf space isn't at eye level for an adult, but a foot or two lower—at the eye level of a toddler sitting in a shopping cart or of a child walking with a parent. Because kids are even more prone to impulse buying than adults, cereal makers are more than happy to pay to have their products stacked at kid-friendly eye levels.

Complementary Explanations at the Supermarket Behavioral economics explains impulse buying and other irrational behaviors as the result of a wide variety of underlying factors, including cognitive biases, heuristics, and ongoing battles between different areas of the brain.

You will learn about these underlying factors in the remainder of this chapter. But for now, take to heart the idea that we typically need both neoclassical *and* behavioral methods to figure out what people are doing. Some behaviors—including the fact that shoppers respond strongly to incentives and prices—can be explained very well by neoclassical models that assume people are perfectly rational. But other behaviors—including impulse buying—are very much inconsistent with rationality and are therefore better explained by using the methods of behavioral economics.

CONSIDER THIS . . .

Wannamaker's Lament

Marketing experts try to increase sales or launch new products by applying what they think they know about consumer behavior. Many people find those efforts spooky and wonder if they are being constantly manipulated into purchasing products that they don't want. But how much do the marketing experts really know?

Judging by their success rate, not so much. Most advertising campaigns show little effect on sales. Eighty percent of newly launched consumer products fail within just three months. And the vast majority of Hollywood films end up as flops despite studios spending billions of dollars each year on market research and advertising.

The difficulties facing marketers were best described in the late 19th century by John Wannamaker, the marketing genius and department store entrepreneur who, among other things, invented the price tag and the money-back guarantee. He famously complained, "Half the money I spend on advertising is wasted—the trouble is, I don't know which half!"

A recent response to Wannamaker's lament has been to run lots of simple experiments to see if anything at all can increase sales. Amazon.com runs hundreds of experiments per month, systematically showing different groups of customers different versions of its website in order to see if any of those different versions can increase sales. Las Vegas casinos also run experiments, systematically varying the scents injected into their air-conditioning systems to see which ones cause the largest increases in gambling. Vanilla apparently works very well and some scents are said to increase revenues by up to 20 percent.

FIGURE 8.1 A visual illusion. The human brain uses a large number of heuristics (shortcuts) to process both visual and other types of information. Many of them utilize context to interpret specific bits of information. When that context changes (as it does here when you put your finger horizontally across the middle of the image), so does the brain's heuristic-filtered interpretation.

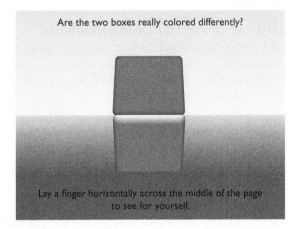

Are the two boxes really colored differently?

Lay a finger horizontally across the middle of the page to see for yourself.

Our Efficient, Error-Prone Brains

LO8.2 Discuss the evidence for the brain being modular, computationally restricted, reliant on heuristics, and prone to various forms of cognitive error.

The human brain is the most complex object in the universe. One hundred billion neurons share 10,000 times as many connections. Working together, they allow you to observe your environment, think creatively, and interact with people and objects.

The brain, however, is rather error-prone. Its many weaknesses are most dramatically illustrated by visual illusions, such as the one shown in Figure 8.1. If you follow the instructions printed in that figure, you will quickly discover that your brain can't consistently tell what color an object is.

This inability to properly process visual information is especially informative about the brain's limitations because the brain devotes more neurons toward processing and interpreting visual information than it does anything else. So, if the brain makes errors with visual processing, we should expect to find errors in everything else it does, too.

Heuristics Are Energy Savers

The brain's information-processing limitations are the result of evolutionary pressures. In particular, it was normally very difficult for our ancestors to get enough food to eat. That matters because our brains are extremely energy intensive. In fact, while your brain accounts for just five percent of your body weight, it burns 20 percent of all the energy you consume each day. So back when our ancestors had to hunt and gather and scavenge to survive, getting enough energy was a constant challenge.

In response, the brain evolved many low-energy mental shortcuts, or **heuristics.** Because they are shortcuts, heuristics are not the most accurate mental-processing options. But in a world where calories were hard to come by, a low-energy "good enough" heuristic was superior to a "perfect but costly" alternative.

Your brain's susceptibility to the visual-processing failure demonstrated in Figure 8.1 is the result of your brain using a host of error-prone heuristics to process visual information. But think about what a good trade-off you are getting. In everyday life, the visual-processing failure demonstrated in Figure 8.1 hardly ever comes up. So, it would be a waste of resources to devote more brainpower to fixing the issue. Put in economic terms, there are diminishing returns to employing additional units of brainpower. Heuristics are used because the opportunity cost of perfection is too high.

Some Common Heuristics The following examples will give you a sense of how the brain employs heuristics for nearly every type of action and decision we make.

Catching a Baseball with the Gaze Heuristic Consider the problem faced by a centerfielder in a baseball game when a ball is hit in his general direction. The mentally expensive way to catch the ball would be for the player to use the laws of physics to determine where the ball is heading so that he could run to that spot before the ball arrives.

What baseball players actually do is lock their eyes on the ball and then adjust their position on the field as necessary to keep the ball in front of them and at the same angle as when they first locked their eyes on it. Just as long as they can run fast enough, this *gaze heuristic* always gets them to the correct place to make the catch. You don't need to learn physics to catch a baseball!

Riding a Bicycle with the Steering Heuristic There is a simple heuristic for staying upright as you ride a bicycle: if you begin to fall, steer in the direction you are falling. This *steering heuristic* works because turning in the direction of a fall generates a centrifugal force that can be used to hold you up long enough for you to steady the bike. This heuristic is almost never articulated, but it is precisely what little kids subconsciously learn to do when they are using training wheels.

Guesstimating Ranks with the Recognition Heuristic Which German city has the larger population, Munich or Stuttgart?

Even people who know nothing about Germany tend to get the right answer to this question. They correctly guess "Munich" by employing the *recognition heuristic*, which says to assume that if one option is more easily recognized, it is probably more important or more highly ranked.

The recognition heuristic isn't foolproof, but it tends to work because relatively important people and places are much more likely to be mentioned in the media. Thus, whichever option is easier to recognize will probably be larger or more important.

Much of advertising is based on exploiting the recognition heuristic. Indeed, companies spend billions to ensure that consumers are familiar with their products because when it comes time to buy, consumers will be biased toward the products that seem the most familiar.

Interpreting Depth with the Shadow Heuristic   The world is three-dimensional, but the light-sensing surfaces at the back of our eyes are two-dimensional. As a result, our brains are forced to use a cluster of heuristics to estimate depth when interpreting the two-dimensional images registered by our eyes.

Figure 8.2 shows how the *shadow heuristic* causes you to interpret shaded, two-dimensional circles as either humps or holes depending upon whether each circle is shaded on the top or on the bottom. Look at Figure 8.2 and count how many of the six shaded circles look like humps rather than holes. Now turn the picture upside down and count again. If your vision is typical, you will find that all the humps have become holes, and vice versa.

Here's what's happening. The shadow heuristic evolved back when sunlight was the only important source of light. As a result, it presumes that light always falls from above. Under that assumption, anything that sticks out from a surface will cast a shadow below it while anything indented will have a shadow on top due to the top of the recessed area casting a shadow on whatever lies below.

FIGURE 8.2 **The shadow heuristic.** The brain processes light with a heuristic that assumes that light always comes from above. Under that assumption, anything that sticks out will have a shadow on the bottom while anything that is recessed will have a shadow on top. As a result, your brain interprets five of the six shaded circles as humps that stick out while the bottom middle circle is interpreted as a recess. See what happens when you turn the picture upside down. Surprised?

Because your brain applies the shadow heuristic no matter what, you are tricked into believing that the shaded circles in Figure 8.2 are three-dimensional and either humps or holes depending upon whether they are shaded on the top or on the bottom.

The Implications of Hardwired Heuristics As you study the rest of the chapter, keep in mind that most heuristics appear to be hardwired into the brain, and, consequently, impossible to unlearn or avoid. That possibility has three important implications:

1. It may be very difficult for people to alter detrimental behaviors or routines even after you point out what they're doing wrong.

2. People may be easy prey for those who understand their hardwired tendencies.

3. If you want people to make a positive behavioral change, it might be helpful to see if you can put them in a situation where a heuristic will kick in and subconsciously lead them toward the desired outcome.

Brain Modularity

The modern human brain is modular, so that specific areas deal with specific sensations, activities, and emotions—such as vision, breathing, and anger.

This modular structure is the result of millions of years of evolution, with the modern human brain evolving in stages from the much less complex brains of our hominid ancestors. The oldest parts of the brain are located in the back of the head, where the spine enters the skull. The newest parts are up front, near the forehead.

The older parts control subconscious activities like breathing and sweating as well as automatic emotional reactions such as fear and joy. The newer parts allow you to think creatively, imagine the future, and keep track of everyone in your social network. They are largely under conscious control.

System 1 and System 2 It is useful to think of the brain's decision-making systems as falling into two categories, which are informally referred to as System 1 and System 2. System 1 uses a lot of heuristics in the older parts of your brain to produce quick, unconscious reactions. If you ever get a "gut instinct," System 1 is responsible. By contrast, System 2 uses the newer parts of your brain to undertake slow, deliberate, and conscious calculations of costs and benefits. If you ever find yourself "thinking things over," you are using System 2.

Conflicts may sometimes arise between our unconscious System 1 intuitions and our conscious System 2 deliberations. For example, System 1 may urge you to eat an entire pile of cookies as fast as possible, while System 2 admonishes you to stick to your diet and have only one. That being said, a large body of evidence suggests that most decisions are probably either fully or mostly the result of System 1 intuitions and heuristics. That matters because those unconscious mental processes suffer from a variety of cognitive biases.

Cognitive Biases **Cognitive biases** are the misperceptions or misunderstandings that cause systematic errors.

There are a wide variety of cognitive biases, but they can be placed into two general categories. The first are mental-processing errors that result from faulty heuristics. As previously discussed, faulty heuristics are the result of evolution trading off accuracy for speed and efficiency.

The second category of cognitive biases consists of mental-processing errors that result from our brains not having any evolved capacities for dealing with modern problems and challenges, such as solving calculus problems or programming computers. Because our ancestors never encountered things like math, engineering, or statistics, our brains have a total absence of System 1 heuristics for dealing with those sorts of problems. In addition, our slower and more deliberative System 2 mental processes are also of only limited assistance because they were evolved to deal with other types of problems, such as keeping track of everyone in a social network or attempting to think through whether it would be better to go hunting in the morning or in the evening.

As a result, most people find recently developed mental challenges like math and physics to be very tiresome. In addition, cognitive biases often result because the System 2 processes that we are recruiting to solve modern problems were in fact designed for other purposes and don't work particularly well when directed at modern problems.

Psychologists have identified scores of cognitive biases. Here are a few that are relevant to economics and decision-making.

Confirmation Bias The term *confirmation bias* refers to the human tendency to pay attention only to information that agrees with one's preconceptions. Information that contradicts those preconceptions is either ignored completely or rationalized away. Confirmation bias is problematic because it allows bad decisions to continue long after an impartial weighing of the evidence would have put a stop to them. When you see someone persisting with a failed policy or incorrect opinion despite overwhelming evidence that he or she should try something else, confirmation bias is probably at work.

Self-Serving Bias The term *self-serving bias* refers to people's tendency to attribute their successes to personal effort or personal character traits while at the same time attributing any failures to factors that were out of their control. While helping to preserve people's self-esteem, this bias makes it difficult for people to learn from their mistakes because they incorrectly assume that anything that went wrong was beyond their control.

Overconfidence Effect The *overconfidence effect* refers to people's tendency to be overly confident about how likely their judgments and opinions are to be correct. As an example, people who rated their answers to a particular quiz as being "99 percent likely to be right" were in fact wrong more than 40 percent of the time. Such overconfidence can lead to bad decisions because people will tend to take actions without pausing to verify if their initial hunches are actually true.

Hindsight Bias People engage in *hindsight bias* when they retroactively believe that they were able to predict past events. As an example, consider an election between candidates named Terence and Philip. Before the election happens, many people will predict that Terence will lose. But after Terence ends up winning, many of those same people will convince themselves that they "knew all along" that Terence was going to win. This faulty "I-knew-it-all-along" perspective causes people to massively overestimate their predictive abilities.

Availability Heuristic The *availability heuristic* causes people to base their estimates about the likelihood of an event not on objective facts but on whether or not similar events come to mind quickly and are readily available in their memories. Because vivid, emotionally charged images come to mind more easily, people tend to think that events like homicides, shark attacks, and lightning strikes are much more common than they actually are. At the same time, they underestimate the likelihood of unmemorable events.

As an example, you are five times more likely to die of stomach cancer than be murdered, but most people rate the likelihood of being murdered as much higher. They do this because they have many vivid memories of both real and fictional murders but almost no recollections whatsoever of anyone dying of stomach cancer.

The availability heuristic causes people to spend too much of their time and effort attempting to protect themselves against charismatic dangers of low actual probability while neglecting to protect themselves against dull threats of substantially higher probability.

Planning Fallacy The *planning fallacy* is the tendency people have to massively underestimate the time needed to

FIGURE 8.3 **The letter illusion is the result of a framing effect.** In each row, the middle symbol is the same. When that symbol is surrounded by the letters A and C in the top row, our brains tend to register the symbol as the letter B. But when it is surrounded by the numbers 12 and 14 in the bottom row, our brains tend to register it as the number 13. What our brain "sees" is largely a matter of context (frame).

complete a task. A good example is when last-minute test cramming gets really frantic. The student doing the cramming probably underestimated by many hours how much time he needed to prepare for the exam. The planning fallacy also helps to explain why construction projects, business initiatives, and government reform efforts all tend to come in substantially behind schedule.

Framing Effects **Framing effects** occur when a change in context (frame) causes people to react differently to a particular piece of information or to an otherwise identical situation.

Figure 8.3 gives an example of a framing effect. The middle symbol is identical in both rows, but it is interpreted differently depending upon whether it is surrounded by letters or numbers. When surrounded by letters in the top row, the brain tends to interpret the symbol as the letter B. When surrounded by numbers in the bottom row, the brain tends to interpret the symbol as the number 13.

Changes in context can also cause extraordinary changes in behavior. Experiments have shown that ordinary people are twice as likely to litter, steal, or trespass if experimenters tag an area with graffiti and scatter lots of trash around. By changing the area's appearance from neat and orderly to rundown and chaotic, experimenters got ordinary people to subconsciously choose to engage in more crime.

Framing effects can also cause consumers to change their purchases. At the local supermarket, apples command a higher price if each one comes with a pretty sticker

and meat sells faster if it is packaged in shiny plastic containers. At a high-end retailer, expensive packaging increases the perceived value of the shop's merchandise. So does having a nice physical space in which to shop. Thus, high-end retailers spend a lot on architecture and displays.

QUICK REVIEW 8.1

- Behavioral economics differs from neoclassical economics because its models of decision-making take into account the fact that heuristics and cognitive biases cause people to make systematic errors.

- To conserve energy, the brain relies on low-energy mental shortcuts, or heuristics, that will usually produce the correct decision or answer.

- Cognitive biases are systematic misperceptions or bad decisions that arise because (1) heuristics are error-prone in certain situations or (2) evolution did not prepare our brains to handle many modern tasks such as solving calculus problems.

Prospect Theory

LO8.3 Relate how prospect theory helps to explain many consumer behaviors, including framing effects, mental accounting, anchoring, loss aversion, and the endowment effect.

Neoclassical economics focuses much of its attention on consumer-choice situations in which people only have to deal with "goods" as opposed to "bads." When deciding on how to spend a budget, a consumer only considers items that would bring her positive marginal utility—that is, "good" things. She then uses the utility-maximizing rule to select how much of each of those good things she should consume to get as much utility as possible from her limited budget.

Unfortunately, life often forces us to deal with bad things, too. Our houses may burn down. A potential investment may go bad. The money we lend out may not be repaid.

How people cope with negative possibilities is a central focus of behavioral economics. Many thousands of observations have been cataloged as to how people actually deal with the prospect of bad things as well as good things. Three very interesting facts summarize how people deal with goods and bads:

- People judge good things and bad things in relative terms, as gains and losses relative to their current situation, or **status quo.**

- People experience both diminishing marginal utility for gains (meaning that each successive unit of gain feels good, but not as good as the previous unit) as well as diminishing marginal disutility for losses (meaning that each successive unit of loss hurts, but less painfully than the previous unit).

- People experience **loss aversion,** meaning that for losses and gains near the status quo, losses are felt *much* more intensely than gains—in fact, about 2.5 times more intensely. Thus, for instance, the pain experienced by an investor who loses one dollar from his status quo level of wealth will be about 2.5 times more intense than the pleasure he would have felt if he had gained one dollar relative to his status quo level of wealth.

Rising Consumption and the Hedonic Treadmill

For many sensations, people's brains are wired to notice changes rather than states. For example, your brain can sense acceleration—your change in speed—but not speed itself. As a result, standing still feels the same as moving at a constant 50 miles per hour. And if you accelerate from one constant speed to another—say, from 50 miles per hour to 70 miles per hour—you will feel the acceleration only while it's happening. Once you settle down at the new higher speed, it will feel like you are standing still again.

Consumption appears to work in much the same way. If you are used to a given level of consumption—say, $50,000 per year—then you will get a lot of enjoyment for a while if your consumption accelerates to $100,000 per year. But, as time passes, you will get used to that higher level of consumption, so that $100,000 per year seems ordinary and doesn't bring you any more pleasure than $50,000 per year used to bring you when it was your status quo.

Economist Richard Easterlin coined the term *hedonic treadmill* (pleasure treadmill) to describe this phenomenon. Just as a person walking on a real treadmill gets nowhere, people trying to make themselves permanently happier by consuming more also get nowhere because they end up getting used to any higher level of consumption. Indeed, except for the extremely poor, people across the income spectrum report similar levels of happiness and satisfaction with their lives. This has led several economists, including Robert Frank, to argue that we should all stop trying to consume more because doing so doesn't make us any happier in the long run. What do you think? Should we all step off of the hedonic treadmill?

These three facts about how people deal with goods and bads form the basis of **prospect theory,** which sheds important light on how consumers plan for and deal with life's ups and downs as well as why they often appear narrow-minded and fail to "see the big picture." To give you an idea of how powerful prospect theory is—and why its pioneer, Daniel Kahneman, was awarded the Nobel Prize in Economics—let's go through some examples of consumer behavior that would be hard to explain without the insights provided by prospect theory.

ORIGIN OF THE IDEA

08.1

Prospect theory

Losses and Shrinking Packages

Because people see the world in terms of gains and losses relative to the status quo situations that they are used to, businesses have to be very careful about increasing the prices they charge for their products. This is because once consumers become used to a given price, they will view any increase in the price as a loss relative to the status quo price they had been accustomed to.

The fact that consumers may view a price increase as a loss explains the otherwise curious fact that many food producers react to rising input costs by shrinking the sizes of their products. The company most famous for doing this is Hershey's chocolates. During its first decades of operation about 100 years ago, it would always charge exactly 5 cents for one of its Hershey's chocolate bars. But the size of the bars would increase or decrease depending on the cost of the company's inputs. When the cost of raw materials rose, the company would keep the price fixed at 5 cents but decrease the size of the bar. When the cost of raw materials fell, it would again keep the price fixed at 5 cents but increase the size of the bar.

This seems rather bizarre when you consider that consumers were not in any way *actually* being shielded from the changes in input prices. That is because what should rationally matter to consumers is the price per ounce that they are paying for Hershey's Bars. And that *does* go up and down when the price remains fixed but the size of the bars changes.

But people aren't being fully rational here. They mentally fixate on the product's price because that is the characteristic that they are used to focusing on when making their purchasing decisions. And because the 5-cent price had become the status quo that they were used to, Hershey's understood that any price increase would be mentally categorized as a loss. Thus, Hershey's wisely chose to keep the price of its product fixed at 5 cents even when input prices were rising.

Other companies employ the same strategy today. In the years following the 2007–2008 recession, the prices of many raw materials, including sugar, soybeans, and corn, rose substantially. Many major manufacturers reacted by reducing product sizes while keeping prices fixed. Häagen-Dazs reduced the size of its supermarket ice cream tubs from 16 to 14 ounces. Kraft reduced the number of slices of cheese in a package of Kraft Singles from 24 to 22 slices. A bottle of Tropicana orange juice shrank from 64 ounces (the traditional half-gallon size) to just 59 ounces. And Procter and Gamble reduced the size of Bounty paper towel rolls from 60 to 52 sheets.

Framing Effects and Advertising

Because people evaluate situations in terms of gains and losses, their decision-making can be very sensitive to the mental frame that they use to evaluate whether a possible outcome should be viewed as a gain or a loss. Here are a couple of examples in which differences in the context or "frame" change the perception of whether a situation should be treated as a gain or loss. See how you react to them.

- Would you be happy with a salary of $100,000 per year? You might say yes. But what if your salary last year had been $140,000? Are you still going to say yes? Now that you know you are taking a $40,000 pay cut, does that $100,000 salary seem as good as it did before?

- Similarly, suppose you have a part-time job. One day, your boss Joe walks in and says that he is going to give you a 10 percent raise. Would that please you? Now, what if he also mentioned that *everyone else* at your firm would be getting a 15 percent raise. Are you still going to be just as pleased? Or does your raise now seem like a loss compared to what everyone else will be getting?

Prospect theory takes into account the fact that people's preferences can change drastically depending on whether contextual information causes them to define a situation as a gain or a loss. These framing effects are important to recognize because they can be manipulated by advertisers, lawyers, and politicians to try to alter people's decisions. For instance, would an advertising company be better off marketing a particular brand of hamburger as "20% fat" or as "80% lean"? Both phrases describe the same meat, but one frames the situation as a loss (20 percent fat) while the other frames it as a gain (80 percent lean).

And would you be more willing to take a particular medicine if you were told that 99.9 percent of the people who take it live or if you were told that 0.1 percent of the people who take it die? Continuing to live is a gain, whereas dying is clearly a loss. Which frame sounds better to you?

Framing effects have major consequences for consumer behavior because any frame that alters whether consumers consider a situation to be a gain or a loss *will* affect their consumption decisions!

Anchoring and Credit Card Bills

Before people can calculate their gains and losses, they must first define the status quo from which to measure those changes. But it turns out that irrelevant information can unconsciously influence people's feelings about the status quo. Here's a striking example. Find a group of people and ask each person to write down the last two digits of his or her Social Security number. Then ask each person to write down his or her best estimate of the value of some object that you display to them—say, a nice wireless keyboard. What you will find is that the people whose Social Security numbers end in higher numbers—say, 67 or 89—will give higher estimates for the value of the keyboard than people whose Social Security numbers end in smaller numbers like 18 or 37. The effect can be huge. Among students in one MBA class at MIT, those with Social Security numbers ending between 80 and 99 gave an average estimate of $56 for a wireless keyboard, while their classmates whose Social Security numbers ended between 00 and 20 gave an average estimate of just $16.

Psychologists and behavioral economists refer to this phenomenon as **anchoring** because people's estimates about the value of the keyboard are influenced, or "anchored," by the recently considered information about the last two digits of their Social Security numbers. Why irrelevant information can anchor subsequent valuations is not fully understood. But the anchoring effect is real and can lead people to unconsciously alter how they evaluate different options.

Unfortunately, credit card companies have figured this out. They use anchoring to increase their profits by showing very small minimum-payment amounts on borrowers' monthly credit card statements. The companies could require larger minimum payments, but the minimum-payment numbers that they present are only typically about 2 percent of what a customer owes. Why such a small amount? Because it acts as an anchor that causes people to unconsciously make smaller payments each month. This can make a huge difference in how long it takes to pay off their bill and how much in total interest they will end up paying. For a customer who owes $1,000 on a credit card that charges the typical interest rate of 19 percent per year, it will take 22 years and $3,398.12 in total payments (including accumulated interest) to pay off the debt if he only makes 2 percent monthly payments. By showing such small minimum-payment amounts, credit card companies anchor many customers into the expensive habit of paying off their debts slowly rather than quickly.

Mental Accounting and Overpriced Warranties

The utility-maximizing rule (Chapter 7) assumes that people will look at all of their potential consumption options simultaneously when trying to maximize the total utility that they can get from spending their limited incomes. But economist Richard Thaler famously noted that people sometimes look at consumption options in isolation, thereby irrationally failing to look at all their options simultaneously. Thaler coined the term **mental accounting** to describe this behavior because it was as if people arbitrarily put certain options into totally separate "mental accounts" that they dealt with without any thought to options outside of those accounts.

As an example of where this suboptimal tendency leads, consider the extended warranties offered by big electronic stores whenever customers purchase expensive products like plasma TVs. These warranties are very much overpriced given that the products they insure hardly ever break down. Personal financial experts universally tell people not to buy them. Yet many people do buy them because they engage in mental accounting.

They do this by mentally labeling their purchase of the TV as an isolated, individual transaction, sticking it into a separate mental account in their brain that might have a title like "Purchase of New TV." Viewing the purchase in isolation exaggerates the size of the potential loss that would come from a broken TV. Customers who view the transaction in isolation see the possibility of a $1,000 loss on their $1,000 purchase as a potential total loss— "Holy cow! I could lose $1,000 on a $1,000 TV!" By contrast, people who can see the big picture are able to compare the potential $1,000 loss with the much larger value of their entire future income stream. That allows them to realize that the potential loss is relatively minor—and thus not a good enough reason to purchase an expensive warranty.

The Endowment Effect and Market Transactions

Prospect theory also offers an explanation for the **endowment effect,** which is the tendency that people have to put a higher valuation on anything that they currently possess (are endowed with) than on identical items that they do not own but might purchase. For instance, if we show a person a new coffee mug and ask him what the maximum amount is that he would pay to buy it, he might say $10. But if we then give the mug to him so that he now owns it, and we then ask how much we would have to pay him to buy it back, he will very likely report a much higher value—say, $15.

The interesting thing is that he is not just bluffing or driving a hard bargain. Rather, the human brain appears wired to put a higher value on things we own than on things we don't. Economist John List has shown that this tendency can moderate if people are used to buying things for resale—that is, buying them with the intention of getting rid of them. But without such experience, the endowment effect can be quite strong. If it is, it can make market transactions between buyers and sellers harder because sellers will be demanding higher prices for the items they are selling ("Hey, *my* mug is worth $15 to me!") than the values put on those items by potential buyers ("Dude, *your* mug is only worth $10 to me").

Several researchers have suggested that loss aversion may be responsible for the endowment effect and the higher values demanded by sellers. They argue that once a person possesses something, the thought of parting with it seems like a potential loss. As a result, the person will demand a lot of money as compensation if he or she is asked to sell the item. On the other hand, potential purchasers do not feel any potential sense of loss, so they end up assigning lower values to the same items.

Status Quo Bias

Prospect theory also explains **status quo bias,** which is the tendency that people have to favor any option that is presented to them as being the default (status quo) option. As an example, consider Global Perspective 8.1. It shows, for a selection of European countries, the percentages of their respective populations that have indicated their willingness to participate in organ-donation programs.

As you can see, seven of the 11 countries have very high participation rates while the other four have low participation rates. You might suspect that cultural differences are at play, but that doesn't make sense when you note that countries like Germany and Austria that are culturally very similar still have massively different participation rates.

What is actually going on is a difference in the default option that people are presented with when they are asked whether they wish to participate. In the seven countries with high participation rates, the default option is participation, so that those who don't want to participate must

GLOBAL PERSPECTIVE 8.1

Percent of Population Consenting to Be Organ Donors

People tend to stick with whatever option is presented as the default option. Thus, the seven countries with high percentages consenting to be organ donors have organ-donation programs in which the default option is participation. By contrast, the four countries with low percentages consenting to be organ donors have organ-donation programs where the default option is *not* participating.

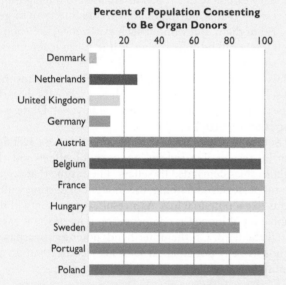

Source: Eric Johnson and Daniel Goldstein, "Defaults and Donation Decisions," *Transplantation* 78, no. 12, December 27, 2004. Used by permission of Wolters Kluwer Health via Copyright Clearance Center.

explicitly check off a box indicating that they don't want to participate. By contrast, in the four countries with low participation rates, the default option is *not* participating, so that those wishing to participate must explicitly check off a box indicating that they want to participate.

What we see in all countries is that nearly everyone chooses to do nothing. They almost never check off the box that would indicate doing the opposite of the default option. Consequently, they end up agreeing to whatever the default option happens to be. Thus, the huge differences in participation rates among the 11 countries are driven almost entirely by what the default option happens to be.

Prospect theory explains this and other examples of status quo bias as a combination of the endowment effect and loss aversion. When people are put into a novel situation, they have no preexisting preferences for any of the options.

As a result, the way the options are framed becomes very important because if any of them is presented as the default option, people will tend to treat it as an endowment that they wish to hold on to. At the same time, they will treat any other option as a prospect that could potentially cause a loss. Loss aversion then kicks in and causes most people to stick with the default option in order to avoid the possibility of incurring a loss. The result is a bias toward the status quo.

Status quo bias can be used to explain several consumer behaviors. Consider brand loyalty. If you have gotten used to eating Heinz ketchup, then status quo bias will make you reluctant to purchase any other brand of ketchup. Overcoming that feeling of potential loss is a difficult challenge for competing brands, as attested to by the fact that rivals seeking to challenge an established brand are often forced to resort to deep discounts or free samples to get consumers to even try their products.

Myopia and Time Inconsistency

LO8.4 Describe how time inconsistency and myopia cause people to make suboptimal long-run decisions.

Our ancient ancestors had little cause to spend much time worrying about anything that would happen in the distant future. Infectious diseases, predatory animals, and the constant threat of starvation made life extremely precarious. Consequently, they had to be almost entirely focused on the present moment and how to get through the next few weeks or the next few months.

Today, however, people living in industrialized countries only rarely die from infectious diseases, mostly see predatory animals in zoos, and are under no threat at all of starvation. Living past 80 is now routine and most of us will die of old age. As a result, long-run challenges like planning for retirement and saving for college are now common tasks that nearly everyone faces.

Unfortunately, our brains were designed for our ancestors' more immediate concerns. Thus, we often have difficulty with long-run planning and decisions that involve trade-offs between the present and the future. Two of the major stumbling blocks are myopia and time inconsistency.

Myopia

In biology, myopia, or nearsightedness, refers to a defect of the eye that makes distant objects appear fuzzy, out of focus, and hard to see. By analogy, economists use the word **myopia** to describe the fact that our brains have a hard time conceptualizing the future. Compared with the present, the future seems fuzzy, out of focus, and hard to see.

As an example, our brains are very good at weighing current benefits against current costs in order to make immediate decisions. But our brains almost seem "future blind" when it comes to conceptualizing either future costs or future benefits. As a result, we have difficulty evaluating possibilities that will occur more than a few weeks or months into the future.

The primary consequence of myopia is that when people are forced to choose between something that will generate benefits quickly and something that won't yield benefits for a long time, they will have a very strong tendency to favor the more immediate option. As an example, imagine that Terence has $1,000 that he can either spend on a vacation next month or save for his retirement in 30 years.

Myopia will cause him to have great difficulty imagining the additional spending power that he will be able to enjoy in 30 years if he saves the money. On the other hand, it is very easy for him to imagine all the fun he could have next month if he were to go on vacation. As a result, he will be strongly biased toward spending the money next month. With myopia obscuring the benefits of the long-term option, the short-term option will seem much more attractive.

Myopia also makes it hard to stick with a diet or follow an exercise plan. Compared with the immediate and clearly visible pleasures of eating doughnuts or hanging out, the future benefits from eating better or exercising consistently are just too hazy in most people's minds to be very attractive.

Time Inconsistency

Time inconsistency is the tendency to systematically misjudge at the present time what you will want to do at some future time. This misperception causes a disconnect between what you currently think you will want to do at some particular point in the future and what you actually end up wanting to do when that moment arrives. It is as though your present self does not understand what your future self will want.

Waking up early is a good example. At 8 p.m. on a Tuesday, you may really like the idea of waking up early the next morning so that you can exercise before starting the rest of your day. So you set your alarm 90 minutes earlier than you normally do. But when your alarm goes off the next morning at that earlier time, you loath the concept, throw the alarm across the room, and go back to sleep. That switch in your preferences from the night

before is the essence of time inconsistency. Your future self ends up disagreeing with your current self.

Self-Control Problems Time inconsistency is important because it is a major cause of **self-control problems.** To see why, imagine that before heading out to a restaurant with friends, you think that you will be happy sticking to your diet and only ordering a salad. After all, that particular restaurant has very tasty salads. But then, after you get there, you find the dessert menu overwhelmingly attractive and end up ordering two servings of cheesecake.

Because you were time inconsistent and didn't understand what your future self would want, you placed yourself into a situation in which it was very difficult for you to stick to your diet. If you had, instead, been able to correctly predict what your future self would want, you might have decided to stay home for the evening rather than putting yourself in temptation's way. Alternatively, you could have gone, but not before making your friends promise to prevent you from ordering dessert.

Time inconsistency also makes it hard for many workers to save money. Before their paychecks arrive, they mistakenly assume that their future selves will want to save money as much as their current selves do. But once the money becomes available, their future selves end up wanting to spend everything and save nothing.

Fighting Self-Control Problems with Precommitments The key to fighting time inconsistency and self-control problems is to have a good understanding of what your future self is likely to want. You can then make **precommitments** and take actions ahead of time to prevent your future self from doing much damage.

Hiding the Alarm Clock Consider again the problem of wanting to wake up 90 minutes early on Wednesday morning so that you can work out before starting the rest of your day. If you understand that your future self is not going to want to cooperate, you can take steps to prevent that future self from flaking out. Some people set multiple alarms. Others put their alarms on the other side of the room, underneath a pile of stuff that will have to be moved if the future self wants to turn the damned thing off. But the point is that each of these methods ensures that it will be nearly impossible for the future self to easily get back to sleep. They set things up so that the future self will be forced to do what the present self desires.

Automatic Payroll Deductions Precommitment strategies have also been used to help future selves save more. Consider automatic payroll deductions. If a worker named

Blaire signs up for such a program, a fixed percentage will be automatically deducted from each of her paychecks and deposited directly into her retirement savings account. Because that money never gets to her checking account, there is no way for Blaire's future self to fall prey to temptation and spend it. As the old saying goes, "Out of sight, out of mind."

Salary Smoothing School teachers and college professors often have the choice of having their annual salaries paid out over 9 larger monthly installments (to match the length of the school year) or 12 smaller monthly installments (to match the length of the calendar year). If we observe which option they actually choose, we find that the vast majority opt to have their salaries spread out over 12 months rather than 9 months.

They do so because they fear self-control problems. In particular, they are afraid that if they opt to be paid over 9 months, they won't have the self control to save enough money during the 9-month period when they will be getting paid to last them through the three months of summer vacation when they won't be getting paid. To avoid that situation, they opt to have their salaries spread out evenly over the entire calendar year. That precommitment ensures that their future selves are never given the chance to blow through all the money too quickly.

Early Withdrawal Penalties Sometimes, one cognitive bias can be used to offset another. Retirement accounts that have early-withdrawal penalties are a good example. They use loss aversion to offset time inconsistency and self-control problems.

In some cases, the penalties on these sorts of accounts are as high as 25 percent, meaning that if a saver wanted to withdraw $1,000 before reaching retirement, he would have to give up an additional $250 (= 25 percent of $1,000) as a penalty. While that amount is substantial in itself, loss aversion makes it even more painful to contemplate. As a result, most people can't bring themselves to make an early withdrawal.

Weight-Loss Competitions Loss aversion also drives the effectiveness of weight-loss competitions. For a person who has agreed to participate, the prospect of losing the competition can be a great motivator because loss aversion applies just as much to future selves as to present selves. Even after the future rolls around and the future self is in charge, the future self won't like the prospect of losing either. Thus, the present self can be confident that the future self will also be motivated to stick to the weight-loss goals that the present self wants to achieve.

CONSIDER THIS . . .

Betting Against Yourself

The website StickK.com makes it easy for people to set up financial incentives that can help them reach their goals. Strangely enough, it does that by getting people to bet against themselves.

Founded by behavioral economist Dean Karlan and fellow Yale University professor Alan Iyers, StickK.com lets each user specify a goal, such as losing 30 pounds in the next year. The user then sets up a "commitment contract" that specifies an amount of money that he or she will have to pay via credit card as a penalty for not reaching his or her goal. That potential penalty gets loss aversion to kick in, thereby helping the user follow through and achieve his or her goal.

As a fun twist, StickK.com also requires each user to specify a recipient for the penalty money. Some users specify that their penalty money go to a charity that they like. But many choose to increase their motivation by designating an "anti-charity" as the recipient. What is an anti-charity? It's a person or group that the user hates.

By letting people designate anti-charities, StickK.com uses deeply seated personal animosities in addition to loss aversion to help people overcome time inconsistency and self-control issues. Those incentives appear to work quite well, as 70 percent of StikK.com users report success in reaching their goals.

The nearby Consider This piece illustrates another effective way to use loss aversion to help overcome self-control problems.

QUICK REVIEW 8.2

- Prospect theory models decision-making by accounting for the fact that people's choices are affected by whether a possible outcome is perceived as a prospective gain or a prospective loss relative to the current status quo situation.

- Because our ancestors were focused on short-term survival, our brains suffer from myopia and are not good at dealing with decisions that involve the future.

- Precommitments can be used to compensate for time inconsistency and the self-control problems that arise when the future self doesn't want to do what the present self prefers.

Fairness and Self-Interest

LO8.5 Define fairness and give examples of how it affects behavior in the economy and in the dictator and ultimatum games.

Neoclassical models assume that people are purely self-interested. They do so because "pure self-interest" seems like a good basis for predicting many economic behaviors, especially those happening in market situations where people are dealing mostly with strangers and are, consequently, unlikely to be particularly sentimental or charity-minded.

Adam Smith, the founder of modern economics, put this line of thinking into words. The most-quoted passage from *The Wealth of Nations* reads,

> It is not from the benevolence of the butcher, the brewer, or the baker that we expect our dinner, but from their regard to their own interest. We address ourselves not to their humanity but to their self-love, and never talk to them of our own necessities but of *their* advantages.

Smith, however, did not believe that people are *exclusively* focused on self-love and their own interests. He believed that we are also strongly motivated by emotions such as charity, selflessness, and the desire to work for the common good. He expressed this view at length in his other influential book, *The Theory of Moral Sentiments*. The most-famous passage from that book reads:

> How selfish soever man may be supposed, there are evidently some principles in his nature which interest him in the fortune of others and render their happiness necessary to him though he derives nothing from it except the pleasure of seeing it.

What behavioral economists have discovered is that this human propensity to care about others extends into every type of economic behavior. While self-interest is always present, most people care deeply about others and how they are interacting with others. As a result, economic transactions are heavily influenced by moral and ethical factors.

Field Evidence for Fairness

Many real-world behaviors support the contention that economic transactions are heavily influenced by beliefs and values. This "field evidence" has helped behavioral economists identify the ethical and moral factors that appear to have the largest influence on economic behavior. Fairness is among the most important.

Fairness is a person's opinion as to whether a price, wage, or allocation is considered morally or ethically acceptable. Standards of fairness vary from person to person

and economists generally take no stand on what people consider to be right or wrong. But fairness has been studied extensively because many everyday economic behaviors indicate that people care substantially about fairness and not just about maximizing what they can get for themselves.

Consider the following examples—none of which would be undertaken by a purely self-interested person.

- *Giving to Charity* Each year, U.S. charities receive over $300 billion of cash donations and 8 billion hours of free labor. These donations of time and money are inconsistent with the idea that people are only interested in themselves. What is more, many of the cash donations are anonymous. That suggests that many donors have extremely pure motives and are not donating just to make themselves look good.

- *Obeying the Law* In many countries, the large majority of citizens are law-abiding despite having many opportunities to break the law without getting caught. In the same way, the large majority of taxpayers complete their tax returns honestly despite having many opportunities to cut corners and hide income.

- *Fixing Prices* During hurricanes and other natural disasters, shortages of crucial products such as gasoline and electric generators often develop. The shortages imply that retailers could raise prices, but they mostly keep prices fixed because they do not want to be thought of as taking advantage of the situation.

- *Purchasing "Fair-Trade" Products* Many consumers are willing to pay premium prices to purchase products that have been certified by the Fair Trade organization as having been produced by companies that meet high standards with respect to workers' rights and environmental sustainability. These customers clearly care about more than just getting the lowest price.

Experimental Evidence for Fairness

Our understanding of fairness and how it affects economic transactions has been reinforced and refined in recent decades by examining experimental games that were specifically designed to test people's feelings about fairness.

The most important feature of these games is that they are played for real money. That matters because if people were only motivated by self-interest, you would expect everyone playing the games to utilize only those strategies that are most likely to maximize their own winnings.

LAST WORD

Nudging People Toward Better Decisions

Behavioral Economists Have Recently Found Success in Using People's Behavioral Biases to "Nudge" Them Toward Making Better Decisions.*

Behavioral economics began as a descriptive science, meaning that its first goal was to develop theories that accurately described human economic behavior. In particular, it sought to explain a number of behaviors that at first glance seemed irrational. Now that behavioral economics has made significant headway in explaining many of those behaviors, some economists are suggesting that its insights be used to nudge people toward choices that are better for themselves and others.

A key feature of "nudges" is that they are subtle. This subtlety means that nudges can cause large changes in behavior without making people feel bullied or coerced—and also without imposing stringent new rules or having to offer people big monetary incentives or disincentives to get them to do what you want.

*The term "nudge" was popularized by Richard Thaler and Cass Sunstein in their book *Nudge: Improving Decisions about Health, Wealth, and Happiness*, Yale University Press, 2008.

Take retirement savings. Myopia and time inconsistency cause many people to consume too much in the present and therefore undersave for retirement. But as it turns out, this unfortunate behavioral tendency can be easily offset by utilizing status quo bias and people's tendency to stick with default options. In terms of retirement savings, this comes down to designing corporate retirement programs in which each worker is "defaulted into" her company's retirement savings program.

Under those savings programs, money is automatically deducted each month from a worker's paycheck and deposited in her retirement savings account. It used to be the case that the default for such programs was for workers to start out *not* enrolled in them. To get enrolled, they would have to request to join the program. That is, they would have to choose to go against the default option of not being enrolled.

As it turns out, however, only a few people behave that way. The majority actually play fairly and generously, often going out of their way to share with less-fortunate players even when they are under no compulsion to do so. That being said, their kindness only goes so far. If other players are acting selfishly, the average person will withhold cooperation and may even retaliate.

The Dictator Game
The strongest experimental evidence against the idea that people are only interested in what they can get for themselves comes from the **dictator game.**

The Rules In the game, two people interact anonymously. One of them is randomly designated as the "dictator." It is his job to split an amount of money that is put up for that purpose by the researcher running the game. A typical amount is $10.

The defining feature of the game is that the dictator can dictate whatever split he prefers. It could be to keep all the money for himself. It could be to give all the money to the other player. It could be to split it in any other possible way, such as $8.67 for himself and $1.33 for the other person.

Because the game is fully anonymous, the dictator doesn't have to worry about retaliation by the other person. He can get away with being as selfish as he wants.

How Players Behave So what actually happens when people play the dictator game? After running the experiment many thousands of times in many different countries, experimenters have found that only one-third of dictators keep all of the money for themselves. The other two-thirds show substantial generosity, allocating an average of 42 percent of the money to the other player. In addition, 17 percent of all dictators split the money perfectly evenly and a little over five percent of all dictators give the other player everything.

Implications for Fairness The way dictators behave suggests two important things about fairness.

First, the majority of people appear to be genuinely concerned about being fair to other people. They are willing to take less for themselves in order to ensure that the other

And because people have the behavioral tendency of sticking with whatever option is presented to them as the default, relatively few workers would make the change and enroll in their company's savings program. That was disappointing. But instead of being deterred, behavioral economists saw an opportunity. Why not change the default? Why not make automatic enrollment the default option? By making that change, people's tendency to stick with default options would work in their own favor—they would stay enrolled and save money for retirement.

When this strategy of switching the default was actually implemented, the number of workers participating in retirement savings programs skyrocketed—jumping from 60 percent to 98 percent. Those workers can now look forward to much more pleasant retirements thanks to this simple change that works *with* people's preference to stick with default options.

People's tendency to look around them for social cues as to what constitutes good behavior can also be exploited to modify their consumption behavior. But you have to be careful about how you do it, as was discovered by Opower, an energy consulting firm that wanted to encourage customers to conserve electricity. Its first attempt to use social cues involved sending each customer in a California town a bill that showed not only his or her own usage of electricity in kilowatt-hours, but also the average usage of nearby houses. Opower hoped that by showing the average usage of neighbors, customers would receive a subtle hint about their own usage. In particular, it was hoped that customers who used more than their neighbors

would feel that they were being wasteful and would thus cut back on their usage.

And that did indeed happen. *But* their reduction in electricity usage ended up being completely swamped by an increase in electricity usage on the part of the customers who had previously been below-average users. Those customers interpreted the new information that they were below-average electricity users to mean that they should feel free to consume more. After all, why should they use so little when their neighbors were using so much more?

Taking that into account, Opower finally hit upon a solution that worked. Smilies. Yes, symbols like ☺ and ☹. In addition to printing people's own usage and the average usage of their neighbors, Opower also started printing a ☺ on a customer's bill if his usage was below average and a ☹ on his bill if his usage was above average. The unhappy smilies embarrassed the heavy users into reducing their consumption even more, while the happy smilies gave a pat on the back to the light users—a pat on the back that kept their usage low.

Bear in mind that both the electricity customers and the workers saving for retirement were being *manipulated* by the people who designed the nudges. This fact is perhaps even more disturbing when you consider that the changes in behavior that were caused by the nudges were most likely *unconscious* on the part of those being manipulated. Keep this in mind as you consider for yourself when and if it is morally or ethically acceptable to use nudges to guide people's behavior.

player receives something, too. And they are willing to give substantially to the other player even though the game's guarantee of anonymity would allow them to take everything for themselves without fear of retaliation.

Second, generosity varies quite widely. Between the third of dictators who keep everything for themselves and the five percent who give everything to the other person lie the large majority who allocate some but not all of the money to the other person. Within that group, every possible split of the money can be found. As a result, behavioral economists believe that individuals vary widely in their beliefs about fairness. Some are incredibly selfish. Others are incredibly generous. And most of us lie somewhere in between.

To help get a better handle on how those widely divergent beliefs affect behavior in more realistic situations, economists designed a slightly more complex game.

The Ultimatum Game
Like the dictator game, the **ultimatum game** involves two players anonymously

splitting an amount of money. But there is no longer a dictator who can arbitrarily decide how the money is spilt. Instead, both players need to agree on any proposed split if it is to take place.

That difference in the rules ensures that the ultimatum game mirrors the many real-world situations in which a project or proposal must obtain the consent and support of all parties if it is to be undertaken. As an example, consider a business transaction between a potential seller and a potential buyer. Even if there are substantial net benefits available to both parties, no transaction will take place unless the buyer and the seller can come to an agreement on the selling price.

The Rules As with the dictator game, the researcher puts up an amount of money to be split. This pot of money is similar in spirit to the net benefits that a buyer and a seller can split if they can agree on a price. It also represents the net benefits that will be forgone if the two parties cannot reach an agreement.

At the start of the experiment, one of the players is randomly assigned to be "the proposer" while the other player is randomly assigned to be "the responder." The game begins with the proposer proposing a split. As in the dictator game, the proposed split can range anywhere from suggesting that all the money go to the proposer to suggesting that all the money go to the responder.

The responder examines the proposed split and decides whether to accept it or reject it. If she accepts it, the split is made and both players are immediately paid their shares by the researcher. But if the responder rejects the proposed split, neither player gets anything. The game simply ends and both players go home without receiving any money at all—a situation similar to when a business negotiation fails and all the potential benefits are forgone.

How Players Behave When the ultimatum game is played, two behaviors stand out.

The more important is that the splits proposed by proposers in the ultimatum game are much more equal on average than the splits imposed by dictators in the dictator game. This is best seen by noting that whereas one-third of dictators keep all the money for themselves in the dictator game, almost no proposers suggest allocating all the money to themselves in the ultimatum game.

This extremely large difference in behavior arises because the people acting as proposers in the ultimatum game realize that suggesting a highly unequal split is almost certain to greatly offend a responder's sense of fairness and lead to a rejection. In addition, most proposers also seem to understand that even moderately unfair offers might also offend responders. As a result, the large majority of proposers suggest either perfectly equal splits or splits that are only slightly biased in the proposer's favor (such as 55 percent going to the proposer).

The second behavior that stands out is the decisiveness and emotional intensity with which responders reject offers that they consider unfair. Of particular interest is the fact that rejection decisions are not made in a cool and calculating fashion. Responders do *not* calmly weigh the costs and benefits of accepting an unfair offer. They actually become extremely angry and reject as a way of retaliating against the proposer. Their rejections are not just negative responses; they are acts of vengeance designed to hurt the proposer by denying him money.

The full extent to which unfair offers make responders angry can be gauged by looking at high-stakes versions of the ultimatum game in which proposers and responders attempt to split hundreds or even thousands of dollars. You might think that when such large amounts of money are on the line, responders would be willing to accept unfair splits.

But what we actually see is responders continuing to reject splits that they consider to be unfair. Their preference for fair treatment is so strong that they will reject unfair offers even when doing so means giving up a *lot* of money.

Why the Threat of Rejection Increases Cooperation Some people won't offer anything to other people unless they are coerced into doing so. This is best understood by comparing the behavior of dictators in the dictator game with the behavior of proposers in the ultimatum game. In the dictator game, a full third of dictators award themselves all the money and leave nothing for the other player. In the ultimatum game, by contrast, nearly every proposer offers a substantial split to the responder.

That dramatic increase in generosity and fairness is, of course, related to the different rules used in the two games. When one person has total control over the split, selfish tendencies are given free reign. But when rejections become possible, the player in charge of proposing the split has to take the other player's feelings into account. That causes even selfish proposers to make generous offers because they quickly realize that the only way they can get any money for themselves is by making proposals that will not be rejected.

Implications for Market Efficiency The willingness of proposers to make more generous offers when faced with the threat of rejection can be thought of as the simplest expression of the invisible hand.

As we discussed in Chapter 2, the invisible hand is a metaphor that summarizes the tendency of the market system to align private interests with social interests and get people behaving in ways that benefit not only themselves but other people, too.

In the case of the ultimatum game, the threat of rejection helps to align private interests with social interests. It does so by motivating selfish people to make substantially more generous offers. The result is a higher level of cooperation and utility as offers get accepted and players split the money.

A similar process can be seen in the real world with respect to consumer sovereignty. As discussed in Chapter 2, consumer sovereignty is the right of consumers to spend their incomes on the goods and services that they are most willing and able to buy. Crucially, that right includes the ability to reject any product that does not meet the consumer's expectations.

That right of rejection leads to substantial social benefits because it motivates producers to work hard at producing products that will be acceptable to consumers. Over time, those efforts lead to increased allocative and productive efficiency as better products get produced at lower prices.

SUMMARY

LO8.1 Define behavioral economics and explain how it contrasts with neoclassical economics.

Neoclassical economics bases its predictions about human behavior on the assumption that people are fully rational decision-makers who have no trouble making mental calculations and no problems dealing with temptation. While some of its predictions are accurate, many are not.

The key difficulty facing neoclassical economics is that people make systematic errors, meaning that they regularly and repeatedly engage in behaviors that reduce their likelihood of achieving what they want.

Behavioral economics attempts to explain systematic errors by combining insights from economics, psychology, and biology. Its goal is to make more accurate predictions about human choice behavior by taking into account the mental mistakes that lead to systematic errors.

LO8.2 Discuss the evidence for the brain being modular, computationally restricted, reliant on heuristics, and prone to various forms of cognitive error.

Our brains make systematic errors for two reasons. First, our brains were not prepared by evolution for dealing with many modern problems, especially those having to do with math, physics, and statistics. Second, our brains also make mistakes when dealing with long-standing challenges (like interpreting visual information) because caloric limitations forced our brains to adopt low-energy heuristics (shortcuts) for completing mental tasks.

Heuristics sacrifice accuracy for speed and low energy usage. In most cases, the lack of accuracy is not important because the errors that result are relatively minor. However, in some cases, those errors can generate cognitive biases that substantially impede rational decision-making. Examples include confirmation bias, the overconfidence effect, the availability heuristic, and framing effects.

LO8.3 Relate how prospect theory helps to explain many consumer behaviors, including framing effects, mental accounting, anchoring, loss aversion, and the endowment effect.

Prospect theory is the behavioral economics theory that attempts to accurately describe how people deal with risk and uncertainty. Its key feature is that it models a person's preferences about uncertain outcomes as being based on whether those outcomes will cause gains or losses relative to the current status quo situation to which the person has become accustomed.

Prospect theory also accounts for loss aversion and the fact that most people perceive the pain of losing a given amount of money as being about 2.5 times more intense than the pleasure they would receive from an equal-sized gain.

LO8.4 Describe how time inconsistency and myopia cause people to make suboptimal long-run decisions.

Myopia refers to the difficulty that most people have in conceptualizing the future. It causes people to put insufficient weight on future outcomes when making decisions.

Time inconsistency refers to the difficulty that most people have in correctly predicting what their future selves will want. It causes self-control problems because people are not able to correctly anticipate the degree to which their future selves may fall prey to various sorts of temptation.

People sometimes utilize precommitments to help them overcome self-control problems. Precommitments are courses of action that would be very difficult for the future self to alter. They consequently force the future self to do what the present self desires.

LO8.5 Define fairness and give examples of how it affects behavior in the economy and in the dictator and ultimatum games.

Behavioral economists have found extensive evidence that people are *not* purely self-interested. Rather, they care substantially about fairness and are often willing to give up money and other possessions in order to benefit other people.

The field evidence for fairness includes donations to charity, law-abiding behavior, the reluctance of retailers to raise prices during natural disasters, and the willingness of many consumers to pay premium prices for Fair Trade products.

The dictator and ultimatum games provide experimental evidence on fairness by showing how pairs of people interact to split a pot of money that is provided by the researcher. In the dictator game, one person has total control over the split. In the ultimatum game, both players must agree to the split.

The dictator game shows that many people will share with others even when anonymity would allow them to be perfectly selfish and keep all the money for themselves. The ultimatum game shows that people put a very high value on being treated fairly. They would rather reject an unfair offer and get nothing than accept it and get something.

TERMS AND CONCEPTS

neoclassical economics	rational	heuristics
behavioral economics	systematic errors	cognitive biases

framing effects	mental accounting	self-control problems
status quo	endowment effect	precommitments
loss aversion	status quo bias	fairness
prospect theory	myopia	dictator game
anchoring	time inconsistency	ultimatum game

The following and additional problems can be found in connect
ECONOMICS

DISCUSSION QUESTIONS

1. Suppose that Joe enjoys and repeatedly does stupid things like getting heavily into debt and insulting police officers. Do these actions constitute systematic errors? If he gets what he wants each time, are his stupid actions even considered to be errors by economists? Explain. **LO8.1**

2. Why do behavioral economists consider it helpful to base a theory of economic behavior on the actual mental processes that people use to make decisions? Why do neoclassical economists not care about whether a theory incorporates those actual mental processes? **LO8.1**

3. Economist Gerd Gigerenzer characterizes heuristics as "fast and frugal" ways of reaching decisions. Are there any costs to heuristics being "fast and frugal"? Explain and give an example of how a fast and frugal method for doing something in everyday life comes at some costs in terms of other attributes forgone. **LO8.2**

4. "There's no such thing as bad publicity." Evaluate this statement in terms of the recognition heuristic. **LO8.2**

5. For each of the following cognitive biases, come up with at least one example from your own life. **LO8.2**
   a. Confirmation bias.
   b. Self-serving bias.
   c. The overconfidence effect.
   d. Hindsight bias.
   e. The availability heuristic.
   f. The planning fallacy.
   g. Framing effects.

6. Suppose that Ike is loss averse. In the morning, Ike's stockbroker calls to tell him that he has gained $1,000 on his stock portfolio. In the evening, his accountant calls to tell him that he owes an extra $1,000 in taxes. At the end of the day, does Ike feel emotionally neutral since the dollar value of the gain in his stock portfolio exactly offsets the amount of extra taxes he has to pay? Explain. **LO8.3**

7. You just accepted a campus job helping to raise money for your school's athletic program. You are told to draft a fundraising letter. The bottom of the letter asks recipients to write down a donation amount. If you want to raise as much money as possible, would it be better if the text of that section mentioned that your school is ranked third in the nation in sports or that you are better than 99 percent of other schools at sports? Explain. **LO8.3**

8. In the early 1990s, New Jersey and Pennsylvania both reformed their automobile insurance systems so that citizens could opt for either a less-expensive policy that did not allow people to sue if they got into accidents or a more-expensive policy that did allow people to sue if they got into accidents. In New Jersey, the default option was the less-expensive policy that did not allow suing. In Pennsylvania, the default option was the more-expensive policy that did allow suing. Given those options, which policy do you think most people in New Jersey ended up with? What about in Pennsylvania? Explain. **LO8.3**

9. Give an example from your own life of a situation where you or someone you know uses a precommitment to overcome a self-control problem. Describe why the precommitment is useful and what it compensates for. Avoid any precommitment that was mentioned in the book. **LO8.4**

10. What does behavioral economics have to say about each of the following statements? **LO8.5**
    a. "Nobody is truly charitable—they just give money to show off."
    b. "America has a ruthless capitalist system. Considerations of fairness are totally ignored."
    c. "Selfish people always get ahead. It's like nobody even notices!"

11. Do people playing the dictator game show only self-interested behavior? How much divergence is there in the splits given by dictators to the other player? **LO8.5**

12. Evaluate the following statement. "We shouldn't generalize from what people do in the ultimatum game because $10 is a trivial amount of money. When larger amounts of money are on the line, people will act differently." **LO8.5**

13. **LAST WORD** What do you think of the ethics of using unconscious nudges to alter people's behavior? Before you answer, consider the following argument made by economists Richard Thaler and Cass Sunstein, who favor the use of nudges. They argue that in most situations, we couldn't avoid nudging even if we wanted to because whatever policy we choose will contain some set of unconscious nudges and incentives that will influence people. Thus, they say, we might as well choose the wisest set of nudges.

REVIEW QUESTIONS

1. Which of the following are systematic errors? **LO8.1**
   a. A colorblind person who repeatedly runs red lights.
   b. An accountant whose occasional math errors are sometimes on the high side and sometimes on the low side.
   c. The tendency many people have to see faces in clouds.
   d. Miranda paying good money for a nice-looking apple that turns out to be rotten inside.
   e. Elvis always wanting to save more but then spending his whole paycheck, month after month.

2. Identify each statement as being associated with neoclassical economics or behavioral economics. **LO8.1**
   a. People are eager and accurate calculators.
   b. People are often selfless and generous.
   c. People have no trouble resisting temptation.
   d. People place insufficient weight on future events and outcomes.
   e. People only treat others well if doing so will get them something they want.

3. Label each of the following behaviors with the correct bias or heuristic. **LO8.3**
   a. Your uncle says that he knew all along that the stock market was going to crash in 2008.
   b. When Fred does well at work, he credits his intelligence. When anything goes wrong, he blames his secretary.

   c. Ellen thinks that being struck dead by lightning is much more likely than dying from an accidental fall at home.
   d. The sales of a TV that is priced at $999 rise after another very similar TV priced at $1,300 is placed next to it at the store.
   e. The sales of a brand of toothpaste rise after new TV commercials announce that the brand "is preferred by 4 out of 5 dentists."

4. Erik wants to save more, but whenever a paycheck arrives, he ends up spending everything. One way to help him overcome this tendency would be to: **LO8.4**
   a. Teach him about time inconsistency.
   b. Tell him that self-control problems are common.
   c. Have him engage in precommitments that will make it difficult for his future self to overspend.

5. Many proposers in the ultimatum game offer half to the responder with whom they are paired. This behavior could be motivated by (select as many as might apply): **LO8.5**
   a. Fear that an unequal split might be rejected by a fair-minded responder.
   b. A desire to induce the responder to reject the offer.
   c. A strong sense of fairness on the part of the proposers.
   d. Unrestrained greed on the part of the proposers.

PROBLEMS

1. One type of systematic error arises because people tend to think of benefits in percentage terms rather than in absolute dollar amounts. As an example, Samir is willing to drive 20 minutes out of his way to save $4 on a grocery item that costs $10 at a local market. But he is unwilling to drive 20 minutes out of his way to save $10 on a laptop that costs $400 at a local store. In percentage terms, how big is the savings on the grocery item? On the laptop? In absolute terms, how big is the savings on the grocery item? On the laptop? If Samir is willing to sacrifice 20 minutes of his time to save $4 in one case, shouldn't he also be willing to sacrifice 20 minutes of his time to save $10? **LO8.2**

2. Anne is a bargain-minded shopper. Normally, her favorite toothpaste costs the same at both of her local supermarkets, but the stores are having competing sales this week. At one store, there is a bonus offer: buy 2, get 1 free. At the other store, toothpaste is being sold at 40 percent off. Anne instantly opts for the first offer. Was that really the less-expensive choice? (Hint: Is "buy 2, get 1 free" the same as 50 percent off?) **LO8.2**

3. The coffee shop near the local college normally sells 10 ounces of roasted coffee beans for $10. But the shop sometimes puts the beans on sale. During some sales, it offers "33 percent more for free." Other weeks, it takes "33 percent off" the normal price. After reviewing the shop's sales data,

the shop's manager finds that "33 percent more for free" sells a lot more coffee than "33 percent off." Are the store's customers making a systematic error? Which is actually the better deal? **LO8.2**

4. Angela owes $500 on a credit card and $2,000 on a student loan. The credit card has a 15 percent annual interest rate and the student loan has a 7 percent annual interest rate. Her sense of loss aversion makes her more anxious about the larger loan. As a result, she plans to pay it off first—despite the fact that professional financial advisors always tell people to pay off their highest-interest-rate loans first. Suppose Angela has only $500 at the present time to help pay down her loans and that this $500 will be the only money she will have for making debt payments for at least the next year. If she uses the $500 to pay off the credit card, how much interest will accrue on the other loan over the coming year? On the other hand, if she uses the $500 to pay off part of the student loan, how much in combined interest will she owe over the next year on the remaining balances on the two loans? By how many dollars will she be better off if she uses the $500 to completely pay off the credit card rather than partly paying down the student loan? (Hint: If you owe X dollars at an annual interest rate of Y percent, your annual interest payment will be $X \times Y$, where the interest rate Y is expressed as a decimal.) **LO8.3**

5. ADVANCED ANALYSIS In the algebraic version of prospect theory, the variable x represents gains and losses. A positive value for x is a gain, a negative value for x is a loss, and a zero value for x represents remaining at the status quo. The so-called value function, $v(x)$, has separate equations for translating gains and losses into, respectively, positive values (utility) and negative values (disutility). The gain or loss is typically measured in dollars while the resulting value (utility or disutility) is measured in utils. A typical person values gains ($x > 0$) using the function $v(x) = x^{0.88}$ and losses ($x < 0$) using the function $v(x) = -2.5*(-x)^{0.88}$. In addition, if she stays at the status quo ($x = 0$), then $v(x) = 0$. First use a scientific calculator (or a spreadsheet program) and the typical person's value functions for gains and losses to fill out the missing spaces in the nearby table. Then answer the questions that follow. **LO8.3**

Gain or Loss	Total Value of Gain or Loss	Marginal Value of Gain or Loss
−3	−6.57	
−2		−2.10
−1	−2.50	−2.50
0	0.00	—
1		1.00
2	1.84	
3		0.79

a. What is the total value of gaining $1? Of gaining $2?

b. What is the marginal value of going from $0 to gaining $1? Of going from gaining $1 to gaining $2? Does the typical person experience diminishing marginal utility from gains?

c. What is the marginal value of going from $0 to losing $1? Of going from losing $1 to losing $2? Does the typical person experience diminishing marginal disutility from losses?

d. Suppose that a person simultaneously gains $1 from one source and loses $1 from another source. What is the person's total utility after summing the values from these two events? Can a *combination* of events that leaves a person with the same wealth as they started with be perceived negatively? Does this shed light on status quo bias?

e. Suppose that an investor has one investment that gains $2 while another investment simultaneously loses $1. What is the person's total utility after summing the values from these two events? Will an investor need to have gains that are bigger than her losses just to feel as good as she would if she did not invest at all and simply remained at the status quo?

6. Ted has always had difficulty saving money, so on June 1, Ted enrolls in a Christmas savings program at his local bank and deposits $750. That money is totally locked away until December 1 so that Ted can be certain that he will still have it once the holiday shopping season begins. Suppose that the annual rate of interest is 10 percent on ordinary savings accounts (that allow depositors to withdraw their money at any time). How much interest is Ted giving up by precommitting his money into the Christmas savings account for six months instead of depositing it into an ordinary savings account? (Hint: If you invest X dollars at an annual interest rate of Y percent, you will receive interest equal to $X \times Y$, where the interest rate Y is expressed as a decimal.) **LO8.4**

developing marketing strategies and a marketing plan

In athletic competitions, the goal is clear: Win! For companies that design, produce, and sell athletic equipment to help runners, players, and competitors achieve their best performance, the idea of victory is similar. However, the competition that takes place between companies aiming to appeal most to their valuable customers—whoever they are—is a little more complicated than who crosses a finish line first.

When it comes to Nike and adidas, for example, the competitive contest spans a wealth of product lines, target markets, and marketing approaches. Thus, the firms must carefully and precisely determine the marketing strategies and plans that they use to appeal to customers and ensure their survival and success.

LEARNING OBJECTIVES

After reading this chapter, you should be able to:

LO 2-1   Define a marketing strategy.

LO 2-2   Describe the elements of a marketing plan.

LO 2-3   Analyze a marketing situation using SWOT analysis.

LO 2-4   Describe how a firm chooses which consumer group(s) to pursue with its marketing efforts.

LO 2-5   Outline the implementation of the marketing mix as a means to increase customer value.

LO 2-6   Summarize portfolio analysis and its use to evaluate marketing performance.

LO 2-7   Describe how firms grow their business.

Created by runners in Oregon, Nike began in the early 1970s as an American company, focused mainly on the American market.[1] Its first running

continued on p. 24

adidas spokesperson and NBA star Dwight Howard at an Adidas Crazy Light Challenge event in Tokyo, Japan.

continued from p. 23

shoes featured a then-innovative design with a waffle-patterned sole. The customers were mainly elite runners, determined to find the lightest shoe they could. But as *Forrest Gump* recounted, running also was gaining popularity among casual athletes, and just like Forrest, many members of this community sported Nikes on their feet.

By 1984, the company had gone public, and it had found Michael Jordan. Thus the entire market—and the very concept of sponsorship—changed forever. The Air Jordan line of basketball shoes turned Nike into a massive success, with broad appeal to sports fans of virtually all ages and profiles. Nike continues to affiliate with high-profile, elite basketball players, including 48 NBA All-Stars such as Dwayne Wade, Kobe Bryant, and LeBron James.[2]

Basketball shoes may be the most well-known site for the brand's famous swoosh logo, but Nike also has branched into other related sectors. For example, it owns Cole-Haan, which makes dress and casual street shoes.[3] It produces other components of athletic uniforms for both professionals (e.g., team jerseys) and casual buyers (e.g., tracksuits, gym bags). It also purchased Umbro, another sports brand that has appealed mainly to soccer enthusiasts in the past.

This purchase of Umbro suggests that Nike is taking on its main competitor, adidas, directly in a market that previously had been dominated by adidas. As a European company, started in Germany in the early twentieth century, adidas began by designing mainly soccer (or in Europe, football) shoes as well as some track and field footwear.

Today it has spread into other sports, though its focus on international sponsorships of the Olympic Games and the World Cup continues to reflect its origins. Yet it also seems determined to challenge Nike's dominance on the basketball court. With young stars such as Derrick Rose and Dwight Howard as spokespeople, adidas has initiated an advertising offensive, mocking Nike's shoes as heavier, less technologically advanced, and bland.[4] It also purchased a third competitor in the market, Reebok, in 2005, in a clear effort to gain U.S. market share.

Although their primary markets continue to differ, Nike and adidas are involved in a turf war in more and more segments. Faced with the resulting challenges, they have struggled to enhance their reputations for innovation while also keeping their costs low. For example, Nike introduced its iPod-focused partnership with Apple. With the Nike+ sensor inserted in their shoes, runners can program their iPods to play a collection of songs that matches their distance or time goals.[5] The sensor also keeps track of their speed and distance, and Nike saves the data and provides platforms for social interactions among runners in the same area. Not to be outdone, adidas has moved to introduce the micro-A smart shoe, whose sensors determine the athlete's performance, together with the environmental conditions, then adjust the cushioning and airflow in the shoe to match the conditions.

To produce these high-tech versions of their footwear, both companies outsource production to countries other than their home base.[6] Nike suffered a major public relations scandal in the 1990s when activists uncovered human rights abuses in some Nike factories. Since then, it has worked actively to improve its reputation, led the way in mandating regulations for overseas continued from p. 24

factories, and donated heavily to philanthropic causes. Although its move to international production is more recent, adidas regards its presence in less developed areas as an inroad to consumers in these markets; its sponsorship of the Beijing Olympics also represented its strong push for dominance in China.

Nike maintains a strong lead in this race: It commands approximately 33 percent of the worldwide market, whereas adidas owns only 22 percent.[7] A count in recent Olympic track and field trials showed that Nike was sponsoring nearly 60 percent of the U.S. athletes present, whereas adidas shoes appeared on less than 13 percent of these elite feet.[8] But this competition is less a 100-yard dash than a super-marathon. When it comes to their race for market share, Nike and adidas have miles to go, and a strong competitor is always in their sights. ▪

> **marketing strategy**
> A firm's target market, marketing mix, and method of obtaining a sustainable competitive advantage.

> **sustainable competitive advantage** Something the firm can persistently do better than its competitors.

> A competitive advantage acts like a wall that the firm has built around its position in a market.

In this chapter, we start by discussing a *marketing strategy,* which outlines the specific actions a firm intends to implement to appeal to potential customers. Then we discuss how to do a *marketing plan,* which provides a blueprint for implementing the marketing strategy. The chapter concludes with a discussion of strategies firms use to grow.

LO 2-1   Define a marketing strategy.

WHAT IS A MARKETING STRATEGY?

A **marketing strategy** identifies (1) a firm's target market(s), (2) a related marketing mix—its four Ps—and (3) the bases on which the firm plans to build a sustainable competitive advantage. A **sustainable competitive advantage** is an advantage over the competition that is not easily copied and thus can be maintained over a long period of time. A competitive advantage acts like a wall that the firm has built around its position in a market. This wall makes it hard for outside competitors to contact customers inside—otherwise known as the marketer's target market. Of course, if the marketer has built a wall around an attractive market, competitors will attempt to break down the wall. Over time, advantages will erode because of these competitive forces, but by building high, thick walls, marketers can sustain their advantage, minimize competitive pressure, and boost profits for a longer time. Thus, establishing a sustainable competitive advantage is key to long-term financial performance.

For Nike, its thickest wall is from its strong brand, based on years of technological breakthroughs, which has created a loyal customer base. These customers know the Nike swoosh well and consider the brand as a first option when they need running, basketball, or even just casual athletic shoes. This appeal reflects Nike's careful targeting and marketing mix implementation. In terms of the four Ps, Nike is constantly trying to come up with new versions of its relatively basic product, namely, shoes and related apparel. To sell these varied products, it relies on multiple channels: online, in dedicated Nike stores and superstores, and through independent retailers such as FootLocker. Its pricing spans a broad range, from lower end, simpler options for casual shoes to the most expensive, technically sophisticated, highly reputed lines associated with big name athletes. And these popular athletes are central to its promotion efforts. Thus it remains dominant in most athletic fields, and it feels confident about expanding further.

There are four macro, or overarching, strategies that focus on aspects of the marketing mix to create and deliver value and develop sustainable competitive advantages, as we depict in Exhibit 2.1:[9]

· **Customer excellence:** Focuses on retaining loyal customers and excellent customer service.

· **Operational excellence:** Achieved through efficient operations and excellent supply chain and human resource management.

· **Product excellence:** Having products with high perceived value and effective branding and positioning.

· **Locational excellence:** Having a good physical location and Internet presence.

" HAVING A STRONG BRAND, UNIQUE MERCHANDISE, AND SUPERIOR CUSTOMER SERVICE ALL HELP SOLIDIFY A LOYAL CUSTOMER BASE. "

▼ **EXHIBIT 2.1** Macro Strategies For Developing Customer Value

Customer Excellence

Customer excellence is achieved when a firm develops value-based strategies for retaining loyal customers and provides outstanding customer service.

Retaining Loyal Customers Sometimes, the methods a firm uses to maintain a sustainable competitive advantage help attract and maintain loyal customers. For instance, having a strong brand, unique merchandise, and superior customer service all help solidify a loyal customer base. In addition, having loyal customers is, in and of itself, an important method of sustaining an advantage over competitors.

Loyalty is more than simply preferring to purchase from one firm instead of another.[10] It means that customers are reluctant to patronize competitive firms. Loyal customers buy Nike apparel for all their sporting and casual endeavors, even if adidas goes on sale or opens a new store right around the corner from their house.

More and more firms thus realize the value of achieving customer excellence through focusing their strategy on retaining loyal customers. Nike doesn't think in terms of selling a single pair of fashionable shoes for $100; instead, it focuses on satisfying the customer who buys track shoes for herself, Cole-Haan dress shoes for her spouse, soccer shoes for her daughter, and basketball shoes for her son. Conservatively, she might buy five

pairs of shoes every year for 20 years. She is not a $100 customer; combining all purchases for her family over the years, she is at least a $10,000 shoe customer—and that doesn't even count the shorts, shirts, and socks she adds on to her purchases. Viewing customers with a lifetime value perspective, rather than on a transaction-by-transaction basis, is key to modern customer retention programs.[11] We will examine how the lifetime value of a customer is calculated in Chapter 10, Appendix 10A, available online.

Marketers also use several methods to build customer loyalty. One way involves developing a clear and precise positioning strategy. With its long history in the sport, adidas is clearly positioned as a provider of soccer cleats, far more so than Nike. That positioning helps explain why Nike might have bought Umbro. But Nike also left the Umbro brand name alone so that it could continue to appeal to players of one of the fastest growing sports in the world.

Another method of achieving customer loyalty creates an emotional attachment through loyalty programs. These loyalty programs, which constitute part of an overall customer relationship management (CRM) program, prevail in many industries, from airlines to hotels to movie theaters to retail stores. With such programs, firms can identify members through the loyalty card or membership information the consumer provides when he or she makes a purchase. Using that purchase information, analysts determine which types of merchandise certain groups of customers are buying and thereby tailor their offering to meet the needs of their loyal customers better. For instance, by analyzing their databases, banks develop profiles of customers who have defected in the past and use that information to identify customers who may defect in the future. Once it identifies these customers, the firm can implement special retention programs to keep them.

Customer Service Marketers also may build sustainable competitive advantage by offering excellent customer service,[12] though consistency in this area can prove difficult. Customer service is provided by employees, and invariably, humans are less consistent than machines. On every visit, for example, Starbucks must attempt to ensure that every single barista greets customers in a friendly way and makes drinks consistently. But what happens when a barista comes to work in a bad mood or

Starbucks' friendly and knowledgeable baristas form a basis for competitive advantage.

simply forgets to add nutmeg to a drink? Firms that offer good customer service must instill its importance in their employees over a long period of time so that it becomes part of the organizational culture. Although it may take considerable time and effort to build a reputation for customer service, once a marketer has earned a good service reputation, it can sustain this advantage for a long time because a competitor is hard pressed to develop a comparable reputation.

Operational Excellence

Firms achieve **operational excellence**, the second way to achieve a sustainable competitive advantage, through their efficient operations, excellent supply chain management, and strong relationships with their suppliers.

All marketers strive for efficient operations to get their customers the merchandise they want, when they want it, in the required quantities, and at a lower delivered cost than that of their competitors. By so doing, they ensure good value to their customers, earn profitability for themselves, and satisfy their customers' needs. In addition, efficient operations enable firms either to provide their consumers with lower-priced merchandise or, even if their prices are not lower than those of the competition, to use the additional margin they earn to attract customers away from competitors by offering even better service, merchandise assortments, or visual presentations.

Firms achieve efficiencies by developing sophisticated distribution and information systems as well as strong relationships with vendors. Like customer relationships, vendor relations must be developed over the long term and generally cannot be easily offset by a competitor.[13]

Furthermore, firms with strong

relationships may gain exclusive rights to (1) sell merchandise in a particular region, (2) obtain special terms of purchase that are not available to competitors, or (3) receive popular merchandise that may be in short supply.

The supply chain for Netflix represented a remarkable innovation when the company first started: With its high-tech distribution centers, it got movies to most of its subscribers overnight. Its current streaming services expand offering even further, allowing subscribers to access various movies and television shows immediately through gaming devices (e.g., Wii), tablets (e.g., iPad), Internet-enabled televisions, or computers. Its supply chain thus continues to evolve and become increasingly efficient. The case study at the end of this chapter provides additional information about the methods Netflix has used to become a dominant player in the movie rental industry—as well as some of the challenges it has faced recently.

Product Excellence

Product excellence, the third way to achieve a sustainable competitive advantage, occurs by providing products with high perceived value and effective branding and positioning. Some firms have difficulty developing a competitive advantage through their merchandise and service offerings, especially if competitors can deliver similar products or services easily. However, others have been able to maintain their sustainable competitive advantage by investing in their brand itself; positioning their product or service using a clear, distinctive brand image; and constantly reinforcing that image through their merchandise, service, and promotion. For instance, *Bloomberg Businessweek*'s top global brands—such as Coca-Cola, IBM, Microsoft, Google, GE, McDonalds, Intel, Apple, Disney, and HP—are all leaders in their respective industries, at least in part because they have strong brands and a clear position in the marketplace.[14]

Locational Excellence

Location is particularly important for retailers and service providers. Many say, "The three most important

Netflix customers can receive videos instantly via the iPad, TV, or computer.

customer excellence Involves a focus on retaining loyal customers and excellent customer service.

operational excellence Involves a firm's focus on efficient operations and excellent supply chain management.

product excellence Involves a focus on achieving high-quality products; effective branding and positioning is key.

location A method of achieving excellence by having a strong physical location and/or Internet presence.

things in retailing are location, location, location." For example, most people will not walk or drive very far when looking to buy a cup of coffee. A competitive advantage based on location is sustainable because it is not easily duplicated. Starbucks has developed a strong competitive advantage with its location selection. The high density of stores it has established in some markets makes it very difficult for a competitor to enter that market and find good locations. Of course, when McDonald's entered the fancy coffee drink battle, it did not need to worry too much about finding new locations; its stores already appear nearly everywhere!

Multiple Sources of Advantage

In most cases, a single strategy, such as low prices or excellent service, is not sufficient to build a sustainable competitive advantage. Firms require multiple approaches to build a wall around their position that stands as high as possible. For example, Southwest Airlines consistently has positioned itself as a carrier that provides good service at a good value—customers get to their destination on time for a reasonable price without having to pay extra for checked luggage. At the same time, its customers don't expect food service or seat assignments. But they do expect—and even more important, get—on-time flights that are reasonably priced. By developing its unique capabilities in several areas, Southwest has built a very high wall around its position as the value player in the airline industry, which has resulted in a huge cadre of loyal customers.

> A written marketing plan provides a reference point for evaluating whether the firm has met its objectives.

---

 check yourself

1. What are the various components of a marketing strategy?

2. List the four macro strategies that can help a firm develop a sustainable competitive advantage.

LO 2-2   Describe the elements of a marketing plan.

THE MARKETING PLAN

Effective marketing doesn't just happen. Firms like Nike and adidas carefully plan their marketing strategies to react to changes in the environment, the competition, and their customers by creating a marketing plan. A **marketing plan** is a written document composed of an analysis of the current marketing situation, opportunities and threats for the firm, marketing objectives and strategy specified in terms of the four Ps, action programs, and projected or pro-forma income (and other financial) statements.[15] The three major phases of the marketing plan are planning, implementation, and control.[16]

Although most people do not have a written plan that outlines what they are planning to accomplish in the next year, and how they expect to do it, firms do need such a document. It is important for everyone involved in implementing the plan to know what the overall objectives for the firm are and how they will be met. Other stakeholders, such as investors and potential investors, also want to know what the firm plans to do. A written marketing plan provides a reference point for evaluating whether the firm has met its objectives.

A marketing plan entails five steps, depicted in Exhibit 2.2. In Step 1 of the **planning phase**, marketing executives, in conjunction with other top managers, define the mission and/or vision of the business. For the second step, they evaluate the situation by assessing how various players, both in and outside the organization, affect the firm's potential for success (Step 2). In the **implementation phase**, marketing managers identify and evaluate different opportunities by engaging in a process known as segmentation, targeting, and positioning (STP) (Step 3). They then are responsible for implementing the marketing mix using the four Ps (Step 4). Finally, the **control phase** entails evaluating the performance of the marketing strategy using marketing metrics and taking any necessary corrective actions (Step 5).

As indicated in Exhibit 2.2, it is not always necessary to go through the entire process for every evaluation (Step 5). For instance, a firm could evaluate its performance in Step 5, then go directly to Step 2 to conduct a situation audit without redefining its overall mission.

We first discuss each step involved in developing a marketing plan. Then we consider ways of analyzing a marketing situation as well as identifying and evaluating marketing opportunities. We also examine some specific strategies marketers use to grow a business. Finally, we consider how the implementation of the marketing mix increases customer value.

Step 1: Define the Business Mission

The **mission statement**, a broad description of a firm's objectives and the scope of activities it plans to undertake,[17] attempts to answer two main questions: What type of business are we? What do we need to do to accomplish our goals and objectives? These fundamental business questions must be answered at the highest corporate levels before marketing executives can get involved. Most firms want to maximize

marketing plan A written document composed of an analysis of the current marketing situation, opportunities and threats for the firm, marketing objectives and strategy specified in terms of the four Ps, action programs, and projected or pro forma income (and other financial) statements.

planning phase The part of the strategic marketing planning process when marketing executives, in conjunction with other top managers, (1) define the mission or vision of the business and (2) evaluate the situation by assessing how various players, both in and outside the organization, affect the firm's potential for success.

implementation phase The part of the strategic marketing planning process when marketing managers (1) identify and evaluate different opportunities by engaging in segmentation, targeting, and positioning (see *STP*) and (2) implement the marketing mix using the four Ps.

control phase The part of the strategic marketing planning process when managers evaluate the performance of the marketing strategy and take any necessary corrective actions.

mission statement A broad description of a firm's objectives and the scope of activities it plans to undertake; attempts to answer two main questions: What type of business is it? What does it need to do to accomplish its goals and objectives?

▼ **EXHIBIT 2.2** The Marketing Plan

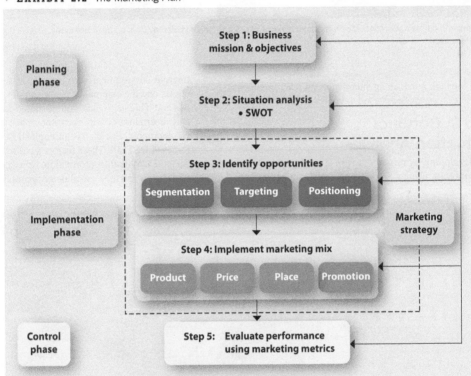

stockholders' wealth by increasing the value of the firms' stock and paying dividends.[18] Let's look at Nike and adidas.

- **Nike's Mission Statement:** "To bring inspiration and innovation to every athlete* in the world," and then with its asterisk, defines an athlete by quoting one of its founders: "If you have a body, you are an athlete."[19]

- **adidas's Mission Statement:** "The adidas group strives to be the global leader in the sporting goods industry with brands built on a passion for sport and a sporting lifestyle."[20]

For both of these firms, marketing is primarily responsible for enhancing the value of the company's offering for its customers and other constituents, whether in pursuit of a profit or not. Another key goal or objective often embedded in a mission statement relates to how the firm is building its sustainable competitive advantage.

However, owners of small, privately held firms frequently have other objectives, such as achieving a specific level of income and avoiding risks. Nonprofit organizations instead have nonmonetary objectives like Teach for America's:

- **Teach for America's** mission is to build the movement to eliminate educational inequity by enlisting our nation's most promising future leaders in the effort.[21]

Both Nike's and adidas's ads reflect their mission statements. Nike's ads (left) consistently inspire athletes to excel; adidas's ads (right) emphasize passion for sports.

LO 2-3   Analyze a marketing situation using SWOT analysis.

Step 2: Conduct a Situation Analysis

After developing its mission, a firm should perform a **situation analysis**, using a **SWOT** analysis that assesses both the internal environment with regard to its **S**trengths and **W**eaknesses and the external environment in terms of its **O**pportunities and **T**hreats. In addition, it should assess the opportunities and uncertainties of the marketplace due to changes in **C**ultural, **D**emographic, **S**ocial, **T**echnological, **E**conomic, and **P**olitical forces (CDSTEP). These factors are discussed in more detail in Chapter 4. With this information, firms can anticipate and interpret change, so they can allocate appropriate resources.

Make history.

It's possible to provide a great education to all kids, despite the challenges of poverty. It begins with committed individuals teaching and leading their students to success.

What role will you play?

TEACHFOR**AMERICA**

Apply now: www.teachforamerica.org

Two year commitment. Full salary and benefits. All majors and career backgrounds.

Teach for America helps provide education to all kids.

▼ EXHIBIT 2.3 Examples of Elements in a SWOT Analysis

		Environment	Evaluation
		Positive	*Negative*
Nike	**Internal**	**Strengths** Strong brand Strong celebrity endorsers Innovative products	**Weakness** Overreliance on footwear
	External	**Opportunity** Emerging countries Other fashion segments	**Threats** Cheaper imports Imitation products Retail becoming price competitive
adidas	**Internal**	**Strengths** Strong brand Portfolio of brands Strong global presence	**Weakness** Management of numerous brands
	External	**Opportunity** Emerging countries	**Threats** Cheaper imports Imitation products Recessionary forces

situation analysis
Second step in a marketing plan; uses a SWOT analysis that assesses both the internal environment with regard to its **S**trengths and **W**eaknesses and the external environment in terms of its **O**pportunities and **T**hreats.

Consider how Nike might conduct a SWOT analysis, as outlined in Exhibit 2.3. We focus on Nike here, but we also recognize that its marketing managers might find it helpful to perform parallel analyses for competitors, such as adidas. Because a company's strengths (Exhibit 2.3, upper left) refer to the positive internal attributes of the firm, in this example we might include Nike's great brand recognition and the visibility of the celebrities who wear its products. Furthermore, its introduction of the Nike+ iPod was the first of its kind, continuing the innovative tradition that has marked Nike since it first came up with waffle-soled running shoes. Its name recognition makes consumers more likely to try out these innovations when they appear on the market—especially when they see their favorite athlete wearing similar apparel on the court or in the field.

Yet every firm has its weaknesses, and Nike is no exception. Weaknesses (Exhibit 2.3, upper right) are negative attributes of the firm. Nike relies heavily—perhaps even too heavily—on its athletic shoe lines, especially for running and basketball. The NBA lockout for the 2012 season put undue stress on its sales in this segment. Not only would players and teams stop buying, but as the old saying goes, "Out of sight, out of mind." If the players are not on the court, their fans aren't thinking about them, and then sales will suffer.[22] In response to the popular emergence of other options, such as toning and barefoot models, Nike has largely suggested they are fads that will not last, stressing instead its traditional athletic shoe models.[23]

Opportunities (Exhibit 2.3, lower left) pertain to positive aspects of the external environment. Among Nike's opportunities, it appears determined to pursue dominance in other, sometime niche, sports markets. For the Olympic Games, it introduced footwear for less familiar sports, including fencing, wrestling, and equestrian events.[24] This goal also aligns with another notable opportunity for Nike, that is, growth in global markets. It sells products in 170 countries worldwide through independent distributors, Nike stores, the website, and licenses.[25] It aims to expand further, and it has devoted significant resources to improving its prominence among European football players and fans.[26]

Finally, threats (Exhibit 2.3, lower right) represent the negative aspects of the company's external environment. For example, its widespread market dominance makes Nike the primary target for all its competitors,[27] from adidas to New

Keke Palmer is wearing her Nikes at a Nickelodeon event.

Nike's strengths include its innovative product tradition. It was the first to introduce the Nike+ iPod, a sensor that when inserted into shoes gives the runner instant feedback on factors such as running time, distance, pace, and calories burned.

Step 3: Identifying and Evaluating Opportunities Using STP (Segmentation, Targeting, and Positioning)

After completing the situation audit, the next step is to identify and evaluate opportunities for increasing sales and profits using **STP** (segmentation, targeting, and positioning). With STP, the firm first divides the marketplace into subgroups or segments, determines which of those segments it should pursue or target, and finally decides how it should position its products and services to meet the needs of those chosen targets best. (More details on the STP process can be found in Chapter 8.)

Segmentation   Many types of customers appear in any market, and most firms cannot satisfy everyone's needs. For

> Hertz uses a variety of demographics—gender, age, income, interests—to identify customers who might want the Fun, Prestige, Green, and SUV/Minivan collections.

Balance to Li Ning, China's largest shoe maker. All of these firms want to take market share from Nike, which means it must constantly be a little bit on the defensive. Furthermore, a perpetual threat for any apparel company is staying fashionable, as Nike itself acknowledges: "We must . . . respond to trends and shifts in consumer preferences by adjusting the mix of existing product offerings, developing new products, styles and categories, and influencing sports and fitness preferences through aggressive marketing. Failure to respond in a timely and adequate manner could have a material adverse effect on our sales and profitability. This is a continuing risk."[28]

instance, among Internet users, some do research online, some shop, some look for entertainment, and many do all three. Each of these groups might be a **market segment** consisting of consumers who respond similarly to a firm's marketing efforts. The process of dividing the market into groups of customers with different needs, wants, or characteristics—who therefore might appreciate products or services geared especially for them—is called **market segmentation**.

Let's look at Hertz, the car rental company. The example in Exhibit 2.4 reveals that some of the segments that Hertz targets includes its Fun Collection, including the Corvette ZHZ and Chevrolet Camaro, to single people and couples wanting to have a bit of fun. Its Prestige Collection, which features the Cadillac Escalade and Infiniti QX56, targets business customers and families who prefer a luxurious ride. With its Green collection of cars such as the Toyota Prius and Ford Fusion, Hertz appeals to environmentally conscious customers, and with its SUV/Minivan collection, it brings in families. It also offers commercial vans for service customers.[29] Thus, Hertz uses a variety of demographics—gender, age, income, interests—to identify customers who might want the Fun, Prestige, Green, and SUV/Minivan collections, but it also applies psychological or behavioral factors, such as a preference for style or a need to move possessions across town, to identify likely consumers of the Fun Collection and its commercial vans.

LO 2-4   Describe how a firm chooses which consumer group(s) to pursue with its marketing efforts.

▼ **EXHIBIT 2.4**   Hertz Market Segmentation

	Segment 1	Segment 2	Segment 3	Segment 4	Segment 5
Segments	Single people and couples wanting to have a bit of fun	Business customers and families who prefer a luxurious ride	Environmentally conscious customers	Families	Commercial customers
	Fun Collection	Prestige Collection	Green Collection	SUV/Minivan & crossover	Commercial Van/Truck
Cars Offered	Corvette ZHZ	Infiniti QX56	Toyota Prius	Toyota Rav 4	
	Chevrolet Camaro	Cadillac Escalade	Ford Fusion	Ford Explorer	Ford Cargo Van

STP The processes of segmentation, targeting, and positioning that firms use to identify and evaluate opportunities for increasing sales and profits.

market segment A group of consumers who respond similarly to a firm's marketing efforts.

market segmentation The process of dividing the market into groups of customers with different needs, wants, or characteristics—who therefore might appreciate products or services geared especially for them.

target marketing/ targeting The process of evaluating the attractiveness of various segments and then deciding which to pursue as a market.

market positioning Involves the process of defining the marketing mix variables so that target customers have a clear, distinctive, desirable understanding of what the product does or represents in comparison with competing products.

Hertz targets several markets. Its Fun Collection (left) appeals to single people and couples wanting to have fun; its Prestige Collection (right) appeals to its business customers and families who prefer a luxurious ride.

Go back to our Nike example; let's look at how it segments its customers based on gender and how the products are used. Nike focuses on the following segments: running, basketball, football (soccer), men's training, women's training, action sports, sportswear, and golf.

Targeting After a firm has identified the various market segments it might pursue, it evaluates each segment's attractiveness and decides which to pursue using a process known as **target marketing or targeting**. For example, Hertz realizes that its primary appeal for the SUV/Minivan collection centers on young families, so the bulk of its marketing efforts for this business is directed toward that group.

Soft drink manufacturers also divide their massive markets into submarkets or segments. Coca-Cola, for instance, makes several types of Coke, including regular, Coke II, and Cherry Coke. Among its diet colas, it targets Coke Zero to men and Diet Coke to women, because men prefer not to be associated with diets. It also markets Sprite to those who don't like dark colas, Fruitopia and Minute Maid for more health-conscious consumers, and Dasani bottled water for purists.

Positioning Finally, when the firm decides which segments to pursue, it must determine how it wants to be positioned within those segments. **Market positioning** involves the process of defining the marketing mix variables so that

Nike targets different segments, such as women's fitness, golf, and running.

target customers have a clear, distinctive, desirable understanding of what the product does or represents in comparison with competing products. Hertz positions itself as a quality car (and truck) rental company that is the first choice for each of its target segments. In its marketing communications, it stresses that customers will get peace of mind when they rent from

Strategies section later in the chapter. Firms typically are most successful when they focus on opportunities that build on their strengths relative to those of their competition. In Step 4 of the marketing plan, the firm implements its marketing mix and allocates resources to different products and services.

> ## Firms typically are most successful when they focus on opportunities that build on their strengths relative to those of their competition.

Hertz, the market leader in the car rental business, and be able to enjoy their journey (e.g., leisure consumers) and reduce travel time (e.g., business consumers).[30]

To segment the coffee drinker market, Starbucks uses a variety of methods, including geography (e.g., college campuses versus shopping/business districts) and benefits (e.g., drinkers of caffeinated versus decaffeinated products). After determining which of those segments represent effective targets, Starbucks positions itself as a firm that develops a variety of products that match the wants and needs of the different market segments—espresso drinks, coffees, teas, bottled drinks, pastries, and cooler foods.

After identifying its target segments, a firm must evaluate each of its strategic opportunities. A method of examining which segments to pursue is described in the Growth

For example, Pizza Hut decided to jump on changing consumer desires for rapid access to its offering by constantly expanding its mobile applications, but it also found its positioning as a convenient option appealing to more markets than it even expected, as Social & Mobile Media 2.1 reveals.

LO 2-5   Outline the implementation of the marketing mix as a means to increase customer value.

Step 4: Implement Marketing Mix and Allocate Resources

When the firm has identified and evaluated different growth opportunities by performing an STP analysis, the real action begins. It has decided what to do, how to do it, and how many resources should be allocated to it. In the fourth step of the planning process, marketers implement the actual marketing mix—product, price, promotion, and place—for each product and service on the basis of what they believe their target markets will value. At the same time, marketers make important decisions about how they will allocate their scarce resources to their various products and services.

Product and Value Creation **Products**, which include services, constitute the first of the four Ps. Because the key to the success of any marketing program is the creation of value,

> **products** Anything that is of value to a consumer and can be offered through a voluntary marketing exchange.

firms attempt to develop products and services that customers perceive as valuable enough to buy. Dyson fans and fan heaters draw in and redirect surrounding air without potentially dangerous or fast spinning blades or visible heating elements. Although more expensive than conventional fans and space heaters, these sculpturally beautiful appliances are perceived by consumers to be a valuable alternative to products that haven't significantly changed since the early 1900s.

Price and Value Capture Recall that the second element of the marketing mix is price. As part of the exchange

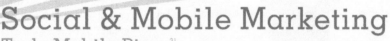

Social & Mobile Marketing 2.1
Truly Mobile Pizza[31]

The pizza delivery business has always been mobile in one sense, but Pizza Hut is making sure that it spreads convenience into mobile commerce as well. This first-mover introduced its mobile website in 2007, an iPhone application in 2009, and apps for the iPad, Android, Windows Mobile 7 in 2010, and an application for Xbox 360 in 2013.

The decision to go mobile was based on a few insights that Pizza Hut gleaned from its market research. In particular, if it did not offer mobile access quickly, its competitors might be first to do so in the competitive pizza delivery market. The Pizza Hut app lets customers order food through a user-friendly experience, but it also

makes sure to identify the closest store locations for delivery or pick-up service to emphasize further convenience.

Without much information about who the consumers who would use the app were, Pizza Hut anticipated more orders from college-aged men, who do not like to cook and want their food on demand, but also are not willing to stop a video game to take the time to order food through more traditional channels. The assumption seemed reasonable—but it also was dead wrong. Further market research, based on the introduction of the app, has shown that there are just as many pizza connoisseurs with iPhones who are older than 55 as there are 13–24-year-olds ordering the pies.

Pizza Hut's mobile app makes ordering pizza a piece of cake.

metric A measuring system that quantifies a trend, dynamic, or characteristic.

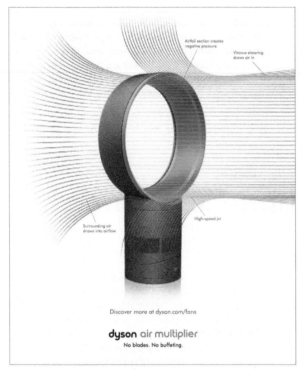

Discover more at dyson.com/fans

dyson air multiplier
No blades. No buffeting.

Dyson creates value with its innovative products.

process, a firm provides a product or a service, or some combination thereof, and in return, it gets money. Value-based marketing requires firms to charge a price that customers perceive as giving them a good value for the product they receive. Clearly, it is important for a firm to have a clear focus in terms of what products to sell, where to sell them, and what methods to use in selling them. But pricing is the only activity that actually brings in money and therefore influences revenues. If a price is set too high, it will not generate much volume. If a price is set too low, it may result in lower-than-optimal margins and profits. Therefore, price should be based on the value that the customer perceives. Dyson fans can retail for $150 or more while conventional fans retail for around $25. Customers thus can decide just what they want from their fan and choose the one at the price they prefer.

Place and Value Delivery For the third P, place, the firm must be able, after it has created value through a product and/or

> Understanding the causes of the performance, regardless of whether that performance exceeded, met, or fell below the firm's goals, enables firms to make appropriate adjustments.

service, to make the product or service readily accessible when and where the customer wants it. Recently, Tesco took an innovative step along these lines when it opened HomePlus virtual stores in several South Korean subway stations. The virtual stores in subway stations look like grocery stores—except that they are just LCD screens! The virtual markets allow customers to shop with just their smartphones.[32] Adding Value 2.1 takes a closer look at how Tesco HomePlus provides consumers great value.

Promotion and Value Communication The fourth and last P of the marketing mix is promotion. Marketers communicate the value of their offering, or the value proposition, to their customers through a variety of media including television, radio, magazines, sales forces, and the Internet. A relatively new promotion channel relies on daily deal websites such as Groupon or LivingSocial to get the word out. Many smaller companies find that these sites give them greater name recognition than they ever could have achieved on their own.

But when a well-known company uses the sites, the effect is even more remarkable. For example, Whole Foods offered a certificate for $20 worth of goods at a cost of only $10 on LivingSocial.com. Consumers snatched up the deal at a rate of 115,000 per hour.[33] Whole Foods capped the offer at 1 million deals, so it exposed itself to costs of around $10–15 million (if we include the fees it had to pay to LivingSocial to post the deal) in this attempt to get more grocery shoppers to visit its stores.

Step 5: Evaluate Performance Using Marketing Metrics

The final step in the planning process includes evaluating the results of the strategy and implementation program using marketing metrics. A **metric** is a measuring system that quantifies a trend, dynamic, or characteristic. Metrics are used to explain why things happened and to project the future. They make it possible to compare results across regions, strategic business units (SBUs), product lines, and time periods. The firm can determine why it achieved or did not achieve its performance goals with the help of these metrics. Understanding the causes of the performance, regardless of whether that performance exceeded, met, or fell below the firm's goals, enables firms to make appropriate adjustments.

Typically, managers begin by reviewing the implementation programs, and their analysis may indicate that the strategy (or even the mission statement) needs to be reconsidered. Problems can arise both when firms successfully implement poor strategies and when they poorly implement good strategies.

Adding Value 2.1
Online Retail Meets Bricks and Mortar: Tesco's HomePlus Virtual Stores

South Korea is known for its tech innovations, introduced by highly creative companies and embraced by a forward-thinking consumer public. But the top app in this tech-savvy nation isn't associated with some space-age fantasy. Instead, it pertains to a seemingly perpetual, distinctly old-fashioned task: grocery shopping.

The international retailer Tesco chose Korea as the site to open its HomePlus virtual stores back in 2011. Virtual stores began appearing on LCD screens in subway stations.[34] Shoppers on their way to or home from work could scan the barcodes or QR codes for the items they wanted to purchase with their smartphones. The virtual stores are laid out in a grid, similar to a brick-and-mortar store, which helped shoppers feel familiar with the radically new approach. Furthermore, the app allows them to schedule home delivery so that fresh produce, food for their pets, replenished cleaning supplies, and maybe even dinner for themselves can be waiting on their doorstep when they get home.

The remarkable success of this app has prompted Tesco to expand the placement of HomePlus stores to bus depots and other commuter routes.[35] Within about six months of the introduction, nearly 1 million consumers had downloaded and used the HomePlus app.

Despite the success and popularity of HomePlus, Tesco continues to keep its physical stores open, with no plans to eliminate them. Two main features demand this dual approach. First, Korea is somewhat special in terms of its significant embrace and acceptance of virtual tools and high-tech options. In many other countries, including Tesco's U.K. home market, and in rural areas where access to public spaces such as bus stops is just as challenging as getting to the local store, acceptance may be less widespread. Even in Korea, consumers tend to use HomePlus for dry goods but still like to be able to touch and feel vegetables and fruit before buying them.

Second, for many people, shopping is an enjoyable pastime that gets them out of their houses or offices for a brief time. Noting this persistent preference, Tesco is seeking to integrate virtual offerings better into some of its stores. For example, it is considering plans to add interactive tablets in its in-store cafes. Customers could take a break, have a cup of tea, and type in a few ingredients that sound appealing to them. The tablets then might produce recipes that match the ingredients, along with a map, showing the customers just where to find each needed item.[36]

The HomePlus Virtual Stores have created a whole new way of providing the third P, place, and value delivery.

Who Is Accountable for Performance? At each level of an organization, the business unit and its manager should be held accountable only for the revenues, expenses, and profits that they can control. Thus, expenses that affect several levels of the organization (such as the labor and capital expenses associated with operating a corporate headquarters) shouldn't be arbitrarily assigned to lower levels. In the case of a store, for example, it may be appropriate to evaluate performance objectives based on sales, sales associate productivity, and energy costs. If the corporate office lowers prices to get rid of merchandise and therefore profits suffer, then it's not fair to assess a store manager's performance based on the resulting decline in store profit.

THE METRICS USED TO EVALUATE A FIRM VARY DEPENDING ON (1) THE LEVEL OF THE ORGANIZATION AT WHICH THE DECISION IS MADE AND (2) THE RESOURCES THE MANAGER CONTROLS.

Performance evaluations are used to pinpoint problem areas. Reasons performance may be above or below planned levels must be examined. If a manager's performance is below planned levels, was it because the sales force didn't do an adequate job, because the economy took a downward turn, because competition successfully implemented a new strategy, or because the managers involved in setting the objectives aren't very good at making estimates? The manager should only be held accountable in the case of the inadequate sales force job or setting inappropriate forecasts.

When it appears that actual performance is going to be below the plan because of circumstances beyond the manager's control, the firm can still take action to minimize the harm. For our chapter exemplar Nike, two situations have arisen recently over which the firm had little control—a global recession and a scandal involving a spokesperson. Many consumers cut their spending on things like apparel in the modern recession. And the Tiger Woods infidelity scandal left Nike in an awkward position. According to researchers at Carnegie Mellon University, for the 10 years prior to the scandal, Woods's endorsement had earned Nike's golf ball division approximately $60 million in additional profits. In the year following widespread media reports of his infidelity, Nike lost approximately 105,000 customers and $1.3 million in profit.[37]

In remarkable cases such as this, marketing managers must ask themselves several relevant questions: How quickly were plans adjusted? How rapidly and appropriately were pricing and promotional policies modified? In short, did I react to salvage an adverse situation, or did my reactions worsen the situation? For the Woods scandal, it appears that marketing managers made the right decision by keeping him as an endorser, despite their short-term losses. The same researchers estimate that "even in the midst of the scandal, the overall profit was greater by $1.6 million for Nike with Tiger Woods than without him."[38]

Performance Objectives and Metrics Many factors contribute to a firm's overall performance, which makes it hard to find a single metric to evaluate performance. One approach is to compare a firm's performance over time or to competing firms, using common financial metrics such as sales and profits. Another method of assessing performance is to view the firm's products or services as a portfolio. Depending on the firm's relative performance, the profits from some products or services are used to fuel growth for others.

Financial Performance Metrics Some commonly used metrics to assess performance include revenues, or sales, and profits. For instance, sales are a global measure of a firm's activity level. However, a manager could easily increase sales by lowering prices, but the profit realized on that merchandise (gross margin) would suffer as a result. An attempt to maximize one metric may lower another. Managers must therefore understand how their actions affect multiple performance metrics. It's usually unwise to use only one metric because it rarely tells the whole story.

In addition to assessing the absolute level of sales and profits, a firm may wish to measure the relative level of sales and profits. For example, a relative metric of sales or profits is its increase or decrease over the prior year. In addition, a firm may compare its growth in sales or profits relative to other benchmark companies (e.g., Coke may compare itself to Pepsi).

The metrics used to evaluate a firm vary depending on (1) the level of the organization at which the decision is made and (2) the resources the manager controls. For example, although the top executives of a firm have control over all of the firm's resources and resulting expenses, a regional sales manager only has control over the sales and expenses generated by his or her salespeople.

Let's look at Nike's sales revenue and profits (after taxes) and compare them with those of adidas (Exhibit 2.5).

Tiger Woods is back.

strategic business unit (SBU) A division of the firm itself that can be managed and operated somewhat independently from other divisions and may have a different mission or objectives.

product lines Groups of associated items, such as those that consumers use together or think of as part of a group of similar products.

market share Percentage of a market accounted for by a specific entity.

▼ **EXHIBIT 2.5** Performance Metrics: Nike vs. adidas

		2011	2012	% Change
Nike	Net Sales	$20.9B	$24.1B	15.30%
	Net Profit	$ 2.1B	$ 2.2B	4.80%
	Net Profit/Net Sales	10.00%	9.10%	−9.00%
adidas	Net Sales	$ 17.6B	$ 19.7B	12.00%
	Net Profit	$809.8M	$694.9M	−14.20%
	Net Profit/Net Sales	4.60%	3.50%	−23.90%

Furthermore, as the corporate consciousness of the importance of social responsibility grows, firms are starting to report corporate social responsibility metrics in major areas, such as their impact on the environment, their ability to diversify their workforce, energy conservation initiatives, and their policies on protecting the human rights of their employees and the employees of their suppliers. Ethical & Societal Dilemma 2.1 examines how dietary supplement and energy drink manufacturers and retailers are wrestling with how best to market their products.

LO 2-6   Summarize portfolio analysis and its use to evaluate marketing performance.

Portfolio Analysis In portfolio analysis, management evaluates the firm's various products and businesses— its portfolio—and allocates resources according to which products are expected to be the most profitable for the firm in the future. Portfolio analysis is typically performed at the **strategic business unit (SBU)** or **product line** level of the firm, though managers also can use it to analyze brands or even individual items. An SBU is a division of the firm itself that can be managed and operated somewhat independently from other divisions and may have a different mission or objectives. For example, Goodyear is one of the largest tire firms in the world, selling its products on six continents in over 180 countries and with sales of approximately $18 billion. Its four SBUs are organized by geography: North America, Europe, Middle East, Africa, Latin America, and Asia/ Pacific.[39]

A product line, in contrast, is a group of products that consumers may use together or perceive as similar in some way. One line of product for Goodyear could be car, van, SUV, and light truck while another line could be racing tires or aviation tires.

One of the most popular portfolio analysis methods, developed by the Boston Consulting Group (BCG), requires firms to classify all their products or services into a two-by-two matrix, as depicted in Exhibit 2.6.[40] The circles represent brands, and their sizes are in direct proportion to the brands' annual sales. The horizontal axis represents the relative market share.

In general, **market share** is the percentage of a market accounted for by a specific entity [41] and is used to establish the product's strength in a particular market. It is usually discussed in units, revenue, or sales. A special type of market

▼ **EXHIBIT 2.6** Boston Consulting Group Matrix

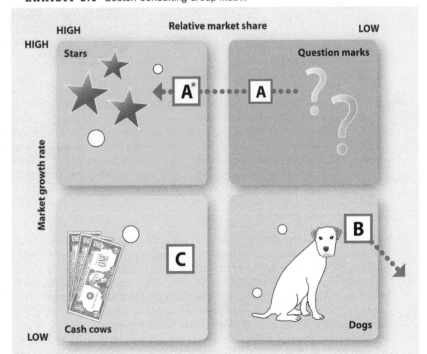

ethical & societal dilemma 2.1

Dangerous Consumption: Is the Consumer or the Company to Blame?

A 22-year-old soldier, with no history of health issues, collapsed while out for a training run, soon after ingesting a dietary supplement he had purchased from GNC.[42] A 14-year-old girl from Maryland drank two 24-ounce Monster Energy Drinks in one day and went into cardiac arrest.[43] Another teen, who drank two cans of Monster Energy every day for three years, ultimately suffered cardiac arrhythmia as well.[44] In response to these tragic deaths, several lawsuits are alleging that the manufacturers and retailers should be held liable.

Energy drinks that contain high levels of caffeine increasingly have come under attack as potential health threats, especially to the youthful consumers that the companies target. Alleging that the companies fail to disclose the risks of drinking such high doses of caffeine, these lawsuits seek to force Monster, Rockstar, and other competitors to carry warnings on their labels. Another lawsuit is attempting to ban the marketing of such products to children under the age of 18 years—a ban supported by the American Medical Association.[45]

The Jack3d dietary supplement contains dimethylalimine (DMAA), a stimulant that promises to increase endurance and stamina among athletes. On the GNC website, promotions of the brand assert that it provides "ultra-intense muscle-gorging strength, energy, power and endurance." In this case, legislators—together with the family of the soldier who died after taking Jack3d—argue that retailers such as GNC should be held responsible for the effects of the products they sell. By creating a sort of scientific or expert image, GNC may signal that the products it sells have been tested and confirmed as safe. Instead, GNC's legal status as a retailer and not a producer of supplements has generally meant that in the past it could not be held responsible for any damages imposed by the products it sells.[46] GNC is defending this position, noting that as a retailer, it must depend on the guarantees offered by the supplement vendors that the ingredients used are safe.

The makers of energy drinks appear to be taking a different tack. Both Rockstar and Monster have repositioned their products, transforming them from dietary supplements to beverages. This move means more than just changing their locations on store shelves. By calling the products beverages instead of dietary supplements, energy drink makers avoid the requirement that they must transmit any reports of health damages or deaths to the U.S. Food and Drug Administration (FDA).[47] However, they face the new requirement that they must list all nutrition information, including caffeine content, on the cans.

Dietary supplements continue to be largely unregulated by national agencies such as the FDA or the U.S. Department of Agriculture (USDA). Furthermore, these products, similar to energy drinks, do not fit obviously into existing product categories, which makes it difficult to determine which federal agency, if any, has responsibility for ensuring their safety. The product makers and retailers argue vigorously that no evidence confirms that the ingredients in their products are harmful. That is, despite the allegations, no one can prove that the three young people died because they ingested the products.

---

share metric, **relative market share**, is used in this application because it provides managers with a product's relative strength, compared with that of the largest firm in the industry.[48] The vertical axis is the **market growth rate**, or the annual rate of growth of the specific market in which the product competes. Market growth rate thus measures how attractive a particular market is. Each quadrant in the matrix has been named on the basis of the amount of resources it generates for and requires from the firm.

Stars. Stars (upper left quadrant) occur in high-growth markets and are high market share products. That is, stars often require a heavy resource investment in such things as promotions and new production facilities to fuel their rapid growth. As their market growth slows, stars will migrate from heavy users of resources to heavy generators of resources and become cash cows.

Cash Cows. Cash cows (lower left quadrant) are in low-growth markets but are high market share products. Because these products have already received heavy investments to develop their high market share, they have excess resources that can be spun off to those products that need it. For example, the firm may decide to use the excess resources generated by Brand C to fund products in the question mark quadrant.

Question Marks. Question marks (upper right quadrant) appear in high-growth markets but have relatively low market shares; thus, they are often the most managerially intensive products in that they require significant resources to maintain and potentially increase their market share. Managers must decide whether to infuse question marks with resources generated by the cash cows, so that they can become stars, or withdraw resources and eventually phase out the products. Brand A, for instance, is currently a question mark, but by infusing it with resources, the firm hopes to turn it into a star.

Dogs. Dogs (lower right quadrant) are in low-growth markets and have relatively low market shares. Although they may generate enough resources to sustain themselves, dogs are not destined for stardom and should be phased out unless they are needed to complement or boost the sales of another product or for competitive purposes. In the case depicted in Exhibit 2.6, the company has decided to stop making Brand B.

Now let's look at Apple and some of its products.[49] The four that we will focus our attention on are:

· iPhone

· iPod

· iMac Desktop

· iPad

relative market share A measure of the product's strength in a particular market, defined as the sales of the focal product divided by the sales achieved by the largest firm in the industry.

market growth rate The annual rate of growth of the specific market in which the product competes.

Goodyear, one of the largest tire firms in the world, organizes its strategic business units by geography.

In which Boston Consulting quadrant do these two products fit?

market penetration strategy A growth strategy that employs the existing marketing mix and focuses the firm's efforts on existing customers.

Let's consider each of these products and place them in the BCG matrix based on these data. The iPhone is clearly a star—a high growth rate (87 percent). In fact, by the end of 2011, Apple returned to its position as the top selling smartphone in the industry, with 16.2 million units sold in their fourth quarter alone, making its relative market share 100 percent.[50]

Apple's iPod is a different story. With a staggering absolute market share consistently above 75 percent, its relative market share is also 100 percent, and with more than 300 million iPods sold in a little over 10 years, it is definitely an important product for Apple. Unfortunately, the MP3 market is contracting (the market shrank by 10 percent from 2010 to 2011). Combine the lack of growth with a large relative market share, and it is likely that the iPod is a cash cow for Apple.[51]

Although popular with graphic designers, the growth rate of the Mac Desktop has slowed to a pitiful 4 percent. Given that it also has a small relative market share in the desktop market, the iMac can be tentatively classified as a dog. Should Apple get rid of the iMac? For at least two reasons, this is probably a bad idea. First, it risks alienating graphic designers and other Apple loyalists who depend on the iMac. Since these customers may also enjoy other Apple products, their dissatisfaction might adversely affect sales of these other products. Second, discontinuing the iMac would leave a gaping hole in its

portfolio, and would therefore hurt its brand image as a computer company.

Then we have the iPad with an incredible sales growth rate from 2010 to 2011 of 333 percent and sales of approximately 55 million units as of early 2012. In 2010, its absolute market share was 95.5 percent, making it the market leader with a relative market share of 100 percent. However, it is also experiencing increasing competition from Android tablets and the Kindle Fire. Looking at 2011 as a whole, the iPad captured 66.6 percent of the tablet market (2 out of every 3 tablets sold was an iPad). But by the end of 2011, its absolute market share had dropped to 57 percent.[52] Where on the BCG matrix would you classify the iPad? Would you argue that a 57 percent absolute market share places it in the star category, or would you be more conservative and put it as a question mark, citing the steady erosion of absolute market share? Will Apple be able to continue to grow and maintain its market share leader position by releasing a new version of the iPad?

Although quite useful for conceptualizing the relative performance of products or services and using this information to allocate resources, the BCG approach and others like it are often difficult to implement in practice. In particular, it is difficult to measure both relative market share and industry growth. Furthermore, other measures easily could serve as substitutes to represent a product's competitive position and the market's relative attractiveness. Another issue for marketers is the potentially

Like the Dalai Lama, Apple approaches the world by thinking differently.

self-fulfilling prophecy of placing a product or service into a quadrant. As we have shown in our Apple iPad example, whether it is classified as a star or a question mark has profound implications on how it is treated and supported within the firm. Question marks require more marketing and production support.

Because of these limitations, many firms have tempered their use of matrix approaches to achieve a more balanced approach to evaluating products and services and allocating their resources. Instead of assigning allocation decisions to the top levels of the organization, many firms start at lower management levels and employ checks and balances to force managers at each level of the organizational hierarchy to negotiate with those above and below them to reach their final decisions.

Strategic Planning Is Not Sequential

The planning process in Exhibit 2.2 suggests that managers follow a set sequence when they make strategic decisions. Namely, after they've defined the business mission, they perform the situation analysis, identify strategic opportunities, evaluate alternatives, set objectives, allocate resources, develop the implementation plan, and, finally, evaluate their performance and make adjustments. But actual planning processes can move back and forth among these steps. For example, a situation analysis may uncover a logical alternative, even though this alternative might not be included in the mission statement, which would mean that the mission statement would need to be revised. The development of the implementation plan also might reveal that insufficient resources have been allocated to a particular product for it to achieve its objective. In that case, the firm would need either to change the objective or increase the resources; alternatively, the marketer might consider not investing in the product at all.

Now that we have gone through the steps of the marketing plan, let's look at some growth strategies that have been responsible for making many marketing firms successful.

check yourself

1. What are the five steps in creating a marketing plan?
2. What tool helps a marketer conduct a situation analysis?
3. What is STP?
4. What do the four quadrants of the portfolio analysis represent?

LO 2-7   Describe how firms grow their business.

▼ **EXHIBIT 2.7**   Market/Product and Services Strategies

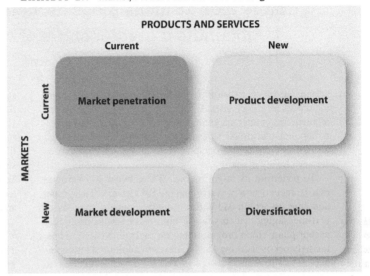

GROWTH STRATEGIES

Firms consider pursuing various market segments as part of their overall growth strategies, which may include the four major strategies in Exhibit 2.7.[53] The rows distinguish those opportunities a firm possesses in its current markets from those it has in new markets, whereas the columns distinguish between the firm's current marketing offering and that of a new opportunity. Let's consider each of them in detail.

Market Penetration

A **market penetration strategy** employs the existing marketing mix and focuses the firm's efforts on existing customers. Such a growth strategy might be achieved by attracting new consumers to the firm's current target market or encouraging

To increase market penetration with its young target audience, MTV produces reality shows like "America's Best Dance Crew."

> MTV develops new online products to engage consumers through more than 25 niche blogs as well as a website that it uses to dominate a greater share of viewers' minds and time.

current customers to patronize the firm more often or buy more merchandise on each visit. A market penetration strategy generally requires greater marketing efforts, such as increased advertising and additional sales and promotions or intensified distribution efforts in geographic areas in which the product or service already is sold.

To penetrate its target market, TV network MTV found that it needed new ways to engage its viewers. The young audience to which MTV traditionally appeals consists of text-messaging, video-gaming multitaskers who no longer accept plain video programming on their televisions. Thus, the network is working hard to develop additional strategies and outlets to retain viewers as well as to encourage them to spend more time interacting with its content. MTV discovered that interactions with the audience through alternative channels increase ratings for its shows. Therefore, in addition to producing and airing reality shows such as *America's Best Dance Crew* and *Jersey Shore*, MTV has partnered with a video game producer Yoostar to offer "Yoostar on MTV" for Xbox 360. The game provides a massive library of constantly updated shows, music videos, and recordings of live events. Using the green screen technology contained in the game, fans of these shows can insert themselves into scenes they've already seen their more famous teen peers undergo. Of course, the game also allows them to upload their completed performance to Facebook, Twitter, or a Yoostar dedicated website.[54] On MTV's website, dedicated forums, blogs, and activities for each show also encourage viewers to connect with characters in their shows. Not only can viewers talk about the characters as if they were friends, but they can buy the products they wear and download the music played during the show.[55]

Market Development

A **market development strategy** employs the existing marketing offering to reach new market segments, whether domestic or international. International expansion generally is riskier than domestic expansion because firms must deal with differences in government regulations, cultural traditions, supply chains, and language. However, many U.S. firms, including MTV, enjoy a competitive advantage in global markets—such as Mexico, Latin America, Europe, China, and Japan—because, especially among young people, U.S. culture is widely emulated for consumer products.

For example, because of rising prosperity worldwide and rapidly increasing access to cable television that offers U.S. programming, fashion trends from the United States have spread to young people in emerging countries. Since its

founding in 1981, MTV has expanded well beyond the United States, with niche sites in more than 20 countries, including the United Kingdom, Japan, Brazil, and India. It is available in 562 million households in 161 countries and 33 languages.[56] Thus, the global MTV generation prefers soft drinks to tea, athletic shoes to sandals, French fries to rice, and credit cards to cash. To achieve such growth, MTV leveraged its existing media content but also delivers culturally relevant content using local DJs and show formats.

Product Development

The third growth strategy option, a **product development strategy**, offers a new product or service to a firm's current target market. Consider MTV's dynamic line-up: The network

MTV's Real World Las Vegas cast members: Heather Marter, Dustin Zito, Naomi Defensor, and Jasmine Reynaud.

market development strategy A growth strategy that employs the existing marketing offering to reach new market segments, whether domestic or international.	**product development strategy** A growth strategy that offers a new product or service to a firm's current target market.	**diversification strategy** A growth strategy whereby a firm introduces a new product or service to a market segment that it does not currently serve.	**related diversification** A growth strategy whereby the current target market and/or marketing mix shares something in common with the new opportunity.	**unrelated diversification** A growth strategy whereby a new business lacks any common elements with the present business.

constantly develops new pilots and show concepts to increase the amount of time viewers can spend watching MTV. For example, each version of *The Real World* reality series and new series such as *Ridiculousness* and *Friendzone* all represent new programs designed to attract and retain existing viewers. Along with its new TV series, MTV develops new online products to engage consumers through more than 25 niche blogs as well as a website that it uses to dominate a greater share of viewers' minds and time. These various MTV-branded niche sites pertain to social, political, and environmental issues that appeal to different segments in its target market. The sites further encourage viewers to get involved in real-world issues (not *The Real World* issues) through mobile technologies. By visiting the sites, MTV promises that consumers can share mobile content, educate themselves, and take action on important issues.[57]

Diversification

A **diversification strategy**, the last of the growth strategies from Exhibit 2.7, introduces a new product or service to a market segment that currently is not served. Diversification opportunities may be either related or unrelated. In a **related diversification** opportunity, the current target market and/or marketing mix shares something in common with the new opportunity.[58] In other words, the firm might be able to purchase from existing vendors, use the same distribution and/or management information system, or advertise in the same newspapers to target markets that are similar to their current consumers. MTV has pursued related diversification by introducing TV series that focus on more positive social messages instead of on wealth, celebrities, and excessive youth culture (e.g., *The Hills, My Super Sweet 16*). In series such as *I Used to Be Fat* and *Made*, recognizable and seemingly similar teens still appeal to viewers and provide a healthy dose of drama. However, the plotlines of these shows focus on how people overcome adversity or struggle with everyday challenges to attain some level of happiness.[59]

In contrast, in an **unrelated diversification**, the new business lacks any common elements with the present business. Unrelated diversifications do not capitalize on either core strengths associated with markets or with products. Thus, they would be viewed as very risky. For instance, if Nike ventured into the child day care service industry, it would be an unrelated diversification because it is so different from its core business, and therefore very risky. ■

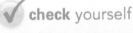

✓ **check** yourself

1. What are the four growth strategies?
2. What type of strategy is growing the business from existing customers?
3. Which strategy is the riskiest?

check it out!

mhhe.com/GrewalM4e
for study materials, including quizzes and videos.

section 2

chapter six

consumer behavior

As first-year students arrive on college campuses to begin the fall semester, they often are greeted by smiling upper-class students, offering to help them locate their rooms or unload their cars.[1] Other experienced students are on hand to assist newcomers with the purchase of a laptop or to invite them to one of the highlights of back-to-school week, a combined party and late-night shopping excursion. Thoughtful people helping rookies settle in? Maybe.

These goodwill ambassadors are also student marketers, paid by companies such as American Eagle Outfitters, Hewlett-Packard, and Red Bull, to hawk products on campus and through social networks. Even the first big college party is a marketing event in this case, sponsored by Target. Bused by the retail giant to a local superstore, first-year students dance to music spun by a DJ, collect free samples of junk food, and win prizes such as

LEARNING OBJECTIVES

After reading this chapter, you should be able to:

LO 6-1 Articulate the steps in the consumer buying process.

LO 6-2 Describe the difference between functional and psychological needs.

LO 6-3 Describe factors that affect information search.

LO 6-4 Discuss postpurchase outcomes.

LO 6-5 List the factors that affect the consumer decision process.

LO 6-6 Describe how involvement influences the consumer decision process.

refrigerators and cases of soda—all while shopping for more room furnishings for their dorms.

Using students to promote goods to their peers and classmates gives manufacturers the credibility of word-of-mouth advertising and direct contact with a market segment worth about $36 billion a year. Students promoting the brand and those experiencing it for

continued on p. 118

The Zipcar/Ford alliance is designed to appeal to college students and get them hooked on Ford products.

continued from p. 117

the first time can become fans and spread the word to their families and high school friends. They can also form a habit and continue purchasing the same brand of toothpaste, smartphone, or jeans as they build their careers and families. This potential to attract new consumers and influence their lifetime shopping behavior, just by marketing to college students, is so significant that two companies that seemingly should function as competitors, Ford Motor Company and Zipcar, have joined forces to take advantage of the opportunities.[2]

A Zipcar, available by the hour for a low rental fee, theoretically might eliminate a student's need to own a car. It thus might steal a customer from Ford. But a Zipcar rental also may be an opportunity for a young driver to test a car model and become comfortable driving it. This familiarity can translate, over time, into a purchase or even repeat purchases. This

logic motivated Ford to provide Zipcar with up to 1,000 Ford Focus sedans for use on 250 U.S. college and university campuses.[3] With its advanced technology features and fuel efficiency, the Focus is particularly alluring to younger drivers. But Ford further sweetened the deal for students by offering $10 off Zipcar's annual membership fee and a $1 per hour discount on the hourly rental fee for students renting a Ford. Zipcar is also purchasing a few Ford Escape sport utility vehicles, which will be available at discounted fees too.

The alliance helps Ford tap into the spending that college students allow themselves. It also gives them a relatively low-cost way to control the early driving experiences of future car buyers, because the deal means that more than half of all Zipcar vehicles available on U.S. campuses will be Fords. The manufacturer's 20 or so rivals are left to divvy up the remains. The relationship helps Zipcar by increasing its presence on college campuses, but also by increasing the number of U.S. cars it can advertise as being in the company's fleet.

As these events and developments show, companies such as Target, Zipcar, and Ford recognize the value of reaching young buyers to shape both their current and future consumer behavior. By using peer-to-peer endorsements and other approaches that resonate with college students, these companies are creating life-long customers, whose behaviors will continue to benefit the firms. ■

> [*To understand consumer behavior, we must ask why people buy goods or services.*]

We are all consumers, and we take this status for granted. But we are also complex and irrational creatures who cannot always explain our own choices and actions. This inability makes the vitally important job of marketing managers even more difficult, in that they must be able to explain consumers' behavior to give marketers as clear an understanding of their customers as possible.

To understand consumer behavior, we must ask *why* people buy goods or services. Using principles and theories from

sociology and psychology, marketers have been able to decipher many consumer choices and develop basic strategies for dealing with consumers' behavior. Generally, people buy one product or service instead of another because they perceive it to be the better value for them; that is, the ratio of benefits to costs is higher for the product or service than for any other.[4]

However, benefits can be subtle and less than rationally assessed, as we shall see. Consider Katie Smith, who is considering a dress purchase for a job interview. She requires something fashionable but professional looking and doesn't want to spend a lot of money. In making the decision about where she should buy the dress, Katie asks herself:

- Which alternative gives me the best overall value—the most appropriate, yet fashionable dress at the lowest price?

- Which alternative is the best investment—the dress that I can get the most use of?

Because Katie might have several reasons to choose a particular store or dress, it is critical for companies such as Ann Taylor or Macy's to key in on the specific benefits that are most important to her. Other factors that might influence Katie go beyond her conscious awareness, which means that the retailers need to be even more well-versed in her decision process than she is.[5] Only then can they create a marketing mix that will satisfy Katie.

In this chapter, we explore the process that consumers go through when they buy products and services. Then we discuss the psychological, social, and situational factors that influence this consumer decision process. Throughout the chapter, we emphasize what firms can do to influence consumers to purchase their products and services.

LO 6-1   Articulate the steps in the consumer buying process.

THE CONSUMER DECISION PROCESS

The consumer decision process model represents the steps that consumers go through before, during, and after making purchases.[6] Because marketers often find it difficult to determine how consumers make their purchasing decisions, it is useful for us to break down the process into a series of steps and examine each individually, as in Exhibit 6.1.

Need Recognition

The consumer decision process begins when consumers recognize they have an unsatisfied need, and they would like to go from their actual, needy state to a different, desired state. The greater the discrepancy between these two states, the greater the **need recognition** will be. For example, your stomach tells you that you are hungry, and you would rather not have that particular feeling. If you are only a little hungry, you may pass it off and decide to eat later. But if your stomach is growling and you cannot concentrate, the *need*—the difference between your actual (hungry) state and your desired (not hungry) state—is greater, and you'll want to eat immediately to get to your desired state. Furthermore, your hunger conceivably could be satisfied by a nice healthy salad, but what you really want is a bowl of ice cream. *Wants* are goods or services that are not necessarily needed but are desired.[7] Regardless of the level of your hunger, your desire for ice cream will never be satisfied by any

need recognition
The beginning of the consumer decision process; occurs when consumers recognize they have an unsatisfied need and want to go from their actual, needy state to a different, desired state.

functional needs Pertain to the performance of a product or service.

▼ **EXHIBIT 6.1** The Consumer Decision Process

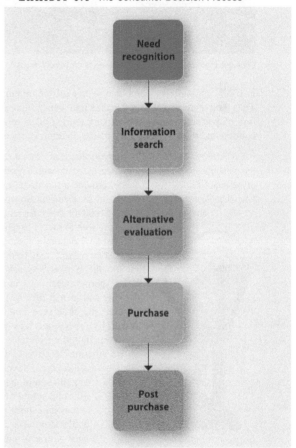

type of salad. Consumer needs like these can be classified as functional, psychological, or both.[8]

LO 6-2   Describe the difference between functional and psychological needs.

Functional Needs **Functional needs** pertain to the performance of a product or service. For years, BMW has made functionally superior motorcycles. BMW's K1600 model has an inline-six cylinder motor, something previously available only

Does this motorcycle satisfy functional or psychological needs?

in BMW automobiles, combined with a stiff aluminum frame. Thus it offers remarkable power on a lightweight bike, enabling it to outperform both the best luxury touring bikes in terms of comfort and serious sporty motorcycles in terms of speed.

Psychological Needs

Psychological needs pertain to the personal gratification consumers associate with a product and/ or service.[9] Shoes, for instance, provide a functional need—to keep feet clean and protect them from the elements. So why would anyone pay more than $1000 for shoes that may do nei-

ther? Because they seek to satisfy psychological needs. Christian Louboutin's shoes, with their signature red sole, may be the hottest shoe on the market.[10] Sarah Jessica Parker sports several pairs in *Sex and the City* and in real life; BMW even featured the shoe in a commercial. Virtually every modern fashion icon, including Penelope Cruz, Catherine Deneuve, Lady Gaga, Ashley Olsen, Beyoncé, and Angelina Jolie, have been photographed wearing Louboutin shoes. And yet a black python-and-lace shoe with a 14-cm heel is not a particularly practical

Do Christian Louboutin's shoes satisfy functional or psychological needs?

means of spending $1500. As a result of all the media attention though, there is a strong demand for Louboutin shoes by women who love exciting (and expensive) shoes.

These examples highlight that the vast majority of goods and services are likely to satisfy both functional and psychological needs, albeit to different degrees. Whereas the functional characteristics of BMW K1600 are its main selling point, it also maintains a fashionable appeal for bikers and comes in several colors to match buyers' aesthetic preferences. In contrast, Christian Louboutin shoes satisfy psychological needs that overshadow the functional needs, though they still ultimately serve the function of a shoe.

Consider another, slightly more realistic example: You can get a $15 haircut at SuperCuts or spend $80 or more to get basically the same thing at an upscale salon. Are the two haircuts objectively different? The answer might vary depending on which you believe represents a good haircut and a good value: One person might value getting a really good deal; another might enjoy the extra attention and amenities associated with a fancy salon.

A key to successful marketing is determining the correct balance of functional and psychological needs that best appeals to the firm's target markets. Marriott is carefully balancing this fine line. In the modern economic environment, Marriott is focusing on what matters most to guests. Many hotel consumers just step on the newspapers delivered to their doors, without ever picking them up to read. The various Marriott brands—including Courtyard, Residence Inn, Fairfield Inn, and the Ritz-Carlton—therefore have discontinued deliveries of approximately 50,000 papers daily. The cost savings enable Marriott to avoid massive layoffs, which supports its core value of taking care of employees and thereby encouraging them to treat customers well. The switch to Edy's brand ice cream, instead of Häagen-Dazs, saves money and facilitates employees' jobs because the less dense dessert is easier to scoop. Yet even as it cuts costs, Marriott recognizes the need to attract more customers, so it offers free nights and discounted rates, including $85 in Medan, Indonesia, and $120 at a casino and beach resort in Curaçao.

Search for Information

The second step, after a consumer recognizes a need, is to search for information about the various options that exist to satisfy that need. The length and intensity of the search are

Marriott focuses on what is really important to its customers. But it saves money by switching from Häagen-Dazs to Edy's brand ice cream.

psychological needs Pertain to the personal gratification consumers associate with a product or service.	internal search for information Occurs when the buyer examines his or her own memory and knowledge about the product or service, gathered through past experiences.	external search for information Occurs when the buyer seeks information outside his or her personal knowledge base to help make the buying decision.	internal locus of control Refers to when consumers believe they have some control over the outcomes of their actions, in which case they generally engage in more search activities.	external locus of control Refers to when consumers believe that fate or other external factors control all outcomes.

based on the degree of perceived risk associated with purchasing the product or service. If the way your hair is cut is important to your appearance and self-image, you may engage in an involved search for the right salon and stylist. Alternatively, an athlete looking for a short buzz cut might go to the closest, most convenient, and cheapest barber shop. Regardless of the required search level, there are two key types of information search: internal and external.

Internal Search for Information In an **internal search for information**, the buyer examines his or her own memory and knowledge about the product or service, gathered through past experiences. For example, every time Katie wants to eat salad for lunch, she and her friends go to Sweet Tomatoes, but if she's craving dessert, she heads straight to The Cheesecake Factory. In making these choices, she relies on her memory of past experiences when she has eaten at these restaurant chains.

External Search for Information In an **external search for information**, the buyer seeks information outside his or her personal knowledge base to help make the buying decision. Consumers might fill in their personal knowledge gaps by talking with friends, family, or a salesperson. They can also scour commercial media for unsponsored and (it is hoped) unbiased information, such as that available through *Consumer Reports,* or peruse sponsored media such as magazines, television, or radio. Sometimes consumers get commercial exposures to products or services without really knowing it. New media such as blogs are steadily becoming a major source of external insformation to consumers, as Adding Value 6.1 notes.

The Internet provides more information than that contained in blogs though.[11] For example, while watching an episode of CW's *Gossip Girl*, Katie saw the character Vanessa wearing a fantastic outfit consisting of a peasant blouse and leggings. She pulled her laptop over, went to Google, and searched for Shop the Look and Gossip Girl. She found a number of websites that carry news items and pictures of the characters. These websites also identify the prices for the various items worn by its characters. A long list of items included both the blouse and the leggings. The

You can find the clothing worn by Gossip Girl characters online.

blouse was designed by Joie and available for sale for $248, and the leggings by LnA cost $105.[12] But Katie is also a savvy shopper, so she searched lna leggings on Google and found that through the company's site, she could get a cropped version on sale for only $45.[13] Satisfied with that purchase, she began flipping through a magazine and saw Reese Witherspoon wearing a pair of jeans she loved. This time, she navigated directly to www .TrueFit.com, which featured those very jeans, designed by 7 for All Mankind, on its homepage.[14] Katie entered her measurements and style preferences, and the website returned recommendations of jeans that would be a good fit for her.

All these types of search are examples of external searches for information. Katie used the television show's dedicated site to find a style she liked; she referred to a magazine for additional style tips; and she found jeans that will be a perfect fit for her using the web. All these events took place without Katie leaving her home to go to the store or try on dozens of pairs of pants.

LO 6-3 Describe factors that affect information search.

Factors Affecting Consumers' Search Processes It is important for marketers to understand the many factors that affect consumers' search processes. Among them are the following three factors.

The Perceived Benefits versus Perceived Costs of Search. Is it worth the time and effort to search for information about a product or service? For instance, most families spend a lot of time researching the housing market in their preferred area before they make a purchase because homes are a very expensive and important purchase with significant safety and enjoyment implications. They likely spend much less time researching which inexpensive dollhouse to buy for the youngest member of the family.

The Locus of Control. People who have an **internal locus of control** believe they have some control over the outcomes of their actions, in which case they generally engage in more search activities. With an **external locus of control**, consumers believe that fate or other external factors control all outcomes. In that case, they believe it doesn't

Adding Value   6.1

How Fashion Blogs Sell Clothes

Sweatpants and T-shirts used to dominate fashion on college campuses. Now students and young professionals are upgrading their wardrobes, seeking ways to stay current with the rapid change in trends while expressing individuality through how they dress.[15] Where do they find their inspiration?

The time-honored approaches are to page through a fashion magazine, keep an eye on how peers dress, or consult with a friend. Now blogs are replacing magazines and expanding style choices, literally putting the world of fashion at a customer's fingertips. These blogs combine the sense of reliability that comes from peer-to-peer advice with the rapid access to information that today's shoppers have come to expect. The result is a marketing channel that is exerting increasing influence over consumer behavior.[16]

Fashion blogs use the Internet to connect designers and styles to the shoppers who are most likely to buy them, but they feature two distinct differences from passive websites: editors who control what appears on the site and contributors who post comments on what they see. One popular blog written by college women, College Fashion, provides fashion tips on subjects ranging from the must-have updates for a fall wardrobe to the top designers for teens and twenty-somethings.[17] Quizzes help site visitors decide which colors would suit their mood on a given day or which celebrity most inspires their style.[18] Clearly the editor's sense of style helps build followers, but the blog also creates a sense of community, providing a place where fashion-conscious young women can contribute their own point of view or proudly announce a new purchase.

At the other end of the fashion blog spectrum are professional sites, such as Refinery29, which offers separate editions for New York, Los Angeles, Chicago, San Francisco, and Washington DC. Multiple editors juggle blogs about various topics of interest, including diet tips and hair and makeup trends. As an added feature, the site goes beyond a discussion format, providing a members-only shopping site with exclusive offers from popular names in fashion, beauty, and decor. In addition to being able to peruse the site to see what's new, members receive e-mails announcing hot designers, stores, and websites.

Professional fashion blogs such as Refinery29 offer a members—only shopping site as well as tips on diet, hair, and makeup trends.

Marketers are recognizing the value of these blogs to reach customers. Like College Fashion, Refinery29 and its competitor, FabSugar, host advertisements—yet another way for retailers to reach target markets. FabSugar, which contains posts on fashion, entertainment, sex and culture, food, money, pets, and even pregnancy and parenting, is considered one of the top 20 most influential fashion blogs.[19] With projected revenues of $8 million in its sixth year of business, Refinery29's blog demonstrates the ability of this marketing channel to generate both followers and sales.[20]

matter how much information they gather; if they make a wise decision, it isn't to their credit, and if they make a poor one, it isn't their fault. People who do a lot of research before purchasing individual stocks have an internal locus of control; those who purchase mutual funds are more likely to believe that they can't predict the market and probably have an external locus of control. These beliefs have widespread effects. For example, when people believe that they can choose their own consumption goals (internal locus of control), they

work harder to achieve them than if those goals feel imposed upon them (external locus of control).[21] Social & Mobile Marketing 6.1 discusses how consumers are gaining a greater internal locus of control over their health by using smartphone apps.

Actual or Perceived Risk. Five types of risk associated with purchase decisions can delay or discourage a purchase: performance, financial, social, physiological, and psychological. The higher the risk, the more likely the consumer is to engage in an extended search.

Performance risk involves the perceived danger inherent in a poorly performing product or service. An example of performance risk is the possibility that Katie Smith's new interview dress is prone to shrinking when dry cleaned.

Financial risk is risk associated with a monetary outlay and includes the initial cost of the purchase as well as the costs of using the item or service.[22] Katie is not only concerned that her new dress will provide her with the

performance risk Involves the perceived danger inherent in a poorly performing product or service.

financial risk Risk associated with a monetary outlay; includes the initial cost of the purchase, as well as the costs of using the item or service.

professional appearance she is seeking but also that the cost of dry cleaning will not be exorbitant. Retailers recognize buying professional apparel can be a financial burden and therefore offer guarantees that the products they sell will perform as expected. Their suppliers are also well aware that dry cleaning is

Social & Mobile Marketing 6.1
The Future of Health Is Mobile[23]

A host of new applications and mobile links make it easier than ever for consumers to maintain their own health and well-being with just a few clicks. Whether the condition is chronic or new, these health-related offerings seek to make it easier for health care consumers to understand their options, consider solutions, and recognize when to seek immediate medical care. They also facilitate providers' efforts to stay up to date with the latest treatments and advances. Consider a few examples:

- An award-winning app, mySugr turns the tedious task of glucose monitoring into a game for diabetics. They earn points for each data entry they make that helps them tame a monster named Diabetes. The app also supports food logging with a snapshot feature, provides immediate data analyses, produces a summary report that users can send their doctors, and maintains the data in a central location.
- Doctor Mole allows people to take a selfie (i.e., self-portrait) of any suspicious skin growth. Using augmented reality technology, the app applies the well-established criteria for assessing the risk associated with each mole (i.e., asymmetry, borders, color, diameter). Thus users can determine whether they have a potentially cancerous malignancy or just a new freckle.
- With BurnMed, users draw on a displayed image of a body to indicate the extent of the burn suffered, whether by themselves, a friend, or a patient. That is, this app seeks to target both laypeople and medical practitioners. In a lay setting, users can determine the seriousness of a burn they might have suffered at home. In a medical practice, emergency staff can quickly determine the appropriate treatment when faced with a crisis such as a tanker explosion that burns hundreds of victims.
- The vCath training tool is expressly for medical students who need to learn to insert neuro-surgical catheters. In patients, this step is critical and risky, such that students have little leeway for practicing their technique. This app enables them to do so virtually, as many times as they wish, before confronting any live patients.

Smartphone apps empower consumers to take control of their health in exciting new ways.

Along with these dedicated apps, various hospitals and doctors are experimenting with software that reminds patients to take their medicine or when their next appointments are. By encouraging positive behaviors, these technology advances should lead to greater consumer health and happiness as well as benefits for society as a whole.

social risk The fears that consumers suffer when they worry others might not regard their purchases positively.

physiological risk The fear of an actual harm should a product not perform properly.

safety risk See *psychological risk.*

psychological risks Associated with the way people will feel if the product or service does not convey the right image.

universal sets Include all possible choices for a product-category.

retrieval sets Includes those brands or stores that the consumer can readily bring forth from memory.

evoked set Comprises the alternative brands or stores that the consumer states he or she would consider when making a purchase decision.

evaluative criteria Consist of a set of salient, or important, attributes about a particular product.

expensive and can limit the life of the garment, so many offer easy-to-care-for washable fabrics.

Social risk involves the fears that consumers suffer when they worry others might not regard their purchases positively. When buying a dress, consumers like Katie consider what their friends would like. Alternatively, because this job interview is so important, Katie might make a conscious effort to assert a distinctive identity or make a statement by buying a unique, more stylish, and possibly more expensive dress than her friends would typically buy.

Physiological risk could also be called **safety risk.** Whereas performance risk involves what might happen if a product does not perform as expected, physiological (or safety) risk refers to the fear of an actual harm should the product not perform properly. Although physiological risk is typically not an issue with apparel, it can be an important issue when buying other products, such as a car. External agencies and government bodies publish safety ratings for cars to help assuage this risk. Consumers compare the safety records of their various choices because they recognize the real danger to their well-being if the

purchase, read several fashion magazines and sought her friends' opinions because she wanted people to think she looked great in the dress, and she wanted to get the job!

Recent research suggests that psychological risks might help explain why consumers enjoy supersizing their menu options. Especially when consumers feel powerless or more vulnerable, they equate larger sizes—whether in televisions, houses, or menu items—with improved status. That is, consumers who feel powerless choose bigger food portions to gain a sense of status.[24]

Evaluation of Alternatives

Once a consumer has recognized a problem and explored the possible options, he or she must sift through the choices available and evaluate the alternatives. Alternative evaluation often occurs while the consumer is engaged in the process of information search. For example, Katie Smith would rule out various stores because she knows they won't carry the style she needs for the job interview. Once in the store, she would try on lots of dresses and eliminate those that don't fit, don't look good on her, or aren't appropriate attire for the occasion. Consumers forgo alternative evaluations altogether when buying habitual (convenience) products; you'll rarely catch a loyal Pepsi drinker buying Coca-Cola.

Attribute Sets Research has shown that a consumer's mind organizes and categorizes alternatives to aid his or her decision process. **Universal sets** include all possible choices for a prod-

> *Recent research suggests that psychological risks might help explain why consumers enjoy supersizing their menu options. Especially when consumers feel powerless or more vulnerable, they equate larger sizes— whether in televisions, houses, or menu items—with improved status.*

automobile they purchase fails to perform a basic task, such as stopping when the driver steps on the brakes or protecting the passengers in the cabin even if the car flips.

Another major physiological risk pertains to growing concerns about health risks associated with the food and beverages we consume. McDonald's has come under a lot of associated scrutiny recently, especially in response to *Supersize Me* and related media (see Ethical & Societal Dilemma 6.1).

Finally, **psychological risks** are those risks associated with the way people will feel if the product or service does not convey the right image. Katie Smith, thinking of her dress

uct category, but because it would be unwieldy for a person to recall all possible alternatives for every purchase decision, marketers tend to focus on only a subset of choices. One important subset is **retrieval sets**, which are those brands or stores that can be readily brought forth from memory. Another is a consumer's **evoked set**, which comprises the alternative brands or stores that the consumer states he or she would consider when making a purchase decision. If a firm can get its brand or store into a consumer's evoked set, it has increased the likelihood of purchase and therefore reduced search time because the consumer will think specifically of that brand when considering choices.

ethical & societal dilemma 6.1

The Obesity Epidemic and Fast Foods

Filmmaker Morgan Spurlock has shown us that a steady fast-food diet can be downright dangerous. Thirty days of eating nothing but McDonald's hamburgers, fries, and shakes turned Spurlock—who started the experiment as a healthy 32-year-old man—into an overweight, depressed, and dysfunctional guy with soaring cholesterol levels and liver trouble.

Today, 42 percent of low-income women in the United States are obese,[25] and there is a growing consensus that an overreliance on fast food and junk food has contributed significantly to this health problem. Although marketing is certainly a major factor in attracting customers to McDonald's and other fast-food restaurants, health experts also have shown that multiple other factors also drive obesity-promoting habits.[26]

In the film Super Size Me, *filmmaker Morgan Spurlock ate nothing but McDonald's food for thirty days. He gained weight, became depressed, and developed high cholesterol and liver trouble.*

In particular, working moms with little time to cook appreciate the convenience of fast foods. Families on a tight budget like these low-cost menus. And the fast-food industry has learned to cater to America's taste for foods high in sugar, salt, and fat, which turn into near-addictive desires. Combine those high-calorie habits with a sedentary or car-dependent lifestyle that rarely includes exercise, and you have a prescription for obesity.

The problem is especially serious among children. One Harvard School of Public Health physician noted that children aged 2 to 19 years consume 7 trillion calories through sugar-sweetened beverages a year, fueling a $24 billion industry for kids.[27] It's just one major factor in the 17 percent obesity rate among U.S. youth.

Efforts to revise food labels so that they clearly tell consumers whether a meal or a supermarket item contains unhealthy ingredients have been blocked successfully by the food industry. But McDonald's—the focus of significant pressures from both health advocates and parents as well as the defendant in at least one lawsuit alleging that its high-fat menu caused obesity-related health damage to two children (*Pelman v. McDonald's Corp.*, 237 F. Supp. 2d 512 [S.D.N.Y. January 22, 2003])—has decided to change some of its ways.

The company has announced a planned 20 percent reduction in the calorie count of its Happy Meals. But it declined to voluntarily jettison the toys that come along with the Happy Meal, a marketing hook that has long made this item one of the most popular on the kids' menu. Lawmakers and parents seeking to break the childhood link between toys and fast food have demanded that such toy giveaways be banned. San Francisco was the first city to enforce such a law; in response, the restaurant chain chose to charge a dime for each toy, so that it could comply with the regulation but still make the toys easily accessible to its youthful customers.[28] McDonald's also has rejected calls to eliminate French fries altogether, along with its traditional soda. But the company says it will include apple slices with every order and reduce salt content by 2015.

Some critics are not impressed. Changes like a one-ounce reduction in French fries won't help kids much. But McDonald's small concessions should generate huge publicity for the company.

Katie Smith knows that there are a lot of apparel stores (universal set). However, only some have the style that she is looking for, such as Macy's, Ann Taylor, The Gap, and Banana Republic (retrieval set). She recalls that Ann Taylor is where her mother shops and The Gap is a favorite of her younger sister. But she is sure that Banana Republic and Macy's carry business attire she would like, so only those stores are in her evoked set.

When consumers begin to evaluate different alternatives, they often base their evaluations on a set of important attributes or evaluative criteria. **Evaluative criteria** consist of salient, or important, attributes about a particular product. For example, when Katie is looking for her dress, she might consider things like the selling price, fit, materials and construction quality, reputation of the brand, and the service support that the retailer offers. At times, however, it becomes difficult to evaluate different brands or stores because there are so many choices,[29] especially when those choices involve aspects of the garment that are difficult to evaluate, such as materials and construction quality.

Ann Taylor is part of the <u>retrieval set</u> of stores available to women for business apparel, but Banana Republic is in the <u>evoked set</u> for young women looking for business apparel.

Consumers use several shortcuts to simplify the potentially complicated decision process: determinant attributes and consumer decision rules. **Determinant attributes** are product or service features that are important to the buyer and on which competing brands or stores are perceived to differ.[30] Because many important and desirable criteria are equal among the various choices, consumers look for something special—a determinant attribute—to differentiate one brand or store from another. Determinant attributes may appear perfectly rational, such as health and nutrition claims offered by certain foods and beverages, or they may be more subtle and psychologically based, such as the red soles on a pair of Christian Louboutin heels. Ethical & Societal Dilemma 6.2 highlights the use of determinant attributes describing food and beverages marketed as natural when in fact they are not.

Consumer Decision Rules **Consumer decision rules** are the set of criteria that consumers use consciously or subconsciously to quickly and efficiently select from among several alternatives. These rules are typically either compensatory or noncompensatory.

Compensatory. A **compensatory decision rule** assumes that the consumer, when evaluating alternatives, trades off one characteristic against another, such that good characteristics compensate for bad characteristics.[31] For instance, Hanna Jackson is looking to buy breakfast cereal and is considering several factors such as taste, calories, price, and natural/organic claims. But even if the cereal is priced a little higher than Hanna was planning to spend, a superb overall rating offsets, or compensates for, the higher price.

Although Hanna probably would not go through the formal process of making the purchasing decision based on the **multi-attribute model** described in Exhibit 6.2, this exhibit illustrates how a compensatory model would work.[32] Hanna assigns weights to the importance of each factor. These weights must add up to 1.0. So, for instance, taste is the most important, with a weight of .4, and calories are least important, with a weight of .1. She assigns weights to how well each of the cereals might perform, with 1 being very poor and 10 being very good. Hanna thinks Cheerios has the best taste, so she assigns it a 10. Then she multiplies each performance rating by its importance rating to get an overall score for each cereal. The rating for

▼ **EXHIBIT 6.2** Compensatory Purchasing Multi-Attribute Model for Buying Cereal

	Taste	Calories	Natural /Organic Claims	Price	Overall Score
Importance Weight	0.4	0.1	0.3	0.2	
Cheerios	10	8	6	8	8.2
Post	8	9	8	3	7.1
Kashi	6	8	10	5	7.2

determinant attributes Product or service features that are important to the buyer and on which competing brands or stores are perceived to differ.	consumer decision rules The set of criteria that consumers use consciously or subconsciously to quickly and efficiently select from among several alternatives.	compensatory decision rule At work when the consumer is evaluating alternatives and trades off one characteristic against another, such that good characteristics compensate for bad ones.	multi-attribute model A compensatory model of customer decision making based on the notion that customers see a product as a collection of attributes or characteristics. The model uses a weighted average score based on the importance of various attributes and performance on those issues.

ethical & societal dilemma   6.2

Wearing the "Healthy" Label: Natural and Organic Foods

With competition for shelf space always at a premium, today's supermarket aisles are more crowded than ever. Much of the new competition comes from natural and organic foods, which comprised more than 4 percent of the $673 billion U.S. food industry in 2010.[33]

For a consumer facing a dizzying array of choices, these natural foods offer a unique appeal: They promise to improve personal and planetary health. Organic and natural food companies claim that their foods are safer and more nutritious because they are produced with only natural ingredients.

Consumers generally believe that these claims mean the food contains no artificial or highly processed ingredients.[34] Yet Snapple's "natural" bottled iced tea contains high-fructose corn syrup, a highly processed, and recently controversial, form of sugar. In California, most organic strawberry farmers use seeds and plants from nurseries that are not organic, including growers producing fruit for Driscoll Strawberry Associates, the largest berry distributor in the world.[35] The farmers argue that once their plants bear fruit, they halt their use of chemical pesticides and herbicides, so the berries themselves are still organic. These companies thus might be contradicting consumer expectations, but they are not actually violating federal requirements.

The U.S. Department of Agriculture (USDA) regulates the production of organic foods. Products bearing the USDA Organic label must be grown using organic, not conventional, farming methods.[36] That regulation means using natural fertilizers, such as manure or compost; beneficial insects or birds to control insects rather than chemical insecticides; and crop rotation or other manual methods to control weeds rather than chemical herbicides. Animals raised for meat production must be given organic feed and access to the outdoors rather than antibiotics, growth hormones, and other medications.

Yet the USDA's National Organic Program (NOP) regulations do not explicitly govern the production of seeds and planting stock. Advocates who want to see sustainable production methods used throughout the food-growing process have called on the USDA to outlaw the use of chemical fumigants, including methyl bromide, a widely used pesticide and soil sterilizer known to deplete the ozone layer.[37] Furthermore, the NOP regulations have not been updated since 2002; they allow conventional agricultural stock to be used whenever organically grown seeds and plants are not commercially available.

Nor does the USDA regulate the production of foods labeled natural, except for meats and poultry,[38]

which must be minimally processed and free of artificial colors, flavors, sweeteners, preservatives, and ingredients. No such specifics govern other foods that choose to carry the natural label rather than an organic claim.

For the consumer, the organic and natural food experience is also about perception. Some shoppers may believe these foods deliver healthful benefits, but studies also reveal that simply identifying a grocery item as a health food may affect their eating experience. Students given snacks labeled health bars reported feeling hungry afterward and craving foods they enjoyed more. In another study, respondents widely perceived "that 'healthy' isn't going to meet enjoyment goals," which likely reflects consumers' assumption that healthy foods won't taste good.[39]

How healthy is Snapple?

> ## CONVERSION RATES TEND TO BE LOWER FOR CONSUMERS USING AN INTERNET CHANNEL BECAUSE THEY ARE ABLE TO LOOK AT PRODUCTS AND THROW THEM IN THEIR CART BUT STILL DELAY THEIR PURCHASE DECISION.

Cheerios in this example is the highest of the three cereals $[(.4 \times 10) + (.1 \times 8) + (.3 \times 6) + (.2 \times 8) = 8.2)]$. This multi-attributes model allows the trade-off between the various factors to be incorporated explicitly into a consumer's purchase decision.

Noncompensatory. Sometimes however, consumers use a **noncompensatory decision rule**, in which they choose a product or service on the basis of one characteristic or one subset of a characteristic, regardless of the values of its other attributes.[40] Thus, though Cheerios received the highest overall score of 8.2, Hanna might still pick Kashi because she is particularly sensitive to claims of natural or organic contents, and this brand earned the highest score on this attribute (i.e., a 10).

Once a consumer has considered the possible alternatives and evaluated the pros and cons of each, he or she can move toward a purchase decision.

Purchase and Consumption

After evaluating the alternatives, customers are ready to buy. However, they don't always patronize the store or purchase the brand or item on which they had originally decided. It may not be available at the retail store, for example. Retailers therefore turn to the **conversion rate** to measure how well they have converted purchase intentions into purchases. One method of measuring the conversion rate is the number of real or virtual abandoned carts in the retailer's store or website.

Retailers use various tactics to increase the chances that customers will convert their positive evaluations into purchases. They can reduce the number of abandoned carts by making it easier to purchase merchandise. Most important, they should have plenty of stock on hand of the merchandise that customers want. They can also reduce the actual wait time to buy merchandise by opening more checkout lanes and placing them conveniently inside the store. To reduce perceived wait times, they might install digital displays to entertain customers waiting in line.[41]

For different types of companies, the conversion rate also refers to rentals (e.g., Netflix) or to outright purchases (e.g., haute couture), though some of these lines appear to be blurring as consumers seek new ways to access the items they want. At Rent the Runway, fashion- and budget-conscious shoppers gain temporary possession of the latest fashions from big names, including Badgley Mischka, Kate Spade, and Vera Wang. As if they were dealing with movies on DVDs, members rent haute couture dresses, handbags, jewelry, and even wedding gowns; pay anywhere between \$50 and \$400 for their chosen items;

receive the glam wear in the mail within a few days; and then return the items after their fabulous affair has ended.[42] At the same time, Warner Bros. is working on a new idea to get movie renters to start buying more of its offerings. It purchased Flixster, the movie buff website, and initiated UltraViolet, a movie storage service that enables viewers to purchase a movie once and then access it on any of their connected devices (e.g., computer, tablet, smartphone, web-ready television).[43]

But conversion rates still tend to be lower for consumers using an Internet channel because they are able to look at products and throw them in their cart but still delay their purchase decision. To encourage customers to make purchase decisions, Zappos.com and Overstock.com create urgency by alerting customers when an item they have put it in their shopping cart is almost sold out. Other sites, such as Gilt, offer items for specified 36-hour periods or until they run out, and Neiman Marcus runs two-hour, online-only sales. Many retailers send reminder e-mails to visitors about items in carts they have abandoned.[44]

LO 6-4 Discuss postpurchase outcomes.

Postpurchase

The final step of the consumer decision process is postpurchase behavior. Marketers are particularly interested in postpurchase behavior because it entails actual rather than potential customers. Satisfied customers, whom marketers hope to create, become loyal, purchase again, and spread positive word of mouth, so they are quite important. There are three possible positive postpurchase outcomes as illustrated in Exhibit 6.3: customer satisfaction, postpurchase cognitive dissonance, and customer loyalty (or disloyalty).

Customer Satisfaction Setting unrealistically high consumer expectations of the product through advertising, personal selling, or other types of promotion may lead to higher initial sales, but it eventually will result in dissatisfaction if the product fails to achieve high performance expectations. (For a related discussion about communication gaps, see Chapter 13.) This failure can lead to dissatisfied customers and the potential for negative word of mouth.[45] Setting customer expectations too low is an equally dangerous strategy. Many retailers don't put their best foot forward. For instance, no matter how good the merchandise and service may be, if a store is not clean and appealing from the entrance, customers are not likely to enter.

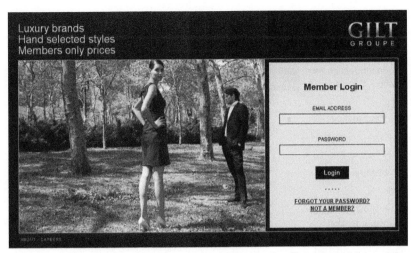

Gilt.com encourages customers to buy now by offering a limited number of items for short time period.

▼ **EXHIBIT 6.3** Components of Postpurchase Outcomes

Marketers can take several steps to ensure postpurchase satisfaction though, such as to:

· Build realistic expectations, not too high and not too low.

· Demonstrate correct product use—improper usage can cause dissatisfaction.

· Stand behind the product or service by providing money-back guarantees and warranties.

· Encourage customer feedback, which cuts down on negative word of mouth and helps marketers adjust their offerings.

· Periodically make contact with customers and thank them for their support. This contact reminds customers that the marketer cares about their business and wants them to be satisfied. It also provides an opportunity to correct any problems. Customers appreciate human contact, though it is more expensive for marketers than e-mail or postal mail contacts.

Postpurchase Cognitive Dissonance **Postpurchase cognitive dissonance** is an internal conflict that arises from an inconsistency between two beliefs or between beliefs and behavior. For example, you might have buyer's remorse after purchasing an expensive TV because you question after all whether a high-price TV is appreciably better quality than a similar size TV at a lower price—or whether you need a television at all, considering your ability to stream content through your computer. Thus, postpurchase cognitive dissonance generally occurs when a consumer questions the appropriateness of a purchase after his or her decision has been made.

Postpurchase cognitive dissonance is especially likely for products that are expensive, are infrequently purchased, do not work as intended, and are associated with high levels of risk. Marketers direct efforts at consumers after the purchase is made to address this issue.[46] General Electric sends a letter to purchasers of its appliances, positively reinforcing the message that the customer made a wise decision by mentioning the high quality that went into the product's design and production. Some clothing manufacturers include a tag on their garments to offer the reassurance that because of their special manufacturing process, perhaps designed to provide a soft, vintage appearance, there may be variations in color that have no effect on the quality of the item. After a pang of dissonance, satisfaction may then set in.

Let's check back in with our friend Katie to recognize these effects. When Katie purchased her interview dress at Macy's, she tried it on for some of her friends. Her boyfriend said he loved it, but several of her girlfriends seemed less impressed. Katie thought it made her look more mature. Because of these mixed signals, some dissonance resulted and manifested itself

as an uncomfortable, unsettled feeling. To reduce the dissonance, Katie could:

- Take back the dress.

- Pay attention to positive information, such as
  looking up ads and articles about this particular dress designer.

- Seek more positive feedback from friends.

- Seek negative information about dresses
  made by designers not selected.

After a while, satisfaction with her experience probably will result.

Customer Loyalty   In the postpurchase
stage of the decision-making process, marketers
attempt to solidify a loyal relationship with their
customers. They want customers to be satisfied
with their purchase and buy from the same company again. Loyal customers will buy only certain brands and shop at certain stores, and they
include no other firms in their evoked set. As we
explained in Chapter 2, such customers are
therefore very valuable to firms, and marketers
have designed customer relationship management (CRM) programs specifically to retain them.

Undesirable Consumer Behavior   Although firms
want satisfied, loyal customers, sometimes they fail to attain
them. Passive consumers are those who don't repeat purchase
or recommend the product to others. More serious and potentially damaging, however, is negative consumer behavior, such
as negative word of mouth and rumors.

Negative word of mouth occurs when consumers spread
negative information about a product, service, or store to others. When customers' expectations are met or even exceeded,
they often don't tell anyone about it. But when consumers believe that they have been treated unfairly in some way, they

Whirlpool posts both good and bad comments on Twitter. It believes that posting negative
comments opens up discussions and emphasizes the proactive measures the company is
taking to remedy service or product failures.

usually want to complain, often to many people. The Internet
has provided an effective method of spreading negative word
of mouth to millions of people instantaneously through personal blogs, Twitter, and corporate websites. To lessen the impact of negative word of mouth, firms provide customer
service representatives—whether online, on the phone, or in
stores—to handle and respond to complaints. Many companies
also allow customers to post comments and complaints to proprietary social media sites.

For example, Whirlpool set up Facebook pages for its appliance brands, Maytag, KitchenAid, and Whirlpool. Customers
may share their thoughts on these sites without fear that their
negative feedback will be deleted from the site. Whirlpool believes that it should keep the bad to open up discussions and emphasize the proactive measures the company is taking to remedy
service or product failures.[47] If a customer believes that positive
action will be taken as a result of the complaint, he or she is less
likely to complain to family and friends or through the Internet.
(A detailed example of word of mouth appears in Chapter 13.)

Stores collect customer information for their CRM programs from
customer credit cards.

 check yourself

1. Name the five stages in the consumer decision process.

2. What is the difference between a need and a want?

3. Distinguish between functional and psychological needs.

4. What are the various types of perceived risk?

5. What are the differences between compensatory and
   noncompensatory decision rules?

▼ **EXHIBIT 6.4** Factors Affecting the Consumer Decision Process

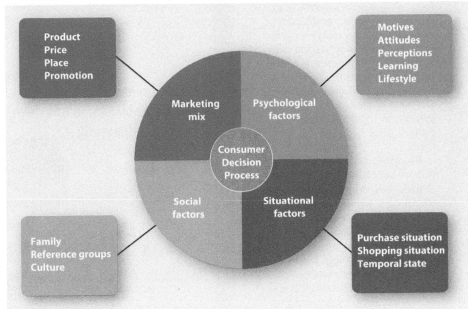

A motive is a need or want that is strong enough to cause the person to seek satisfaction.

LO 6-5 List the factors that affect the consumer decision process.

FACTORS INFLUENCING THE CONSUMER DECISION PROCESS

The consumer decision process can be influenced by several factors, as illustrated in Exhibit 6.4. First are the elements of the marketing mix, which we discuss throughout this book. Second are psychological factors, which are influences internal to the customer, such as motives, attitudes, perception, and learning. Third, social factors, such as family, reference groups, and culture, also influence the decision process. Fourth, there are situational factors, such as the specific purchase situation, a particular shopping situation, or temporal state (the time of day), that affect the decision process.

Every decision people make as consumers will take them through some form of the consumer decision process. But, like life itself, this process does not exist in a vacuum.

Psychological Factors

Although marketers can influence purchase decisions, a host of psychological factors affect the way people receive marketers' messages. Among them are motives, attitudes, perception, learning, and lifestyle. In this section, we examine how such psychological factors can influence the consumer decision process.[48]

Motives In Chapter 1, we argued that marketing is all about satisfying customer needs and wants. When a need, such as thirst, or a want, such as a Diet Pepsi, is not satisfied, it motivates us, or drives us, to get satisfaction. So, a **motive** is a need or want that is strong enough to cause the person to seek satisfaction.

People have several types of motives. One of the best known paradigms for explaining these motive types was developed by Abraham Maslow more than 30 years ago, called **Maslow's Hierarchy of Needs.**[49] Maslow categorized five groups of needs, namely, physiological (e.g., food, water, shelter), safety (e.g., secure employment, health), love (e.g., friendship, family), esteem (e.g., confidence, respect), and self-actualization (people engage in personal growth activities and attempt to meet their intellectual, aesthetic, creative, and other such needs). The pyramid in Exhibit 6.5 illustrates the theoretical progression of those needs.

Physiological needs deal with the basic biological necessities of life—food, drink, rest, and shelter. Although for most people in developed countries these basic needs are generally met, there are those in both developed and less-developed countries who are less fortunate. However, everyone remains concerned with meeting these basic needs.[50] Marketers seize every opportunity to convert these needs into wants by reminding us to eat at Taco Bell, drink milk, sleep on a Beautyrest mattress, and stay at a Marriott.

Safety needs pertain to protection and physical well-being. The marketplace is full of products and services that are designed to make you safer, such as airbags in cars and burglar alarms in homes, or healthier, such as vitamins and organic meats and vegetables.

Love needs relate to our interactions with others. Haircuts and makeup make you look more attractive, and deodorants prevent odor. Greeting cards help you express your feelings toward others.

▼ **EXHIBIT 6.5** Maslow's Hierarchy of Needs

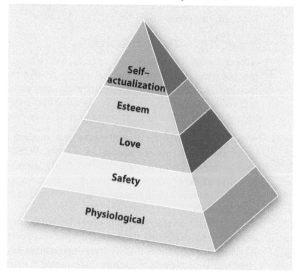

Taco Bell satisfies physiological needs.

Ads for crime prevention satisfy safety needs.

Yoga satisifies esteem needs by helping people satisy their inner desires.

Esteem needs allow people to satisfy their inner desires. Yoga, meditation, health clubs, and many books appeal to people's desires to grow or maintain a happy, satisfied outlook on life.

Finally, **self-actualization** occurs when you feel completely satisfied with your life and how you live. You don't care what others think. You drive a Ford Fusion because it suits the person you are, not because some celebrity endorses it or because you want others to think better of you.

Which of these needs applies when a consumer purchases a magazine? Magazines such as *Weight Watchers,* for instance, help satisfy physiological needs like how to eat healthy but also esteem needs like how to be happy with one's life.[51] Magazines such as *Family Circle* provide tips on how to make the home a safer place to live, and magazines such as *Weddings* help satisfy love and belonging needs because they provide instructions on how to prepare gracious invitations for friends and family, for example. Many of these magazines fulfill several needs simultaneously, of course. Good marketers add value to their products or services by nudging

Which categories of Maslow's *hierarchy of needs* do these magazines fulfill?

people up the needs hierarchy and offering information on as many of the pyramid of needs as they can.

Attitude We have attitudes about almost everything. For instance, we like this class, but we don't like the instructor. We like where we live, but we don't like the weather. An **attitude** is a person's enduring evaluation of his or her feelings about and behavioral tendencies toward an object or idea. Attitudes are learned and long lasting, and they might develop over a long period of time, though they can also abruptly change. For instance, you might like your instructor for much of the semester—until she returns your first exam. The one thing attitudes have in common for everyone is their ability to influence our decisions and actions.

An attitude consists of three components. The **cognitive component** reflects a person's belief system, or what we believe to be true; the **affective component** involves emotions, or what we feel about the issue at hand, including our like or dislike of something; and the **behavioral component** pertains to the actions we undertake based on what we know and feel. For example, Matt and Lisa Martinez see an advertisement for the latest *Pirates of the Caribbean* movie, showing Johnny Depp dueling with Geoffrey Rush. The ad lists quotes from different movie critics who call it a great and exciting film. Matt and Lisa therefore come to believe that the critics must be correct and that the new *Pirates of the Caribbean* will be a good movie (cognitive component). Later they catch an interview with Johnny Depp, who talks about making the movie and his enjoyment playing Captain Jack Sparrow. Therefore, Matt and Lisa start to believe the movie will be fun and engaging, because they appreciate action adventures and have enjoyed previous Johnny Depp films (affective component). After weighing their various options—which include various other movies, other entertainment options such as attending a concert instead, or just staying home—Matt and Lisa decide to go see the movie (behavioral component).

> **attitude** A person's enduring evaluation of his or her feelings about and behavioral tendencies toward an object or idea; consists of three components: *cognitive, affective,* and *behavioral.*
>
> **cognitive component** A component of *attitude* that reflects what a person believes to be true.
>
> **affective component** A component of *attitude* that reflects what a person feels about the issue at hand—his or her like or dislike of something.
>
> **behavioral component** A component of *attitude* that comprises the actions a person takes with regard to the issue at hand.

perception The process by which people select, organize, and interpret information to form a meaningful picture of the world.

learning Refers to a change in a person's thought process or behavior that arises from experience and takes place throughout the consumer decision process.

Ideally, agreement exists among these three components. But when there is incongruence among the three—if Matt and Lisa read positive reviews and like action films but do not find Johnny Depp an appealing actor—cognitive dissonance might occur. Matt and Lisa might decide their reviews and their liking of action films will outweigh their dislike of Johnny Depp and go see the movie. If they then find the movie unenjoyable because Johnny Depp is the primary star, they may feel foolish for having wasted their money.

Such dissonance is a terrible feeling, which people try to avoid, often by convincing themselves that the decision was a good one in some way.[52] In this example, Matt and Lisa might focus on the special effects and the romantic elements of the movie while mentally glossing over the parts that featured the actor they did not enjoy. In this way, they can convince themselves that the parts they liked were good enough to counterbalance the part they didn't like, and thus, they make their movie-going experience a positive event overall.

Although attitudes are pervasive and usually slow to change, the important fact from a marketer's point of view is that they can be influenced and perhaps changed through persuasive communications and personal experience. Marketing communication—through salespeople, advertisements, free samples, or other such methods—can attempt to change what people believe to be true about a product or service (cognitive) or how they feel toward it (affective). If the marketer is successful, the cognitive and affective components work in concert to affect behavior. Continuing with our example, suppose that prior to viewing the movie ad, Matt and Lisa thought that *Cowboys & Aliens* would be the next movie they would go see, but they had heard good things about *Pirates of the Caribbean*. The ad positively influenced the cognitive component of their attitude toward *Pirates of the Caribbean*, making it consistent with their affective component.

Perception Another psychological factor, **perception**, is the process by which we select, organize, and interpret information to form a meaningful picture of the world. Perception in marketing influences our acquisition and consumption of goods and services through our tendency to assign meaning to such things as color, symbols, taste, and packaging. Culture, tradition, and our overall upbringing determine our perception of the world. For instance, Lisa Martinez has always wanted an apartment in the Back Bay neighborhood of Boston because her favorite aunt had one, and they had a great time visiting for Thanksgiving one year. However, from his past experiences, Matt has a different perception. Matt thinks Back Bay apartments are small, expensive, and impractical for a couple thinking about having children—though they would be convenient for single people who work in downtown Boston. The city of Boston has

Based on positive review (cognitive component) and positive feelings (affective component), many people went to see the latest Pirates of the Caribbean movie (behavioral component) and came away with a positive attitude.

worked hard in recent years to overcome the long-standing negative perceptual bias that Matt and many others hold by working with developers to create larger, modern, and more affordable apartments and using promotion to reposition the perception of apartments in the Back Bay for young couples.[53]

Learning **Learning** refers to a change in a person's thought process or behavior that arises from experience and takes place throughout the consumer decision process. For instance, after Katie Smith recognized that she needed a dress for her job interview, she started looking for ads and searching for reviews and articles on the Internet. She learned from each new piece of information, so her thoughts about the look she wanted in a dress were different from those before she had read anything. She liked what she learned about the clothing line from Macy's. She learned from her search, and it became part of her memory to be used in the future, possibly so she could recommend the store to her friends.

Learning affects both attitudes and perceptions. Throughout the buying process, Katie's attitudes shifted. The cognitive component came into play for her when she learned Macy's had one of the most extensive collections of career apparel. Once she was in the store and tried on some dresses, she realized how much she liked the way she looked and felt in them, which involved the affective component. Then she purchased it, which involved the behavioral component. Each time she was exposed to information about the store or the dresses, she learned something different that affected her perception. Before she tried them on, Katie hadn't realized how easy it would be to find exactly what she was looking for; thus, her perception of Macy's line of dresses changed through learning.

Lifestyle **Lifestyle** refers to the way consumers spend their time and money to live. For many consumers, the question of whether the product or service fits with their actual lifestyle, which may be fairly sedentary, or their perceived lifestyle, which might be outdoorsy, is an important one. Some of the many consumers sporting North Face jackets certainly need the high-tech, cold weather gear because they are planning their next hike up Mount Rainier and want to be sure they have sufficient protection against the elements. Others, however, simply like the image that the jacket conveys—the image that they might be leaving for their own mountain-climbing expedition any day now—even if the closest they have come has been shoveling their driveway.

A person's perceptions and ability to learn are affected by their social experiences, which we discuss next.

Social Factors

The consumer decision process is influenced from within by psychological factors, but also by the external, social environment, which consists of the customer's family, reference groups, and culture.[54] (Refer to Exhibit 6.4.)

Family Many purchase decisions are made about products or services that the entire family will consume or use. Thus, firms must consider how families make purchase decisions and understand how various family members might influence these decisions.

When families make purchase decisions, they often consider the needs of all the family members. In choosing a restaurant, for example, all the family members may participate in the decision making. In other situations, however, different members of the family may take on the purchasing role. For example, the husband and teenage child may look through car magazines and *Consumer Reports* to search for information about a new car. But once they arrive at the dealership, the husband and wife, not the child, decide which model and color to buy, and the wife negotiates the final deal.[55]

Children and adolescents play an increasingly important role in family buying decisions. Kids in the United States spend over $200 billion a year on personal items such as snacks, soft drinks, entertainment, and apparel. They directly influence the purchase of another $300 billion worth of items such as food, snacks, beverages, toys, health and beauty aids, clothing, accessories, gifts, and school supplies. Their indirect influence on family spending is even higher—$600 billion for items such as

---

lifestyle A component of *psychographics;* refers to the way a person lives his or her life to achieve goals.

reference group One or more persons whom an individual uses as a basis for comparison regarding beliefs, feelings, and behaviors.

---

recreation, vacations, technology, and even the family car.[56] Even grandparents contribute to the economic impact of children in the United States. It is estimated that grandparents spend $52 billion dollars on purchases for grandchildren.[57]

Influencing a group that holds this much spending power is vitally important. Traditional food retailers are already caught in a squeeze between Walmart, which lures low-end customers, and specialty retailers like Whole Foods, which target the high end. Knowing how children influence food buying decisions is a strategic opportunity for traditional supermarkets and their suppliers to exploit. Currently, the age cohorts referred to as Gen X and Millennials (remember from Chapter 5 that these groups were born anywhere between 1966 and 1994) tend to shop at Target, Kmart, and Walmart more and spend more at those stores than other generational groups.[58] Getting this group to prefer one store, chain, or product over another can make a difference in the bottom line as well as in the chances for survival in a difficult marketplace.

Reference Groups A **reference group** is one or more persons whom an individual uses as a basis for comparison

Children influence parents' purchasing decisions.

> ## Customers who want to be seen as earthy might buy Birkenstock sandals, whereas those wanting to be seen as high fashion might buy Christian Louboutin shoes.

regarding beliefs, feelings, and behaviors. A consumer might have various reference groups, including family, friends, coworkers, or famous people the consumer would like to emulate. These reference groups affect buying decisions by (1) offering information, (2) providing rewards for specific purchasing behaviors, and (3) enhancing a consumer's self-image.

Reference groups provide information to consumers directly through conversation or indirectly through observation. For example, Katie received valuable information from a friend about where she should shop for her interview dress. On another occasion, she heard a favorite cousin who is a fashionista praising the virtues of shopping at Macy's, which solidified her decision to go there.

Some reference groups also influence behaviors by rewarding behavior that meets with their approval or chastising behavior that doesn't. For example, smokers are often criticized or even ostracized by their friends and made to smoke outside or in restricted areas.

Consumers can identify and affiliate with reference groups to create, enhance, or maintain their self-image. Customers who want to be seen as earthy might buy Birkenstock sandals, whereas those wanting to be seen as high fashion might buy Christian Louboutin shoes, as we discussed previously in this chapter. If they purchase a gift for someone else and that gift conflicts with their self-image, they also seek to reestablish their preferred affiliation quickly by purchasing something more in line with their identity.[59]

Some stores, such as Abercrombie & Fitch, play on these forms of influence and hire sales associates they hope will serve as a reference group for customers who shop there. These cool, attractive, and somewhat aloof employees are encouraged to wear the latest store apparel—thereby serving as living mannequins to emulate.[60]

Culture   We defined **culture** in Chapter 5 as the shared meanings, beliefs, morals, values, and customs of a group of people. As the basis of the social factors that affect your buying decisions, the culture or cultures in which you participate are not markedly different from your reference groups. That is, your cultural group might

be as small as your reference group at school or as large as the country in which you live or the religion to which you belong. Like reference groups, cultures influence consumer behavior. For instance, the culture at Katie's college is rather fashion conscious. This influences, to some extent, the way she spends, how she dresses, and where she shops.

Situational Factors

Psychological and social factors typically influence the consumer decision process the same way each time. For example, your motivation to quench your thirst usually drives you to drink a Coke or a Pepsi, and your reference group at the workplace coerces you to wear appropriate attire. But sometimes, **situational factors**, or factors specific to the situation, override, or at least influence, psychological and social issues. These situational factors are related to the purchase and shopping situation as well as to temporal states.[61]

Famous people, like Sarah Jessica Parker, can be part of your reference group, influencing your purchases.

Purchase Situation   Customers may be predisposed to purchase certain products or services because of some underlying psychological trait or social factor, but these factors may change in certain purchase situations. For instance, Samantha Crumb considers herself a thrifty, cautious shopper—someone who likes to get a good deal. But her best friend is getting married, and she wants to buy the couple a silver tray. If the tray were for herself, she would probably go to Crate & Barrel or possibly even Walmart. But since it is for her best friend, she went to Tiffany & Co. Why? To purchase something fitting for the special occasion of a wedding.

Shopping Situation   Consumers might be ready to purchase a product or service but be completely derailed once they arrive in the store. Marketers use several techniques to influence consumers at this choice stage of the decision process. Consider the following techniques.

Store Atmosphere. Some retailers and service providers have developed unique images that are based at least in part on their internal environment, also known as their atmospherics.[62] Research has shown that, if used in concert with other aspects of a

The Cheesecake Factory has developed atmospherics that are not only pleasant, but consistent with their image, menu, and service.

culture The set of values, guiding beliefs, understandings, and ways of doing things shared by members of a society; exists on two levels: visible artifacts (e.g., behavior, dress, symbols, physical settings, ceremonies) and underlying values (thought processes, beliefs, and assumptions).

situational factors Factors affecting the consumer decision process; those that are specific to the situation that may override, or at least influence, psychological and social issues.

retailer's strategy, music, scent, lighting, and even color can positively influence the decision process.[63] Restaurants such as Outback Steakhouse and The Cheesecake Factory have developed internal environments that are not only pleasant but also consistent with their food and service.

Some Wegmans and Whole Foods stores have built bars and restaurants inside their stores, where customers can stop and relax, have a glass of wine or a bite to eat, but still get their shopping done for the week. Whole Foods has cutting edge culinary centers that offer cooking classes in over 30 stores. Other grocery store chains are following suit; the Brewers Yard Kroger in Ohio has a band play in the store on Friday nights. Still other grocery stores offer flat-screen televisions, comfortable chairs, free Wi-Fi hotspots, in-store cooking classes, or wine tasting events to create interactive atmospheres that will appeal to customers.[64]

Salespeople. Well-trained sales personnel can influence the sale at the point of purchase by educating consumers about product attributes, pointing out the advantages of one item over another, and encouraging multiple purchases. The salesperson at Tiffany & Co., for instance, explained to Samantha why one platter was better than another and suggested some serving pieces to go with it.

Jordan's Furniture, a New England–based chain, has worked hard to make furniture shopping fun by offering in-store entertainment and food outlets. But after going through all the effort to make the store atmospheres inviting, Jordan's also realized that the quality of its salespeople could mean all the difference between a consumer just visiting the store for fun or making a purchase. It

In-store demonstrations entice people to buy.

therefore initiated an extensive training program for its entire sales staff to guarantee that salespeople were knowledgeable about anything and everything customers may want to know. The regular training modules take place during workshops at the individual stores, usually before hours over three consecutive days. The sessions focus on various topics, including the differences between solid wood and veneers or the introduction of a new fabric line by a certain manufacturer.

Crowding. Customers can feel crowded because there are too many people, too much merchandise, or lines that are too long. If there are too many people in a store, some people become distracted and may even leave.[65] Others have difficulty purchasing if the merchandise is packed too closely together. This issue is a particular problem for shoppers with mobility disabilities.

In-Store Demonstrations. The taste and smell of new food items may attract people to try something they normally wouldn't. Similarly, some fashion retailers offer trunk shows, during which their vendors show their whole line of merchandise on a certain day. During these well-advertised events, customers are often enticed to purchase that day because they get special assistance from the salespeople and can order merchandise that the retailer otherwise does not carry.

Promotions. Retailers employ various promotional vehicles to influence customers once they have arrived in the store. An unadvertised price promotion can alter a person's preconceived buying plan. Multi-item discounts, such as buy 1, get 1 free sales, are popular means to get people to buy more

Adding Value   6.2

Judging a Product by Its Cover[66]

In stores, customers spend just 3 to 10 seconds standing in front of products as they decide whether to buy them. Regardless of the significant time and money put into marketing products in places outside store walls, customers evaluate most products based mainly on their appearance in the store. That means that packaging is tremendously important.

Packaging must sell itself to the customer, over and above any competitors on the shelf. Redesigned packages offer the excitement of exhibiting something new, but they also might alienate customers who find them unfamiliar. Yet increasing the visibility of any package on the shelf helps increase sales—which may be why Pringles keeps packaging its chips in tubes that differ greatly from the formless bags farther down the aisle.

But not all product packaging can, or should, remain the same, the way Pringles has. Doublemint Gum undertook its first packaging redesign in 2006—nearly a century after its 1914 product launch. The move was designed to help the chewing gum appeal to a younger audience, even while it maintained its loyal base of older consumers. Another aging brand, Kraft's Macaroni & Cheese, similarly redesigned its packaging, which it launched originally in 1937.

For Nonni's Biscotti, the most recent package redesign involved adding a window to the front of the box, so customers could see the texture of the baked treats. The biscotti, stacked vertically

Nonni's redesigned its biscotti packages to include a window so customers could see the products.

instead of horizontally, now help give a grander impression of the product. Furthermore, by adding decorative touches to make the packaging more visually appealing, Nonni's could encourage customers to leave the box right on their countertops, easily accessible to snackers.

---

than they normally would.[67] Because many people regard clipping coupons from the newspaper as too much trouble, some stores make coupons available in the store, on the Internet, or on their cell phones. Another form of promotion is offering a free gift with the purchase of a good or service. This type of promotion is particularly popular with cosmetics.

Packaging. It is difficult to make a product stand out in the crowd when it competes for shelf space with several other brands. This problem is particularly difficult for consumer packaged goods, such as groceries and health and beauty products (see Adding Value 6.2). Marketers therefore spend millions of dollars designing and updating their packages to be more appealing and eye catching.[68]

Temporal State Our state of mind at any particular time can alter our preconceived notions of what we are going to purchase. For instance, some people are morning people, whereas others function better at night. A purchase situation may thus have different appeal levels depending on the time of day and the type of person the consumer is. Mood swings can alter consumer behavior.[69] Suppose Samantha received a parking ticket just prior to shopping at Tiffany & Co. It is likely that she would be less receptive to the salesperson's influence than if

she came into the store in a good mood. Her bad mood might even cause her to have a less positive postpurchase feeling about the store. Since retailers can't affect what happens outside the store very much, they should do everything possible to make sure their customers have a positive shopping experience once they are in the store.

The factors that affect the consumer decision process—the marketing mix, psychological factors, social factors, and situational factors—are all affected by the level of consumer involvement, the subject of the next section.

 check yourself

1. What are some examples of specific needs suggested by Maslow's Hierarchy of Needs?

2. Which social factors likely have the most influence on (a) the purchase of a new outfit for a job interview and (b) the choice of a college to attend?

3. List some of the tactics stores can use to influence consumers' decision processes.

▼ **EXHIBIT 6.6** Elaboration Likelihood Model

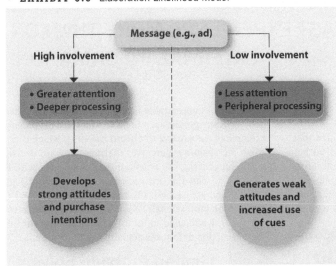

who is researching buying a dress for a job interview) will scrutinize all the information provided (price, fabric quality, construction) and process the key elements of the message more deeply. As an involved consumer, Katie likely ends up judging the ad as truthful and forming a favorable impression of the product, or else she regards the message as superficial and develops negative product impressions (i.e., her research suggests the product is not as good as it is being portrayed).

In contrast, a low-involvement consumer will likely process the same advertisement in a less thorough manner. Such a consumer might pay less attention to the key elements of the message (price, fabric quality, construction) and focus on heuristic elements such as brand name (Macy's I·N·C) or the presence of a celebrity endorser. The impressions of the low-involvement consumer are likely to be more superficial.

LO 6-6 Describe how involvement influences the consumer decision process.

INVOLVEMENT AND CONSUMER BUYING DECISIONS

Consumers make two types of buying decisions depending on their level of involvement: extended problem solving; and limited problem solving, which includes impulse buying and habitual decision making. **Involvement** is the consumer's degree of interest in the product or service.[70] Consumers may have different levels of involvement for the same type of product. One consumer behavior theory, the elaboration likelihood model, illustrated in Exhibit 6.6, proposes that high- and low-involvement consumers process different aspects of a message or advertisement.

If both types of consumers viewed ads for career dresses, the high-involvement consumer (e.g., Katie,

What type of buying decision does each of these products represent?

[Consumers may have different levels of involvement for the same type of product.]

LIMITED PROBLEM SOLVING USUALLY RELIES ON PAST EXPERIENCE MORE THAN ON EXTERNAL INFORMATION.

Extended Problem Solving

The buying process begins when consumers recognize that they have an unsatisfied need. Katie Smith recognized her need to buy a new dress for a job interview. She sought information by asking for advice from her friends, reading fashion magazines, and conducting research online. She visited several stores to determine which had the best options for her.

Picking up a hamburger at a drive-through fast-food restaurant like In-N-Out Burger requires little thought. It is a habitual decision.

Finally, after considerable time and effort analyzing her alternatives, Katie purchased a dress at Macy's. This process is an example of **extended problem solving**, which is common when the customer perceives that the purchase decision entails a lot of risk. The potential risks associated with Katie's decision to buy the dress include financial (did I pay too much?) and social (will my potential employer and friends think I look professional?) risks. To reduce her perceived risk, Katie spent a lot of effort searching for information before she actually made her purchase.

Limited Problem Solving

Limited problem solving occurs during a purchase decision that calls for, at most, a moderate amount of effort and time. Customers engage in this type of buying process when they have had some prior experience with the product or service and the perceived risk is moderate. Limited problem solving usually relies on past experience more than on external information. For many people, an apparel purchase, even a dress for a job interview, could require limited effort.

A common type of limited problem solving is **impulse buying**, a buying decision made by customers on the spot when they see the merchandise.[71] When Katie went to the grocery store to do her weekly shopping, she saw a display case of popcorn and Dr Pepper near the checkout counter. Knowing that some of her friends were coming over to watch a movie, she stocked up. The popcorn and soda were an impulse purchase. Katie didn't go through the entire decision process; instead, she recognized her need and jumped directly to purchase without spending any time searching for additional information or evaluating alternatives. The grocery store facilitated this impulse purchase by providing easily accessible cues (i.e., by offering the popcorn and soda in a prominent display, at a great location in the store, and at a reasonable price).

Some purchases require even less thought. **Habitual decision making** describes a purchase decision process in which consumers engage in little conscious effort. On her way home from the grocery store, for example, Katie drove past an In-N-Out Burger and swung into the drive-through for a cheeseburger and Diet Coke. She did

extended problem solving A purchase decision process during which the consumer devotes considerable time and effort to analyzing alternatives; often occurs when the consumer perceives that the purchase decision entails a lot of risk.

limited problem solving Occurs during a purchase decision that calls for, at most, a moderate amount of effort and time.

impulse buying A buying decision made by customers on the spot when they see the merchandise.

habitual decision making A purchase decision process in which consumers engage with little conscious effort.

not ponder the potential benefits of going to Wendy's instead for lunch. Rather, she simply reacted to the cue provided by the sign and engaged in habitual decision making. Marketers strive to attract and maintain habitual purchasers by creating strong brands and store loyalty (see Chapters 11 and 12) because these customers don't even consider alternative brands or stores. ■

 check yourself

1. How do low- versus high-involvement consumers process the information in an advertisement?
2. What is the difference between extended versus limited problem solving?

check it out!

mhhe.com/GrewalM4e
for study materials,
including quizzes
and videos.

section 3

chapter nine

segmentation, targeting, and positioning

K nown for its highly watched fashion shows, Angel models, and assortment of sexy intimate apparel and sleepwear, Victoria's Secret has reached annual net sales of more than $4 billion and opened more than 1,000 stores.[1] Most of the undergarments that Victoria's Secret sells attempt to conjure romance and seduction, which means they are likely to involve discretionary expenses. Yet women need bras and panties, so the offerings also represent basic necessities.

Determining who its customers are and then balancing the discrepancies between their needs and wants is part of what makes Victoria's Secret so successful. Given the changes in the economy, the company introduced lower-priced offerings, simultaneously reducing inventory.[2] The chain's Everyday line of bras retail for $29.50, about half the price of other styles. Its popular Seven-Way bra functions well with various clothing silhouettes, so that women do not need to purchase separate bras to wear with T-shirts, strapless tops, racer-back shirts, sheer clothing, and so on. After discontinuing it briefly to encourage sales of the various alternatives, Victoria's Secret was quick to expand the line, such that women could buy multi-use bras across various product lines, including its BioFit and Showstopper selections.[3]

continued on p. 186

LEARNING OBJECTIVES

After reading this chapter, you should be able to:

LO 9-1   Outline the different methods of segmenting a market.

LO 9-2   Describe how firms determine whether a segment is attractive and therefore worth pursuing.

LO 9-3   Articulate the differences among targeting strategies: undifferentiated, differentiated, concentrated, or micromarketing.

LO 9-4   Determine the value proposition.

LO 9-5   Define positioning and describe how firms do it.

Victoria's Secret created different product lines to appeal to various consumer segments.

continued from p. 185

Moving beyond these long-running offerings, Victoria's Secret Pink product line, launched in 2004, is designed to appeal to younger shoppers with brightly colored sweatshirts, T-shirts, pajamas, pillows and bedding, sandals, and swimwear as well as undergarments.[4] The Wear Everywhere bra costs $32 for a package of two, and rather than going for glamorous or sexy, Pink clothing is intended to be comfortable and cute.

In Chapter 1, we learned that marketing is about satisfying consumers' wants and needs. Chapter 2 noted how companies analyze their markets to determine the different kinds of products and services people want. But it is not sufficient just to produce such an offering. Firms must also position their offerings in the minds of customers in their target market in such a way that these consumers understand why the thing the company is providing meets their needs better than other, competitive offerings.

This process requires a marketing plan, as we discussed in Chapter 2. As you should recall, the third step of this plan is identifying and evaluating opportunities by performing an STP (segmentation, targeting, and positioning) analysis. This chapter focuses on that very analysis.

The Pink line also aims to expand the reach of Victoria's Secret through cobranding. Pink offers merchandise imprinted with the logos and names of most major U.S. colleges and universities (though it stumbled when it mistakenly printed the University of Michigan slogan, "Hail to the Victors," beneath the Spartan logo of rival Michigan State University).[5] With these options, the brand may attract more male consumers, who enjoy purchasing gifts for their significant others that are both feminine and indicative of support for a favorite National Football League or Major League Baseball team.[6]

Even with these extensions though, Victoria's Secret remains true to its core offering: appealing to women who are more concerned with curves than cost. Its Miraculous push-up bra promises to add two cup sizes to a wearer's bust. And its annual fashion show is a widely anticipated event that features top models sporting ornate, handmade wings (to invoke the image of angels) along with minuscule lingerie. There is nothing cozy or price-conscious on display on the runway. Instead, Miranda Kerr hoisted a heavy, clam-shaped set of wings, surrounding her diamond-encrusted bra worth $2.5 million.[7]

Using price points to segment its market; customizing color, fabrics, and styles to appeal to various target audiences; associating its brand with supermodels, baseball and football teams, and colleges; reaching different shoppers through different stores and assortments; and promoting products through multiple selling channels all help Victoria's Secret, and its varied customers, feel quite in the pink. ▦

LO 9-1   Outline the different methods of segmenting a market.

THE SEGMENTATION, TARGETING, AND POSITIONING PROCESS

In this chapter, we discuss how a firm conducts a market segmentation or STP analysis (see Exhibit 9.1). We first outline a firm's overall strategy and objectives, methods of segmenting

▼ **EXHIBIT 9.1** The Segmentation, Targeting, and Positioning Process

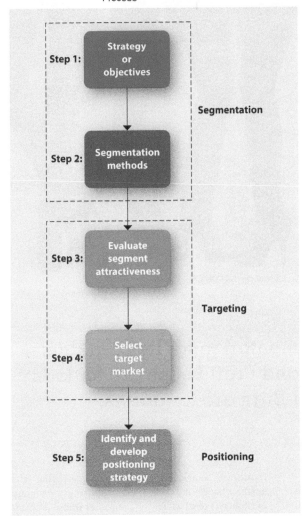

a firm could start with a strategy but then modify it as it gathers more information about various segments' attractiveness.

Step 1: Establish Overall Strategy or Objectives

The first step in the segmentation process is to articulate the vision or objectives of the company's marketing strategy clearly. The segmentation strategy must be consistent with and derived from the firm's mission and objectives as well as its current situation—its strengths, weaknesses, opportunities, and threats (SWOT). Coca-Cola's objective, for instance, is to increase sales in a mature industry. The company knows its strengths are its brand name and its ability to place new products on retailers' shelves, but its primary weakness is that it may not have a product line for newer market segments. Identifying this potentially large and profitable market segment, before many of its mainstream competitors can do so, offers a great opportunity. However, following through on that opportunity could lead to a significant threat: competitive retaliation. Coca-Cola's recent choice to pursue health-conscious men with products such as Coke Zero is consistent with its overall strategy and objectives. (See the case study on this text's website for more discussion of Coke's strategy.)

Coke Zero targets health-conscious men.

Now let's take a look at methods for segmenting a market.

Step 2: Segmentation Methods

The second step in the segmentation process is to use a particular method or combination of methods to segment the market.

> [Marketers use geographic, demographic, psychographic, benefits, and behavioral segmentation methods.]

the market, and which segments are worth pursuing. Then we discuss how to choose a target market or markets by evaluating each segment's attractiveness and, on the basis of this evaluation, choose which segment or segments to pursue. Finally, we describe how a firm develops its positioning strategy.

Although the STP process in Exhibit 9.1 implies that the decision making is linear, this need not be the case. For instance,

This step also develops descriptions of the different segments, which helps firms better understand the customer profiles in each segment. With this information, they can distinguish customer similarities within a segment and dissimilarities across segments. Marketers use geographic, demographic, psychographic, benefits, and behavioral segmentation methods, as Exhibit 9.2 details.

Denizen jeans by Levi's are made exclusively for Target. What segmentation method is Target using?

> Kellogg's uses age segmentation for its breakfast cereals: Cocoa Krispies and Fruit Loops are for kids; Special K and All-Bran are for adults.

Soft-drink marketers, for instance, divide the carbonated beverage landscape into caffeinated or decaffeinated, regular (with sugar) or diet, and cola versus something else. This segmentation method is based on the *benefits* that consumers derive from the products.

Geographic Segmentation **Geographic segmentation** organizes customers into groups on the basis of where they live. Thus, a market could be grouped by country, region (northeast, southeast), or areas within a region (state, city, neighborhoods, zip codes). Not surprisingly, geographic segmentation is most useful for companies whose products satisfy needs that vary by region.

Firms can provide the same basic goods or services to all segments even if they market globally or nationally, but better marketers make adjustments to meet the needs of smaller geographic groups.[8] A national grocery store chain such as Safeway or Kroger runs similar stores with similar assortments in various locations across the United States. Within those similar stores, though, a significant percentage of the assortment of goods will vary by region, city, or even neighborhood, depending on the different needs of the customers who surround each location.

Demographic Segmentation **Demographic segmentation** groups consumers according to easily measured,

▼ **EXHIBIT 9.2** Methods for Describing Market Segments

Segmentation Method	Sample Segments
Geographic	Continent: North America, Asia, Europe, Africa Within U.S.: Pacific, mountain, central, south, mid-Atlantic, northeast
Demographic	Age, gender, income
Psychographic	Lifestyle, self-concept, self-values
Benefits	Convenience, economy, prestige
Behavioral	Occasion, loyalty

objective characteristics such as age, gender, income, and education. These variables represent the most common means to define segments because they are easy to identify and demographically segmented markets are easy to reach. Kellogg's uses age segmentation for its breakfast cereals: Cocoa Krispies and Fruit Loops are for kids; Special K and All-Bran are for adults. It also tends to adopt a gender-based segmentation, such that marketing communications about Special K almost exclusively appeal to women.

Gender plays a very important role in how most firms market products and services.[9] For instance, TV viewing habits vary significantly between men and women. Men tend to channel surf—switching quickly from channel to channel—and watch prime-time shows that are action oriented and feature physically attractive cast members. Women, in contrast, tend to view shows to which they can personally relate through the situational plot or characters and those recommended by friends. Print media is similar: A company such as Lululemon, which sells fitness clothing for both men and women, therefore considers the gender appeal of various magazines when it buys advertising space.

However, demographics may not be useful for defining the target segments for other companies. They are poor predictors of the users of activewear, such as jogging suits and athletic shoes. At one time, firms such as Nike assumed that activewear would be purchased exclusively by young, active people, but the health and fitness trend has led people of all ages to buy such merchandise. And even relatively inactive consumers of all ages, incomes, and education find activewear more comfortable than traditional street clothes.

Rethinking some stereotypical ideas about who is buying thus has become a relatively common trend among firms that once thought their target market was well defined. Adding Value 9.1 highlights how Skechers has broadened its appeal by aiming marketing communications at various segments of potential consumers.

> **geographic segmentation** The grouping of consumers on the basis of where they live.
>
> **demographic segmentation** The grouping of consumers according to easily measured, objective characteristics such as age, gender, income, and education.

Adding Value   9.1

Skechers Broadening Its Appeal

In its earliest days, Skechers was mostly a lifestyle brand, with hip styles and vibrant designs that appealed to young trendsetters and hipsters, both men and women. When its Shape-Up line arrived in 2010, it offered promises that even if they were a little older and perhaps not quite as in shape as Christina Aguilera, women could improve muscle tone in their legs and buttocks by wearing the rocker-shaped shoe. It began running advertisements in *AARP the*

Magazine as well as in *Cosmopolitan* and *GQ*.[10] It hired Kris Jenner as a spokesperson, along with her daughter Kim Kardashian. This success among older women prompted further extensions, including Shape-Ups for men and girls.[11]

Skechers has expanded into more athletic arenas to market itself as an alternative for sports, not just lifestyle. Joe Montana appears in televised ads, and the 2012 Super Bowl featured a prominent commercial with Mark Cuban, the outspoken owner of the Dallas Mavericks, introducing Skechers' latest GOrun line of shoes.[12]

The comparison of its Super Bowl commercials is telling. Whereas in 2011, the ad featured Kim Kardashian, which prominently focused on her physique, the 2012 version puts a small dog in sneakers. Thus the company is trying to appeal to multiple segments.

Skechers creates shoes that appeal to several target markets, including kids.

psychographics
Used in segmentation; delves into how consumers describe themselves; allows people to describe themselves using those characteristics that help them choose how they occupy their time (behavior) and what underlying psychological reasons determine those choices.

Psychographic Segmentation Of the various methods for segmenting, or breaking down, the market, **psychographics** is the one that delves into how consumers actually describe themselves. Usually marketers determine (through demographics, buying patterns, or usage) into which segment an individual consumer falls. Psychographics studies how people self-select, as it were, based on the characteristics of how they choose to occupy their time (behavior) and what underlying psychological reasons determine those choices.[13] For example, a person might have a strong need for inclusion or belonging, which motivates him or her to seek out activities that involve others, which in turn influences the products he or she buys to fit in with the group. Determining psychographics involves knowing and understanding three components: self-values, self-concept, and lifestyles.

Self-values are goals for life, not just the goals one wants to accomplish in a day. They are the overriding desires that drive how a person lives his or her life. Examples might be the need for self-respect, self-fulfillment, or a specific sense of belonging.

> A person who has a goal to belong may see, or want to see, himself as a fun-loving, gregarious type whom people wish to be around.

This motivation causes people to develop self-images of how they want to be and then images of a way of life that will help them arrive at these ultimate goals. From a marketing point of view, self-values help determine the benefits the target market may be looking for from a product. The underlying, fundamental, personal need that pushes a person to seek out certain products or brands stems from his or her desire to fulfill a self-value.

People's self-image, or **self-concept**, is the image people ideally have of themselves.[14] For instance, a person who has a goal to belong may see, or want to see, himself as a fun-loving, gregarious type whom people wish to be around. Marketers often make use of this particular self-concept through communications that show their products being used by groups of laughing people who are having a good time. The connection emerges between the group fun and the product being shown and connotes a lifestyle that many consumers seek.

Lifestyles, the third component of people's psychographic makeup, are the way we live.[15] If values provide an end goal and self-concept is the way one sees oneself in the context of that goal, lifestyles are how we live our lives to achieve goals.

One of the most storied lifestyles in American legend is the Harley way of life. The open road, wind in your hair, rebelling against conventions—the image nearly always depicted men like Dennis Hopper in *Easy Rider*. But the notions of freedom, rebellion, and standing out from a crowd vastly appeal to all sorts of people. In response, Harley-Davidson has shifted its STP methods to define four main target markets: core (white men older than 35 years), young adults (both genders, 18–34 years), women (white and older than 35 years), and diverse (men and women, African American and Hispanic, older than 35 years).[16]

For women, for example, it encourages lifestyle events such as Garage Parties, women's-only social gatherings hosted in the evenings at dealerships to teach women the basics of motorcycling. The company publication *We Ride* focuses solely on female Hogs, and the HD-1 Customization website offers a separate process for women to build their cycles to match their build, power preferences, and color desires.[17]

The most widely used tool to support such psychographic segmentation efforts is **Value and Lifestyle Survey, VALS™**, owned and operated by Strategic Business Insights (SBI).[18] Consumers can be classified into the eight segments shown in Exhibit 9.3 based on their answers to the questionnaire

Marketers such as Benetton want their ads to appeal to people's self-concepts: "I'm like them (or I want to be like them), so I should buy their products."

(http://www.strategicbusinessinsights.com/vals/presurvey
.shtml). The vertical dimension of the VALS framework indicates level of resources, including income, education, health,
energy level, and degree of innovativeness. The upper segments
have more resources and are more innovative than those on the
bottom.

The horizontal dimension shows the segments' primary
psychological motivation for buying. Consumers buy products and services because of their primary motivations—
that is, how they see themselves in the world and how that
self-image governs their activities. The three primary motivations of U.S. consumers are ideals, achievement, and self-
expression. People who are primarily motivated by ideals are
guided by knowledge and principles. Those who are motivated by achievement look for products and services that
demonstrate success to their peers. Consumers who are primarily motivated by self-expression desire social or physical
activity, variety, and risk.

VALS also enables firms to identify target segments and
their underlying motivations. It shows correlations between
psychology and lifestyle choices. For instance, a European
luxury automobile manufacturer used VALS to identify online, mobile applications that would appeal to affluent, early-
adopter consumers within the next five years.[19] The VALS

analysis enabled the company to
prioritize the most promising applications to develop. In another
case, VALS was used to help a
medical center identify customers
most interested and able to afford
cosmetic surgery. Based on the underlying motivations of its target
customers, the center and its ad
agency developed an ad campaign
so successful that it had to be
pulled early to avoid overbooking
at the surgical center.

Firms are finding that psychographic segmentation schemes like
VALS are often more useful for predicting consumer behavior than are
demographics. This is because people who share demographics often
have very different psychological
traits. Take, for example, Jack and
John, both 30-year-old, married,
college graduates. Demographically, they are the same, but Jack is

self-values Goals for
life, not just the goals one
wants to accomplish in a
day; a component of
psychographics that refers
to overriding desires that
drive how a person lives
his or her life.

self-concept The
image a person has of
him- or herself; a component
of *psychographics.*

lifestyles A component
of *psychographics;* refers to
the way a person lives his
or her life to achieve goals.

**Value and Lifestyle
Survey (VALS™)**
A psychographic tool
developed by SRI Consulting
Business Intelligence;
classifies consumers into
eight segments: innovators,
thinkers, believers, achievers,
strivers, experiencers,
makers, or survivors.

*Using lifestyle segmentation, Harley-Davidson has four main target markets: On
the left is its core segment, consisting of white men older than 35 years. On the
right are white women older than 35 years.*

> ## BECAUSE MARKETING IS ALL ABOUT SATISFYING CONSUMERS' NEEDS AND WANTS, DIVIDING THE MARKET INTO SEGMENTS WHOSE NEEDS AND WANTS ARE BEST SATISFIED BY THE PRODUCT BENEFITS CAN BE A VERY POWERFUL TOOL.

▼ **EXHIBIT 9.3** VALS Framework

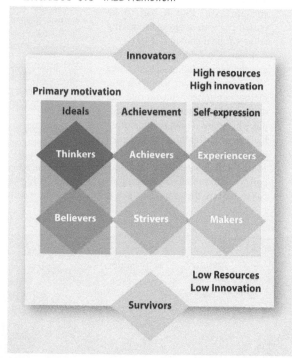

Source: Reprinted with permission of Strategic Business Insights (SBI); www.strategicbusinessinsights.com/VALS.

risk-averse and John is a risk taker. Jack is socially conscious and John is focused on himself. Lumping Jack and John together as a target does not make sense because the ways they think and act are totally different from each other.

There are limitations to using psychographic segmentation, however. Psychographics are more expensive as a means to identify potential customers. With demographics, for example, a firm like Nike can easily identify its customers as, say, men or women and then direct its marketing strategies to each group differently. The problem is that not all men are alike, as we saw with Jack and John. Women are not all alike either! To identify VALS Thinkers or Makers, companies use the VALS questionnaire in surveys or focus groups. Then VALS provides segment descriptions, linkages with consumer product and media data, communication styles, and zip code locations.[20]

Benefit Segmentation **Benefit segmentation** groups consumers on the basis of the benefits they derive from products or services. Because marketing is all about satisfying consumers' needs and wants, dividing the market into segments whose needs and wants are best satisfied by the product benefits can be a very powerful tool.[21] It is effective and relatively easy to portray a product's or service's benefits in the firm's communication strategies. Social & Mobile Marketing 9.1 describes how Heinz is using social media to convey the specific benefits of its new balsamic vinegar ketchup.

Hollywood in particular is a constant and effective practitioner of benefit segmentation. Although all movies may seem

It is just as easy to identify Thinkers (left) as it is Makers (right). A person is given the VALS questionnaire, and the VALS program at SRIC-BI runs the answers through the computer for scoring to determine the VALS type.

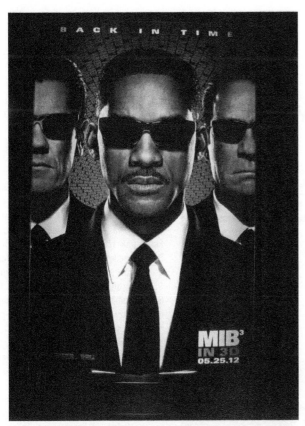

Hollywood uses benefit segmentation to segment moviegoers. Fans of Men in Black *go because they love action movies.*

to provide the same service—entertainment for a couple of hours—film producers know that people visit the theater or rent films to obtain a vast variety of benefits, and market them accordingly. Need a laugh? Try the latest comedy from Adam Sandler or Melissa McCarthy. Want to cry and then feel warm and fuzzy? Go to a romantic movie starring Katherine Heigl, for by the time you leave the theater, you are likely to feel quite happy because the lead characters will have faced obstacles, overcome them, and ultimately found love.

Behavioral Segmentation **Behavioral segmentation** divides customers into groups on the basis of how they use the product or service. Some common behavioral measures include occasion and loyalty.

Occasion. Behavioral segmentation based on when a product or service is purchased or consumed is called **occasion segmentation**. Men's Wearhouse uses this type of segmentation to develop its merchandise selection and its promotions. Sometimes men need a suit for their everyday work, but other suits are expressly for special occasions such as a prom or a wedding. Snack food companies such as Frito-Lay also make and promote snacks for various occasions—individual servings of potato chips for a snack on the run but 16-ounce bags for parties.

Loyalty. Firms have long known that it pays to retain loyal customers. Loyal customers are those who feel so strongly that the firm can meet their relevant needs best that any competitors are virtually excluded from their consideration; that is, these

customers buy almost exclusively from the firm. These loyal customers are the most profitable in the long term.[22] In light of the high cost of finding new customers and the profitability of loyal customers, today's companies are using **loyalty segmentation** and investing in retention and loyalty initiatives to retain their most profitable customers.

Airlines definitely believe that not all customers are created equal. At United Airlines, customers who have flown the most miles with the company, the Premier Executive 1K, receive guaranteed reservations even on sold-out flights, priority check-in, special seating priorities, dedicated reservation services and priority waitlist status.[23] According to Hollywood, flying 10 million miles, like George Clooney's character in *Up in the Air,* even gets you a dedicated customer service line.[24] None of these special services are available to the occasional flyer.

benefit segmentation The grouping of consumers on the basis of the benefits they derive from products or services.

behavioral segmentation A segmentation method that divides customers into groups based on how they use the product or service. Some common behavioral measures include occasion and loyalty.

occasion segmentation A type of behavioral segmentation based on when a product or service is purchased or consumed.

loyalty segmentation Strategy of investing in loyalty initiatives to retain the firm's most profitable customers.

Using Multiple Segmentation Methods Although all segmentation methods are useful, each has its unique advantages and disadvantages. For example, segmenting by demographics and geography is easy because information about who the customers are and where they are located is readily available, but these characteristics don't help marketers determine their customers' needs. Knowing what benefits customers are seeking or how the product or service fits a particular lifestyle is important for designing an overall marketing strategy, but such segmentation schemes present a problem for marketers

Airlines use a loyalty segmentation strategy to attract frequent fliers. *It costs less for frequent flyer members with more miles to have access to airlines' elite lounges.*

Social & Mobile Marketing   9.1
Trials of a Bottle of Ketchup[25]

Heinz extensively used Facebook to introduce its new Ketchup Blended with Balsamic Vinegar.

When you sell a product whose recipe has not ever really changed, it can be hard to create much excitement or buzz. But the rarity of changes also means that virtually any move you make provokes commentary. When Heinz Ketchup changed its label in 2009, replacing the picture of a gherkin that had been there since the 1890s with a ripe tomato, there were some complaints. But the brand also enjoyed a bit more press than was usual, which helped it emphasize a key selling point: that all its ketchup was made from tomatoes the company had grown from seed.

The change in that case was related to packaging, not the contents of the bottle. To build buzz about an entirely new flavor—Heinz Tomato Ketchup Blended with Balsamic Vinegar—Heinz realized it needed an entirely new approach. As consumer goods firms have learned from several examples of failed flavor changes (e.g., New Coke), it's never a good idea to eliminate old favorites. Rather, Heinz left traditional bottles on shelves and offered a limited release of the balsamic version to its faithful fan base. To define those customers, it went beyond simple purchase counts or segmentation based on any demographic considerations. It prioritized people who followed the Heinz Ketchup Facebook page.

For those who had already indicated their loyalty, Heinz granted the right to order a $2.49 bottle of the limited-edition ketchup (with a $2 shipping fee), compared with $1.89 for the regular flavor. If consumers purchased a bottle online through Facebook, they received

25 cents off and a free sample of the new Heinz Dip 'N Squeeze Ketchup package. Heinz Ketchup Blended with Balsamic Vinegar was available for purchase on Facebook from November 14 through December, when it also became available at select retailers (including Walmart, Safeway, and other regional stores). The limited edition offering would be available in stores through March, then offered permanently, depending on the demand.

At least, that was the plan. On November 14, the Facebook launch of Heinz Ketchup Blended with Balsamic Vinegar was disrupted by unforeseen technical difficulties. Heinz received an overwhelming response from consumers placing orders for the balsamic ketchup via Facebook, which led to the technical difficulties. The plan was to resume the offering within 24 hours. The online buzz began, but not quite in the way Heinz had hoped. Consumers complained directly on the page. Heinz responded to fans on the Facebook page, notifying them of the technical difficulties. Everyone who contacted Heinz on the Heinz Ketchup Facebook wall on November 14 and 15 received a free bottle with their order plus free shipping. On a social network, even a few hours' delay seems like an eternity.

The Heinz Ketchup Facebook page received 86,000 new likes during the balsamic ketchup promotion period. Clearly, these potential customers do not fit into the other segmentation schemes. They have self-selected into a segment based on a perceived *benefit*.

attempting to identify specifically which customers are seeking these benefits. Thus, firms often employ a combination of segmentation methods, using demographics and geography to identify and target marketing communications to their customers, then using benefits or lifestyles to design the product or service and the substance of the marketing message.

One very popular mixture of segmentation schemes is geodemographic segmentation. Based on the adage "birds of a feather flock together," **geodemographic segmentation** uses a combination of geographic, demographic, and lifestyle characteristics to classify consumers. Consumers in the same neighborhoods tend to buy the same types of cars, appliances, and apparel and shop at the same types of retailers. Two of the

most widely used tools for geodemographic segmentation are PRIZM (Potential Rating Index by Zip Market), developed by Nielsen Claritas (www.mybestsegments.com), and ESRI's (www.esri.com) Tapestry. Using detailed demographic data and information about the consumption and media habits of people who live in each U.S. block tract (zip code + 4), PRIZM can identify 66 geodemographic segments or neighborhoods. Each block group then can be analyzed and sorted by more than 60 characteristics, including income, home value, occupation, education, household type, age, and several key lifestyle variables. The information in Exhibit 9.4 describes two PRIZM clusters.

Geodemographic segmentation can be particularly useful for retailers because customers typically patronize stores close to

geodemographic segmentation The grouping of consumers on the basis of a combination of geographic, demographic, and lifestyle characteristics.

▼ **EXHIBIT 9.4** PRIZM Clusters

Segment Name	Bohemian Mix	Big Sky Families
Segment Number	16	33
Demographics Traits:		
Urbanicity:	Urban	Rural
Median household income:	$55,665	$57,074
Age ranges:	<55	25–44
Presence of kids:	Family mix	HH w/kids
Homeownership:	Renters	Mostly owners
Employment levels:	White collar, Mix	Blue collar, Service, Mix
Education levels:	College grad	Some college
Ethnic diversity:	White, Black, Asian, Hispanic	White
Lifestyle Traits:		
	Shop at Express, 3mo	Own horse
	Own/lease new Volkswagen	Buy children's clothes, 6mos
	Go Snowboarding, 1yr	Own satellite dish
Food & Drink:		
	Drink Corona Extra beer, 1wk	Use baby foods, 1wk
	Buy from Au Bon Pain, 1mo	Buy from family restaurant, child decides, 6mo
	Buy from Dunkin Donuts, 1mo	Buy from Hardee's, 1mo
Media Usage:		
	Read *The New Yorker,* last issue	Read *Hunting,* last issue
	Visit Internet Movie Database (imdb.com), 1mo	Visit nascar.com, 1mo
	Write a blog online, 1mo	Watch The Disney Channel, 1wk

Source: Reprinted with permission of The Nielsen Company.

their neighborhood. Thus, retailers can use geodemographic segmentation to tailor each store's assortment to the preferences of the local community. If a toy store discovers that one of its stores is surrounded by Big Sky Families, it might adjust its offering to include less expensive toys. This kind of segmentation is also useful for finding new locations; retailers identify their best locations and determine what types of people live in the area surrounding those stores, according to the geodemographic clusters. They can then find other potential locations where similar segments reside.

✓ **check** yourself

1. What are the various segmentation methods?

LO 9-2   Describe how firms determine whether a segment is attractive and therefore worth pursuing.

Step 3: Evaluate Segment Attractiveness

The third step in the segmentation process involves evaluating the attractiveness of the various segments. To undertake this

evaluation, marketers first must determine whether the segment is worth pursuing, using several descriptive criteria: Is the segment identifiable, substantial, reachable, responsive, and profitable (see Exhibit 9.5)?

Identifiable Firms must be able to identify who is within their market to be able to design products or services to meet their needs. It is equally important to ensure that the segments are distinct from one another because too much overlap between segments means that distinct marketing strategies aren't necessary to meet segment members' needs. Thus, Conde Nast is able to identify its market for *Modern Bride* magazine by purchasing mailing lists of people who have bridal registries. It also knows that *Modern Bride* customers tend to be distinct from those who subscribe to *GQ*.

Substantial Once the firm has identified its potential target markets, it needs to measure their size. If a market is too small or its buying power insignificant, it won't generate sufficient profits or be able to support the marketing mix activities. As China's economy started growing, there were not enough middle-class car buyers to push foreign automakers to design an entry-level vehicle. It was only after that number reached substantial numbers that it became worthwhile for them to market to these identified consumers.

▼ **EXHIBIT 9.5** Evaluation of Segment Attractiveness

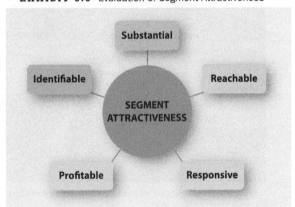

undifferentiated targeting strategy (mass marketing)
A marketing strategy a firm can use if the product or service is perceived to provide the same benefits to everyone, with no need to develop separate strategies for different groups.

differentiated targeting strategy
A strategy through which a firm targets several market segments with a different offering for each.

> [If, through the firm's distinctive competencies, it cannot provide products or services to that segment, it should not target it.]

Reachable   The best product or service cannot have any impact, no matter how identifiable or substantial the target market is, if that market cannot be reached (or accessed) through persuasive communications and product distribution. The consumer must know the product or service exists, understand what it can do for him or her, and recognize how to buy it. If Victoria's Secret fails to tell women that it is offering some less luxurious, more affordable options, shoppers will just walk right past the store and buy basic bras from the Macy's store in the same mall, for example.

Responsive   For a segmentation strategy to be successful, the customers in the segment must react similarly and positively to the firm's offering. If, through the firm's distinctive competencies, it cannot provide products or services to that segment, it should not target it. For instance, General Motors (GM) has introduced a line of cars to the large and very lucrative luxury car segment. People in this market typically purchase Porsches, BMWs, Audis, and Lexuses. In contrast, GM has been somewhat successful competing for the middle-priced family-oriented car and light truck segments. Thus, though the luxury car segment meets all the other criteria for a successful segment, GM took a big risk in attempting to pursue this market.

Profitable   Marketers must also focus their assessments on the potential profitability of each segment, both current and future. Some key factors to keep in mind in this analysis include

Can General Motors compete with other luxury car companies for the very lucrative luxury car segment?

market growth (current size and expected growth rate), market competitiveness (number of competitors, entry barriers, product substitutes), and market access (ease of developing or accessing distribution channels and brand familiarity). Some straightforward calculations can help illustrate the profitability of a segment:[26]

$$
\begin{aligned}
\text{Segment profitability} = &(\text{Segment size} \\
&\times \text{Segment adoption percentage} \\
&\times \text{Purchase behavior} \\
&\times \text{Profit margin percentage}) \\
&- \text{Fixed costs}
\end{aligned}
$$

where

Segment size = Number of people in the segment

Segment adoption percentage = Percentage of customers in the segment who are likely to adopt the product/service

Purchase behavior = Purchase price × number of times the customer would buy the product/service in a year

Profit margin percentage = (Selling price − variable costs) ÷ selling price

Fixed costs = Advertising expenditure, rent, utilities, insurance, and administrative salaries for managers

To illustrate how a business might determine a segment's profitability, consider Camillo's start-up lawn service. He is trying to determine whether to target homeowners or businesses in a small Midwestern town. Exhibit 9.6 estimates the profitability of the two segments. The homeowner segment is much larger than the business segment, but there are already several lawn services with established customers. There is much less competition in the business segment. So, the segment adoption rate for the homeowner segment is only 1 percent,

▼ **EXHIBIT 9.6**   Profitability of Two Market Segments for Camillo's Lawn Service

	Homeowners	Businesses
Segment size	75,000	1,000
Segment adoption percentage	1%	20%
Purchase behavior		
Purchase price	$100	$500
Frequency of purchase	12 times	20 times
Profit margin percentage	60%	80%
Fixed costs	$400,000	$1,000,000
Segment profit	$140,000	$600,000

compared with 20 percent for the business segment. Camillo can charge a much higher price to businesses, and they use lawn services more frequently. The profit margin for the business segment is higher as well because Camillo can use large equipment to cut the grass and therefore save on variable labor costs. However, the fixed costs for purchasing and maintaining the large equipment are much higher for the business segment. Furthermore, he needs to spend more money obtaining and maintaining the business customers, whereas he would use less expensive door-to-door flyers to reach household customers. On the basis of these informed predictions, Camillo decides the business segment is more profitable for his lawn service.

This analysis provides an estimate of the profitability of two segments at one point in time. It is also useful to evaluate the profitability of a segment over the lifetime of one of its typical customers, as Social & Mobile Marketing 9.2 highlights in a different context, namely, the modern music business.

To address such issues, marketers consider factors such as how long the customer will remain loyal to the firm, the defection rate (percentage of customers who switch on a yearly basis), the costs of replacing lost customers (advertising, promotion), whether customers will buy more or more expensive merchandise in the future, and other such factors.

Now that we've evaluated each segment's attractiveness (Step 3), we can select the target markets to pursue (Step 4).

> **LO 9-3** Articulate the differences among targeting strategies: undifferentiated, differentiated, concentrated, or micromarketing.

Step 4: Select Target Market

The fourth step in the STP process is to select a target market. The key factor likely to affect this decision is the marketer's ability to pursue such an opportunity or target segment. Thus, as we mentioned in Chapter 2, a firm assesses both the attractiveness of the target market (opportunities and threats based on the SWOT analysis and the profitability of the segment) and its own competencies (strengths and weaknesses based on SWOT analysis) very carefully.

Determining how to select target markets is not always straightforward. Exhibit 9.7 illustrates several targeting strategies, which we discuss in more detail next.

Undifferentiated Targeting Strategy, or Mass Marketing

When everyone might be considered a potential user of its product, a firm uses an **undifferentiated targeting strategy**. (See Exhibit 9.7.) Clearly, such a targeting strategy focuses on the similarities in needs of the customers as opposed to the differences. If the product or service is perceived to provide

▼ **EXHIBIT 9.7** Targeting Strategies

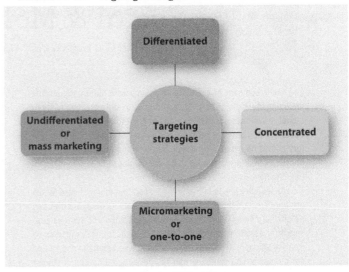

similar benefits to most consumers, there simply is little need to develop separate strategies for different groups.

Although not a common strategy in today's complex marketplace, an undifferentiated strategy is used for many basic commodities such as salt or sugar. However, even those firms that offer salt and sugar now are trying to differentiate their products. Similarly, everyone with a car needs gasoline. Yet gasoline companies have vigorously moved from an undifferentiated strategy to a differentiated one by targeting their offerings to low-, medium-, and high-octane gasoline users.

Differentiated Targeting Strategy

Firms using a **differentiated targeting strategy** target several market segments with a different offering for each (see again Exhibit 9.2). Condé Nast has more than 20 niche magazines focused on different aspects of life—from *Vogue* for fashionistas to *Bon Appetit* for foodies to *GQ* for fashion-conscious men to *The*

Condé Nast has more than 20 niche magazines focused on different aspects of life.

Social & Mobile Marketing   9.2
Spinning Records Takes on a Totally New Meaning[27]

The music business has long been a microcosm that demonstrates changing technology. From record albums to eight-tracks to CDs to digital downloads, its history summarizes the history of changing customer demand and reinventions of the offerings. And that history shows no signs of changing as the industry once again leads the way in shifting its approach by reimagining what it means to sell to customers.

The industry keeps learning the lesson that major record labels are unnecessary if a band can attract fans on its own. But that can be challenging as a band gets started, so companies such as Topspin offer assistance. With Topspin web applications, bands have a route to upload and sell recordings, along with tickets to shows and merchandise. The company handles the accounting and customer contact details, while also offering detailed advice and suggestions about how best to build a fan base.

Perhaps the most notable of Topspin's recommendations is the notion that bands should reject the $.99 single download model popularized by iTunes. Rather than encouraging fans to buy one single for less than a dollar, bands should give away their product for free in the hope of encouraging those fans to buy a $15 T-shirt, a $50 deluxe set of recordings, or even a $100 concert ticket.

Whereas the recent trend has been to unbundle music—that is, rather than buying the entire album, consumers can pick and choose which singles they prefer—Topspin encourage rebundling. Thus it combines free digital downloads with offers for physical products such as posters as well as services such as ticket sales. The average value of transactions on the Topspin website, even when the music is available for free, is $26. If the measure includes sales when customers bought tickets, the average jumps to $88.

The chief executive of Topspin summarizes the idea succinctly:

> You are talking to your fans so you probably know what they want but if you're not sure, ask them! Create something of value for them. It could be as simple as a T-shirt or vinyl or as elaborate as a box set or an in-person experience. But remember not everyone has the same level of fandom or depth of pocketbook. Every day there are people coming to your website who are just entering the "Awareness" phase and there's nothing you're going to do to get them to open their wallet for you. Offer something free, something in the $10 price range, something in the $25 price range, something in the $50 price range, and something in the superfan price range. It turns out the Internet isn't about "going digital" after all, it's about consumer choice. Give your fans a valuable product that fits their budget and level of fandom and they will be happy to support you.

Another digital firm takes a different approach to help musicians evaluate the attractiveness of their fans and potential customers. With the FanTrail application, those musicians set up an easily accessible site for fans. The sites include features such as LoveMail—a function that allows the artist to record a message that gets sent automatically to registered fans' smartphones. Then with the LoveMeter function, that same artist can determine just how active each fan is, measured in terms of purchases and check-ins at concerts. The messages can be precisely targeted, based on fans' location or LoveMeter ranking, which allows artists to reward their biggest, most loyal fans with invitations to secret shows, advance ticket sales, and so forth.

Ian Rogers, CEO of Topspin, believes that if you give customers a valuable product, even if it is free music at first, they will be happy and support you as your fandom and depth of pocketbook increases.

New Yorker for literature lovers to *Golf Digest* for those who walk the links.

Firms embrace differentiated targeting because it helps them obtain a bigger share of the market and increase the market for their products overall. Readers of *Golf Digest* probably are unlike readers of *Architectural Digest* in their interests, as well as in their demographics, such as gender, age, and income. Providing products or services that appeal to multiple segments helps diversify the business and therefore lowers the company's (in this case, Conde Nast's) overall risk. Even if one magazine suffers a circulation decline, the impact on the firm's profitability can be offset by revenue from another publication that continues to do well. But a differentiated strategy is likely to be more costly for the firm.

Concentrated Targeting Strategy When an organization selects a single, primary target market and focuses all its energies on providing a product to fit that market's needs, it is using a **concentrated targeting strategy**.

Micromarketing[28] Take a look at your collection of belts. Have you ever had one made to match your exact specifications? (If you're interested, try www.leather-goodsconnection.com.) When a firm tailors a product or service to suit an individual customer's wants or needs, it is undertaking an extreme form of segmentation called **micromarketing** or **one-to-one marketing**.

Such small producers and service providers generally can tailor their offerings to individual customers more easily. But it is far more difficult for larger companies to achieve this degree of segmentation. Major players such as Dell (computers) and Lands' End (shirts) tried to capitalize on Internet technologies to offer

concentrated targeting strategy
A marketing strategy of selecting a single, primary target market and focusing all energies on providing a product to fit that market's needs.

micromarketing
An extreme form of segmentation that tailors a product or service to suit an individual customer's wants or needs; also called *one-to-one marketing*.

one-to-one marketing See *micromarketing*.

> " Readers of *Golf Digest* probably are unlike readers of *Architectural Digest* in their interests, as well as in their demographics, such as gender, age, and income. "

Entrepreneurial start-up ventures often benefit from using a concentrated strategy, which allows them to employ their limited resources more efficiently. Newton Running, for instance, has concentrated its targeting strategy to runners—but not all runners. It focuses only on those who prefer to land on their forefeet while running, a style that recently has been suggested as more natural, efficient, and less injury-prone than the style encouraged by more traditional running shoes with their heel-first construction and substantial cushioning. In comparison, though it also is known for its running shoes, Nike uses a differentiated targeting strategy (recall the opening vignette about Nike in Chapter 2). It makes shoes for segments that include basketball and football players and skateboarders as well as fashion-conscious white-collar workers with its subsidiary brand Cole-Haan.

Newton Running has concentrated its targeting strategy on runners who seek to land on the forefront.

custom products. Lands' End let customers choose from a variety of options in the fabric, type of collar, sleeve, shape, and based on the customer's specific measurements—but it halted this service when it could not manage to achieve profitable sales. Dell still allows customers to choose the size, color, and speed of their laptops, though it has backed off its promotions and limits the choice of software included. These adjustments demonstrate the difficulty of micromarketing.

The Internet clearly helps facilitate such a segmentation strategy.[29] Companies can cater to very small segments, sometimes as small as one customer at a time, relatively efficiently and inexpensively (e.g., mortgage and insurance sites provide personalized quotes). An Internet-based company can offer one-to-one service more inexpensively than can other venues, such as retail stores or telephone-based businesses. For example,

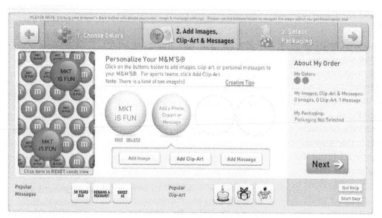

www.mymms.com allows customers to customize their candy.

made especially for them, which means they'll meet the person's needs exactly. If a tailor measures you first and then sews a suit that fits your shoulders, hips, and leg length exactly, it probably will fit better than an off-the-rack suit that you pick up at a department store. But such products and services are typically more expensive than ready-made offerings and often take longer to obtain. You can purchase a dress shirt in your size at Macy's and wear it out of the store. Ordering a tailored shirt from an online site that allows you to enter in your measurements might take five to six weeks to receive delivery. And if you visited an old-fashioned tailor, the processes of measuring you, ordering the material, and sewing the pants might take several months—at a much higher cost.

frequent fliers of American Airlines can check prices and choose special services online at a fraction of the cost that the company would incur for a phone consultation with a ticket agent.

The Internet also simplifies customer identification. **Cookies**, or small text files a website stores in a visitor's browser, provide a unique identification of each potential customer who visits and details how the customer has searched the site. Marketers also can ask visitors to fill out an online registration form. Using such information, the company can make a variety of recommendations to customers. Amazon.com is renowned for the algorithms it uses to provide recommendations for related products to customers as they browse the site, which match customer profiles to those of other customers. The marketing strategy therefore is customized in real time, using known and accurate data about the customer. Staples offers merchandise at different prices in different parts of the country—simply by asking customers to enter their zip codes.

Customers can even do the work themselves, both to create items for themselves and to find the perfect gifts for others.[30] Mars Chocolate North America's MY M&M's® Brand site (www.mymms.com) lets customers customize their own M&M's® Chocolate Candies with personalized greetings, including messages for birthday parties, sporting events, graduations, and weddings—as well as wedding proposals! Both online and in stores, Build-A-Bear lets young (or not so young) customers design their very own stuffed furry friend with unique clothes, accessories, sounds, and the name printed on its birth certificate.

Some consumers appreciate such custom-made goods and services because they are

LO 9-4   Determine the value proposition.

Step 5: Develop Positioning Strategy

The last step in developing a market segmentation strategy is positioning. Market positioning involves a process of defining the marketing mix variables so that target customers have a clear, distinctive, desirable understanding of what the product does or represents in comparison with competing products.

Build-A-Bear lets customers design their own stuffed furry friend with unique clothes, accessories, sounds, and the name printed on its birth certificate.

The positioning strategy can help communicate the firm's or the product's **value proposition**, which communicates the customer benefits to be received from a product or service and thereby provides reasons for wanting to purchase it.

To visualize the value proposition, examine the Circles for a Successful Value Proposition framework in Exhibit 9.8A.[31] The first circle represents the customer needs and wants, the second circle represents the benefits that the company provides (i.e., its capabilities), and the final circle represents the benefits provided by competitors. The best situation is if a firm's product or service offering overlaps with customer needs and wants but suffers no overlap with competitors' offerings (Exhibit 9.8A). The shaded portion reflects the value proposition, or the intersection of what the customer needs and wants with what the firm can offer. Unfortunately, even if the situation depicted in Exhibit 9.8A existed, the product or service then would be successful, so it likely would not be sustainable because competitors would attempt to copy the important product or service attributes and therefore begin to encroach on the firm's value proposition. Maintaining a unique value

proposition can be sustained in the long term only in monopoly situations or possibly monopolistic competition situations.

In Exhibit 9.8B, the intersection of customer needs, the benefits provided by our focal firm, and the benefits provided by a competing firm reveal seven specific spaces where a product or service might be located. Let's look at each one in turn, using the offerings of the airline industry as hypothetical examples to understand each space.

Space 1. Representing the firm's value proposition, this space reveals which customer needs are effectively met by the benefits that the firm provides but not by the benefits provided by competitors. That is, there is no overlap between competitors. When airline customers prefer a cattle-call approach to seating, which allows them to choose their own seats on the plane as long as they get an early check-in, they turn to Southwest, and Southwest alone, for their flights.

cookies Computer program, installed on hard drives, that provides identifying information.

value proposition The unique value that a product or service provides to its customers and how it is better than and different from those of competitors.

[The best situation is if a firm's product or service offering overlaps with customer needs and wants but suffers no overlap with competitors' offerings.]

▼ **EXHIBIT 9.8** Circles for a Successful Value Proposition

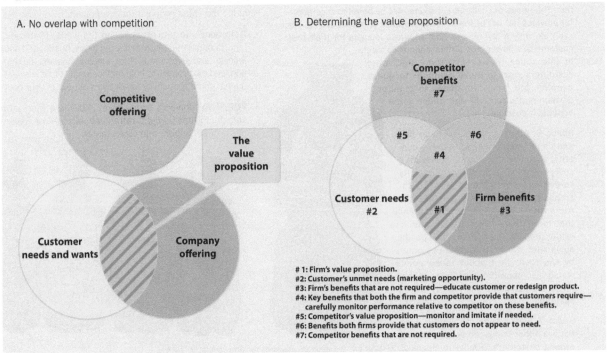

A. No overlap with competition

- Competitive offering
- The value proposition
- Customer needs and wants
- Company offering

B. Determining the value proposition

- Competitor benefits #7
- #5
- #6
- #4
- Customer needs #2
- #1
- Firm benefits #3

1: Firm's value proposition.
#2: Customer's unmet needs (marketing opportunity).
#3: Firm's benefits that are not required—educate customer or redesign product.
#4: Key benefits that both the firm and competitor provide that customers require—carefully monitor performance relative to competitor on these benefits.
#5: Competitor's value proposition—monitor and imitate if needed.
#6: Benefits both firms provide that customers do not appear to need.
#7: Competitor benefits that are not required.

> ## REGARDLESS OF THEIR EXISTING SPACE THOUGH, FIRMS MUST CONSTANTLY AND CLOSELY MONITOR THEIR COMPETITORS' OFFERINGS.

Space 2. These customer needs are unmet. It represents an important marketing opportunity in that the firm could create new products or augment existing services to satisfy these needs better. A direct route between two cities that currently are not connected by any airline represents a prime example of such a space.

Space 3. Customers express little need or desire for these company benefits. The firm thus has several options. It might educate customers about the importance and benefits that it provides with this space, to encourage customers to develop a sense of their need. Alternatively, it could reengineer its approach to stop providing these unwanted benefits, which likely would enable it to save money. For example, when airlines realized that passengers cared little about the appearance of a piece of lettuce underneath the in-flight sandwiches they were served, they saved millions of dollars they had previously spent on unwanted produce.

Space 4. These needs are being met by the benefits of the firm as well as by competitors. Many customers make frequent trips between major cities, like New York and Washington, DC, and many airlines offer multiple direct flights each day between these hubs. Each firm therefore works to compete effectively, such as by offering convenient flight times or striving to increase its on-time rates to make it easier for customers to compare firms on these specific features.

Space 5. This space constitutes the competitor's value proposition: The needs of customers that are met by benefits a competitor provides but not by the benefits provided by our focal firm. For example, only a few airlines host separate lounges for their best customers; a lower-cost airline cannot compete in this space. However, if more and more customers start to make demands for these benefits, the focal firm needs to monitor developments carefully and match some benefits if possible.

Space 6. Although both the focal firm and its competitors provide these benefits, they somehow are not meeting customer needs. The stringent security screening requirements aim to increase passenger safety, but they also represent a significant inconvenience that many fliers associate with airlines rather than federal regulators. Expending significant efforts to educate customers by the focal firm about these needs would also benefit competitors, so they likely are lower in the priority list of spending.

Space 7. Finally, some competitor benefits are either undesired or unnecessary among customers. Similar to Space 3,

the competitor could invest money to educate customers about the importance of these benefits and highlight their needs through advertising and promotional campaigns. If so, the focal firm should recognize that this need is moving to Space 5. Alternatively, the competitor could reengineer its products to eliminate these benefits, in which case it requires no response from the focal firm.

Regardless of their existing space though, firms must constantly and closely monitor their competitors' offerings. If competitors offer features that the firm does not, it is important to determine their importance to customers. Important attributes should be considered for inclusion in the firm's offering—or else they will provide a unique value proposition for competitors.

In Exhibit 9.9, we highlight the elements of developing and communicating a firm's value proposition. The main value proposition components are:

1. Target market

2. Offering name or brand

3. Product/service category or concept

4. Unique point of difference/benefits

Let's focus on a couple of well-known products, Gatorade and 7-Up, and their potential value propositions (brackets added to separate the value proposition components):

- **Gatorade:**[32] To [athletes around the world] [Gatorade] is the [sports drink] that [represents the heart, hustle, and soul of athleticism and gives the fuel for working muscles, fluid for hydration, and electrolytes to help replace what is lost in sweat before, during, and after activity to get the most out of your body].

- **7UP:**[33] To [non-cola consumers] [7UP] is a [non-caffeinated soft drink] that [is light, refreshing, lemon-lime flavored, and has a crisp, bubbly, and clean taste].

What are the value propositions for Gatorade and 7UP?

value Reflects the relationship of benefits to costs, or what the consumer *gets* for what he or she *gives*.

▼ **EXHIBIT 9.9** Value Proposition Statement Key Elements

	Gatorade	7UP
Target market:	To athletes around the world	To non-cola consumers
Offering name or brand:	Gatorade	7UP
Product/service category or concept:	is the sports drink	is a non-caffeinated soft drink
Unique point of difference/ benefits:	representing the heart, hustle, and soul of athleticism and gives the fuel for working muscles, fluid for hydration, and electrolytes to help replace what is lost in sweat before, during, and after activity to get the most out of your body.	that is light, refreshing, lemon-lime flavored and has a crisp, bubbly, and clean taste.

LO 9-5   Define positioning and describe how firms do it.

Positioning Methods

Firms position products and services based on different methods such as the value proposition, salient attributes, symbols, and competition.

The positioning strategy can help communicate the firm's or the product's value proposition, the unique value that a product or service provides to its customers, and how it is better than and different from those of competitors. Firms thus position their products and services according to value and salient attributes. **Value** is a popular positioning method because the relationship of price to quality is among the most important considerations for consumers when they make a purchase decision.

Remember that value does not necessarily mean low priced. The watchmaker Patek Philippe uses the advertising tagline, "You never actually own a Patek Philippe. You merely take care of it for the next generation," to encourage buyers to consider its arm candy an investment.[34] The long-running campaign takes on added effectiveness in the modern economic downturn, especially as a way to market a luxury brand in a necessity-focused economy. Other brands that rely on a similar idea of luxury value include Hermès, Chanel, and Mercedes-Benz.

Another common positioning strategy focuses on the product attributes that are most important to the target market. Volvo, the car company traditionally positioned for the safety-conscious driver, wants to stretch its safety image to one focused on driving performance and excitement. The company expects the positioning adjustment to be a long and concentrated effort because so many of Volvo's boxier vehicles remain on the road today, which reinforces its more conservative image. Volvo's goal is not

French retailer Hermès is positioned as a luxury brand, which makes its customers less price-sensitive for its products like this handmade Birkin bag which retails for $9,000.

to abandon the safety notions associated with the brand but rather to expand its image to compete with other top luxury brands.[35]

A well-known symbol can also be used as a positioning tool. What comes to mind when you think of Colonel Sanders, the Jolly Green Giant, the Gerber Baby, or Tony the Tiger? Or consider the Texaco star, the Nike swoosh, or the Ralph Lauren polo player. These symbols are so strong and well known that they create a position for the brand that distinguishes it from its competition. Many such symbols are registered trademarks that are legally protected by the companies that developed them.

Firms can choose to position their products or services against a specific competitor or an entire product/service classification. For instance, 7UP positioned its product as the Uncola to differentiate it from caramel-colored cola beverages such as Pepsi and Coke. Goodrich tires were promoted as the other guys, or the ones without the blimp, to set them apart from Goodyear tires.

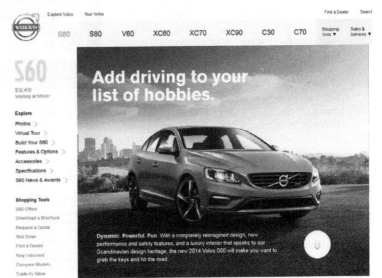

Volvo is repositioning its cars from safe to safe plus performance.

Goodrich positions its tires as the ones without the blimp to set them apart from Goodyear.

steps. Before you read about these steps, though, examine Exhibit 9.10 (Charts A–D), a hypothetical perceptual map of the soft drink industry. A **perceptual map** displays, in two or more dimensions, the position of products or brands in the consumer's mind. We have chosen two dimensions for illustrative purposes: strong versus light taste (vertical) and fun versus healthy (horizontal). Also, though this industry is quite complex, we have simplified the diagram to include only a few players in the market. The position of each brand is denoted by a small circle, and the numbered circles denote consumers' **ideal points**—where a particular market segment's ideal product would lie on the map. The larger the numbered circle, the larger the market size.

To derive a perceptual map such as shown in Exhibit 9.10, marketers follow six steps.

1. **Determine consumers' perceptions and evaluations of the product or service in relation to competitors'.** Marketers determine their brand's position by asking consumers a series of questions about their and competitors' products. For instance, they might ask how the consumer uses the existing product or services, what items the consumer regards as alternative sources to satisfy his or her needs, what the person likes or dislikes about the brand in relation to competitors, and what might

Marketers must be careful, however, that they don't position their product too closely to their competition. If, for instance, their package or logo looks too much like a competitor's, they might be opening themselves up to a trademark infringement lawsuit. Many private-label and store brands have been challenged for using packaging that appears confusingly similar to that of the national brand leaders in a category. Similarly, McDonald's sues anyone who uses the Mc prefix, including McSleep Inns and McDental Services, even though in the latter case there was little possibility that consumers would believe the fast-food restaurant company would branch out into dental services.

Positioning Using Perceptual Mapping

Now that we have identified the various methods by which firms position their products and services, we discuss the actual steps they go through to establish that position. When developing a positioning strategy, firms go through six important

Gatorade uses athletes to compete for target markets in Exhibit 9.10.

make that person choose one brand over another. Exhibit 9.10A depicts the six products using two dimensions (light taste–sweet taste; and less natural–healthy).

2. **Identify the market's ideal points and size.** On a perceptual map, marketers can represent the size of current and potential markets. For example, Exhibit 9.10B uses differently sized ovals that correspond to the market size. Ideal point 1 represents the largest market, so if the firm does not already have a product positioned close to this point, it should consider an introduction. Point 3 is the smallest market, so there are relatively few customers who want a healthy, light-tasting drink. This is not to suggest that this market should be ignored; however, the company might want to consider a niche, rather than mass, market strategy for this group of consumers.

3. **Identify competitors' positions.** When the firm understands how its customers view its brand relative to competitors', it must study how those same competitors position themselves. For instance, POWERade positions itself closely to Gatorade, which means they appear next to each other on the perceptual map and appeal to target market 2 (see Exhibit 9.10C). They are also often found next to each other on store shelves, are similarly priced, and are viewed by customers as sports drinks. Gatorade also knows that its sports drink is perceived to be more like POWERade than like its own Propel

> **perceptual map**
> Displays, in two or more dimensions, the position of products or brands in the consumer's mind.
>
> **ideal points**
> The position at which a particular market segment's ideal product would lie on a *perceptual map.*

▼ **EXHIBIT 9.10A** Perceptual Maps

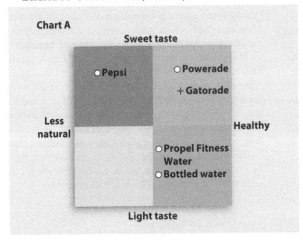

▼ **EXHIBIT 9.10C** Perceptual Maps

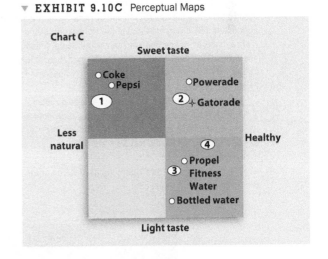

▼ **EXHIBIT 9.10B** Perceptual Maps

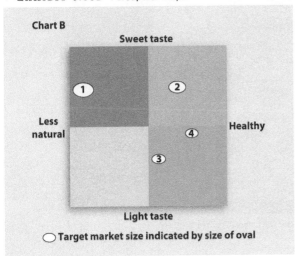

▼ **EXHIBIT 9.10D** Perceptual Maps

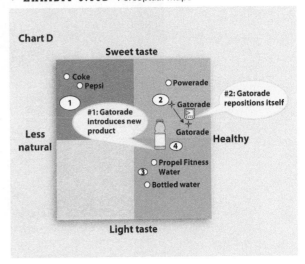

Fitness Water (located near target market 3) or Coke (target market 1).

4. **Determine consumer preferences.** The firm knows what the consumer thinks of the products or services in the marketplace and their positions relative to one another. Now it must find out what the consumer really wants, that is, determine the ideal product or service that appeals to each market. For example, a huge market exists for traditional Gatorade, and that market is shared by POWERade. Gatorade also recognizes a market, depicted as the ideal product for segment 4 on the perceptual map, of consumers who would prefer a less sweet, less calorie-laden drink that offers the same rejuvenating properties as Gatorade. Currently, no product is adequately serving market 4.

Adding Value   9.2

Striving to Encourage the Strivers to Stay[36]

The InterContinental Hotels Group owns several well-known brands, including the Holiday Inn and Crowne Plaza hotel chains. It conducted a $1 billion overhaul of the Holiday Inn brand—only to realize that the Crowne Plaza image was outdated, unfocused, and apparently unappealing to customers. In particular, it identified a target market of young travelers, or strivers, whose needs Crowne Plaza was not meeting.

Using a combination of promotions and advertisements aimed directly at this target market, Crowne Plaza has worked to highlight its key attractions and events likely to captivate their interest. For example, noting that young travelers are highly likely to book their rooms online and through mobile applications, Crowne Plaza allows people to book same-day reservations through their Android, Blackberry, or iPhone applications.

Beyond age and usage, strivers are interesting in terms of their international character. Richard Solomons, the chief executive of the InterContinental Group, noted the chain's recognition that "there is a big customer base in China that wants a brand that gives them the comfort of being part of an international group but is designed in our China office, by our China team, for our Chinese customers." This group also has specific demands for service, including spaces for entertaining for both business and social contacts in their hotels. By including such spaces in the designs of Crowne Plaza hotels, the brand appeals directly to such customers, without doing anything that would damage its image among strivers from other cultures.

The turbulent state of the hotel industry also suggests that Crowne Plaza will need to reconsider some of its offerings, including whether to shut down underperforming sites. Careful marketing research has suggested that segmentation will increase as customers express increasingly specific preferences and demands.

At the same time, there are some appeals that seem almost universal. All the redesigned hotels therefore will feature a pancake-making machine, available for customers' use any time of the day. It may seem like just a pancake, but it's also fun, different, and playful, and that's exactly the image Crowne Plaza is pursuing.

Repositioning isn't easy! But Crowne Plaza is attempting to reposition itself with an exciting image to appeal to young travelers.

5. **Select the position.** Continuing with the Gatorade example, the company has some choices to appeal to the "less sweet sports drink" target market 4. It could develop a new product to meet the needs of market 4 (see Exhibit 9.10D, option 1). Alternatively, it could adjust or reposition its marketing approach—its product and promotion—to sell original Gatorade to market 4 (option 2). Finally, it could ignore what target market 4 really wants and hope that consumers will be attracted to the original Gatorade because it is closer to their ideal product than anything else on the market.

6. **Monitor the positioning strategy.** Markets are not stagnant. Consumers' tastes shift, and competitors react to those shifts. Attempting to maintain the same position year after year can spell disaster for any company. Thus, firms must always view the first three steps of the positioning process as ongoing, with adjustments made in step four as necessary.

Despite the apparent simplicity of this presentation, marketers should recognize that changing their firm's positioning is never an easy task. Some firms might try to change their image in response to a shift in the target market, such as when Skechers realized that older consumers wanted hip lifestyle shoes too. Crowne Plaza has attempted to reposition itself in the other direction, namely, to gain a more vital, exciting image among younger travelers, as Adding Value 9.2 describes. ◼

✓ check yourself

1. What is a perceptual map?
2. Identify the six positioning steps.

check it out!

mhhe.com/GrewalM4e
for study materials,
including quizzes
and videos.

10 Motivation, Personality, and Emotion

LEARNING OBJECTIVES

L01 Define motivation and summarize the motivation sets put forth by Maslow and McGuire

L02 Articulate motivation's role in consumer behavior and marketing strategy

L03 Define personality and the various theories of personality

L04 Discuss how brand personality can be used in developing marketing strategies

L05 Define emotions and list the major emotional dimensions

L06 Discuss how emotions can be used in developing marketing strategies

Brands, like people, have personalities. Brand personality, as we will see later in the chapter, is a set of human characteristics that become associated with a brand. These characteristics contribute to a brand's image. Personality traits and other brand associations can be affected in positive and negative ways by numerous factors including advertising, word of mouth, direct product experience, and so on. Toyota, which has enjoyed amazing success in the United States, has found itself struggling with brand image since safety issues relating to its accelerator pedal and system resulted in a recall of nearly 6 million vehicles. The overall result was a major reduction in Toyota perceptions as shown below.[1]

For both owners and nonowners, perceptions of reliability and quality went down after the recall and these effects were stronger for nonowners. Owners appear to be giving Toyota a bit more of the benefit of the doubt, although even there, the declines are substantial. Specifically, among Toyota owners, there was a 23 point drop in reliability and a 44 point drop in those who perceived Toyota to be of higher quality than domestics. Reliability is a brand personality trait associated with competence. Clearly Toyota's image has suffered, and that has translated into reduced quality perceptions and purchase intentions, as the percentage of Toyota owners who would consider buying a Toyota in the future dropped 16 points after the recall.

Toyota is working hard to fix its image problem. Among other things, it has a "recall information" page on its website and has launched its "Safety First" advertising campaign that states, in part:

At Toyota, we're committed to providing our customers with safe, reliable cars. That's why we're currently

	Toyota Owners		Toyota Nonowners	
	Before Recall	**After Recall**	**Before Recall**	**After Recall**
Reliable Brand	95%	72%	89%	61%
Unreliable Brand	5	28	6	39
Quality Lower than Domestics	4	18	5	34
Quality Equal to Domestics	25	49	43	53
Quality Higher than Domestics	70	33	47	13

Source: Adapted from B. Steinberg, "Lightspeed Survey: Toyota's Loss of Consumer Trust is Domestic Rivals' Gain," *Advertising Age*, February 8, 2010, p. 2.

spending $1 million per hour to enhance the technology and safety of our vehicles. And we've also made our comprehensive star safety system standard on every vehicle we make.

There is evidence that Toyota is coming back. Although they dropped as far as fourth place in U.S. sales after the recall, more recent sales numbers put them in third place behind Ford and GM.

As the opening example suggests, brand personality is critical to brand image and consumer behavior. It is also part of three interrelated aspects of consumer behavior, namely motivation, personality, and emotions. *Motivation* is the energizing force that activates behavior and provides purpose and direction to that behavior. It helps answer the question of "why" consumers engage in specific behaviors. *Personality* reflects the relatively stable behavioral tendencies that individuals display across a variety of situations. It helps answer the question of "what" behaviors consumers choose to engage in to achieve their goals. *Emotions* are strong, relatively uncontrollable feelings that affect our behavior. Emotions are triggered by a complex interplay between motives, personality, and external factors. Indeed, the three concepts are closely interrelated and are frequently difficult to separate.

THE NATURE OF MOTIVATION

Motivation is the reason for behavior. A **motive** is a construct representing an unobservable inner force that stimulates and compels a behavioral response and provides specific direction to that response. A motive is why an individual does something. The terms *need* and *motivation* are often used interchangeably. This is because when a consumer feels a gap between a desired state and his or her actual current state, a need is recognized and experienced as a drive state referred to as motivation. Needs and motives influence what consumers perceive as relevant and also influence their feelings and emotions. For example, a consumer who feels hungry is motivated to satisfy that need, will view food and ads for food as personally relevant, and will experience negative emotions prior to eating and positive emotions after eating.

There are numerous theories of motivation. This section describes two particularly useful approaches. The first approach, *Maslow's need hierarchy,* is a macro theory designed to account for most human behavior in general terms. The second approach, based on McGuire's work, uses a fairly detailed set of motives to account for specific aspects of consumer behavior.

Maslow's Hierarchy of Needs

Maslow's hierarchy of needs is based on four premises:[2]

1. All humans acquire a similar set of motives through genetic endowment and social interaction.
2. Some motives are more basic or critical than others.
3. The more basic motives must be satisfied to a minimum level before other motives are activated.
4. As the basic motives become satisfied, more advanced motives come into play.

Thus, Maslow proposed a need hierarchy shared by all. Table 10-1 illustrates this hierarchy, briefly describes each level, and provides marketing examples.

Marketing Strategies and Maslow's Need Hierarchy	TABLE 10-1

I. Physiological: Food, water, sleep, and, to an extent, sex, are physiological motives.

Products   Health foods, medicines, sports drinks, low-cholesterol foods, and exercise equipment.

Themes   BAND-AID—"Blister-proof your feet."

Quaker Oats—"Eating oatmeal is good for your heart."

NordicTrack—"Only NordicTrack gives you a total-body workout."

II. Safety: Seeking physical safety and security, stability, familiar surroundings, and so forth are manifestations of safety needs.

Products   Smoke detectors, preventive medicines, insurance, retirement investments, seat belts, burglar alarms, and sunscreen.

Themes   Sleep Safe—"We've designed a travel alarm that just might wake you in the middle of the night—because a fire is sending smoke into your room. You see, ours is a smoke alarm as well as an alarm clock."

Partnership for a Drug-Free America—"Heroin: Dying's the Easy Part."

State Street Investing—"Precise in a world that isn't."

III. Belongingness: Belongingness motives are reflected in a desire for love, friendship, affiliation, and group acceptance.

Products   Personal grooming, foods, entertainment, clothing, and many others.

Themes   Olive Garden Restaurants—"When You're Here, You're Family."

Tums—"You are important. You are loved. You should take your calcium."

Grand Marnier—"Add flavor to good company."

IV. Esteem: Desires for status, superiority, self-respect, and prestige are examples of esteem needs. These needs relate to the individual's feelings of usefulness and accomplishment.

Products   Clothing, furniture, liquors, hobbies, stores, cars, and many others.

Themes   Sheaffer—"Your hand should look as contemporary as the rest of you."

New Balance—"One more woman chasing a sunset. One more woman going a little farther. One more woman simply feeling alive. One less woman relying on someone else."

BMW—"The Ultimate Driving Machine."

V. Self-Actualization: This involves the desire for self-fulfillment, to become all that one is capable of becoming.

Products   Education, hobbies, sports, some vacations, gourmet foods, museums.

Themes   U.S. Navy—"Accelerate Your Life."

Gatorade—"Is it in you?"

Outward Bound School—"Minds in Motion."

Maslow's theory is a good guide to general behavior. It is not an ironclad rule, however. Numerous examples exist of individuals who sacrificed their lives for friends or ideas, or who gave up food and shelter to seek self-actualization. However, we do tend to regard such behavior as exceptional, which indicates the general validity of Maslow's overall approach.[3] It is important to remember that any given consumption behavior can satisfy more than one need. Likewise, the same consumption behavior can satisfy different needs at different times. For example, a number of motives could cause one to join the U.S. Army. The ad in Illustration 10–1 appeals to self-actualization.

McGuire's Psychological Motives

Maslow presented a hierarchical set of five basic motives, and other researchers have proposed hundreds of additional, very specific motives. McGuire developed a classification system that organizes these various theories into 16 categories.[4] This system helps marketers

ILLUSTRATION 10–1

Appeals to self-actualization focus on individuals challenging themselves and reaching their full potential.

isolate motives likely to be involved in various consumption situations. McGuire first divides motivation into four main categories using two criteria:

1. Is the mode of motivation cognitive or affective?
2. Is the motive focused on preservation of the status quo or on growth?

Cognitive motives focus on the person's need for being adaptively oriented toward the environment and achieving a sense of meaning. *Affective* motives deal with the need to reach satisfying feeling states and to obtain personal goals. *Preservation-oriented* motives emphasize the individual as striving to maintain equilibrium, while *growth* motives emphasize development. These four main categories are then further subdivided on the bases of source and objective of the motive:

3. Is this behavior actively initiated or in response to the environment?
4. Does this behavior help the individual achieve a new internal or a new external relationship to the environment?

The third criterion distinguishes between motives that are actively or internally aroused versus those that are a more passive response to circumstances. The final criterion is used to categorize outcomes that are internal to the individual and those focused on a relationship with the environment.

McGuire's 16 motives and their implications for marketing are briefly described in the following sections.

Cognitive Preservation Motives   *Need for Consistency (active, internal)*   A basic desire is to have all facets of oneself consistent with one another.[5] These facets include attitudes, behaviors, opinions, self-images, views of others, and so forth. *Cognitive dissonance* is a common motive of this type. For example, making a major purchase is not consistent with the need to save money. This inconsistency motivates the individual to reduce it (see Chapter 18).

Understanding the need for consistency is also important for structuring advertising messages relating to attitude change. A need for internal consistency means consumers are reluctant to accept information that disagrees with existing beliefs. Thus, marketers wishing to change attitudes must use highly credible sources or other techniques to overcome this (see Chapter 11).

Need for Attribution (active, external)   This set of motives deals with our need to determine who or what causes the things that happen to us and relates to an area of research called **attribution theory.**[6] Do we attribute the cause of a favorable or unfavorable outcome to ourselves or to some outside force?

Need for attribution is extremely relevant to consumer reactions to promotional messages (in terms of credibility). Because consumers do not passively receive messages but rather attribute "selling" motives and tactics to ads and the advice of sales personnel, they

do not believe or they discount many sales messages.[7] Marketers use a variety of means to overcome this. One approach is to use a credible spokesperson, as seen in Illustration 10–2. This technique is discussed in depth in Chapter 11.

Need to Categorize (passive, internal)   People have a need to categorize and organize the vast array of information and experiences they encounter in a meaningful yet manageable way.[8] So they establish categories or mental partitions to help them do so. Prices are often categorized such that different prices connote different categories of goods. Automobiles over $20,000 and automobiles under $20,000 may elicit two different meanings because of information categorized on the basis of price level. Many firms price items at $9.95, $19.95, $49.95, and so forth. One reason is to avoid being categorized in the over $10, $20, or $50 group.

Need for Objectification (passive, external)   These motives reflect needs for observable cues or symbols that enable people to infer what they feel and know. Impressions, feelings, and attitudes are subtly established by viewing one's own behavior and that of others and drawing inferences as to what one feels and thinks. In many instances, clothing plays an important role in presenting the subtle meaning of a desired image and consumer lifestyle. Brands play a role in this as shown in Figure 10-1.

Cognitive Growth Motives   ***Need for Autonomy (active, internal)***   The need for independence and individuality is a characteristic of the American culture, as described in Chapter 2. All individuals in all cultures have this need at some level. Americans are taught that it is proper and even essential to express and fulfill this need (in contrast to Eastern countries such as Japan, which value affiliation).

Owning or using products and services that are unique is one way consumers express their autonomy.[9] Marketers have responded to this motive by developing limited editions of products and providing wide variety and customization options. In addition, many products are advertised and positioned with independence, uniqueness, or individuality themes, as shown in Illustration 10–3.

Need for Stimulation (active, external)   People often seek variety and difference out of a need for stimulation.[10] Such variety-seeking behavior may be a prime reason for brand switching and some so-called impulse purchasing.[11] The need for stimulation is curvilinear and changes over time.[12] That is, individuals experiencing rapid change generally become satiated and desire stability, whereas individuals in stable environments become bored and desire change.

Teleological Need (passive, internal)   Consumers are pattern matchers who have images of desired outcomes or end states with which they compare their current situation. Behaviors are changed and the results are monitored in terms of movement toward the desired end state. This motive propels people to prefer mass media such as movies, television programs, and books with outcomes that match their view of how the world should work (e.g., the good guys win). This has obvious implications for advertising messages.

Utilitarian Need (passive, external)   These theories view the consumer as a problem solver who approaches situations as opportunities to acquire useful information or new skills. Thus, a consumer watching a situation comedy on television not only is being entertained but is learning clothing styles, lifestyle options, and so forth. Likewise, consumers may approach ads and salespeople as a source of learning for future decisions as well as for the current one.

Affective Preservation Motives   *Need for Tension Reduction (active, internal)*   People encounter situations in their daily lives that create uncomfortable levels of stress. In order to effectively manage tension and stress, people are motivated to seek ways to reduce arousal. Recreational products and activities are often promoted in terms of tension relief. Illustration 10–4 contains a product and appeal focused on this need.

Need for Expression (active, external)   This motive deals with the need to express one's identity to others. People feel the need to let others know who and what they are by their actions, which include the purchase and use of goods. The purchase of many products, such as clothing and automobiles, allows consumers to express an identity to others, because the products have symbolic meanings. For example, fashion-oriented watches such as Swatch satisfy more than the functional need to tell time—they allow consumers to express who they are.

Need for Ego Defense (passive, internal)   The need to defend one's identity or ego is another important motive. When one's identity is threatened, the person is motivated to protect his or her self-concept and utilize defensive behaviors and attitudes. Many products can provide ego defense. A consumer who feels insecure may rely on well-known brands for socially visible products to avoid any chance of making a socially incorrect purchase.

Need for Reinforcement (passive, external)   People are often motivated to act in certain ways because they were rewarded for behaving that way in similar situations in the past. This

ILLUSTRATION 10–4

Today's hurried life-styles often produce uncomfortable levels of tension. Products that relieve this stress fulfill a fundamental need.

is the basis for operant learning. Products designed to be used in public situations (clothing, furniture, and artwork) are frequently sold on the basis of the amount and type of reinforcement that will be received. Keepsake Diamonds have exploited this motive with an ad that states, "Enter a room and you are immediately surrounded by friends sharing your excitement."

Affective Growth Motives *Need for Assertion (active, internal)* Many people are competitive achievers who seek success, admiration, and dominance. Important to them are power, accomplishment, and esteem. As Illustration 10–5 shows, the need for assertion underlies numerous ads.

Need for Affiliation (active, external) Affiliation refers to the need to develop mutually helpful and satisfying relationships with others. It relates to altruism and seeking acceptance and affection in interpersonal relations. As we saw in Chapter 7, group membership is a critical part of most consumers' lives, and many consumer decisions are based on the need to maintain satisfying relationships with others. Marketers frequently use such affiliation-based themes as "Your kids will love you for it" in advertisements.[13]

Need for Identification (passive, internal) The need for identification results in the consumer's playing various roles. A person may play the role of college student, sorority member, bookstore employee, fiancée, and many others. One gains pleasure from adding new, satisfying roles and by increasing the significance of roles already adopted. Marketers encourage consumers to assume new roles (become a skateboarder) and position products as critical for certain roles ("No working mother should be without one").

Need for Modeling (passive, external) The need for modeling reflects a tendency to base behavior on that of others. Modeling is a major means by which children learn to become consumers. The tendency to model explains some of the conformity that occurs

ILLUSTRATION 10–5

Consumer need for
assertion underlies the
strategy for this ad.

within reference groups. Marketers use this motive by showing desirable types of individuals using their brands. American Express, for example, used Kate Winslet and Beyoncé in its "My life. My card" campaign.

MOTIVATION THEORY AND MARKETING STRATEGY

 Consumers do not buy products; instead, they buy motive satisfaction or problem solutions. For example, a study of Porsche buyers in the United States found that some were motivated by power and status (need for assertion), others by excitement and adventure (need for stimulation), others by escapism (need for tension reduction). Such motives are not constrained to the United States. A study of car buyers in India found fairly similar motives. For example, they found a "Potency" buyer group interested in power (need for assertion), a "Utility" buyer group interested in basic transportation (utilitarian need), an "Adventure" buyer group interested in fun (need for stimulation), and a "Liberation" buyer group interested in freedom (need for autonomy).[14] Thus, firms must discover the motives that their products and brands can satisfy and develop marketing mixes around these motives.

An important question that often arises is, "Do marketers create needs?" The answer depends in part on what is meant by the term *need.* If it is used to refer to the basic motives described in this chapter, it is clear that marketers seldom if ever *create* a need. Human genetics and experience basically determine motives. Long before marketing or advertising appeared, individuals used perfumes, clothing, and other items to gain acceptance, display status, and so forth. However, marketers do create **demand.** Demand is *the willingness to buy a particular product or service.* It is caused by a need or motive, but it is not the

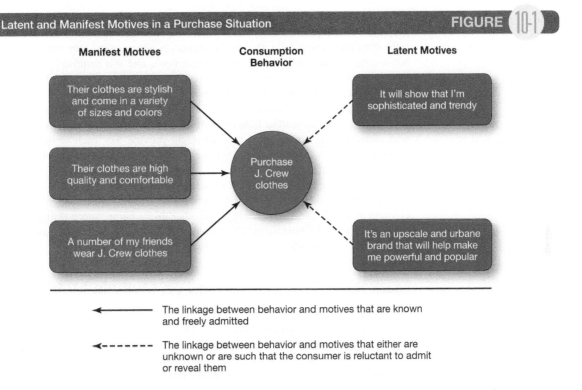

Latent and Manifest Motives in a Purchase Situation   FIGURE 10-1

Manifest Motives   Consumption   Latent Motives
                            Behavior

Their clothes are stylish
and come in a variety   It will show that I'm
of sizes and colors   sophisticated and trendy

                            Purchase
Their clothes are high   J. Crew
quality and comfortable   clothes

A number of my friends   It's an upscale and urbane
wear J. Crew clothes   brand that will help make
                                                      me powerful and popular

⟵———————— The linkage between behavior and motives that are known
            and freely admitted

⟵- - - - - - The linkage between behavior and motives that either are
            unknown or are such that the consumer is reluctant to admit
            or reveal them

motive. For example, a mouthwash ad might use a theme suggesting that without mouthwash people will not like you because you have bad breath. This message ties mouthwash to an existing need for affiliation in hopes of creating demand for the brand.

The following sections examine how motives relate to various aspects of marketing strategy.

Discovering Purchase Motives

Suppose a marketing researcher asked a consumer why he wears J. Crew clothes (or owns a mountain bike, or uses cologne, or whatever). Odds are the consumer would offer several reasons, such as "They're in style," "My friends wear them," "I like the way they fit," or "They look good on me." However, there may be other reasons that the consumer is reluctant to admit or perhaps is not even aware of: "They show that I have money," "They make me sexually desirable," or "They show I'm trendy and urbane." All or any combination of the above motives could influence the purchase of clothes or many other items.

The first group of motives mentioned above were known to the consumer and admitted to the researcher. Motives that are known and freely admitted are called **manifest motives.** Any of the motives we have discussed can be manifest; however, motives that conform to a society's prevailing value system are more likely to be manifest than are those in conflict with such values.

The second group of motives described above either were unknown to the consumer or were such that she was reluctant to admit them. Such motives are **latent motives.** Figure 10-1 illustrates how the two types of motives might influence a purchase.

The first task of the marketing manager is to determine the combination of motives influencing the target market. Manifest motives are relatively easy to determine. Direct questions (Why do you purchase J. Crew clothing?) will generally produce reasonably accurate assessments of manifest motives.

Determining latent motives is substantially more complex. Motivation research or **projective techniques** are designed to provide information on latent motives. One example is the third-person technique whereby consumers provide reasons why "other people" might buy a certain brand. Oreo used projective techniques and was surprised to find that "many regarded Oreo as almost 'magical.'" As a result, "Unlocking the Magic of Oreo" became a campaign theme.[15] For more details on projective techniques, see Appendix A and Table A-1.

Beyond projective techniques, a popular tool for identifying motives is **laddering,** or constructing a **means–end** or **benefit chain.**[16] A product or brand is shown to a consumer, who names all the benefits that product might provide. For each of these benefits, the respondent is then asked to identify further benefits. This is repeated until no additional benefits are identified.

For example, a respondent might mention "fewer colds" as a benefit of taking a daily vitamin. When asked the benefit of fewer colds, one respondent might identify "more efficient at work" and "more energy." Another might name "more skiing" and "looking better." Both use the vitamin to reduce colds but as a means to different ultimate benefits. *How should vitamin ads aimed at each of these two consumers differ?*

Marketing Strategies Based on Multiple Motives

Once a manager has isolated the combination of motives influencing the target market, the next task is to design the marketing strategy around the appropriate set of motives. This involves everything from product design to marketing communications. The nature of these decisions is most apparent in the communications area. Suppose the motives shown in Figure 10-1 are an accurate reflection of a desired target market. *What communications strategy should the manager use?*

One consideration is the extent to which more than one motive is important. If multiple motives are important, the product and ads must provide and communicate them, respectively. A second consideration is whether the motive is manifest or latent. Communicating manifest benefits is relatively easy. For example, J. Crew's website provides

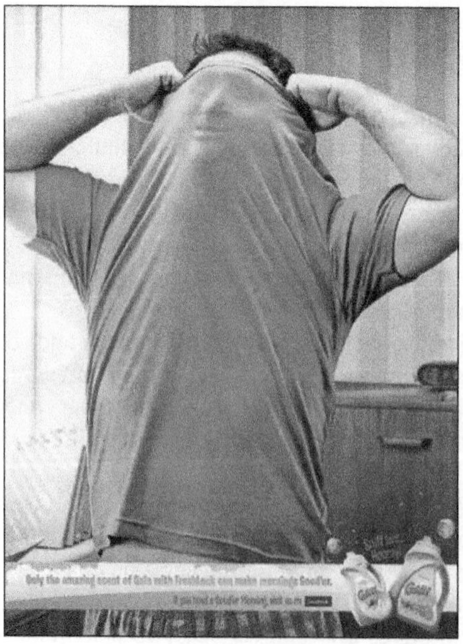

ILLUSTRATION 10–6

Most ads appeal to multiple motives and desires. Both the picture and the text should be based on the set of motives associated with acquiring and using the brand.

hundreds of thumbnails of its many different products by category so that consumers can visually evaluate their products in terms of style, color, and quality. This is a *direct appeal* to manifest motives. However, since latent motives often are less than completely socially desirable, *indirect appeals* frequently are used. So J. Crew's website uses font, white space, designer collections, and so forth, to *indirectly suggest* its upscale and trendy nature.

Any given ad may focus on only one or a few purchasing motives. However, the campaign needs to cover all the important purchase motives of the target market to position the product in their schematic memory in a manner that corresponds to their manifest and latent motives for the product. *To what motives does the ad shown in Illustration 10–6 appeal?*

Motivation and Consumer Involvement

As we have seen in previous chapters, involvement is an important determinant of how consumers process information and learn. We will also see in future chapters that involvement is an important determinant of how consumers form attitudes and make purchase decisions. **Involvement** is a motivational state caused by consumer perceptions that a product, brand, or advertisement is relevant or interesting.[17] Needs play a strong role in determining what is relevant or interesting to consumers. For example, watches may be involving because they tell time (utilitarian need), because they allow for self-expression (expressive need), or because they provide a way to fit in (affiliation need).[18] In addition, the situation itself may influence involvement. For example, some consumers may be involved with computers on an ongoing basis (enduring involvement), while others may only be involved in specific situations such as an upcoming purchase (situational involvement).

Involvement is important to marketers because it affects numerous consumer behaviors. For example, consumer involvement increases attention, analytical processing, information search, and word of mouth.[19] Involvement is also important to marketers because it affects marketing strategies. For example, high-involvement consumers tend to be product experts and are more persuaded by ads that include detailed product information. On the other hand, low-involvement consumers lack product expertise and are more persuaded by images, emotion, and message source. As a consequence, you will often find highly informational ads for automobiles in magazines, such as *Car and Driver,* that are targeted at high-involvement consumers. Alternatively, image and emotional approaches are often the norm in general interest magazines where involvement is likely moderate to low.

Marketing Strategies Based on Motivation Conflict

With the many motives consumers have, there are frequent conflicts between motives. Resolution of a motivational conflict often affects consumption patterns. In many instances, the marketer can analyze situations that are likely to result in a motivational conflict, provide a solution to the conflict, and thus encourage purchase of their brand. We address the three key types of motivation conflict next.

Approach–Approach Motivational Conflict   A consumer who must choose between two attractive alternatives faces **approach–approach conflict.** The more equal the attractions, the greater the conflict. A consumer who recently received a large cash gift for graduation (situational variable) might be torn between a trip to Hawaii (perhaps powered by a need for stimulation) and a new mountain bike (perhaps driven by the need for assertion). This conflict could be resolved by a timely ad designed to encourage one or the other action. Or a price modification, such as "buy now, pay later," could result in a resolution whereby both alternatives are selected.

Approach–Avoidance Motivational Conflict   A consumer facing a purchase choice with both positive and negative consequences confronts **approach–avoidance conflict.** Consumers who want a tan but don't want to risk the skin damage and health risks associated with extended sun exposure face this situation. Neutrogena's Instant Bronze sunless tanner resolves this problem by allowing consumers the aesthetic and social benefits of having a tan (approach) without the risk of skin cancer (avoidance).

Avoidance–Avoidance Motivational Conflict   A choice involving only undesirable outcomes produces **avoidance–avoidance conflict.** When a consumer's old washing machine fails, this conflict may occur. The person may not want to spend money on a new washing machine, or pay to have the old one repaired, or go without one. The availability of credit is one way of reducing this motivational conflict. Advertisements emphasizing the importance of regular maintenance for cars, such as oil filter changes, also use this type of motive conflict: "Pay me now, or pay me (more) later."

Marketing Strategies Based on Regulatory Focus

Consumers are often strategic in terms of the behaviors they choose to attain a desired outcome. Some of this, we will see later, is a function of personality. Some of this relates to the particular set of motives that happen to be salient or important when consumers are reacting to stimuli and making decisions. The salience of particular sets of motives triggers consumers to regulate their behavior in different ways in order to achieve desired outcomes. Two prominent sets of motives are termed promotion and prevention. **Promotion-focused motives** revolve around a desire for growth and development and are related to consumers' hopes and aspirations. **Prevention-focused motives** revolve around a desire for safety and security and are related to consumers' sense of duties and obligations.[20]

Regulatory focus theory suggests that consumers will react differently depending on which broad set of motives is most salient. When promotion-focused motives are more salient, consumers seek to gain positive outcomes, think in more abstract terms, make decisions based more on affect and emotion, and prefer speed versus accuracy in their decision making. When prevention-focused motives are more salient, consumers seek to avoid negative outcomes, think in more concrete terms, make decisions based more on factual substantive information, and prefer accuracy over speed in their decision making. In essence, when promotion-focused motives are most salient, consumers are "eager," more risk-seeking decision makers looking for ways to maximize the possibility that they will attain the most positive possible outcomes. When prevention-focused motives are most salient, consumers are "vigilant," more risk-averse decision makers looking for ways to minimize the chances that they will experience negative outcomes and attempt to avoid making mistakes.

Considerable insight has been gained into the motives, characteristics, and decision-making styles that distinguish a promotion focus from a prevention focus. These differences have important marketing consequences, some of which we have already addressed, and some of which will be addressed in later chapters. Table 10-2 describes differences and the marketing-related dimensions to which they relate.

Whether promotion or prevention motives are most salient depends both on the individual and on the situation. Both prevention and promotion motives reside in each person simultaneously. However, as a result of early childhood experiences, one or the other tends to dominate in each person. This aspect is called *chronic accessibility*. That is, these aspects have been a key focus for so long for these consumers that they tend to be brought to mind when stimuli and decisions are encountered. One aspect of this that has important implications for marketers and market segmentation is the fact that promotion-focused individuals tend to possess more independent self-concepts while prevention-focused individuals tend to possess more interdependent self-concepts. As we saw in Chapter 2, such differences relate to global differences across Western (individualistic) and Eastern (interdependent) cultures. Thus, marketers in Asia should expect that on average, consumers will be more naturally prevention focused than those in the United States and Western Europe and would benefit from adapting their strategies accordingly. For example, it appears that ads which "frame" the message in terms of acquiring positive outcomes work better in the United

Differences in Regulatory Focus		TABLE 10-2
Dimension	**Promotion-Focused**	**Prevention-Focused**
Motives	Hopes, wishes, aspirations	Obligations, responsibilities
	Regulate nurturance needs	Regulate security needs
	Growth and development	Status quo
Characteristics		
• Time	Long-term focus	Short-term focus
• Mental imagery	Abstract	Concrete
• Desired steady state	Change	Stability
• Desired feelings	Fun and enjoyment	Safety and security
• Failure emotions	Dejection	Agitation
• Desired self trait	Creativity	Self-control
• Self-concept	Independent	Interdependent
Decision Making		
• Style	Eager style to maximize gains	Vigilant style to minimize losses
• Meta-goals	Speed over accuracy	Accuracy over speed
• Ad cue effects	Affect and emotion	Product facts
• Choice of compromise brand	Lower probability	Higher as compromise brand is less extreme and thus less risky
• Importance of "fit" in brand extensions	Less important	More important as fit reduces risk

States than in China, whereas ads which frame the message in terms of avoiding losses work better in China than in the United States.

Situational factors, such as characteristics of the decision, the environment, and so on, can also *temporarily* make one orientation more prominent. Examples that marketers can use include:

- *Ad theme*—achievement (promotion) versus avoidance (prevention).
- *Message frame*—benefits to be gained (promotion) versus losses to be avoided (prevention).
- *Advertising context*—ad placement in shows, magazines, or websites that are likely to elicit a promotion focus (e.g., *O Magazine,* which focuses on ideals and aspirations) versus those likely to elicit a prevention focus (e.g., *The Evening News,* which tends to focus on negative events).

Consumer Insight 10-1 examines one situational component related to regulatory focus.

PERSONALITY

While motivations are the energizing and directing force that makes consumer behavior purposeful and goal directed, the personality of the consumer helps guide and further direct the behaviors chosen to accomplish goals in different situations. **Personality** is *an individual's characteristic response tendencies across similar situations.* Thus, two consumers might have equal needs for tension reduction, but differ in their level of extroversion, and as a consequence, engage in very different behaviors designed to satisfy that need.

While there are many theories of personality, those found to be most useful in a marketing context are called trait theories. Trait theories examine personality as an individual difference and thus allow marketers to segment consumers as a function of their personality differences. Trait theories assume that (1) all individuals have internal characteristics or

When Consumers Wait Until the Last Minute to Buy

Sometimes consumers put off purchase decisions until the last minute. Have you ever still been shopping on Christmas Eve? Have you ever waited until right before a vacation to book a flight and hotel? Well, you are not alone and the consequences are significant. A recent study examined how people react to different advertising themes when they were either booking a last-minute summer vacation or planning for a winter break vacation many months away. Two ad themes for an online travel service were created, with differing taglines as follows:[21]

- Prevention-focused ad: *Don't get stuck at home! Don't get ripped off!*
- Promotion-focused ad: *Give yourself a memorable vacation! Get the best deals!*

After viewing the ads, consumers were asked how much they would pay for a ticket from the service. The results may surprise you, since scaring people sometimes led to a willingness to pay more, but not always. *Can you predict when the prevention-focused ad worked better and when the promotion-focused ad worked better?* Here are the results:

- Last-minute summer vacation (how much would you pay for a ticket?)
  - Prevention-focused ad—$672
  - Promotion-focused ad—$494
- Future winter break vacation (how much would you pay for a ticket?)
  - Prevention-focused ad—$415
  - Promotion-focused ad—$581

This may seem odd until you consider the fact that when consumers are shopping at the last minute (last-minute summer vacation in the example above), their goals are prevention focused, such as minimizing losses and mistakes. The prevention-focused ad worked best in this situation because it played into consumer fears about those losses. Alternatively, when consumers are shopping well in advance (future winter break vacation in the example above), their goals are promotion-focused goals such as personal growth and aspirations. The promotion-focused ad worked best in this situation because it played into those consumer desires and aspirations.

According to Jennifer Aaker, an expert in this area: [It's] about how people are motivated by hope and optimism on one hand and by fear on the other.

For holiday marketers, the results seem clear—utilize positive (promotion-focused) messages early on, and negative (prevention-focused) messages close to the holiday. Last-minute shoppers beware!

Critical Thinking Questions

1. Why is it that fear-based appeals are not always the most effective?
2. How might airlines and hotels be able to determine and utilize decision timing in their online marketing efforts?
3. Do you see any ethical issues associated with applying knowledge of decision timing to decisions about promotional themes? Explain.

traits related to action tendencies, and (2) there are consistent and measurable differences between individuals on those characteristics. To demonstrate, imagine how you might respond if you were asked to describe the personality of a friend. You might say that one of your friends is aggressive, competitive, and outgoing. What you have described are the behavioral tendencies or *traits* your friend has exhibited over time across a variety of situations. Most trait theories state that traits are inherited or formed at an early age and are relatively unchanging over the years. Differences between personality theories center on which traits or characteristics are the most important.

The Five-Factor Model of Personality	TABLE 10-3

Core Trait	Manifestation
Extroversion	Prefer to be in a large group rather than alone Talkative when with others Bold
Instability	Moody Temperamental Touchy
Agreeableness	Sympathetic Kind to others Polite with others
Openness to experience	Imaginative Appreciative of art Find novel solutions
Conscientiousness	Careful Precise Efficient

Multitrait Approach

Some trait research attempts to examine a consumer's entire personality profile across a set of relatively exhaustive dimensions. Specifically, *multitrait personality theory* identifies several traits that in combination capture a substantial portion of the personality of the individual. The multitrait theory used most commonly by marketers is the **Five-Factor Model.**[22] This theory identifies five basic traits formed by genetics and early learning. These core traits interact and manifest themselves in behaviors triggered by situations. Table 10-3 lists the five traits and some of their manifestations.

The Five-Factor Model has proven useful in such areas as understanding bargaining and complaining behavior[23] and compulsive shopping.[24] There is evidence that it may have validity across cultures.[25] The advantage of a multitrait approach such as this is the broad picture it allows of the determinants of behavior. For example, suppose research focused on the single dimension of extroversion and found that those who complained about a dissatisfactory purchase tended to be extroverts. *What insights does this provide for training those who deal with consumer complaints? What training insights are added if we also learn such people are conscientious?* Clearly, the more we know, the better we can satisfy these customers.

Single-Trait Approach

Single-trait theories emphasize one personality trait as being particularly relevant to understanding a particular set of behaviors. They do not suggest that other traits are nonexistent or unimportant. Rather, they study a single trait for its relevance to a set of behaviors, in our case, consumption-related behaviors. Three such consumer traits are described next. We emphasize that given the strong interrelationship between motivation and personality, it is not uncommon for personality traits to evidence motivational aspects.[26] Traits labeled as "needs" often reflect these motivational bases.

Consumer Ethnocentrism   **Consumer ethnocentrism** *reflects an individual differ-ence in consumers' propensity to be biased against the purchase of foreign products.*[27] Consumers low in ethnocentrism tend to be more open to other cultures, less conservative, and more open to purchasing foreign-made products. Consumers high in ethnocentrism tend to be less open to other cultures, more conservative, and more likely to reject foreign-made products in favor of domestics. As a consequence, Lexington Furniture is tapping into pro-American sentiments by actively promoting the "Made in America" status of its Bob Timberlake line to retailers and consumers.[28] Consumer ethnocentrism is a global phenomenon, thus also affecting perceptions of American brands doing business in other countries.[29]

Need for Cognition   *Need for cognition (NFC)* reflects an individual difference in consumers' propensity to engage in and enjoy thinking.[30] Compared with low-NFC individuals, those high in NFC engage in more effortful processing of persuasive communications, prefer verbal to visual information, and are less swayed by the opinions of others. NFC has obvious implications for marketing communications. In addition, research linking NFC to demographic characteristics such as gender (e.g., women are generally higher in NFC) helps to make this personality factor more actionable in terms of media targeting.[31]

Consumers' Need for Uniqueness   *Consumers' need for uniqueness* reflects an individual difference in consumers' propensity to pursue differentness relative to others through the acquisition, utilization, and disposition of consumer goods.[32] It affects what consumers own and value, why they own it, and how they use it. The concept fits with the increasingly common marketing practice of deliberate scarcity—producing less of an item than the predicted demand. Such a strategy helps preserve the uniqueness of the product and enhances the distinctiveness and status of those who own it.

THE USE OF PERSONALITY IN MARKETING PRACTICE

Sometimes consumers choose products that fit their personality. For example, a timid person might forgo a flashy car because "it's just not me." Other times, consumers use products to bolster an area of their personality where they feel weak. Thus, a timid person who wants to feel more assertive might drive a powerful, flashy sports car. Clearly, products and brands help consumers express their personality.

Brand image is what people think of and feel when they hear or see a brand name (Chapter 9). A particular type of image that some brands acquire is a **brand personality.** Brand personality is *a set of human characteristics that become associated with a brand.* Consumers perceive brand personalities in terms of five basic dimensions, each with several facets as shown in Figure 10-2. A scale has been developed to measure brand personality in the United States and, with adaptations, in countries such as Russia and Chile.[33]

Researchers have drawn the following conclusions about brand personality:[34]

- Consumers readily assign human characteristics to brands.
- Brand personalities create expectations about key brand characteristics.
- Brand personalities are often the basis for a long-term relationship with the brand.

Not surprisingly, marketers are paying increasing attention to brand personality. Jaguar, Reebok, and Sprite are just a few of the many companies that are currently attempting to enhance their brand personalities to better target key customer groups. Jaguar is trying to be less "aloof," Reebok wants to be "hip and aggressive," and Sprite wants more "street cred."[35]

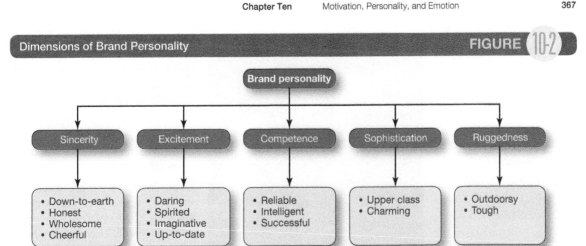

Dimensions of Brand Personality   FIGURE 10-2

The ability of a brand's personality to affect customer relationships is critical, and one study provides key insights. Specifically, consumer relationships with "sincere" brands were found to deepen over time along the lines of a "friendship." Alternatively, consumer relationships with "exciting" brands were found to weaken over time along the lines of a "short-lived fling." This advantage for sincere brands required, however, that the brand consistently deliver high quality.[36]

Nonprofits can also benefit from understanding and managing brand personality. One study shows that nonprofits (compared to for-profits) are generally seen as warmer but less competent. Warmth is related to the sincerity dimension of Figure 10-2. Competence is related to reliability and effectiveness as shown in Figure 10-2. The perceived lack of competence hinders consumer willingness to buy from (or donate to) a nonprofit despite perceptions of the organizations good intentions. However, cues that enhance credibility, such as an endorsement from a credible source, can bridge this gap and therefore increase purchase/donation intentions for the nonprofit firm.[37]

Communicating Brand Personality

Since brand personality can serve as a way to target specific market segments, marketers need to manage and communicate brand personality. Bourjois, a French cosmetics company, created unique makeup sets that communicate distinctive personalities. It used "various cocktails, holiday destinations, [and] fashion statements that have different personality attributes" on its packaging. One set, for example, used the martini and the name *Fabulous Flirtini.* According to Bourjois's branding company Dragon Rouge, the strategy was to

[offer] several different color stories with the same theme to capture as many consumers as possible and to promote a range of personalities to connect with a range of consumers. At the same time the sets reflected the core attributes of Bourjois: profusion of color, joi de vivre, whimsy, sassy and fun.[38]

As you can see, numerous elements can be used to communicate brand personality. Three important advertising tactics are celebrity endorsers, user imagery, and executional factors.[39]

ILLUSTRATION 10–7

People assign personalities to brands whether marketers want them to or not. Therefore, marketing managers increasingly try to manage the brand personalities of their products.

Celebrity Endorsers Celebrity endorsers are often a useful way to personify a brand since the characteristics and meanings of the celebrity can be transferred to the brand. Examples include:[40]

- Nike and Serena Williams—edgy, individualistic brand.
- Revlon and Halle Berry—sexy, confident brand.

User Imagery User imagery involves showing a typical user along with images of the types of activities they engage in while using the brand. User imagery helps define who the typical user is in terms of his or her traits, activities, and emotions. The emotion and tone of the activities can also transfer to the brand. Examples include:[41]

- Mountain Dew—features young, active users engaged in fun and exciting activities.
- Hush Puppies—features "hip young people in a wooded setting."

Executional Factors Executional factors go beyond the core message to include "how" it is communicated. The "tone" of the ad (serious vs. quirky), the appeal used (fear vs. humor), the logo and typeface characteristics (*scripted font* may signal sophistication), the pace of the ad, and even the media outlet chosen can all communicate a brand's personality. Examples include:[42]

- *Tone.* Listerine in Canada wanted a way to be both lighthearted and powerful, so it leveraged an action-hero theme from a popular movie. Listerine went from "old-fashioned and serious," to "powerful and larger than life."
- *Media.* Hush Puppies placed ads in fashion magazines such as *W* and *InStyle* to establish a more hip, fashionable personality.
- *Pace.* Molson in Canada wanted a "spirited, adventurous and slightly naughty" personality. So it created TV ads in which "a festive Latin beat is punctuated with fast-moving, sexually charged party scenes."
- *Logo.* Reebok wanted to invigorate its brand toward a younger, hipper image. So it created the new "Rbk" logo. According to one executive, "Creating a short code gave permission to the youth culture to look at the brand again without the old baggage."

What type of brand personality is created by the ad in Illustration 10–7? What advertising elements are being used?

 LO5

EMOTION

Emotions are strong, relatively uncontrolled feelings that affect behavior.[43] Emotions are strongly linked to needs, motivation, and personality. Unmet needs create motivation, which is related to the arousal component of emotion. Unmet needs generally yield negative emotions, while met needs generally yield positive emotions. As a result, products and brands that generate positive consumption emotions increase consumer satisfaction and loyalty.[44] Personality also plays a role. For example, some people are more emotional than others, a consumer trait termed *affect intensity.*

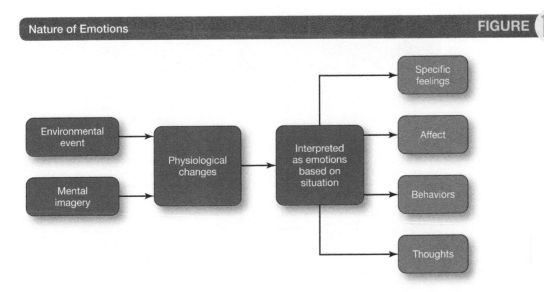

Nature of Emotions   FIGURE 10-3

Consumers higher in affect intensity experience stronger emotions and are more influenced by emotional appeals.[45]

All emotional experiences tend to have several common elements. First, emotions are often triggered by environmental events (e.g., viewing an ad, consuming a product that meets a need). However, they can also be initiated by internal processes such as imagery. As we have seen, advertisers frequently use imagery to evoke specific emotional responses.

Second, emotions are accompanied by *physiological changes* such as (1) eye pupil dilation, (2) increased perspiration, (3) more rapid breathing, (4) increased heart rate and blood pressure, and (5) enhanced blood sugar level. Third, emotions generally, though not necessarily, are accompanied by *cognitive thought*.[46] The types of thoughts and our ability to think rationally vary with the type and degree of emotion.[47]

A fourth characteristic is that emotions have associated *behaviors*. While the behaviors vary across individuals and within individuals across time and situations, there are unique behaviors characteristically associated with different emotions: fear triggers fleeing (avoidance) responses, anger triggers striking out (approach), grief triggers crying, and so forth.[48]

Finally, emotions involve *subjective feelings*. In fact, it is the feeling component we generally refer to when we think of emotions. Grief, joy, anger, and fear feel very different. These subjectively determined feelings are the essence of emotion. These feelings have a specific component we label as the emotion, such as sad or happy. In addition, emotions carry an evaluative, or a like–dislike, component.

We use **emotion** to refer to the identifiable, specific feeling, and *affect* to refer to the liking–disliking aspect of the specific feeling. Emotions are generally evaluated (liked and disliked) in a consistent manner across individuals and within individuals over time, but there are cultural, individual, and situational variations.[49] For example, few of us generally want to be sad or afraid, yet we occasionally enjoy a movie or book that scares or saddens us.

Figure 10-3 reflects current thinking on the nature of emotions.

Types of Emotions

If asked, you could doubtless name numerous emotions. Thus, it is not surprising that researchers have attempted to categorize emotions into manageable clusters. Some researchers have suggested that three basic dimensions—pleasure, arousal, and dominance (PAD)—underlie

TABLE 10-4	Emotional Dimensions, Emotions, and Emotional Indicators	
Dimension	**Emotion**	**Indicator/Feeling**
Pleasure	Duty	Moral, virtuous, dutiful
	Faith	Reverent, worshipful, spiritual
	Pride	Proud, superior, worthy
	Affection	Loving, affectionate, friendly
	Innocence	Innocent, pure, blameless
	Gratitude	Grateful, thankful, appreciative
	Serenity	Restful, serene, comfortable, soothed
	Desire	Desirous, wishful, craving, hopeful
	Joy	Joyful, happy, delighted, pleased
	Competence	Confident, in control, competent
Arousal	Interest	Attentive, curious
	Hypoactivation	Bored, drowsy, sluggish
	Activation	Aroused, active, excited
	Surprise	Surprised, annoyed, astonished
	Déjà vu	Unimpressed, uninformed, unexcited
	Involvement	Involved, informed, enlightened, benefited
	Distraction	Distracted, preoccupied, inattentive
	Surgency	Playful, entertained, lighthearted
	Contempt	Scornful, contemptuous, disdainful
Dominance	Conflict	Tense, frustrated, conflictful
	Guilt	Guilty, remorseful, regretful
	Helplessness	Powerless, helpless, dominated
	Sadness	Sad, distressed, sorrowful, dejected
	Fear	Fearful, afraid, anxious
	Shame	Ashamed, embarrassed, humiliated
	Anger	Angry, agitated, enraged, mad
	Hyperactivation	Panicked, confused, overstimulated
	Disgust	Disgusted, revolted, annoyed, full of loathing
	Skepticism	Skeptical, suspicious, distrustful

Source: Adapted from M. B. Holbrook and R. Batra, "Assessing the Role of Emotions on Consumer Responses to Advertising," *Journal of Consumer Research*, December 1987, pp. 404–20. Copyright © 1987 by the University of Chicago. Used by permission.

all emotions. Specific emotions reflect various combinations and levels of these three dimensions. Table 10-4 lists the three primary PAD dimensions, a variety of emotions or emotional categories associated with each dimension, and indicators or items that can be used to measure each emotion.

EMOTIONS AND MARKETING STRATEGY

Emotions play a role in a wide range of marketing situations relating to products, retailing, consumer coping, and advertising. We examine each of these in the following sections.

Emotion Arousal as a Product and Retail Benefit

Emotions are characterized by positive or negative evaluations. Consumers actively seek products whose primary or secondary benefit is emotion arousal.[50] Movies, books, and music are obvious examples,[51] as are resort destinations such as Las Vegas and adventure travel programs. Recent advertisements designed to fuel consumer emotion and excitement about brands include Bacardi rum's "Shake up your night," Pontiac G6's "Move like a shaker," and Chevrolet's "An American Revolution." Beyond products and brands, retailers also feature events and environments that arouse emotions such as excitement. For example, websites using avatars are perceived as more social, which enhances pleasure, arousal, perceived hedonic value, and purchase intentions.[52]

One specific emotion that is getting increased attention in terms of relationship marketing is **gratitude.** Gratitude in a consumer context is *the emotional appreciation for benefits received.* Firms can invest in relationship improvements in many ways, including time, effort, investments in equipment specific to the customer, and so on. Research shows that these relationship marketing efforts on the part of the firm lead to the following outcomes:

* Increased consumer gratitude
* Increased consumer trust in the firm
* Increased customer purchases
* Increased "gratitude-based reciprocity" behaviors

Gratitude-based reciprocity behaviors include (a) buying products based on gratitude for the relationship marketing efforts, (b) giving more business to the firm due to feelings of "owing" them, (c) buying a broader set of products from the firm as a "payback" for their prior relationship marketing efforts, and positive word of mouth. Gratitude, it turns out, is a powerful emotion. It causes consumers to want to reward firms for their relationship marketing efforts in ways that lead to greater sales and positive word of mouth.[53]

Although consumers seek positive emotions the majority of the time, this is not always the case, as when we enjoy a sad movie. Additionally, products can arouse negative emotions, such as the frustration and anger we feel when high-tech gadgets are difficult to use.[54]

Emotion Reduction as a Product and Retail Benefit

Few people like to feel sad, powerless, humiliated, or disgusted. Responding to this, marketers design or position many products to prevent or reduce the arousal of unpleasant emotions. The most obvious of these products are the various over-the-counter medications designed to deal with anxiety or depression. Food and alcohol are consumed, often harmfully, to reduce stress. Flowers are heavily promoted as an antidote to sadness. Weight-loss products and other self-improvement products are frequently positioned primarily in terms of guilt-, helplessness-, shame-, or disgust-reduction benefits. Personal grooming products often emphasize anxiety reduction as a major benefit. Charities frequently stress guilt reduction or avoidance as a reason for contributing.[55]

Consumer Coping in Product and Service Encounters

Consumers must cope with the negative emotions they experience in various marketing situations. **Coping** *involves consumer thoughts and behaviors in reaction to a stress-inducing situation designed to reduce stress and achieve more desired positive emotions.*[56] Avoidance is a common mechanism. For example, when a decision involves a trade-off that evokes strong negative emotions (e.g., price versus safety), consumers will often delay the purchase to avoid making a decision.[57] In retail settings, consumers in a bad mood attempt to cope by avoiding salespeople they perceive as happy. However, if they are forced to deal with a happy salesperson, it makes them feel worse, which reduces salesperson effectiveness.[58] *What marketing and training aspects relating to service personnel does this suggest?*

One typology of coping strategies categorizes three broad types in response to negative emotions emanating from stressful events such as bad customer service or product failure. The three types are:[59]

- *Active coping.* Thinking of ways to solve the problem, engaging in restraint to avoid rash behavior, and making the best of the situation.
- *Expressive support seeking.* Venting emotions and seeking emotional and problem-focused assistance from others.
- *Avoidance.* Avoiding the retailer mentally or physically or engaging in complete self-denial of the event.

Each strategy can have positive and negative marketing consequences. Active coping may involve working with the company to resolve the situation or switching from the firm altogether. Likewise, consumers may vent to the company (expressive support seeking), which is desirable, or they may vent to friends (negative WOM), which is damaging. Finally, denial (avoidance) may result in customer retention, but physical avoidance of the retailer will result in lost sales. As you can see, proper training of service personnel to handle product and service failures as well as the careful design of retail and service facilities to reduce stressors are critical.

Consumer ability to *effectively* cope with stressful situations relates to the concept of **consumer emotional intelligence.** Consumer emotional intelligence is defined as *a person's ability to skillfully use emotional information to achieve a desirable consumer outcome.* It is an ability variable rather than a personality trait. Consumers higher in emotional intelligence are better at perceiving, facilitating, understanding, and managing emotional information. For example, consumers with higher emotional intelligence may understand better how to channel their feelings of anger over a service failure to obtain a solution that is desirable to them.[60] A failure to appropriately channel such feelings can result in "rage episodes," which appear to be on the increase in the United States. In response, firms need to better understand what triggers rage episodes and train their employees so they can (a) engage in behaviors to minimize their likelihood, and (b) train their employees to effectively and safely handle such rage episodes when they do occur.[61]

EMOTION IN ADVERTISING

Emotion arousal is often used in advertising regardless of whether it is specifically relevant to the brand's performance. Consider the following recent headlines:

- Under Armour taps raw emotion.
- Kleenex for Men to play on emotion in TV return.
- Emotional appeal of laundry to replace performance claims in ads.

Illustration 10–8 provides an example of the effective use of emotion to attract attention to an ad and to position a brand.

Emotions can play a variety of roles in advertising. Emotional content in ads *enhances their attention, attraction, and maintenance capabilities.* Advertising messages that trigger the emotional reactions of joy, warmth, and suspense[62] are more likely to be attended to than are more neutral ads. As we saw in Chapter 8, attention is a critical early step in the perception process.

Emotions are characterized by a state of heightened physiological arousal. Individuals become more alert and active when aroused. Given this enhanced level of arousal,

emotional messages may be processed more thoroughly than neutral messages. More effort and increased elaboration activities may occur in response to the emotional state.[63] As a consequence of this greater attention and processing, emotional ads *may be remembered better than neutral ads.*[64]

Emotional advertisements that *trigger a positively evaluated emotion will enhance liking of the ad itself.*[65] For example, warmth is a positively valued emotion that is triggered by experiencing directly or vicariously a love, family, or friendship relationship. Ads high in warmth are liked more than neutral ads. Liking an ad has a positive impact on liking the product and purchase intentions.[66] As you might suspect, ads that irritate or disgust consumers can create negative reactions to the advertised brand.[67]

Repeated exposure to positive-emotion-eliciting ads *may increase brand preference through classical conditioning.*[68] Repeated pairings of positive emotion (unconditioned response) with the brand name (conditioned stimulus) may result in the positive affect occurring when the brand name is presented. *Brand preference may also occur in a direct, high-involvement way.* A person having a single or few exposures to an emotional ad may simply decide they like the product. This is a much more conscious process than implied by classical conditioning. Such a process seems more likely for hedonic products involving high levels of emotional value rather than utilitarian products. For hedonic products, ad-evoked emotion is a relevant cue on which to base a product evaluation.[69]

Advertising using emotional appeals continues to be popular. For example, Zippo launched an emotion-based campaign for its lighters. It used eight print ads, each with a picture of an engraved lighter and a simple headline "True Love Is Not Disposable." A spokesperson said of the campaign, "We wanted to make a human, emotional attachment."[70] Illustration 10–9 shows how Geico taps into emotions through the use of nostalgia.

SUMMARY

LO1: Define motivation and summarize the motivation sets put forth by Maslow and McGuire

Consumer motivations are energizing forces that activate behavior and provide purpose and direction to that behavior. There are numerous motivation theories. Maslow's need hierarchy states that basic motives must be minimally satisfied before more advanced motives are activated. It proposes five levels of motivation: physiological, safety, belongingness, esteem, and self-actualization.

McGuire developed a more detailed set of motives—the needs for consistency, attribution, categorization, objectification, autonomy, stimulation, desired outcomes (teleological), utility, tension reduction, expression, ego defense, reinforcement, assertion, affiliation, identification, and modeling.

LO2: Articulate motivation's role in consumer behavior and marketing strategy

Consumers are often aware of and will admit to the motives causing their behavior. These are *manifest motives*. They can be discovered by standard marketing research techniques such as direct questioning. Direct advertising appeals can be made to these motives. At other times, consumers are unable or unwilling to admit to the motives that are influencing them. These are *latent motives*. They can be determined by motivation research techniques such as word association, sentence completion, and picture response (see Appendix Table A-1). Although direct advertising appeals can be used, indirect appeals are often necessary. Both manifest and latent motives are operative in many purchase situations.

Involvement is a motivational state caused by consumer perceptions that a product, brand, or advertisement is relevant or interesting. Consumer needs play a strong role in shaping involvement and marketers must adapt their strategies depending on the level (high versus low) and type (enduring versus situational) of involvement exhibited by their target audience.

Because of the large number of motives and the many different situations that consumers face, motivational conflict can occur. In an *approach–approach conflict,* the consumer faces a choice between two attractive alternatives. In an *approach–avoidance conflict,* the consumer faces both positive and negative consequences in the purchase of a particular product. And finally, in an *avoidance–avoidance conflict,* the consumer faces two undesirable alternatives.

Regulatory focus theory suggests that consumers react differently depending on whether promotion-focused or prevention-focused motives are most salient. When promotion-focused motives are more salient, consumers seek to gain positive outcomes, think in more abstract terms, make decisions based more on affect and emotion, and prefer speed versus accuracy in their decision making. When prevention-focused motives are more salient, consumers seek to avoid negative outcomes, think in more concrete terms, make decisions based more on factual substantive information, and prefer accuracy over speed in their decision making. Which motive set is more salient can depend on individual and situational factors and has numerous marketing implications.

LO3: Define personality and the various theories of personality

The *personality* of a consumer guides and directs the behavior chosen to accomplish goals in different situations. Trait theories of personality assume that (1) all individuals have internal characteristics or traits related to action tendencies, and (2) there are consistent and measurable differences between individuals on those characteristics. Most of these theories assume that traits are formed at an early age and are relatively unchanging over the years.

Multitrait theories attempt to capture a significant portion of a consumer's total personality using a set of personality attributes. The Five-Factor Model of personality is the most widely used multitrait approach. Single-trait theories focus on one aspect of personality in an attempt to understand a limited part of consumer behavior. Various traits related specifically to consumer behavior include consumer ethnocentricity, need for cognition, and consumers' need for uniqueness.

LO4: Discuss how brand personality can be used in developing marketing strategies

Brands, like individuals, have personalities, and consumers tend to prefer products with brand personalities that are pleasing to them. Consumers also prefer advertising messages that portray their own or a desired personality. Brand personality can be communicated in a number of ways, including celebrity endorsers, user imagery, and executional ad elements such as tone and pace.

LO5: Define emotions and list the major emotional dimensions

Emotions are strong, relatively uncontrollable feelings that affect our behavior. Emotions occur when environmental events or our mental processes trigger physiological changes such as increased heart rate. These changes are interpreted as specific emotions resulting from the situation. They affect consumers' thoughts and behaviors. The major dimensions of emotion are pleasure, arousal, and dominance. Each of these major dimensions has specific emotions and feelings associated with it.

LO6: Discuss how emotions can be used in developing marketing strategies

Marketers design and position products to both arouse and reduce emotions. In addition, consumers must cope with stressful marketing situations such as service and product failures. The various coping mechanisms can be beneficial or detrimental to the firm depending on various factors and requires that marketers consider not only their responses to failure but also service-setting design to reduce consumer stressors. Advertisements include emotion-arousing material to increase attention, degree of processing, remembering, and brand preference through classical conditioning or direct evaluation.

KEY TERMS

Approach–approach conflict 361
Approach–avoidance conflict 361
Avoidance–avoidance conflict 361
Attribution theory 354
Benefit chain 360
Brand personality 366
Consumer emotional
   intelligence 372
Consumer ethnocentrism 366

Coping 371
Demand 359
Emotion 369
Five-Factor Model 365
Gratitude 371
Involvement 361
Laddering 360
Latent motives 359
Manifest motives 359

Maslow's hierarchy of needs 352
Means–end chain 360
Motivation 352
Motive 352
Personality 363
Prevention-focused motives 362
Projective techniques 360
Promotion-focused motives 362
Regulatory focus theory 362

INTERNET EXERCISES

1. Visit several company websites. Find and describe one that makes effective use of an appeal or theme based on the following:
   a. One of Maslow's need hierarchy levels
   b. One of McGuire's motives
   c. An emotional appeal

2. Visit several general interest or entertainment sites on the Internet that contain ads. Find and describe an ad that uses the following:
   a. One of Maslow's need hierarchy levels
   b. One of McGuire's motives
   c. An emotional appeal

3. Monitor a hobby- or product-based interest group for a week. What types of motives and emotions are involved with the activity or product? What are the marketing implications of this?

4. Go to http://www.ceis-research.com. Complete the Consumer Emotional Intelligence Questionnaire on Survey Monkey. Write and report about the questionnaire and its dimensions. *Is this a good survey instrument to capture CEI as defined in the text?* Explain.

DDB LIFE STYLE STUDY™ DATA ANALYSES

1. Examine the DDB data in Tables 1B through 7B. What characterizes someone who *wants to look a little different from others*? Which factors contribute most? Which of McGuire's motives does this most relate to, and what are the marketing implications of your findings?

2. What characterizes someone who *views shopping as a form of entertainment* (Tables 1B through 7B)? Which factors contribute most? How do your

findings relate to the information presented in Consumer Insight 10-1?

3. Some people feel (and act) more self-confident than others. Based on the DDB data (Tables 1B through 7B), what factors are most characteristic of highly confident individuals? Which of the Big Five personality dimensions does self-confidence relate most to, and what are the marketing implications of your findings?

REVIEW QUESTIONS

1. What is a *motive*?

2. What is meant by a *motive hierarchy*? How does Maslow's hierarchy of needs function?

3. Describe each level of Maslow's hierarchy of needs.

4. Describe each of McGuire's motives.

5. Describe *attribution theory.*

6. What is meant by *motivational conflict,* and what relevance does it have for marketing managers?

7. What is a *manifest motive*? A *latent motive*? How is each measured?

8. How do you appeal to manifest motives? Latent motives?

9. Describe the following motivation research techniques (see Appendix A and Appendix Table A-1 for details):
   a. Association
   b. Completion
   c. Construction

10. What is the relationship between *involvement* and *motivation*?

11. Describe *regulatory focus theory.*

12. What is *personality*?

13. What is *consumer ethnocentrism* and why is it important to global marketers?

14. How can knowledge of personality be used to develop marketing strategy?

15. What is an *emotion*? What are the basic dimensions of emotion?

16. What physiological changes accompany emotional arousal?

17. What factors characterize emotions?

18. What is consumer *gratitude,* and what outcomes are associated with this emotion?

19. How do marketers use emotions in product design and advertising?

20. What is *coping* and what are the general types of coping mechanisms used by consumers?

DISCUSSION QUESTIONS

21. How could Maslow's motive hierarchy be used to develop marketing strategy for the following?
    a. American Bird Conservancy
    b. Redken shampoo
    c. Purell hand sanitizer
    d. Chipotle Mexican Grill
    e. BlackBerry
    f. Crest Whitestrips

22. Which of McGuire's motives would be useful in developing a promotional campaign for the following? Why?
    a. Cadillac CTS
    b. Precision Cuts (hair salon chain)
    c. Nokia cell phones
    d. Just for Men hair coloring
    e. Twitter
    f. Habitat for Humanity

23. Describe how motivational conflict might arise in purchasing, patronizing, or giving to the following:
    a. Greenpeace
    b. Chevy Volt
    c. Walmart
    d. Red Bull energy drink
    e. Taco Bell restaurant
    f. Home security system

24. Describe the manifest and latent motives that might arise in purchasing, shopping at, or giving to the following:
    a. Yukon hybrid
    b. Saks Fifth Avenue

c. Bose sound system
d. Kitten
e. Mercedes-Benz convertible
f. iPhone

25. Do marketers create needs? Do they create demand? What ethical issues are relevant?

26. Respond to the questions in Consumer Insight 10-1.

27. How might knowledge of personality be used to develop an advertising campaign for the following?
    a. Rainforest Action Network (an environmental group)
    b. Smartphones
    c. American Express financial services
    d. Ready-to-drink iced tea
    e. J. Crew women's shoes
    f. Clinique cosmetics

28. Using Table 10-3, discuss how you would use one of the core personality source traits in developing a package design for an organic, shade-grown coffee.

29. How would the media preferences of those on each end of the consumer need for uniqueness continuum differ?

30. How would the shopping behaviors of those on each end of the ethnocentrism continuum differ?

31. How would you use emotion to develop a marketing strategy for each of the following?
    a. Visa card use
    b. Sky diving
    c. Orthodontist
    d. Silk (soy milk)
    e. Honda Civic Hybrid
    f. Iceland

32. List all the emotions you can think of. Which ones are not explicitly mentioned in Table 10-4? Where would you place them in this table?

APPLICATION ACTIVITIES

33. Develop an advertisement for one of the items in Question 21 based on relevant motives from McGuire's set.

34. Repeat Question 33 using Maslow's need hierarchy.

35. Repeat Question 33 using emotions.

36. Find and copy or describe two advertisements that appeal to each level of Maslow's hierarchy. Explain why the ads appeal to the particular levels, and speculate on why the firm decided to appeal to these levels.

37. Find and copy or describe an ad that contains direct appeals to manifest motives and indirect appeals to latent motives. Explain how and why the ad is using each approach.

38. Select a product of interest and use motivation research techniques to determine the latent purchase motives for five consumers (see Appendix A and Appendix Table A-1 for details).

39. Have five students describe the personality of the following. To what extent are their descriptions similar? Why are there differences?
    a. Swatch watches
    b. Prada sunglasses
    c. Toyota
    d. Dell computer
    e. Cheesecake Factory restaurant
    f. The university bookstore

40. Find and copy an ad that you feel communicates a strong brand personality. Describe that personality in terms of the dimensions in Figure 10-2. Describe the various techniques used in the ad (e.g., celebrity endorser, user imagery, and executional factors) and how that links to the personality they are communicating.

41. Find and copy an ad with strong emotional appeals and another ad from the same product category with limited emotional appeals. Why do the companies use different appeals?
    a. Have 10 students rank or rate the ads in terms of their preferences and then explain their rankings or ratings.
    b. Have 10 different students talk about their reactions to each ad as they view it. What do you conclude?

42. Ask two students to describe the coping mechanisms they use when dealing with product or service failures. Identify factors that cause their coping to be beneficial (e.g., complaining to the company) rather than detrimental (e.g., negative WOM) to the firm.

REFERENCES

1. This insight is based on B. Ellis and P. Valdes-Dapena, "Toyota's Big Recall Halts Sales, Production of 8 Models," *CNNMoney.com*, February 10, 2010; "Toyota Announces January 2010 Recall for 2.3 Million Vehicles to Fix Sticky Accelerator Pedal," www.autos.aol.com, January 21, 2010, accessed June 6, 2011; B. Steinberg, "Lightspeed Survey," *Advertising Age*, February 2010, pp. 2 and 18; "U.S. Auto Sales by Brand—February 2011," www.goodcarbadcar.net, accessed June 6, 2011; and information from Toyota's website at www.toyota.com.

2. A. H. Maslow, *Motivation and Personality*, 2nd ed. (New York: Harper & Row, 1970).

3. See R. Yalch and F. Brunel, "Need Hierarchies in Consumer Judgments of Product Designs," *Advances in Consumer Research*, vol. 23, ed. K. P. Corfman and J. G. Lynch (Provo, UT: Association for Consumer Research, 1996), pp. 405–10.

4. W. J. McGuire, "Psychological Motives and Communication Gratification," in *The Uses of Mass Communications*, ed. J. G. Blumler and C. Katz (Newbury Park, CA: Sage, 1974), pp. 167–96; and W. J. McGuire, "Some Internal Psychological Factors Influencing Consumer Choice," *Journal of Consumer Research*, March 1976, pp. 302–19.

5. See A. G. Woodside and J.-C. Chebat, "Updating Heider's Balance Theory in Consumer Behavior," *Psychology & Marketing,* May 2001, pp. 475–95.

6. M. C. Campbell and A. Kirmani, "Consumers' Use of Persuasion Knowledge," *Journal of Consumer Research,* June 2000, pp. 69–83; and R. N. Laczniak, T. E. DeCarlo, and S. N. Ramaswami, "Consumers' Responses to Negative Word-of-Mouth Communication," *Journal of Consumer Psychology* 11, no. 31 (2001), pp. 57–73.

7. See M. Friestad and P. Wright, "Persuasion Knowledge," *Journal of Consumer Research,* June 1995, pp. 62–74.

8. See B. H. Schmit and S. Zhang, "Language Structure and Categorization," *Journal of Consumer Research,* September 1998, pp. 108–22; and J. A. Rosa and J. F. Porac, "Categorization Bases and Their Influence on Product Category Knowledge Structures," *Psychology & Marketing,* June 2002, pp. 503–32.

9. M. Lynn and J. Harris, "The Desire for Unique Consumer Products," *Psychology & Marketing,* September 1997, pp. 601–16.

10. R. K. Ratner, B. E. Kahn, and D. Kahneman, "Choosing Less-Preferred Experiences for the Sake of Variety," *Journal of Consumer Research,* June 1999, pp. 1–15; and R. K. Ratner and B. E. Kahn, "The Impact of Private versus Public Consumption on Variety-Seeking Behavior," *Journal of Consumer Research,* September 2002, pp. 246–57.

11. M. Trivedi, "Using Variety-Seeking-Based Segmentation to Study Promotional Response," *Journal of the Academy of Marketing Science,* Winter 1999, pp. 37–49; M. Trivedi and M. S. Morgan, "Promotional Evaluation and Response among Variety Seeking Segments," *Journal of Product and Brand Management* 12, no. 6 (2003), pp. 408–25; and J. Chen and S. Paliwoda, "The Influence of Company Name in Consumer Variety Seeking," *Brand Management,* February 2004, pp. 219–31.

12. See D. Goldman, "Pain? It's a Pleasure," *American Demographics,* January 2000, pp. 60–61; and J. J. Inman, "The Role of Sensory-Specific Satiety in Attribute-Level Variety Seeking," *Journal of Consumer Research,* June 2001, pp. 105–19.

13. See G. M. Zinkhan, J. W. Hong, and R. Lawson, "Achievement and Affiliation Motivation," *Journal of Business Research,* March 1990, pp. 135–43.

14. Porsche example from A. Taylor III, "Porsche Slices Up Its Buyers," *Fortune,* January 6, 1995, p. 24. Indian car example from "New Car Buyers in India Seek Emotive Needs," *indiatelevision .com,* December 21, 2004, at www.indiatelevision.com, accessed June 7, 2011.

15. C. Rubel, "Three Firms Show That Good Research Makes Good Ads," *Marketing News,* March 13, 1995, p. 18.

16. T. J. Reynolds and J. C. Olson, *Understanding Consumer Decision Making* (Mahwah, NJ: Erlbaum, 2001); G. S. Mort and T. Rose, "The Effect of Product Type on Value Linkages in the Means-End Chain," *Journal of Consumer Behaviour,* March 2004, pp. 221–34; and F. Huber, S. C. Beckmann, and A. Herrmann, "Means-End Analysis," *Psychology & Marketing,* September 2004, pp. 715–37.

17. See J. L. Zaichkowsky, "The Personal Involvement Inventory," *Journal of Advertising,* December 1994, pp. 59–70.

18. See P. Quester and A. L. Lim, "Product Involvement/Brand Loyalty," *Journal of Product and Brand Management* 12, no. 1 (2003), pp. 22–38.

19. See U. M. Dholakia, "A Motivational Process Model of Product Involvement and Consumer Risk Perception," *European Journal of Marketing* 35, no. 11/12 (2001), pp. 1340–60; and C.-W. Park and B.-J. Moon, "The Relationship between Product Involvement and Product Knowledge," *Psychology & Marketing,* November 2003, pp. 977–97.

20. This section on regulatory focus, including Table 10-2, is based on the following: E. T. Higgins, "Beyond Pleasure and Pain," *American Psychologist,* December 1997, pp. 1280–1300; J. L. Aaker and A. Y. Lee, " 'I' Seek Pleasures and 'We' Avoid Pains," *Journal of Consumer Research,* June 2001, pp. 33–49; A. Chernev, "Goal-Attribute Compatibility in Consumer Choice," *Journal of Consumer Psychology* 14, nos. 1 & 2 (2004), pp. 141–50; M. T. Pham and T. Avnet, "Ideals and Oughts and the Reliance on Affect versus Substance in Persuasion," *Journal of Consumer Research,* March 2004, pp. 503–18; A. Bosmans and H. Baumgartner, "Goal-Relevant Emotional Information," *Journal of Consumer Research,* December 2005, pp. 424–34; J. L. Aaker and A. Y. Lee, "Understanding Regulatory Fit," *Journal of Marketing Research,* February 2006, pp. 15–19; T. Avnet and E. T. Higgins, "How Regulatory Fit Affects Value in Consumer Choices and Opinions," *Journal of Marketing Research,* February 2006, pp. 1–10; Y-J. Kim, "The Role of Regulatory Focus in Message Framing in Antismoking Advertisements for Adolescents," *Journal of Advertising,* Spring 2006, pp. 143–51; J. Yeo and J. Park, "Effects of Parent-Extension Similarity and Self Regulatory Focus on Evaluations of Brand Extensions," *Journal of Consumer Psychology* 16, no. 3 (2006), pp. 272–82; M. Mourali, U. Bockenholt, and M. Laroche, "Compromise and Attraction Effects under Prevention and Promotion Motivations," *Journal of Consumer Research,* August 2007, pp. 234–47; and A. Y. Lee, P. A. Keller, and B. Sternthal, "Value from Regulatory Construal Fit," *Journal of Consumer Research,* February 2010, pp. 735–74.

21. This insight is based on "No Time Before Valentine's Day?" *Science Daily,* January 27, 2008; C. Mogilner, J. L. Aaker, and G. L. Pennington, "Time Will Tell," *Journal of Consumer Research,* February 2008, pp. 670–81; and S. Vedantam, "Care to Know the Motivation Behind That Gift, Love?" *The Washington Post,* February 11, 2008, p A3.

22. See J. S. Wiggins, *The Five-Factor Model of Personality* (New York: Guilford Press, 1996).

23. E. G. Harris and J. C. Mowen, "The Influence of Cardinal-, Central-, and Surface-Level Personality Traits on Consumers' Bargaining and Complaint Behaviors," *Psychology & Marketing,* November 2001, pp. 1155–85.

24. J. C. Mowen and N. Spears, "Understanding Compulsive Buying among College Students," *Journal of Consumer Psychology* 8, no. 4 (1999), pp. 407–30.

25. W. Na and R. Marshall, "Validation of the 'Big Five' Personality Traits in Korea," *Journal of International Consumer Marketing* 12, no. 1 (1999), pp. 5–19.

26. See N. Brody and H. Ehrlichman, *Personality Psychology* (Englewood Cliffs, NJ: Prentice Hall, 1998); and A. Deponte, "Linking Motivation to Personality," *European Journal of Personality* 18 (2004), pp. 31–44.

27. See S. Sharma, T. A. Shimp, and J. Shin, "Consumer Ethnocentrism," *Journal of the Academy of Marketing Science,* Winter 1995, pp. 26–37; and G. Balabanis and

A. Diamantopoulos, "Domestic Country Bias, Country-of-Origin Effects, and Consumer Ethnocentrism," *Journal of the Academy of Marketing Science,* Winter 2004, pp. 80–95.

28. J. Linville, "Lexington Touts Timberlake as "Made in America" Line," *Furniture Today,* October 13, 2003, p. 98.

29. M. Supphellen and K. Gronhaug, "Building Foreign Brand Personalities in Russia," *International Journal of Advertising* 22, no. 2 (2003), pp. 203–26; and H. Kwak, A. Jaju, and T. Larsen, "Consumer Ethnocentrism Offline and Online," *Journal of the Academy of Marketing Science,* Summer 2006, pp. 367–85.

30. C. S. Areni, M. E. Ferrell, and J. B. Wilcox, "The Persuasive Impact of Reported Group Opinions on Individuals Low vs. High in Need for Cognition," *Psychology & Marketing,* October 2000, pp. 855–75; J. Z. Sojka and J. L. Giese, "The Influence of Personality Traits on the Processing of Visual and Verbal Information," *Marketing Letters,* February 2001, pp. 91–106.

31. See, e.g., L. K. Waters and T. D. Zakrajsek, "Correlates of Need for Cognition Total and Subscale Scores," *Educational and Psychological Measurement,* Spring 1990, pp. 213–17.

32. K. T. Tian, W. O. Bearden, and G. L. Hunter, "Consumers' Need for Uniqueness," *Journal of Consumer Research,* June 2001, pp. 50–66. See also K. T. Tian and K. McKenzie, "The Long-Term Predictive Validity of the Consumers' Need for Uniqueness Scale," *Journal of Consumer Psychology* 10, no. 3 (2001), pp. 171–93.

33. J. L. Aaker, "Dimensions of Brand Personality," *Journal of Marketing Research,* August 1997, pp. 347–56. For international adaptations, see Supphellen and Gronhaug, "Building Foreign Brand Personalities in Russia"; J. I. Rojas-Mendez, I. ErenchunPodlech, and E. Silva-Olave, "The Ford Brand Personality in Chile," *Corporate Reputation Review,* Fall 2004, pp. 232–51; and Y. Sung and S. F. Tinkham, "Brand Personality Structures in the United States and Korea," *Journal of Consumer Psychology* 15, no. 4, (2005), pp. 334–50.

34. Ibid. Also see T. Triplett, "Brand Personality Must Be Managed or It Will Assume a Life of Its Own," *Marketing News,* May 9, 1994, p. 9.

35. K. Greenberg, "Levinson: Jaguar Ads to Stress Quality, Youth, a Bit of Humor," *Brandweek,* April 26, 2004, p. 32; B. Russak, "Calling the Shots," *Footwear News,* October 25, 2004, p. 42; and K. MacArthur and J. Neff, "Sprite Shifts Gears in Quest for Street Cred," *Advertising Age,* January 26, 2004, p. 1.

36. J. Aaker, S. Fournier, and S. A. Brasel, "When Good Brands Do Bad," *Journal of Consumer Research,* June 2004, pp. 1–16.

37. J. Aaker, K. D. Vohs, and C. Mogilner, "Nonprofits Are Seen as Warm and For-Profits as Competent," *Journal of Consumer Research,* August 2010, pp. 224–37.

38. From http://dragonrouge-usa.com/, accessed February 24, 2008.

39. For a detailed discussion, see D. A. Aaker, R. Batra, and J. G. Meyers, *Advertising Management,* 4th ed. (Englewood Cliffs, NJ: Prentice Hall, 1992), chap. 8. See also T. T. Wee, "Extending Human Personality to Brands," *Brand Management,* April 2004, pp. 317–30.

40. A. Nagel and M. Prior, "Revlon Gets Ready for 2005," *WWD,* August 13, 2004, p. 8; and S. Kang, "Nike, Serena Williams Partner Up," *The Wall Street Journal,* December 12, 2003, p. B2.

41. S. O'Loughlin, "Hush Puppies Steps into a New Image," *Brandweek,* June 23, 2003, p. 14.

42. Russak, "Calling the Shots"; O'Loughlin, "Hush Puppies Steps into a New Image"; "Listerine Mouthwash and PocketPaks," *Marketing Magazine,* November 18, 2002, p. C9; and M. Warren, "Molson Debuts a Saucy Brazilian," *Marketing Magazine,* March 24, 2003, p. 2.

43. For a thorough discussion, see R. P. Bagozzi, M. Gopinath, and P. U. Nyer, "The Role of Emotions in Marketing," *Journal of the Academy of Marketing Science,* Spring 1999, pp. 184–207. See also M. E. Hill et al., "The Conjoining Influences of Affect and Arousal on Attitude Formation," *Research in Consumer Behavior* 9 (2000), pp. 129–46.

44. See, e.g., D. M. Phillips and H. Baumgartner, "The Role of Consumption Emotions in the Satisfaction Response," *Journal of Consumer Psychology* 12, no. 3 (2002), pp. 243–52; and D. Martin et al., "The Role of Emotion in Explaining Consumer Satisfaction and Future Behavioural Intention," *Journal of Services Marketing* 22, no. 3 (2008), 224–36.

45. See, e.g., Moore and Homer, "Dimensions of Temperament."

46. J. A. Ruth, F. F. Brunel, and C. C. Otnes, "Linking Thoughts to Feelings," *Journal of the Academy of Marketing Science,* Winter 2002, pp. 44–58.

47. See B. J. Babin, J. S. Boles, and W. R. Darden, "Salesperson Stereotypes, Consumer Emotions, and Their Impact on Information Processing," *Journal of the Academy of Marketing Science,* Spring 1995, pp. 94–105.

48. For a discussion of coping strategies, see S. Yi and H. Baumgartner, "Coping with Negative Emotions in Purchase-Related Situations," *Journal of Consumer Psychology* 14, no. 3 (2004), pp. 303–17.

49. See L. Dube and M. S. Morgan, "Trend Effects and Gender Differences in Retrospective Judgments of Consumption Emotions," *Journal of Consumer Research,* September 1996, pp. 156–62; J. L. Aaker and P. Williams, "Empathy versus Pride," *Journal of Consumer Research,* December 1998, pp. 241–61; and M. Geuens and P. D. Pelsmacker, "Affect Intensity Revisited," *Psychology & Marketing,* May 1999, pp. 195–209.

50. J. A. Ruth, "Promoting a Brand's Emotion Benefits," *Journal of Consumer Psychology* 11, no. 2 (2001), pp. 99–113.

51. See K. T. Lacher and R. Mizerski, "An Exploratory Study of the Responses and Relationships Involved in the Evaluation of, and in the Intention to Purchase, New Rock Music," *Journal of Consumer Research,* September 1994, pp. 366–80.

52. L. C. Wang et al., "Can a Retail Web Site Be Social?" *Journal of Marketing,* July 2007, pp. 143–57.

53. I. Soscia, "Gratitude, Delight, or Guilt," *Psychology and Marketing,* October 2007, pp. 871–94; and R. W. Palmatier et al., "The Role of Customer Gratitude in Relationship Marketing," *Journal of Marketing,* September 2009, pp. 1–18.

54. S. L. Wood and C. Page Moreau, "From Fear to Loathing?" *Journal of Marketing,* July 2006, pp. 44–57.

55. B. A. Huhmann and T. P. Brotherton, "A Content Analysis of Guilt Appeals in Popular Magazine Advertisements," *Journal of Advertising,* Summer 1997, pp. 35–45.

56. Based on A. Duhachek, "Coping," *Journal of Consumer Research,* June 2005, pp. 41–53.

57. M. F. Luce, "Choosing to Avoid," *Journal of Consumer Research,* March 1998, pp. 409–33.

58. N. M. Puccinelli, "Putting Your Best Face Forward," *Journal of Consumer Psychology* 16, no. 2, (2006), pp. 156–62.

59. A. Duhachek, "Coping."

60. B. Kidwell, D. M. Hardesty, and T. L. Childers, "Consumer Emotional Intelligence," *Journal of Consumer Research,* June 2008, pp. 154–66.

61. J. R. McColl-Kennedy et al., "Consumer Rage Episodes," *Journal of Retailing* 85, no. 2 (2009), 222–37.

62. See L. F. Alwitt, "Suspense and Advertising Responses," *Journal of Consumer Psychology* 12, no. 1 (2002), pp. 35–49.

63. H. Mano, "Affect and Persuasion," *Psychology & Marketing,* July 1997, pp. 315–35; and A. M. Isen, "An Influence of Positive Affect on Decision Making in Complex Situations," *Journal of Consumer Psychology* 11, no. 2 (2001), pp. 75–85.

64. A. Y. Lee and B. Sternthal, "The Effects of Positive Mood on Memory," *Journal of Consumer Research,* September 1999, pp. 115–27; K. R. Lord, R. E. Burnkrant, and H. R. Unnava, "The Effects of Program-Induced Mood States on Memory for Commercial Information," *Journal of Current Issues and Research in Advertising,* Spring 2001, pp. 1–14; and S. J. Newell, K. V. Henderson, and B. T. Wu, "The Effects of Pleasure and Arousal on Recall of Advertisements during the Super Bowl," *Psychology & Marketing,* November 2001, pp. 1135–53.

65. M. Royo-Vela, "Emotional and Informational Content in Commercials," *Journal of Current Issues and Research in Advertising,* Fall 2005, pp. 13–38; and C. Chang, "Context-Induced and Ad-Induced Affect," *Psychology & Marketing,* September 2006, pp. 757–82.

66. W. Janssens and P. De Pelsmacker, "Emotional or Informative?" *International Journal of Advertising* 24, no. 3 (2005), pp. 373–94; and J. Kim and J. D. Morris, "The Power of Affective Response and Cognitive Structure in Product-Trial Attitude Formation," *Journal of Advertising,* Spring 2007, pp. 95–106.

67. B. M. Fennis and A. B. Bakker, "Stay Tuned—We Will Be Right Back After These Messages," *Journal of Advertising,* Fall 2001, pp. 15–25; J. D. Morris et al., "The Power of Affect," *Journal of Advertising Research,* May–June 2002, pp. 7–17; and T. A. Shimp and E. W. Stuart, "The Role of Disgust as an Emotional Mediator of Advertising Effects," *Journal of Advertising,* Spring 2004, pp. 43–53.

68. E. Walther and S. Grigoriadis, "Why Sad People Like Shoes Better," *Psychology & Marketing,* October 2004, pp. 755–73; and P. R. Darke, A. Chattapadhyay, and L. Ashworth, "The Importance and Functional Significance of Affective Cues in Consumer Choice," *Journal of Consumer Research,* December 2006, pp. 322–28.

69. See R. Adaval, "Sometimes It Just Feels Right," *Journal of Consumer Research,* June 2001, pp. 1–17.

70. C. Beardi, "Zippo's Eternal Flame," *Advertising Age,* August 13, 2001, p. 4.

Chapter Eleven

11 Attitudes and Influencing Attitudes

LEARNING OBJECTIVES

LO1 Define attitude and its role in consumer behavior

LO2 Summarize the three components of attitudes

LO3 Discuss attitude change strategies associated with each attitude component

LO4 Describe the elaboration likelihood model of persuasion

LO5 Describe the role of message source, appeal, and structure on attitudes

LO6 Discuss segmentation and product development applications of attitudes

Companies like Nike, Gatorade, and American Express spend billions on celebrity endorsements each year. In fact, it is estimated that 25 percent or more of ads in the United States contain a celebrity and that spending on celebrity endorsers is roughly $30 billion annually. In many ways, the use of celebrities as product endorsers makes sense. As we will discuss later in the chapter, celebrities can break through the clutter and grab consumer attention as well as enhance consumer perceptions and attitudes toward the brands they endorse. The downside is when endorsers engage in questionable personal behaviors. What is particularly interesting, however, is which companies decide to stick with their endorsers through scandals while others fire them. Let's look at three recent examples.[1]

Michael Phelps—This Olympic swimmer, who has broken most if not all of the swimming records, has had problems in his personal life. The most recent was a picture that surfaced after the Beijing Olympics showing Phelps smoking a marijuana pipe. Kellogg dropped Phelps, while Speedo did not. Here are statements from each company:

KELLOGG: Michael's most recent behavior is not consistent with the image of Kellogg.
SPEEDO: In light of Michael Phelps's statement yesterday, Speedo would like to make it clear that it does not condone such behavior and we know

that Michael truly regrets his actions. Michael Phelps is a valued member of the Speedo team and a great champion. We will do all that we can to support him and his family.

Tiger Woods—Perhaps the most gifted golfer of his generation, if not of all time, Tiger Woods has performed miracles on the golf course. Unfortunately, personal scandals involving infidelity came crashing down recently. Tag Heuer dropped Tiger; Nike did not. Here are statements from each company:

TAG HEUER: We recognize Tiger Woods as a great champion, but we have to take account of the sensitivity of some consumers in relation to recent events.
NIKE: Tiger has been a part of Nike for more than a decade. He is the best golfer in the world and one of the greatest athletes of his era. We look forward to his return to golf. He and his family have Nike's full support.

Why such different reactions by each company? No one knows for sure, but in looking at these examples, it appears that it may be a function of what the company gains or loses from the endorser and the scandal. Speedo and Nike arguably gain the most from Phelps and Woods because of the product performance credibility they bring to their sports brands. Personal scandals may do little to damage this dimension. Alternatively, Kellogg and Tag Heuer appear to have used Phelps and Woods for general credibility and image, and these clearly took a hit when the scandals broke.

Outside of sports, Subway has been dealing with the undesirable behavior of its main endorser, Jared Fogle. Jared lost 245 pounds eating low-fat Subway sandwiches, but had recently gained back 40 pounds. Rather than walking away from Jared, they took it as an opportunity to highlight the humanness of Jared in having weight struggles. They entered and trained him for the New York City Marathon. According to Subway:

> Jared is kind of like the everyman. He has his ups and downs, and though he hasn't had crazy ups, this one got a lot of attention.

Researchers in sports have reached similar conclusions. Namely, sports fans love the human side of athletes and love a great "comeback" story.

 As the chapter's opening example indicates, brands and organizations attempt to influence consumer attitudes and their resulting consumption behaviors.

An **attitude** is an enduring organization of motivational, emotional, perceptual, and cognitive processes with respect to some aspect of our environment. It is a learned predisposition to respond in a consistently favorable or unfavorable manner with respect to a given object. Thus, an attitude is the way one thinks, feels, and acts toward some aspect of his or her environment, such as a retail store, television program, or product.[2] Attitudes are formed as the result of all the factors we have discussed in previous chapters, and they represent an important influence on an individual's lifestyle. In this chapter, we examine attitude components, general attitude change strategies, and the effect of marketing communications on attitudes.

ATTITUDE COMPONENTS

 As Figure 11-1 illustrates, it is useful to consider attitudes as having three components: cognitive (beliefs), affective (feelings), and behavioral (response tendencies). Each of these attitude components is discussed in more detail below.

Cognitive Component

The **cognitive component** consists of *a consumer's beliefs about an object.* For most attitude objects, people have a number of beliefs. For example, an individual may believe that AMP beverages

- Are popular with younger consumers.
- Provide consumers with lots of energy.
- Contain a lot of vitamins.
- Are priced competitively with other energy drinks.
- Are made by a sports-oriented company.

The total configuration of beliefs about this beverage brand represents the cognitive component of an attitude toward AMP. Beliefs can be about the emotional benefits of owning or using a product (one can believe it would be exciting to own or drive a convertible) as well as about objective features.[3] Many beliefs about attributes are evaluative in nature; for example, high gas mileage, attractive styling, and reliable

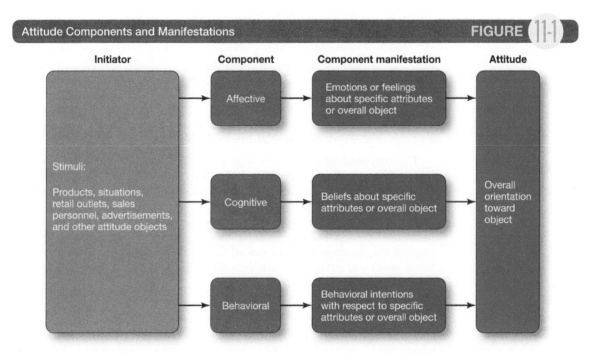

Attitude Components and Manifestations   FIGURE 11-1

Initiator	Component	Component manifestation	Attitude
	Affective	Emotions or feelings about specific attributes or overall object	
Stimuli: Products, situations, retail outlets, sales personnel, advertisements, and other attitude objects	Cognitive	Beliefs about specific attributes or overall object	Overall orientation toward object
	Behavioral	Behavioral intentions with respect to specific attributes or overall object	

performance are generally viewed as positive beliefs. This brings up the distinction between a *feature* and a *benefit,* both of which are beliefs. A product may have five milligrams of sodium per serving (a nonevaluative *feature* belief), which means that it is low in sodium and better for your health (both evaluative *benefit* beliefs). Marketers must promote benefits rather than features, especially for less knowledgeable consumers and for complex products. Otherwise consumers will not know how to evaluate and respond to the claims.[4] For example, Quaker Oats helps consumers interpret the nutritional information on their package with statements such as "the soluble fiber in oatmeal helps reduce cholesterol."

The more positive beliefs associated with a brand, the more positive each belief is; and the easier it is for the individual to recall the beliefs, the more favorable the overall cognitive component is presumed to be.[5] And because all the components of an attitude are generally consistent, the more favorable the overall attitude is. This logic underlies what is known as the **multiattribute attitude model.**

Multiattribute Attitude Model   There are several versions of this model. The simplest is

$$A_b = \sum_{i=1}^{n} X_{ib}$$

where

A_b = Consumer's attitude toward a particular brand b
X_{ib} = Consumer's belief about brand b's performance on attribute i
n = Number of attributes considered

This version assumes that all attributes are equally important in determining our overall evaluation. However, a moment's reflection suggests that frequently a few attributes, such as price, quality, or style, are more important than others. Thus, it is often necessary to add an importance weight for each attribute:

$$A_b = \sum_{i=1}^{n} W_i X_{ib}$$

where

W_i = The importance the consumer attaches to attribute i

This version of the model is useful in a variety of situations. However, it assumes that more (or less) is always better. This is frequently the case. More miles to the gallon is always better than fewer miles to the gallon, all other things being equal. This version is completely adequate for such situations.

For some attributes, more (or less) is good up to a point, but then further increases (decreases) become bad. For example, adding salt to a saltless pretzel will generally improve the consumer's attitude toward the pretzel up to a point. After that point, additional amounts of salt will decrease the attitude. Thus, we need to introduce an *ideal point* into the multiattribute attitude model:

$$A_b = \sum_{i=1}^{n} W_i |I_i - X_{ib}|$$

where

I_i = Consumer's ideal level of performance on attribute i

Because multiattribute attitude models are widely used by marketing researchers and managers, we will work through an example using the weighted, ideal point model. The simpler models would work in a similar manner.

Imagine that Coca-Cola gathers data on a set of beliefs about Diet Coke from a segment of consumers (more details on measuring the various attitude components can be found in Appendix A and Appendix Table A-3). These consumers perceive Diet Coke to have the following levels of performance (the Xs) and desired performance (the Is) on four attributes:

	(1)	(2)	(3)	(4)	(5)	(6)	(7)	
Low price			I	X				High price
Sweet taste		I				X		Bitter taste
High status			I		X			Low status
Low calories	IX							High calories

This segment of consumers believes (the Xs) that Diet Coke is average priced, very bitter in taste, somewhat low in status, and extremely low in calories. Their ideal soda (the Is) would be slightly low priced, very sweet in taste, somewhat high in status, and extremely low in calories. Since these attributes are not equally important to consumers, they are assigned weights based on the relative importance a segment of consumers attaches to each.

A popular way of measuring importance weights is with a 100-point *constant-sum scale*. For example, the importance weights shown below express the relative importance of the four soft-drink attributes such that the total adds up to 100 points.

Attribute	Importance
Price	10
Taste	30
Status	20
Calories	40
	100 points

In this case, calories are considered the most important attribute, with taste slightly less important. Price is given little importance.

From this information, we can index this segment's attitude toward Diet Coke as follows:

$$^A Diet\ Coke = (10)(|3-4|) + (30)(|2-6|) + (20)(|3-5|) + (40)(|1-1|)$$
$$= (10)(1) + (30)(4) + (20)(2) + (40)(0)$$
$$= 170$$

This involves taking the absolute difference between the consumer's ideal soft-drink attributes and beliefs about Diet Coke's attributes and multiplying these differences by the importance attached to each attribute. In this case, the attitude index is computed as 170. Is this good or bad? Since an attitude index is relative, to fully evaluate it, we must compare it with the segment's attitudes toward competing brands. However, if Diet Coke were perceived as the ideal soft drink, an attitude index of zero would result. Thus, the closer an attitude index calculated in this manner is to zero, the better. It is important to note that, in general, the multiattribute attitude model merely *represents* a process that is much less precise and structured than implied by the model.

Affective Component

Feelings or *emotional reactions to an object* represent the **affective component** of an attitude. A consumer who states "I like Diet Coke" or "Diet Coke is a terrible soda" is expressing the results of an emotional or affective evaluation of the product. This overall evaluation may be simply a vague, general feeling developed without cognitive information or beliefs about the product. Or it may be the result of several evaluations of the product's performance on each of several attributes. Thus, the statements "Diet Coke tastes bad" and "Diet Coke is not good for your health" imply a negative affective reaction to specific aspects of the product that, in combination with feelings about other attributes, will determine the overall reaction to the brand.

Marketers are increasingly turning their attention to the affective or "feeling" component of attitudes to provide a richer understanding of attitudes than that based solely on the cognitive or "thinking" component. As a consequence, marketers now commonly distinguish *utilitarian* or functional benefits and attitudes from *hedonic* or emotional benefits and attitudes.[6] For example, one study found that consumer acceptance of handheld Internet devices was influenced by both utilitarian benefits such as usefulness and hedonic aspects such as fun to use.[7] Another study found that in some cases hedonic aspects of giving blood such as fear and joy were stronger determinants of overall attitude toward blood donation than utilitarian beliefs.[8]

In addition, marketers are beginning to consider both form *and* function in product designs and focus considerable attention on the aesthetic aspects of design (appearance, sensory

388   **Part Three**   Internal Influences

experience). The iPod and iPad are examples of products with high **aesthetic appeal** that tap consumers' affective reactions by going beyond the cognitive associations of functionality.[9] Illustration 11–1 shows an ad for a product high in aesthetic appeal.

Affective reactions to a specific product or benefit can vary by situation and individual. For example, a consumer's belief that Diet Coke has caffeine may result in positive feelings if he or she needs to stay awake to work late but negative feelings if he or she wants to get to sleep quickly. Would you enjoy an experience that induced the following? Illustration 11–2 is an example of an affective ad.

Marketers sometimes measure the affective component on verbal scales much like those used to measure the cognitive component (for more detail, see Appendix A and Appendix Table A-3). So, consumers might be asked to rate Diet Coke overall (or specific attributes such as taste) on the following dimensions by placing an X in the appropriate space:

	(1)	(2)	(3)	(4)	(5)	(6)	(7)	
Good	_____	_____	_____	_____	_____	_____	_____	Bad
Like	_____	_____	_____	_____	_____	_____	_____	Dislike
Happy	_____	_____	_____	_____	_____	_____	_____	Sad
Pleasant	_____	_____	_____	_____	_____	_____	_____	Unpleasant

SAM and AdSAM®   However, sometimes marketers want to tap feelings and emotions more directly and bypass the cognitive processing that often goes along with verbal scales. One such measure is based on the pleasure-arousal-dominance (PAD) approach to emotions discussed in Chapter 10. This measure, termed SAM (Self-Assessment Manikin), provides visual representations of 232 "emotional adjectives" underlying PAD. SAM (and AdSAM®, which applies SAM to ad planning) is a graphical character that is manipulated to portray emotions and more directly tap emotional responses. From a global standpoint, SAM is effective across different cultures and languages because the pictorial representations don't require translation or alteration.[10] Examples of AdSAM® for each dimension of PAD are shown below (top panel—pleasure; middle—arousal; bottom—dominance):

ILLUSTRATION 11–2

Individuals differ in their affective reactions to product characteristics. Likewise, the same individual will react differently to the same attribute in different situations.

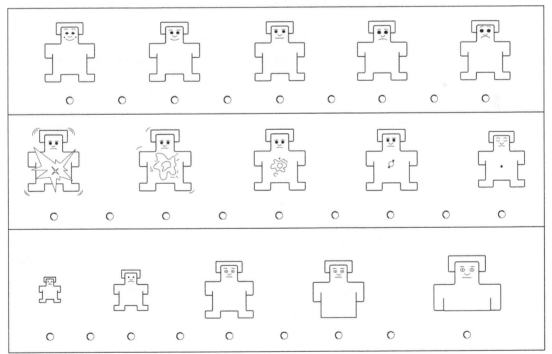

Source: Copyright 2000 AdSAM Marketing LLC.

Behavioral Component

The **behavioral component** of an attitude is *one's tendency to respond in a certain manner toward an object or activity.* A series of decisions to purchase or not purchase Diet Coke or to recommend it or other brands to friends would reflect the behavioral component. Brand

FIGURE 11-2   Attitude Component Consistency

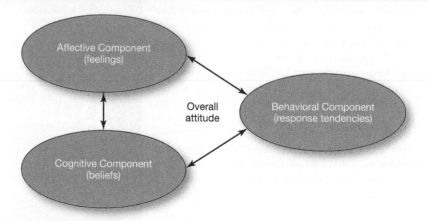

interest, as represented by tendencies to seek out the brand on store shelves or search for brand information, also reflects the behavioral component. The behavioral component provides response tendencies or behavioral intentions. *Actual behaviors reflect these intentions as they are modified by the situation in which the behavior will occur.*

Direct versus Indirect Approach   Actual behaviors and response tendencies are most often measured by fairly direct questioning (for more detail, see Appendix A and Appendix Table A-3). For example, consumers might be asked about their intentions to buy Diet Coke, as follows:

How likely is it that you will buy Diet Coke the next time you purchase a soft drink (put an X in the appropriate space)?

Definitely Will	Probably Will	Might	Probably Will Not	Definitely Will Not
____	____	____	____	____

Such direct questioning may work well for most consumption, but not so well for sensitive topics such as alcohol, pornography, and eating patterns where consumers may understate negative behaviors or intentions. In these cases, asking *indirect* questions such as estimating the behaviors of other people similar to themselves (neighbors, those with similar jobs, etc.) may help reduce the bias.

Component Consistency

Figure 11-2 illustrates a critical aspect of attitudes: *All three attitude components tend to be consistent.*[11] This means that a change in one attitude component tends to produce related changes in the other components. This tendency is the basis for a substantial amount of marketing strategy.

Marketing managers are ultimately concerned with influencing behavior. But it is often difficult to influence behavior directly. Marketers generally are unable to directly cause consumers to buy, use, or recommend their products. However, consumers will often listen to sales personnel, attend to advertisements, or examine packages. Marketers can, therefore, indirectly influence behavior by providing information, music, or other stimuli that influence a belief or feeling about the product if the three components are indeed consistent with each other.

Some research has found only a limited relationship among the three components.[12] Let's examine the sources of this inconsistency by considering an example. Suppose an individual reports positive beliefs and affect toward the iPod but does not own an iPod or purchases another brand. At least six factors may account for inconsistencies between *measures* of beliefs and feelings and *observations* of behavior.

1. *Lack of need.* A favorable attitude requires a need or motive before it can be translated into action. Thus, the consumer may not feel a need for a portable player or might already own an acceptable, though less preferred, brand.

2. *Lack of ability.* Translating favorable beliefs and feelings into ownership requires ability. The consumer might not have sufficient funds to purchase an iPod, thus she might purchase a less expensive brand.

3. *Relative attitudes.* In the prior example, only attitudes toward the iPod were considered. However, purchases often involve trade-offs across competing brands. Thus, a consumer may have a relatively high attitude toward iPod, but a slightly higher attitude toward a competing brand. In a choice situation, relative attitudes are a stronger predictor of behavior.

4. *Attitude ambivalence.* While consumers often strive to hold consistent beliefs, feelings, and intentions toward a specific attitude object, this is not always the case. Sometimes a consumer has an **ambivalent attitude,** which involves *holding mixed beliefs and/or feelings about an attitude object.* Think of seafood. A consumer with an ambivalent attitude toward seafood would agree that "Sometimes I feel seafood tastes good, but other times I feel it tastes bad." Ambivalent attitudes are less stable over time and less predictive of behavior. Firms should avoid ambivalent attitudes by creating consistent messages and experiences over time. Firms may also attempt to gain market share by creating ambivalence among customers of competing brands.[13]

5. *Weak beliefs and affect.* If the cognitive and affective components are weakly held, and if the consumer obtains additional information while shopping, then the initial attitudes may give way to new ones. Specifically, stronger attitudes or those attitudes held with more confidence tend to be stronger predictors of behavior. Attitudes can be weak because of ambivalence. However, they can also be weak because of a general lack of experience with the brand. Thus, direct (and consistently positive) experience tends to yield attitudes that are more strongly and confidently held.[14] As a consequence, companies often spend enormous amounts of money on coupons and free samples to generate direct product experience.

    In addition to direct experience, factors related to strength of learning such as importance, message involvement, reinforcement, and repetition (see Chapter 9) are also related to attitude strength since attitudes are generally learned.

6. *Interpersonal and situational influences.* An individual's attitudes were measured above. However, many purchase decisions involve others directly or indirectly. Thus, a shopper may purchase something other than an iPod to better meet the needs of the entire family. Situation and other consumers' expectations in those situations can also play a role. For example, it may be seen by some as more desirable to purchase and use an iPod in front of friends (even though they themselves like another brand better) because their friends think the iPod is the coolest brand.

In summary, attitude components—cognitive, affective, and behavioral—tend to be consistent. However, as we see, the degree of apparent consistency can be reduced by a variety of factors. Marketers must incorporate these factors when developing persuasive messages and strategies.

ATTITUDE CHANGE STRATEGIES

Marketers often attempt to influence consumer behavior by changing one or more of the underlying attitude components. Such influence can be positive, as we saw in the chapter's opening vignette. However, social, ethical, and regulatory concerns arise when companies attempt to promote potentially harmful consumption behaviors or when persuasion attempts are deemed deceptive.

Change the Cognitive Component

A common and effective approach to changing attitudes is to focus on the cognitive component.[15] Four basic marketing strategies are used for altering the cognitive structure of a consumer's attitude.

Change Beliefs This strategy involves shifting beliefs about the performance of the brand on one or more attributes.[16] Illustration 11–3 shows one example. Another example is Radio Shack, which is repositioning itself as a more modern and contemporary retailer. They have nicknamed the store "The Shack" and are trying to change existing merchandise beliefs as follows:[17]

> Consumers thought this was a place that had private labels and off brands, when in fact we've got leading national brands across every one of our categories. So the goal from the outset was to close those gaps in brand perception [beliefs] and business reality.

Attempts to change beliefs generally involve providing facts or statements about performance. It is important to realize that some beliefs are strongly held and thus hard to change. As a consequence, marketers may have more success changing overall brand attitudes by targeting weaker brand beliefs that are more vulnerable to persuasion attempts.[18]

Shift Importance Most consumers consider some product attributes to be more important than others. Marketers often try to convince consumers that those attributes on which their brands are relatively strong are the most important. For example, General Motors uses detailed narratives of drivers in distress to emphasize the importance of instant communications and emergency assistance, which its proprietary OnStar system provides.

Sometimes evaluative factors that would otherwise not be prominent to consumers can be enhanced by cues in the ad. One study created ads with references to Asian culture (e.g., picture of the Great Wall of China) to enhance "ethnic self-awareness." When ethnic self-awareness was enhanced, Asian consumers reacted more positively to ads containing an Asian spokesperson.[19]

Add Beliefs Another approach to changing the cognitive component of an attitude is to add new beliefs to the consumer's belief structure. For example, the California Pomegranate Council wants consumers to know that beyond possessing vitamins and minerals (already known), new research shows that pomegranates contain "powerful antioxidants [that] help retard aging and can neutralize almost twice as many free radicals as red wine and seven times as many as green tea."[20]

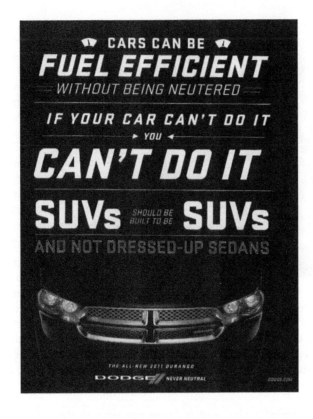

ILLUSTRATION 11–3

The cognitive component of an attitude can be altered by changing current beliefs, adding new beliefs, shifting the importance of beliefs, or changing the beliefs about the ideal product. This ad focuses primarily on changing beliefs.

Change Ideal   The final strategy for changing the cognitive component is to change the perceptions of the ideal brand or situation. Thus, many conservation organizations strive to influence our beliefs about the ideal product in terms of minimal packaging, nonpolluting manufacturing, extensive use of recycled materials, and nonpolluting disposition after its useful life.

Change the Affective Component

Firms increasingly attempt to influence consumers' liking of their brands without directly influencing either beliefs or behavior. If the firm is successful, increased liking will tend to lead to increased positive beliefs,[21] which could lead to purchase behavior should a need for the product arise. Or, perhaps more common, increased liking will lead to a tendency to purchase the brand should a need arise,[22] with purchase and use leading to increased positive beliefs. Marketers use three basic approaches to directly increase affect: classical conditioning, affect toward the ad itself, and mere exposure.

Classical Conditioning   One way of directly influencing the affective component is through classical conditioning (see Chapter 9). In this approach, a stimulus the audience likes, such as music, is consistently paired with the brand name. Over time, some of the positive affect associated with the music will transfer to the brand.[23] Other liked stimuli, such as pictures, are frequently used for this reason.

Affect toward the Ad or Website   As we saw in Chapter 10, liking the advertisement (attitude toward the ad, or Aad) generally increases the tendency to like the brand (attitude

ILLUSTRATION 11–4

Ads can change the affective component of an attitude toward a brand without altering the belief structure if the ad itself elicits a positive response (is liked). Ads that are primarily pictorial are often used for this purpose, though the pictures themselves convey cognitive as well as emotional meanings.

toward the brand, or Abr).[24] Somewhat similar results are associated with liking the website on which an ad appears (Aweb).[25] Using humor, celebrities, or emotional appeals increases Aad and Aweb. For example, vivid websites with rich sensory content that appeal to multiple senses produce more positive Aweb than do less vivid sites.[26] Illustration 11–4 contains an ad that relies on positive affect.

Ads that arouse negative affect or emotions such as fear, guilt, or sorrow can also enhance attitude change. For example, an ad for a charity assisting refugees could show pictures that would elicit a variety of unpleasant emotions such as disgust or anger and still be effective.[27]

Mere Exposure   While controversial, there is evidence that affect or brand preference may also be increased by **mere exposure.**[28] That is, simply presenting a brand to an individual on a large number of occasions might make the individual's attitude toward the brand more positive. A common explanation of the mere exposure effect is that "familiarity breeds liking." Thus, the repetition of advertisements for low-involvement products may well increase liking (through enhanced familiarity) and subsequent purchase of the advertised brands without altering the initial belief structure. Mere exposure effects underlie the use of simple reminder ads as well as product placements.[29]

Classical conditioning, Aad, and mere exposure can alter affect directly and, by altering affect, alter purchase behavior without first changing beliefs. This has a number of important implications:

- Ads designed to alter affect need not contain any cognitive (factual or attribute) information.
- Classical conditioning principles should guide such campaigns.
- Aad and ad-evoked affect are critical for this type of campaign unless mere exposure is being used.
- Repetition is critical for affect-based campaigns.
- Cognitively based measures may be inappropriate to assess advertising effectiveness.

As these guidelines suggest, classical conditioning, Aad, and mere exposure tend to occur in low-involvement situations (see Chapter 9). There is at least one major exception, however. When emotions and feelings are important product performance dimensions, then such feelings and emotions are relevant to the evaluation. In these situations, Aad can readily influence Abr under high involvement. As we discussed earlier in the chapter, hedonic (versus utilitarian) products are those for which affect and emotion are relevant performance criteria. Not surprisingly, hedonic products are those for which affect, emotions, and Aad can play a role in more conscious, high-involvement settings.[30]

Change the Behavioral Component

Behavior, specifically purchase or use behavior, may precede the development of cognition and affect. Or it may occur in contrast to the cognitive and affective components. For example, a consumer may dislike the taste of diet soft drinks and believe that artificial sweeteners are unhealthy. However, rather than appear rude, the same consumer may accept a diet drink when offered one by a friend due to social norms. Drinking the beverage may alter her perceptions of its taste and lead to liking; this in turn may lead to increased learning, which changes the cognitive component.

Behavior can lead directly to affect, to cognitions, or to both simultaneously.[31] Consumers frequently try new brands or types of low-cost items in the absence of prior knowledge or affect. Such purchases are as much for information (Will I like this brand?) as for satisfaction of some underlying need such as hunger.

Internet marketers have been particularly concerned about their ability to simulate direct experiences for products in a virtual context. A recent study finds that for experiential products such as sunglasses, creating a *virtual direct experience* (in this case, a video that simulated viewing the content with and without the sunglasses) led to more positive beliefs, affect, and purchase intentions.[32] The ability to simulate experiences with products in an online context relates to the issue of "touch," which is a major online purchasing factor discussed in Chapter 17.

Changing behavior prior to changing affect or cognition is based primarily on operant conditioning (see Chapter 9). Thus, the key marketing task is to induce people to purchase or consume the product while ensuring that the purchase or consumption will indeed be rewarding.[33] Coupons, free samples, point-of-purchase displays, tie-in purchases, and price reductions are common techniques for inducing trial behavior. Since behavior often leads to strong positive attitudes toward the consumed brand, a sound distribution system (limited stockouts) is important to prevent current customers from trying competing brands.

INDIVIDUAL AND SITUATIONAL CHARACTERISTICS THAT INFLUENCE ATTITUDE CHANGE

Attitude change is determined by individual and situational factors as well as marketing activities.[34] Individual factors include gender, need for cognition, consumer knowledge, ethnicity, and as we saw in Chapter 10, regulatory focus. Situational factors include program context, level of viewer distraction, and buying occasion.

Marketers continue to focus considerable attention on consumer involvement, which has both an individual (intrinsic interest) and situational (current need to make a purchase decision) component. Consumer involvement is an important motivational factor that influences elaborative processing, learning, and attitudes. The **elaboration likelihood model (ELM)** is a theory about how attitudes are formed and changed under varying conditions of involvement. Thus, the ELM integrates select individual, situational, and marketing factors to understand attitudes.[35]

The ELM suggests that involvement is a key determinant of how information is processed and attitudes are changed. High involvement results in a *central route* to attitude change by which consumers deliberately and consciously process those message elements that they believe are relevant to a meaningful and logical evaluation of the brand (see Figure 11-3). These elements are elaborated on and combined into an overall evaluation. The multiattribute attitude model represents a high-involvement view of attitude change.

In contrast, low involvement results in a *peripheral route* to attitude change in which consumers form impressions of the brand based on exposure to readily available cues in the message regardless of their relevance to the brand or decision. Attitudes formed through the peripheral route are based on little or no elaborative processing. Classical conditioning, Aad, and mere exposure represent low-involvement views of attitude change.

FIGURE 11-3   The Elaboration Likelihood Model

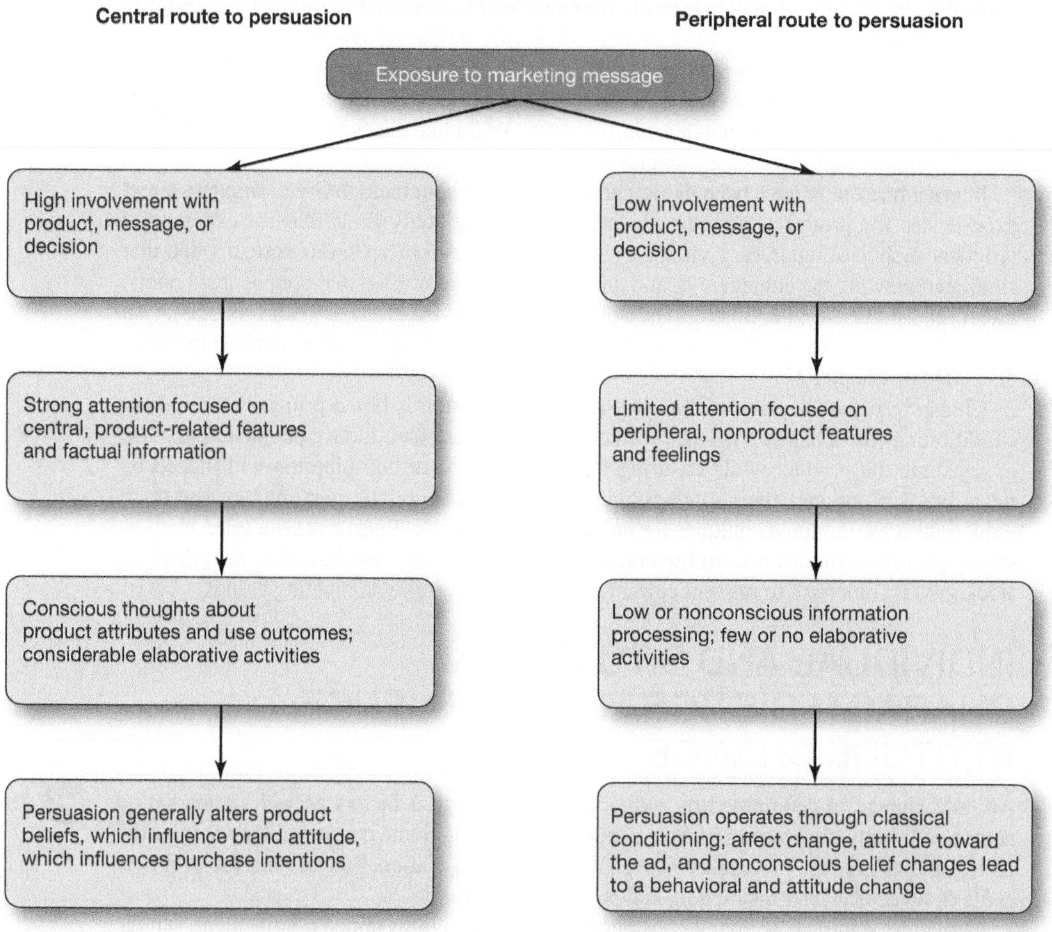

Central route to persuasion

Peripheral route to persuasion

Exposure to marketing message

Central route to persuasion	Peripheral route to persuasion
High involvement with product, message, or decision	Low involvement with product, message, or decision
Strong attention focused on central, product-related features and factual information	Limited attention focused on peripheral, nonproduct features and feelings
Conscious thoughts about product attributes and use outcomes; considerable elaborative activities	Low or nonconscious information processing; few or no elaborative activities
Persuasion generally alters product beliefs, which influence brand attitude, which influences purchase intentions	Persuasion operates through classical conditioning; affect change, attitude toward the ad, and nonconscious belief changes lead to a behavioral and attitude change

The ELM suggests that vastly different communications strategies are required to communicate effectively with high- versus low-involvement consumers. In general, detailed factual information (central cues) is effective in high-involvement, central-route situations. Low-involvement, peripheral-route situations generally require limited information and instead rely on simple affective and cognitive cues such as pictures, music, and characteristics of people in the ad (peripheral cues). *Which persuasion route is most likely being used in Illustration 11–4?*

Cue Relevance and Competitive Situation

Generally speaking, compared with attitudes formed under the peripheral route, attitudes formed under the central route tend to be stronger, more resistant to counterpersuasion attempts, more accessible from memory, and more predictive of behavior.[36]

However, it is important to realize that central-route processing involves extensive processing of *decision-relevant* information or cues. And what consumers find relevant can vary by product and situation. For example, an attractive picture can be peripheral or central. In an ad for orange soda, a picture of cute puppies would be a peripheral cue (and influence attitudes under low involvement) while a picture of fresh, juicy orange slices would be a central cue (and influence attitudes under high involvement).[37] Similarly, emotions likely represent a central cue for hedonic products and thus influence attitudes under high involvement.

In addition, the competitive situation can also work to enhance the role of peripheral cues even under high involvement. For example, if competing brands are comparable in terms of their product features (central cues), highly involved consumers prefer the brand with the strongest peripheral cues in its advertising.[38] The basic idea is that relative attitudes are critical in competitive settings and peripheral cues become the tiebreaker between otherwise equivalent (parity) brands. As you can see, the role of peripheral cues can extend beyond low-involvement settings in certain competitive situations.

Consumer Resistance to Persuasion

Consumers are not passive to persuasion attempts. Instead, consumers are often skeptical (an individual characteristic) and resist persuasion.[39] Also, consumers frequently infer an advertiser's intent and respond in light of that presumed selling intent.[40] For example, a recent ad for California Almonds stated, "It's uncanny how we raise indulgence and lower cholesterol." A consumer could respond to the ad as follows: "Of course they're going to tell me almonds are healthy for me. They're trying to sell more almonds. I'm still not convinced." To help reduce the likelihood of such responses, the ad makes use of the American Heart Association and scientific research to bolster its health claims.

Strongly held attitudes are harder to change than weakly held attitudes. Think of something you feel strongly about—perhaps your school or your favorite sports team. What would be required to change your attitude? Clearly, it would be difficult. Consumers tend to avoid messages that are counter to their attitudes (e.g., committed smokers tend to avoid antismoking ads). And if they do encounter such messages, they tend to discount them. Consumer Insight 11-1 examines various strategies that consumers use to resist persuasion attempts.

COMMUNICATION CHARACTERISTICS THAT INFLUENCE ATTITUDE FORMATION AND CHANGE

In this section, we describe communication techniques that can be used to form and change attitudes. Obviously, as with all aspects of consumer behavior, individual and situational characteristics interact with the communication features to determine effectiveness.

Source Characteristics

The source of a communication represents "who" delivers the message. Sources include people (celebrities, typical consumers), animated spokescharacters (Jolly Green Giant, Mr. Peanut), and organizations (the company, a third-party endorser). The source of a message is important because consumers respond differently to the same message delivered by different sources.

Source Credibility   Persuasion is easier when the target market views the message source as highly credible. **Source credibility** consists of *trustworthiness* and *expertise*. A source that has no ulterior motive to provide anything other than complete and accurate

Resisting Brand Attacks

Loyal users of a brand have highly developed associative networks regarding their favored brand. As a consequence, the attitude components are highly consistent and their brand attitudes are both positive and strongly held. Why is this important? One reason is that brands are often attacked by competitors or the media. Competitors can use comparative ads to suggest that a brand is weak in specific ways. The media might pick up a story regarding a potential scandal involving the brand. Either way, when a brand is under attack, customers loyal to that brand use a number of defense mechanisms to avoid changing their attitudes. These include:[41]

- *Discrediting.* When a consumer's favorite brand is attacked, the first strategy they use is to discredit the negative information. This is done through counterarguments, whereby consumers look for weaknesses in the attack. For example, if a competitor claimed that a customer's favorite running shoe was inferior in terms of shock absorption, but the evidence came from an unknown research firm with low credibility, it would be relatively easy for the customer to discredit this claim ("the competitor is biased," "the research was shoddy," and so on). Discrediting gets more difficult when the negative information is harder to refute, as when it comes from a highly credible source.
- *Discounting.* When discrediting won't work, loyal consumers will often resort to discounting. That is, they will, perhaps without even being aware of it, protect their brand by decreasing the importance they put on the attribute in question. For example, if it is hard to refute that their favorite brand is inferior in shock absorption, a loyal customer might simply reduce the importance placed on that attribute.

- *Containment.* If an attack can't be discredited, loyal consumers also engage in containment. It's as if they "seal off" the negative information as a way to quarantine it and avoid having it spill over and spoil their existing positive attitude. This is particularly important when the negative information is on an attribute that is highly correlated with other important product features. In the case of running shoes, other attributes you would expect to be related to shock absorption would be support and comfort. Loyal customers use containment by not changing their beliefs about other related and important attributes such as support and comfort.

As you can see, loyal customers are active defenders of their brands. If the attack is weak, they discredit it. If the attack is strong, they discount and contain it. On the other hand, consumers who are not loyal to the brand under attack do not engage in these behaviors. Thus, most marketers do not generally try to capture sales from consumers who are committed to competing brands. Rather, they focus on those who are less committed, as these consumers are more attentive and responsive to their messages.

Critical Thinking Questions

1. How is discounting by consumers related to marketer's use of the cognitive attitude change strategy of "shifting importance"?
2. Can you think of any situations where loyal customers might be converted by competing brands?
3. Discuss how this insight relates to the difficulty marketers have when trying to get consumers to stop engaging in behaviors that are dangerous for them such as the use of illegal drugs?

information would generally be considered trustworthy. However, product knowledge is required for a source to have expertise. Thus a friend might be trustworthy but lack expertise. Alternatively, salespeople and advertisers may have ample knowledge but be viewed with skepticism by consumers.

Individuals who are recognized experts and who have no apparent motive to mislead can be powerful sources because of their ability to reduce risk.[42] An example is 1-800-PetMeds®, with its TV advertisements in which a veterinarian discusses pain management options for your pet. Relatively unknown individuals similar to those in the target market can be effective spokespersons as well, but for different reasons. In a **testimonial ad,** *a person, generally a typical member of the target market, recounts his or her successful use of the product, service, or idea.*[43] Testimonials are important on the web as well. Amazon and other online marketers offer customer reviews, which appear to be important determinants of attitudes and purchase behavior.[44] Similarity of the source enhances the believability and relevance of these testimonials.

Independent *third-party endorsements* by organizations such as the American Dental Association (ADA) are widely viewed as both trustworthy and expert by consumers and are actively sought by marketers. Such endorsements appear to be used by consumers as brand quality cues.[45] The remarkable success of Crest toothpaste is largely attributable to the ADA endorsement. Other examples include:

* The American Heart Association—Quaker Oats and Subway.
* J.D. Power and Associates—Edward Jones.
* Good Housekeeping Seal of Approval—LiftMaster garage doors.

Of course, the company itself is the most obvious source of most marketing messages. This means developing a corporate reputation or image for trustworthiness can greatly enhance the impact of the firm's marketing messages.[46]

Source credibility can influence persuasion in various situations. First, a credible source can enhance attitudes when consumers lack the ability or motivation to form direct judgments of the product's performance.[47] This is more of a low-involvement process. Second, a credible source can enhance message processing and acceptance. In fact, expert sources can increase attitudes in some high-involvement settings as a result of their perceived decision relevance.[48]

Cultural differences can also play a role. For example, Thai consumers are more influenced by expert sources than are Canadian consumers. Thai consumers are more risk averse and more likely to defer to authority, thus making them more prone to external sources of influence.[49]

One factor that can diminish the credibility of any source is if consumers believe that the firm is paying the source for his or her endorsement.[50] This is especially relevant for celebrities and athletes who are paid large sums for their endorsements.

Celebrity Sources   Celebrities are widely used in advertising. Marketers are increasingly using culturally diverse celebrities to reach an ethnically diverse U.S. population. Eva Mendes (Pantene), Kobe Bryant (Nike), Penelope Cruz (Lancome Tresor Fragrance), and Michelle Wie (Omega watches) are just a few such celebrities with endorsement contracts or their own product lines.

A visible use of celebrity endorsers in recent years has been the mustache campaign for milk. Illustration 11–5 clearly targets the growing ethnic market in the United States.

Celebrity sources are effective for a variety of reasons:[51]

* *Attention.* Celebrities may attract attention to the advertisement. Consumers tend to be curious about celebrities and are drawn to ads in which they appear.
* *Attitude toward the ad.* A celebrity's likability and popularity often translate into higher Aad, which can enhance brand attitudes.
* *Trustworthiness.* Despite being paid for their endorsements, celebrities often develop strong and credible public personas that consumers trust. And this trust translates into

Ethnic celebrities are increasingly common in U.S. advertisements as a way to target specific ethnic subcultures.

purchases. One study finds that private actions are just as important as professional achievements for many consumers, which explains why personal scandals can lead to a company firing an endorser as we saw in the opener.[52]

- *Expertise.* Some celebrities are also experts. This occurs frequently in areas such as music and sports. Sabian's partnership with Neil Peart is an example in music. Nike's partnership with Tiger Woods in golf equipment is an example in sports.
- *Aspirational aspects.* Consumers may identify with or desire to emulate the celebrity. As a consequence, they may imitate the behavior and style of a celebrity through purchases of similar brands and styles. For example, popular actresses often lead the way in terms of clothing and hair styles for young women.
- *Meaning transfer.* Consumers may associate known characteristics of the celebrity with attributes of the product that coincide with their own needs or desires. For example, urban youth looking for "street cred" see celebrity athletes like Alan Iverson as powerful icons. As one executive states, "He's from the streets. They admire him."[53]

As the last point suggests, effectiveness of a celebrity endorser can generally be improved by matching the image of the celebrity with the personality of the product and the actual or desired self-concept of the target market.

When the three components shown in Figure 11-4 are well matched, effective attitude formation or change can result.[54] For example, "Avril Lavigne, known for her pairing of frilly dresses and combat boots, will bring her style to the juniors department at Kohl's department stores. The edgy, pop-rock star's clothing line 'Abbey Dawn' was named after her childhood nickname."[55] In this case, there should be a strong match between the celebrity, the clothing line, and the teen and tween female consumers who want to emulate the singer's style and personality. Sometimes images don't mesh and should be avoided. For

FIGURE 11-4   Matching Endorser with Product and Target Audience

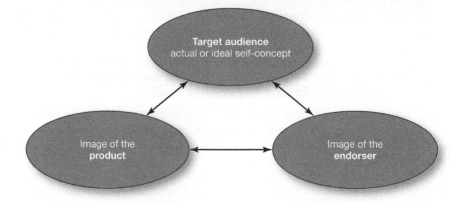

ILLUSTRATION 11–6

Spokescharacters are gaining popularity. They can add credibility to a message as well as attract attention. Some come to serve as a symbol of the product.

example, Burger King canceled talks with Paris Hilton when it decided her racy image might be too extreme for the franchise.[56] A recent study also supports the importance of matchup in sports marketing in China.[57]

Using a celebrity as a company spokesperson creates special risks. One risk is overexposure. If a celebrity endorses many products, consumers' reactions may become less positive. Thus, marketers might consider limiting the number of products "their" celebrities endorse.[58] An additional risk, as we saw in the opening example, is that negative behavior involving the spokesperson will affect the individual's credibility and, in turn, damage the firm's image.[59] Rawlings and Nike terminated their deals with Michael Vick after his indictment for dog fighting. And to protect its family image, NASCAR was quick to penalize Dale Earnhardt, Jr., for using profanity in an interview. And PLBS, a Pittsburgh company that made Big Ben Beef Jerky, terminated its contract with Ben Roethlisberger after several off-field scandals, citing their "morals clause."

Rather than use celebrities, many firms are creating **spokescharacters.**[60] Tony the Tiger and the Green Giant are perhaps the most famous, although Geico's gecko and Aflac's duck have quickly become household names. Spokescharacters can be animated animals, people, products, or other objects. A major advantage of spokescharacters is complete image control. This eliminates many of the problems associated with real celebrities. Such characters come to symbolize the brand and give it an identity that competitors cannot easily duplicate. Illustration 11–6 shows how spokescharacters are used as product symbols.

Sponsorship   **Sponsorship,** *a company providing financial support for an event* such as the Olympics or a concert, is one of the most rapidly growing marketing activities and a multibillion-dollar industry.[61] Sponsorships in North America continue to grow and total spending exceeds $16 billion per year.[62] One high-profile example is Nextel's replacement of Winston as NASCAR's title sponsor.[63] Another example is Coke's sponsorship of the FIFA World Cup.[64] The potential to generate goodwill in sports sponsorships is particularly high among rabid fans.[65] These fans may react along these lines: "Reebok supports my team, so I'm going to support Reebok."

Sponsorships often work in much the same manner as using a celebrity endorser and the matchup described in Figure 11-4 is important (where the sponsor replaces the endorser in Figure 11-4). Mismatches can generate consumer backlash such as the negative reactions over an Ohio hospital's plan to name its children's emergency and trauma center after Abercrombie & Fitch, a company that advocacy groups see as engaging in "not-exactly-child-friendly advertising."[66] Sponsor matchup is important in countries such as France and Australia as well.[67]

Finally, it is important to remember that sponsorships should be promoted through offline, online, and social media to maximize awareness and effectiveness.

Appeal Characteristics

As you would expect, the nature of the appeal, or "how" a message is communicated, affects attitude formation and change.

Fear Appeals

> The picture at the top of an ad is a snapshot of a young couple sitting together on their back deck. The headline reads: "I woke up in the hospital. Patti never woke up." The copy describes how carbon monoxide poisoning caused the tragedy. The ad, one of a series of similar ads, is for First Alert carbon monoxide detector.

Fear appeals use *the threat of negative (unpleasant) consequences if attitudes or behaviors are not altered.* Fear appeals have been studied primarily in terms of physical fear (physical harm from smoking, unsafe driving, and eating genetically modified foods), but social fears (disapproval of one's peers for incorrect clothing, bad breath, or smoking) are also used in advertising.[68]

There is some evidence that individuals avoid or distort extremely threatening messages. At the same time, fear appeals tend to be more effective as higher levels of fear are aroused. Thus, those using fear appeals want to maximize the level of fear aroused while not presenting a threat so intense as to cause the consumer to distort, reject, or avoid the message. This task is difficult because individuals respond differently to threats. Thus, the same "threatening" advertisement may arouse no fear in one individual or group and a high level of fear in another.[69] To further complicate matters, creating fear may not be enough. Recent research suggests that making people feel *accountable* to act by playing on guilt or regret emotions (e.g., ad for heart attack prevention medicine showing what the family goes through if you fail to act and die from a heart attack) may also be necessary to induce desired behaviors.[70]

Examine Illustration 11–7. *Is this an effective use of a fear appeal?*

Fear appeals are frequently criticized as unethical. Frequent targets of such criticisms are fear appeals based on social anxieties about bad breath, body odor, dandruff, or soiled clothes. The thrust of these complaints is that these appeals raise anxieties unnecessarily; that is, the injury or harm that they suggest will occur is unlikely to occur or is not really harmful. Fear appeals used to produce socially desirable behaviors such as avoiding drug use or avoiding acknowledged physical risks such as carbon monoxide poisoning are subject to much less criticism.[71]

Humorous Appeals   At almost the opposite end of the spectrum from fear appeals are **humorous appeals.**[72] Ads built around humor appear to increase attention to and liking of the ad, particularly for those individuals high in *need for humor.*[73] It also increases attitude toward the brand.[74] The overall effectiveness of humor is generally increased when the humor relates to the product or brand in a meaningful way and is viewed as appropriate for the product by the target audience.[75]

Illustration 11–8 shows an ad that makes effective use of humor.

Another effective use of humor is:

> Snickers' "You're just not you when you're hungry," featured Betty White whining during a touch football game, before eating a Snickers bar offered by a friend, and then turning back into himself. This ad aired during the Super Bowl and won *USA Today*'s ad meter award.[76] The humor points to how being hungry makes one grumpy and that Snickers satisfies that hunger.

While it is generally recommended that humor be relevant, companies have been successful using humor that is only loosely tied to the product (e.g., Geico's gecko ads in which the confusion between the two creates the humor even though the gecko has nothing to do with auto insurance). In these cases, humor attracts attention, and the positive emotional response may transfer to the brand via classical conditioning or Aad.[77] Humorous ads also involve risk. What is considered funny varies across individuals, cultures, and situations.[78] Humor viewed as demeaning or insulting can cost a company image and sales.

Comparative Ads   **Comparative ads** *directly compare the features or benefits of two or more brands* (see Illustration 11–9). Comparative ads are often more effective than

ILLUSTRATION 11–7

Fear appeals can be effective at forming, reinforcing, and/or changing attitudes. The ethics of such appeals should be examined carefully before they are used.

ILLUSTRATION 11–8

Humor is widely used in advertising to attract attention and alter attitudes.

There's a reason nobody's ever been called a couch peanut.

A friendly reminder from America's Peanut Farmers™
www.nationalpeanutboard.org

noncomparative ads in generating attention, message and brand awareness, greater message processing, favorable sponsor brand attitudes, and increased purchase intentions and behaviors. However, comparative ads can also have negative consequences for the sponsor brand such as lower believability, lower attitude toward the ad and sponsor brand, and more positive attitude toward the competitor brand(s).[79] Available evidence suggests that comparative ads should follow these guidelines:[80]

- Comparative advertising may be particularly effective for promoting new or little-known brands with strong product attributes to create their position or to upgrade their image by association. When established brands use comparative ads, they may appear "defensive." This may be particularly true if comparisons are seen as overly derogatory.
- Comparative advertising is likely to be more effective if its claims are substantiated by credible sources. Also, research should be used to determine the optimal number of claims.
- Audience characteristics, especially brand loyalty associated with the sponsoring brand, are important. Users of the named competitor brands appear to resist comparative claims.
- Since comparative ads are more interesting than noncomparatives (and more offensive), they may be effective in stagnant categories where noncomparative ads have ceased to be effective.

ILLUSTRATION 11–9

Comparison ads can be very effective at changing attitudes about lesser-known brands.

TASTE FOR YOURSELF.

A LOT OF HYPE.

OR

A LOT OF FLAVOR.

NESCAFÉ
Taster's Choice

For a free sample of all six varieties go to tasterschoice.com/thesmartchoice or facebook.com/nescafeusa

- Print media appear to be better vehicles for comparative advertisements, because print lends itself to more thorough comparisons.
- Care must be used with *partially* comparative ads because of their misleading potential. A partially comparative ad contains comparative and noncomparative information and may lead consumers to believe the sponsor brand is superior on all attributes not just the compared attributes.

Emotional Appeals   Emotional or feeling ads are being used with increasing frequency. **Emotional ads** are *designed primarily to elicit a positive affective response rather than to provide information or arguments.* Emotional ads such as those that arouse feelings of warmth trigger physiological reactions (see Chapter 10). Emotional advertisements may enhance persuasion by increasing[81]

- Attention and processing of the ad and, therefore, ad recall.

- Liking of the ad.
- Product liking through classical conditioning.
- Product liking through high-involvement processes.

As we discussed previously, whether emotional ads operate through classical conditioning and Aad (low involvement) or through more analytical high-involvement processes depends on the relevance of the emotion to evaluating key aspects of the product.

In addition, emotional ads appear to work better than rational or informational ads for heavy (versus light) users of a brand and more established (versus new) brands in a market. This effect may be due to the fact that heavy users and established brands already have an established knowledge base for attribute information, making emotions a more compelling differentiating feature.[82]

Illustration 11–10 is designed to elicit emotional responses.

Value-Expressive versus Utilitarian Appeals   **Value-expressive appeals** attempt to build a personality for the product or create an image of the product user. **Utilitarian appeals** involve informing the consumer of one or more functional benefits that are important to the target market. Which is best under what conditions?

Both theory and some empirical evidence indicate that *utilitarian* appeals are most effective for functional products and *value-expressive* appeals are most effective for products designed to enhance self-image or provide other intangible benefits.[83] Which to use can be difficult when, as in the case of automobiles, many consider the product primarily utilitarian and many consider it primarily value-expressive. Some marketers hedge their bets in such situations by appealing to both aspects simultaneously. Illustration 11–11 contains an example of each approach.

Research also indicates that banner ads on websites should differ for the two types of products. For utilitarian products, banner ads serve primarily to transport consumers to the more detailed target ads or sites. For value-expressive products, banner ads should influence attitudes on the basis of exposure to the banner ad itself, not on click-through to the target ad.[84]

Message Structure Characteristics

One-Sided versus Two-Sided Messages   In advertisements and sales presentations, marketers generally present only the benefits of their product without mentioning any negative characteristics it might possess or any advantages a competitor might have. These are **one-sided messages,** since only one point of view is expressed. The idea of a **two-sided message,** presenting both good and bad points, is counterintuitive, and most marketers are reluctant to try such an approach. However, two-sided messages are generally more effective than one-sided messages in changing a strongly held attitude. One reason is because they are unexpected and increase consumer trust in the advertiser. They are particularly effective with highly educated consumers. One-sided messages are most effective at reinforcing existing attitudes. However, product type, situational variables, and advertisement format influence the relative effectiveness of the two approaches.[85]

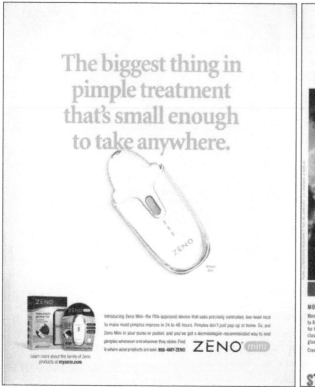

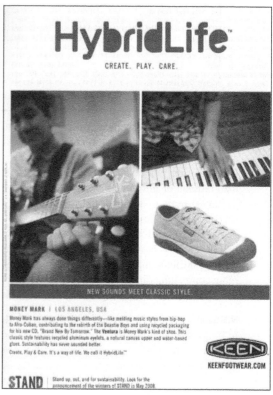

ILLUSTRATION 11–11

Utilitarian appeals generally work best with functional products; value-expressive appeals work best with products designed to enhance one's image or provide other intangible benefits.

Positive versus Negative Framing   **Message framing** refers to presenting one of two equivalent value outcomes either in positive or gain terms (positive framing) or in negative or loss terms (negative framing). There are various *types* of message frames, and the type of frame influences whether positive or negative framing is best.[86] The simplest form appears to be **attribute framing** where only a single attribute is the focus of the frame. A classic example is describing ground beef as either 80 percent fat free (positive frame) or 20 percent fat (negative frame). In attribute framing situations, positive framing yields the most positive evaluations because it emphasizes the desirable aspects of the specific attribute.

Goal framing is where "the message stresses either the positive consequences of performing an act or the negative consequences of not performing the act."[87] The act could be purchasing a specific brand, having a yearly mammogram, and so on. In both cases the act is beneficial. However, in the positive frame, the benefits of the act are emphasized (e.g., increased chance of finding tumor) while in the negative frame, the risks of not engaging in the act are emphasized (e.g., decreased chance of finding tumor). In goal framing situations the *negative* frame is generally more effective. This is likely due to the risk-averse nature of consumers coupled with the risk-enhancing nature of the negative goal frame.

Framing effects can vary across products, consumers, and situations. Thus, decisions to use positive or negative framing should ultimately be based on research for the specific product and market.[88]

Nonverbal Components   In Chapter 9, we discussed how pictures enhance imagery and facilitate learning. Pictures, music, surrealism, and other nonverbal cues are also effective in attitude change. Emotional ads, described earlier, often rely primarily or exclusively on nonverbal content to arouse an emotional response. Nonverbal ad content can also affect cognitions about a product. For example, an ad showing a person drinking a new beverage after exercise provides information about appropriate usage situations without stating "good to use after exercise." Thus, nonverbal components can influence attitudes through affect, cognition, or both.

MARKET SEGMENTATION AND PRODUCT DEVELOPMENT STRATEGIES BASED ON ATTITUDES

Market Segmentation

Identifying market segments is a key aspect of marketing. Properly designed marketing programs should be built around the unique needs of each market segment. The importance of various attributes is one way of defining customer needs for a given product. *Segmenting consumers on the basis of their most important attribute or attributes* is called **benefit segmentation.**[89]

To define benefit segments, a marketer needs to know the importance that consumers attached to various product or service features. This allows consumers who seek the same benefits to be grouped into segments. Additional information about consumers within each segment can then be obtained to develop a more complete picture of each segment. Based on this information, separate marketing programs can be developed for each of the selected target segments.

Product Development

While the importance consumers attach to key attributes provides a meaningful way to understand needs and form benefit segments, the ideal levels of performance indicate the consumers' desired level of performance in satisfying those needs. These ideal levels of performance can provide valuable guidelines in developing a new product or reformulating an existing one.

Table 11-1 describes how Coca-Cola used this approach in developing a new soft drink.[90] The first step is constructing a profile of a consumer segment's ideal level of performance on key soft drink attributes. As shown in Table 11-1, four attributes were identified for a particular type of soft drink, and ideal performance was obtained from consumer ratings as shown in section A.

A second step is creating a product concept that closely matches the ideal profile. The concept could be a written description, picture, or actual prototype. As section B in Table 11-1 shows, consumers evaluated the product concept developed by Coca-Cola as being fairly close to their ideal on each of the four attributes. Only color appears to be off target slightly by being a little too dark.

The next step is translating the concept into an actual product. When Coca-Cola did this and presented the product to the consumers, they did not perceive it to be similar to either the product concept or their ideal (see section C in Table 11-1). Although the actual product achieved a reasonable attitude rating, the product concept scored higher (section D, Table 11-1). Thus, the product could benefit from further improvements to better align it with the ideal profile. This same basic procedure can be used to help design ads, packages, or retail outlets.

TABLE **Using the Multiattribute Attitude Model in the Product Development Process**

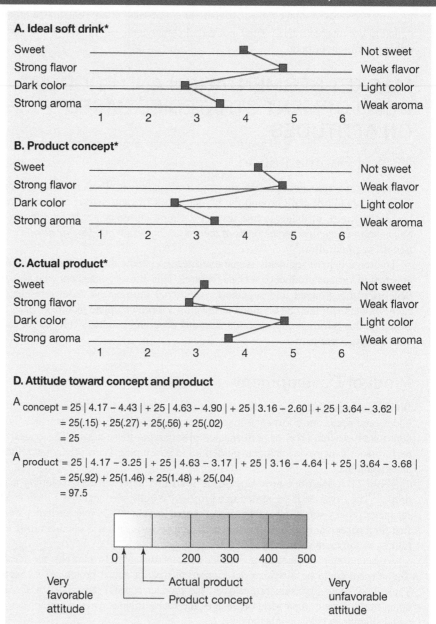

A. Ideal soft drink*

Sweet	Not sweet
Strong flavor	Weak flavor
Dark color	Light color
Strong aroma	Weak aroma

(scale 1 2 3 4 5 6)

B. Product concept*

Sweet	Not sweet
Strong flavor	Weak flavor
Dark color	Light color
Strong aroma	Weak aroma

(scale 1 2 3 4 5 6)

C. Actual product*

Sweet	Not sweet
Strong flavor	Weak flavor
Dark color	Light color
Strong aroma	Weak aroma

(scale 1 2 3 4 5 6)

D. Attitude toward concept and product

$$A_{concept} = 25 \mid 4.17 - 4.43 \mid + 25 \mid 4.63 - 4.90 \mid + 25 \mid 3.16 - 2.60 \mid + 25 \mid 3.64 - 3.62 \mid$$
$$= 25(.15) + 25(.27) + 25(.56) + 25(.02)$$
$$= 25$$

$$A_{product} = 25 \mid 4.17 - 3.25 \mid + 25 \mid 4.63 - 3.17 \mid + 25 \mid 3.16 - 4.64 \mid + 25 \mid 3.64 - 3.68 \mid$$
$$= 25(.92) + 25(1.46) + 25(1.48) + 25(.04)$$
$$= 97.5$$

(scale 0 — 200 300 400 500)

Very favorable attitude — Actual product / Product concept — Very unfavorable attitude

*Measured on a six-point semantic differential scale.

SUMMARY

LO1: Define attitude and its role in consumer behavior

Attitudes can be defined as the way people think, feel, and act toward some aspect of their environment. A result of all the factors discussed so far in the text, attitudes influence, as well as reflect, the lifestyle individuals pursue.

LO2: Summarize the three components of attitudes

Attitudes have three components: cognitive, affective, and behavioral. The *cognitive component* consists of the individual's beliefs or knowledge about the object. It is generally assessed by using a version of the multiattribute attitude model. Feelings or emotional reactions to an object represent the *affective component* of the attitude and can be assessed in various ways including AdSAM®. The *behavioral component* reflects overt actions and statements of behavioral intentions with respect to specific attributes of the object or the overall object. In general, all three components tend to be consistent with each other. However, a number of factors can create inconsistencies, and marketers must understand and incorporate these in their marketing research and communications strategies.

LO3: Discuss attitude change strategies associated with each attitude component

Attitude change strategies can focus on affect, behavior, cognition, or some combination. Attempts to change affect generally rely on classical conditioning. Change strategies focusing on behavior rely more on operant conditioning. Changing cognitions usually involves information processing and cognitive learning. It can involve changing beliefs about such things as a brand's attribute levels, shifting the importance of a given attribute, adding beliefs about new attributes, or changing the perceived ideal point for a specific attribute or for the brand concept overall.

LO4: Describe the elaboration likelihood model of persuasion

The *elaboration likelihood model (ELM)* is a theory about how attitudes are formed and changed under varying conditions of involvement. The ELM suggests different communications strategies depending on involvement.

In general, detailed factual information (central cues) is effective in high-involvement, central-route situations. Low-involvement, peripheral-route situations generally require limited information and instead rely on simple affective and cognitive cues such as pictures, music, and characteristics of people in the ad (peripheral cues). The ELM has found general support. However, what is perceived as relevant can depend on the situation (e.g., attractive model and hair may be "central" in shampoo ad but "peripheral" in car ad) and the nature of competition can bolster the role of peripheral cues even under high involvement.

LO5: Describe the role of message source, appeal, and structure on attitudes

Three communication characteristics are important to attitudes. They are source characteristics, message appeal characteristics, and message structure characteristics.

In terms of source characteristics, *source credibility* is composed of two dimensions: trustworthiness and expertise. Persuasion is much easier when the message source is viewed as highly credible. Celebrities are widely used as product or company spokespersons. They are most effective when their image matches the personality of the product and the actual or desired self-concept of the target market.

In terms of message appeals, the appeals used to change attitudes are important and are varied. *Fear appeals* use threat of negative consequences if attitudes or behaviors are not altered. *Humorous appeals* can also be effective in influencing attitudes. However, the humorous message must remain focused on the brand or main selling point to be maximally effective. *Comparative ads* produce mixed results. They are most effective for unknown brands having a strong functional advantage. The decision to use a *value-expressive* or *utilitarian appeal* depends on whether the brand fills value-expressive or utilitarian needs. However, this is complicated when the brand fills both types of needs. *Emotional appeals* have been found to have a strong effect on attitudes toward both the ad and the product.

Message structure has three facets. *Two-sided* (versus *one-sided*) *messages* can increase trust and message acceptance, but effects depend on characteristics of the individual and situation. *Message framing* effects—presenting equivalent value outcomes either in positive (positive framing) or negative (negative framing) terms—depend on type of frame. Positive *attribute framing* tends to work best whereas negative *goal framing* tends to work best. *Nonverbal* aspects of the ad, such as pictures, surrealism, and music, also affect attitudes.

LO6: Discuss segmentation and product development applications of attitudes

Consumer evaluations, feelings, and beliefs about specific product features form the basis for market segmentation strategies, such as *benefit segmentation,* and for new-product development strategies.

KEY TERMS

Aesthetic appeal 388
Affective component 387
Ambivalent attitude 391
Attitude 384
Attribute framing 406
Behavioral component 389
Benefit segmentation 407
Cognitive component 384
Comparative ads 403

Elaboration likelihood model
  (ELM) 395
Emotional ads 404
Fear appeals 402
Goal framing 406
Humorous appeals 403
Mere exposure 394
Message framing 406
Multiattribute attitude model 385

One-sided messages 405
Source credibility 397
Spokescharacters 401
Sponsorship 401
Testimonial ad 399
Two-sided message 405
Utilitarian appeals 405
Value-expressive appeals 405

INTERNET EXERCISES

1. Visit several general interest or entertainment sites on the Internet that contain ads. Find and describe an ad that attempts to change each of the following to help form or change attitudes:
   a. Affective component
   b. Cognitive component
   c. Behavioral component
2. Visit several company websites. Find and describe one that uses one of the following to help form or change attitudes:
   a. Credible source
   b. Celebrity source
   c. Humorous appeal

   d. Fear appeal
   e. Comparative appeal
   f. Emotional appeal
3. Visit www.adsam.com. Go to the "Take a Sample Survey" section, read the instructions, and take a survey that involves ratings using the AdSAM approach. Evaluate AdSAM® compared with more cognitive approaches that utilize verbal scales.
4. Visit the Intergovernmental Panel on Climate Change (IPCC) website (www.ipcc.ch/). What attitude change techniques does it use? Are they effective?

REVIEW QUESTIONS

1. What is an *attitude*?
2. What are the components of an attitude?
3. Are the components of an attitude consistent? What factors reduce the apparent consistency among attitude components?
4. What is the *multiattribute attitude model*?
5. What is *attitude ambivalence*?

6. What strategies can be used to change the following components of an attitude?
   a. Affective
   b. Behavioral
   c. Cognitive
7. What is meant by *mere exposure*?
8. What is the *elaboration likelihood model*?

9. What strategies can consumers use to resist persuasion? Which consumers are most likely to do so?

10. What are the two characteristics of the source of a message that influence its ability to change attitudes? Describe each.

11. What is *source credibility*? What causes it?

12. Why are celebrity sources sometimes effective? What risks are associated with using a celebrity source?

13. Name five possible characteristics of an appeal that would influence or change attitudes. Describe each.

14. Are *fear appeals* always effective in changing attitudes? Why?

15. What characteristics should *humorous ads* have?

16. Are *emotional appeals* effective? Why?

17. Are *comparative appeals* effective? Why?

18. What is a *value-expressive appeal*? A *utilitarian appeal*? When should each be used?

19. What are the three characteristics of the message structure that influence its ability to change attitudes? Describe each.

20. What is meant by *positive message framing* and *negative message framing*? How does the effectiveness of a positive versus negative frame vary depending on whether it's a *goal frame* or *attribute frame*?

21. What are the nonverbal components of an ad? What impact do they have on attitudes?

22. When is a *two-sided message* likely to be more effective than a *one-sided message*?

23. How can attitudes guide new-product development?

24. What is a *benefit segment*?

DISCUSSION QUESTIONS

25. Which version of the multiattribute attitude model, and which attributes, would you use to assess student attitudes toward the following? Justify your answer.
    a. Student health system
    b. Target store
    c. Hybrid automobiles
    d. Cats as pets
    e. AMP

26. Respond to the questions in Consumer Insight 11-1.

27. Assume you wanted to improve or create favorable attitudes among college students toward the following. Would you focus primarily on the affective, cognitive, or behavioral component? Why?
    a. ASPCA
    b. BMW motorcyles
    c. Organic eggs
    d. Sky diving
    e. Not driving after drinking
    f. Using the bus for most local trips
    g. Oreo cookies
    h. Volunteering for Habitat for Humanity

28. Suppose you used the multiattribute attitude model and developed a fruit-based carbonated drink that was successful in the United States. Could you use the same model in the following countries? If not, how would it have to change?
    a. India
    b. Chile
    c. Qatar

29. Suppose you wanted to form highly negative attitudes toward smoking among college students.
    a. Which attitude component would you focus on? Why?
    b. Which message characteristic would you use? Why?
    c. What type of appeal would you use? Why?

30. What communications characteristics would you use in an attempt to improve college students' attitudes toward the following?
    a. Buick
    b. Levis
    c. Volunteering at a local shelter
    d. Gmail
    e. MADD
    f. White-water rafting

31. Is it ethical to use fear appeals to increase demand for the following?
    a. Complexion medication among teenagers
    b. Dandruff-control shampoos among adults

c. Emergency response devices among elderly consumers

d. Weight-loss supplements for young women

32. Name two appropriate and two inappropriate celebrity spokespersons for each of the products or causes in Question 27. Justify your selection.

33. What benefit segments do you think exist for the following?
   a. Crossroads Guitar Festival
   b. NASCAR
   c. Major art museums
   d. Jazz concert

APPLICATION ACTIVITIES

34. Find and copy two magazine or newspaper advertisements, one based on the affective component and the other on the cognitive component. Discuss the approach of each ad in terms of its copy and illustration and what effect it creates in terms of attitude. Also discuss why the marketer might have taken that approach in each advertisement.

35. Repeat Activity 34 for utilitarian and value-expressive appeals.

36. Identify a television commercial that uses a humorous appeal. Then interview five individuals not enrolled in your class and measure their
   a. Awareness of this commercial.
   b. Recall of the brand advertised.
   c. Recall of relevant information.
   d. Liking of the commercial.
   e. Preference for the brand advertised.

   Evaluate your results and assess the level of communication that has taken place in terms of these five consumers' exposure, attention, interpretation, and preferences for this product and commercial.

37. Describe a magazine, Internet, or television advertisement, or a package that uses the following. Evaluate the effectiveness of the ad or package.
   a. Aesthetic appeal
   b. Source credibility
   c. Celebrity source
   d. Testimonial
   e. Fear appeal
   f. Humorous appeal
   g. Emotional appeal
   h. Comparative approach
   i. Extensive nonverbal elements
   j. A two-sided appeal
   k. Positive message framing
   l. Negative message framing

38. Measure another student's ideal beliefs and belief importance for the following. Examine these ideal beliefs and importance weights and then develop a verbal description (i.e., concept) of a new brand for these items that would satisfy this student's needs. Next, measure that student's attitude toward the concept you have developed in your verbal description.
   a. Sunglasses
   b. Spa
   c. Automobile
   d. Credit card
   e. Dietary supplements
   f. Charity

39. Use the multiattribute attitude model to assess 10 students' attitudes toward several brands in the following product categories. Measure the students' behavior with respect to these brands. Are they consistent? Explain any inconsistencies.
   a. Television news program
   b. Sports drinks
   c. Healthy dinners
   d. Fast-food restaurants
   e. Exercise
   f. Coffee shops

40. Develop two advertisements for the following with college students as the target. One ad should focus on the cognitive component and the other on the affective component.
   a. Timex sport watches
   b. Toyota Prius
   c. Red Bull energy drink
   d. Reducing smoking
   e. Increasing exercise
   f. Reebok athletic shoes

41. Repeat Activity 40 using utilitarian and value-expressive appeals.

42. Develop a positively framed and an equivalent negatively framed message about a product attribute. Have five students react to these messages. What do you conclude?

REFERENCES

1. This opener is based on "Michael Phelps' Sponsors Sticking with Him After Bong Photo," *Associated Press,* February 2, 2009; K. Hein, "Are Celebrity Endorsers Really Worth the Trouble?" *Brandweek,* February 9, 2009; "Nike Won't Drop Tiger Woods," www.x17online.com/celebrities, December 12, 2009, accessed June 6, 2011; Y. Upadhyay and S. K. Singh, "When Sports Celebrity Doesn't Perform," *Vision,* January–June 2010; E. B. York, "Celeb Dieters," *Advertising Age,* February 15, 2010, p. 10; D. Tilkin, "Study on Tiger," www.kval.com/news/business, February 11, 2011, accessed June 6, 2011; and L. I. Alpert, "Tag Heuer Drops Tiger," *New York Post,* June 10, 2011.

2. See R. E. Petty, D. T. Wegener, and L. R. Fabriger, "Attitudes and Attitude Change," *Annual Review of Psychology* 48 (1997), pp. 609–38.

3. J. A. Ruth, "Promoting a Brand's Emotional Benefits," *Journal of Consumer Psychology* 11, no. 2 (2001), pp. 99–113.

4. B. Wansink and M. M. Cheney, "Leveraging FDA Health Claims," *Journal of Consumer Affairs* 39, no. 2 (2005), pp., 386–98.

5. See M. Wanke, G. Bohner, and A. Jurkowitsch, "There Are Many Reasons to Drive a BMW," *Journal of Consumer Research,* September 1997, pp. 170–77.

6. K. E. Voss, E. R. Spangenberg, and B. Grohmann, "Measuring the Hedonic and Utilitarian Dimensions of Consumer Attitude," *Journal of Marketing Research,* August 2003, pp. 310–20; T. Lageat, S. Czellar, and G. Laurent, "Engineering Hedonic Attributes to Generate Perceptions of Luxury," *Marketing Letters,* July 2003, pp. 97–109; and R. Chitturi, R. Raghunathan, and V. Mahajan, "Delight by Design," *Journal of Marketing,* May 2008, pp. 48–63.

7. G. C. Bruner II and A. Kumar, "Explaining Consumer Acceptance of Handheld Internet Devices," *Journal of Business Research* 58 (2005), pp. 553–58.

8. C. T. Allen et al., "A Place for Emotion in Attitude Models," *Journal of Business Research* 58 (2005), pp. 494–99.

9. C. Page and P. M. Herr, "An Investigation of the Processes by Which Product Design and Brand Strength Interact to Determine Initial Affect and Quality Judgments," *Journal of Consumer Psychology* 12, no. 2 (2002), pp. 133–47; and H. Hagtvedt and V. M. Patrick, "Art Infusion," *Journal of Marketing Research,* June 2008, pp. 379–89.

10. J. D. Morris et al., "The Power of Affect," *Journal of Advertising Research,* May–June 2002, pp. 7–17; and J. D. Morris, "Observations: SAM," *Journal of Advertising Research,* November–December 1995, pp. 63–68.

11. For an excellent review, see P. A. Dabholkar, "Incorporating Choice into an Attitudinal Framework," *Journal of Consumer Research,* June 1994, pp. 100–18. See also Morris et al., "The Power of Affect"; and P. E. Grimm, "A$_b$ Components' Impact on Brand Preference," *Journal of Business Research* 58 (2005), pp. 508–17; and P. M. Homer, "Relationships among Ad-Induced Affect, Beliefs, and Attitudes," *Journal of Advertising,* Spring 2006, pp. 35–51.

12. R. E. Petty and J. A. Krosnick, *Attitude Strength* (Mahwah, NJ: Erlbaum, 1995); S. J. Kraus, "Attitudes and the Prediction of Behavior," *Personality and Social Psychology Bulletin* 21 (1995), pp. 58–75; R. Madrigal, "Social Identity Effects in a Belief-Attitude-Intentions Hierarchy," *Psychology & Marketing,* February 2001, pp. 145–65; and W. E. Baker, "The Diagnosticity of Advertising Generated Brand Attitudes in Brand Choice Contexts," *Journal of Consumer Psychology* 11, no. 2 (2001), pp. 129–39.

13. S. O. Olsen, J. Wilcox, and U. Olsson, "Consequences of Ambivalence on Satisfaction and Loyalty," *Psychology & Marketing,* March 2005, pp. 247–69; and C. Homburg, N. Koschate, and W. D. Hoyer, "The Role of Cognition and Affect in the Formation of Customer Satisfaction," *Journal of Marketing,* July 2006, pp. 21–31. See also C. A. Roster and M. L. Richins, "Ambivalence and Attitudes in Consumer Replacement Decisions," *Journal of Consumer Psychology* 19 (2009), pp. 48–61.

14. See, e.g., J. R. Priester et al., "The $A^2 SC^2$ Model," *Journal of Consumer Research,* March 2004, pp. 574–87; and B. Johnson, "Consumers Cite Past Experience as the No. 1 Influencer When Buying," *Advertising Age,* November 20, 2006, p. 21.

15. See S. A. Hawkins, S. J. Hoch, and J. Meyers-Levy, "Low-Involvement Learning," *Journal of Consumer Psychology* 11, no. 31 (2001), pp. 1–11.

16. For guidelines on structuring message arguments to enhance beliefs, see C. S. Areni, "The Proposition–Probability Model of Argument Structure and Message Acceptance," *Journal of Consumer Research,* September 2002, pp. 168–87.

17. N. Zmuda, "Rebranding Resuscitates 90-year-old Radio Shack," *Advertising Age,* April 12, 2010, p. 16.

18. See A. Drolet and J. Aaker, "Off-Target?" *Journal of Consumer Psychology* 12, no. 1 (2002), pp. 59–68; and A. H. Tangari et al., "How Do Antitobacco Campaign Advertising and Smoking Status Affect Beliefs and Intentions?" *Journal of Public Policy and Marketing,* Spring 2007, pp. 60–74.

19. M. R. Forehand and R. Deshpande, "What We See Makes Us Who We Are," *Journal of Marketing Research,* August 2001, 336–48. See also J. K. Maher and M. Hu, "The Priming of Material Values on Consumer Information Processing of Print Advertisements," *Journal of Current Issues and Research in Advertising,* Fall 2003, pp. 21–30.

20. From website at http://www.pomegranates.org/techinfo.html, accessed June 10, 2011.

21. For a discussion of program-induced affect and extremity of beliefs, see R. Adaval, "How Good Gets Better and Bad Gets Worse," *Journal of Consumer Research,* December 2003, pp. 352–67.

22. See M. J. J. M. Candel and J. M. E. Pennings, "Attitude-Based Models for Binary Choices," *Journal of Economic Psychology* 20 (1999), pp. 547–69; and H.-P. Erb, Antoine Bioy, and D. J. Hilton, "Choice Preferences without Inferences," *Journal of Behavioral Decision Making,* July 2002, pp. 251–62.

23. See, e.g., W. E. Baker, "When Can Affective Conditioning and Mere Exposure Directly Influence Brand Choice?" *Journal of Advertising,* Winter 1999, pp. 31–46; and B. D. Till and R. L. Priluck, "Stimulus Generalization in Classical Conditioning," *Psychology & Marketing,* January 2000, pp. 55–72.

24. See, e.g., R. E. Goldsmith, B. A. Lafferty, and S. J. Newell, "The Impact of Corporate Credibility and Celebrity Credibility on Consumer Reaction to Advertisements and Brands," *Journal of Advertising,* Fall 2000, pp. 43–54; and K. S. Coulter, "An Examination of Qualitative vs. Quantitative Elaboration Likelihood Effects," *Psychology & Marketing,* January 2005, pp. 31–49.

25. J. S. Stevenson, G. C. Bruner II, and A. Kumard, "Webpage Background and Viewer Attitudes," and G. C. Bruner II and A. Kumard, "Web Commercials and Advertising Hierarchy-of-Effects," both in *Journal of Advertising Research,* January 2000, pp. 29–34 and 35–43, respectively. See also L. Dailey, "Navigational Web Atmospherics," *Journal of Business Research* 57 (2004), 795–803.

26. J. R. Coyle and E. Thorson, "The Effects of Progressive Levels of Interactivity and Vividness in Web Marketing Sites," *Journal of Advertising,* Fall 2001, pp. 65–77.

27. See M.-H. Huang, "Is Negative Affect in Advertising General or Specific?" *Psychology Marketing,* May 1997, pp. 223–40. See also P. S. Ellen and P. F. Bone, "Does It Matter If It Smells?" *Journal of Advertising,* Winter 1998, pp. 29–39.

28. A. Rindfleisch and J. J. Inman, "Explaining the Familiarity-Liking Relationship," *Marketing Letters* 1 (1998), pp. 5–19; E. L. Olson and H. M. Thjomoe, "The Effects of Peripheral Exposure to Information on Brand Preference," *European Journal of Marketing* 37, no. 1/2 (2003), pp. 243–55; and G. Menon and P. Raghubir, "Ease-of-Retrieval as an Automatic Input in Judgments," *Journal of Consumer Research,* September 2003, pp. 230–43.

29. S. Auty and C. Lewis, "Exploring Children's Choice," *Psychology & Marketing,* September 2004, pp. 697–713.

30. See Ruth, "Promoting a Brand's Emotional Benefits"; R. Adaval, "Sometimes It Just Feels Right," *Journal of Consumer Research,* June 2001, pp. 1–17; M. T. Pham et al., "Affect Monitoring and the Primacy of Feelings in Judgment," *Journal of Consumer Research,* September 2001, pp. 167–88; and C. W. M. Yeung and R. S. Wyer Jr., "Affect, Appraisal, and Consumer Judgment," *Journal of Consumer Research,* September 2004, pp. 412–24.

31. See D. S. Kempf, "Attitude Formation from Product Trial," *Psychology & Marketing,* January 1999, pp. 35–50.

32. D. A. Griffith and Q. Chen, "The Influence of Virtual Direct Experience (VDE) on On-line Ad Message Effectiveness," *Journal of Advertising,* Spring 2004, pp. 55–68.

33. See G. J. Gaeth et al., "Consumers' Attitude Change across Sequences of Successful and Unsuccessful Product Usage," *Marketing Letters* 1 (1997), pp. 41–53; and L. A. Brannon and T. C. Brock, "Limiting Time for Response Enhances Behavior Corresponding to the Merits of Compliance Appeals," *Journal of Consumer Psychology* 10, no. 3 (2001), pp. 135–46.

34. See, e.g., M. L. Roehm and B. Sternthal, "The Moderating Effect of Knowledge and Resources on the Persuasive Impact of Analogies," *Journal of Consumer Research,* September 2001, pp. 257–72; M. Moorman, P. C. Neijens, and E. G. Smit, "The Effects of Magazine-Induced Psychological Responses and Thematic Congruence on Memory and Attitude toward the Ad in a Real-Life Setting," *Journal of Advertising,* Winter 2002, pp. 27–40; and S. Putrevu, J. Tan and K. R. Lord "Consumer Responses to Complex Advertisements," *Journal of Current Issues and Research in Advertising,* Spring 2004, pp. 9–24.

35. See R. E. Petty, J. T. Cacioppo, and D. Schumann, "Central and Peripheral Routes to Advertising Effectiveness," *Journal of Consumer Research,* September 1993, pp. 135–46; J. Meyers-Levy and P. Malaviya, "Consumers' Processing of Persuasive Advertisements," *Journal of Marketing* 63 (1999), pp. 45–60; C. S. Areni, "The Effects of Structural and Grammatical Variables on Persuasion," *Psychology & Marketing,* April 2003, pp. 349–75; and D. D. Rucker and R. E. Petty, "Increasing the Effectiveness of Communications to Consumers," *Journal of Public Policy and Marketing,* Spring 2006, 39–52. For additional perspectives, see T. P. Novak and D. L. Hoffman, "The Fit of Thinking Style and Situation," *Journal of Consumer Research,* June 2009, pp. 56–72; and M. L. Cronley, S. P. Mantel, and F. R. Kardes, "Effects of Accuracy Motivation and Need to Evaluate on Mode of Attitude Formation and Attitude-Behavior Consistency," *Journal of Consumer Psychology* 20 (2010), pp. 274–81.

36. See, e.g., Petty and Krosnick, *Attitude Strength.* For a discussion of attitude persistence under low involvement, see J. Sengupta, R. C. Goodstein, and D. S. Boninger, "All Cues Are Not Created Equal," *Journal of Consumer Research,* March 1997, pp. 351–61.

37. P. W. Miniard et al., "Picture-based Persuasion Processes and the Moderating Role of Involvement," *Journal of Consumer Research,* June 1991, pp. 92–107.

38. P. W. Miniard, D. Sirdeshmukh, and D. E. Innis, "Peripheral Persuasion and Brand Choice," *Journal of Consumer Research,* September 1992, pp. 226–39; and T. B. Heath, M. S. McCarthy, and D. L. Mothersbaugh, "Spokesperson Fame and Vividness Effects in the Context of Issue-Relevant Thinking," *Journal of Consumer Research,* March 1994, pp. 520–34; see also B. Yoo and R. Mandhachitara, "Estimating Advertising Effects on Sales in a Competitive Setting," *Journal of Advertising Research,* September 2003, pp. 310–21; and S. S. Posavac et al., "The Brand Positivity Effect," *Journal of Consumer Research,* December 2004, pp. 643–51.

39. T. F. Mangleburg and T. Bristol, "Socialization and Adolescents' Skepticism toward Advertising," *Journal of Advertising,* Fall 1998, pp. 11–21; C. Obermiller and E. R. Spangenberg, "On the Origin and Distinctiveness of Skepticism toward Advertising," *Marketing Letters,* November 2000, pp. 311–22; and D. M. Hardesty, J. P. Carlson, and W. O. Bearden, "Brand Familiarity and Invoice Price Effects on Consumer Evaluations," *Journal of Advertising,* Summer 2002, pp. 1–15.

40. M. C. Campbell and A. Kirmani, "Consumers' Use of Persuasion Knowledge," *Journal of Consumer Research,* June 2000, pp. 69–83; R. Ahluwalia and R. E. Burnkrant, "Answering Questions about Questions," *Journal of Consumer Research,* June 2004, pp. 26–42; and D. M. Hardesty, W. O. Bearden, and J. P. Carlson, "Persuasion Knowledge and Consumer Reactions to Pricing Tactics," *Journal of Retailing* 83, no. 2 (2007), pp. 199–210.

41. Consumer Insight 11-1 is based on R. Ahlusalia, "Examination of Psychological Processes Underlying Resistance to Persuasion," *Journal of Consumer Research,* September 2000, pp. 217–32; R. D. Jewell and H. R. Unnava, "Exploring Differences in Attitudes between Light and Heavy Brand Users," *Journal of Consumer Psychology* 14, nos. 1 & 2 (2004), pp. 75–80; and Z. L. Tormala and R. E. Petty, "Source Credibility and Attitude Certainty," *Journal of Consumer Psychology* 14, no. 4 (2004), pp. 427–42.

42. A. Wang, "The Effects of Expert and Consumer Endorsements on Audience Response," *Journal of Advertising Research,* December 2005, pp. 402–12; R. Arora, C. Stoner, and A. Arora, "Using Framing and Credibility to Incorporate Exercise and Fitness in Individual's Lifestyle," *Journal of Consumer Marketing* 23, no. 4 (2006), pp. 199–207; and D. Biswas, A. Biswas, and N. Das, "The Differential Effects of Celebrity and Expert Endorsements on Consumer Risk Perceptions," *Journal of Advertising,* Summer 2006, pp. 17–31.

43. R. D. Reinartz, "Testimonial Ads," *Bank Marketing,* March 1996, pp. 25–30; and J. Nicholson, "Testimonial Ads Defend Client Turf," *Editor & Publisher,* October 23, 1999, p. 33; and O. Appiah, "The Effectiveness of 'Typical-User' Testimonial Advertisements on Black and White Browsers' Evaluations of Products on Commercial Websites," *Journal of Advertising Research,* March 2007, pp. 14–27.

44. A. Wang, "The Effects of Expert and Consumer Endorsements on Audience Response."

45. D. H. Dean, "Brand Endorsement, Popularity, and Event Sponsorship as Advertising Cues Affecting Pre-Purchase Attitudes," *Journal of Advertising,* Fall 1999, pp. 1–11; and D. H. Dean and A. Biswas, "Third-Party Organization Endorsement of Products," *Journal of Advertising,* Winter 2001, pp. 41–57.

46. Goldsmith, Lafferty, and Newell, "The Impact of Corporate Credibility and Celebrity Credibility on Consumer Reaction to Advertisements and Brands"; B. A. Lafferty, R. E. Goldsmith, and S. J. Newell, "The Dual Credibility Model," *Journal of Marketing Theory and Practice,* Summer 2002, pp. 1–12; and Z. Gurhan-Canli and R. Batra, "When Corporate Image Affects Product Evaluations," *Journal of Marketing Research,* May 2004, pp. 197–205.

47. S. P. Jain and S. S. Posavac, "Prepurchase Attribute Verifiability, Source Credibility, and Persuasion," *Journal of Consumer Psychology* 11, no. 3 (2001), pp. 169–80.

48. See P. M. Homer and L. R. Kahle, "Source Expertise, Time of Source Identification, and Involvement in Persuasion," *Journal of Advertising* 19, no. 1 (1990), pp. 30–39.

49. C. Pornpitakpan and J. N. P. Francis, "The Effect of Cultural Differences, Source Expertise, and Argument Strength on Persuasion," *Journal of International Consumer Marketing* 13, no. 1 (2001), pp. 77–101.

50. D. J. Moore, J. C. Mowen, and R. Reardon, "Multiple Sources in Advertising Appeals," *Journal of the Academy of Marketing Science,* Summer 1994, pp. 234–43. See also N. Artz and A. M. Tybout, "The Moderating Impact of Quantitative Information on the Relationship between Source Credibility and Persuasion," *Marketing Letters* 10, no. 1 (1999), pp. 51–62.

51. Sengupta, Goodstein, and Boninger, "All Cues Are Not Created Equal"; B. Z. Erdogan, M. J. Baker, and S. Tagg, "Selecting Celebrity Endorsers," *Journal of Advertising Research,* May–June 2001, pp. 39–48; M. R. Stafford, N. E. Spears, and C.-K. Hsu, "Celebrity Images in Magazine Advertisements," *Journal of Current Issues and Research in Advertising,* Fall 2003, pp. 13–20; and A. J. Bush, C. A. Martin, and V. D. Bush, "Sports Celebrity Influence on the Behavioral Intentions of Generation Y," *Journal of Advertising Research,* March 2004, pp. 108–18.

52. "Michael Jordon Trumps Tiger, Lance in Influence on Purchase Consideration," press release, Knowledge Networks, October 27, 2003, www.knowledgenetworks.com.

53. M. Tenser, "Endorser Qualities Count More than Ever," *Advertising Age,* November 8, 2004, p. S2.

54. B. D. Till and M. Busler, "The Match-Up Hypothesis," *Journal of Advertising,* Fall 2000, pp. 1–13; Erdogan, Baker, and Tagg, "Selecting Celebrity Endorsers"; A. B. Bower and S. Landreth, "Is Beauty Best?" *Journal of Advertising,* Spring 2001, pp. 1–12; and R. Batra and P. M. Homer, "The Situational Impact of Brand Image Beliefs," *Journal of Consumer Psychology* 14, no. 3 (2004), pp. 318–30.

55. "Avril Lavigne's Style Comes to Kohl's," *StarNewsOnline.com,* March 12, 2008. See also J. Chebatoris, "Avril Lavigne Is Sew Cool," *Newsweek,* March 17, 2008, p. 69.

56. K. Macarthur, "BK and Paris," *Advertising Age,* August 30, 2004, p. 6.

57. M. T. Liu, Y. Huang, and J. Minghua, "Relations Among Attractiveness of Endorsers, Match-up, and Purchase Intention in Sport Marketing in China," *Journal of Consumer Marketing* 24, no. 6 (2007), pp. 358–65.

58. C. Tripp, T. D. Jensen, and L. Carlson, "The Effects of Multiple Product Endorsements by Celebrities on Consumers' Attitudes and Intentions," *Journal of Consumer Research,* March 1994, pp. 535–47; and J. R. Priester and R. E. Petty, "The Influence of Spokesperson Trustworthiness on Message Elaboration, Attitude Strength, and Advertising Effectiveness," *Journal of Consumer Psychology* 13, no. 4 (2003), pp. 408–21.

59. B. D. Till and T. A. Shimp, "Endorsers in Advertising," *Journal of Advertising,* Spring 1998, pp. 67–82; and T. A. Louie, R. L. Kulik, and R. Jacobson, "When Bad Things Happen to the Endorsers of Good Products," *Marketing Letters,* February 2001, pp. 13–23.

60. J. A. Garretson and R. W. Niedrich, "Spokes-Characters," *Journal of Advertising,* Summer 2004, pp. 25–36; and J. A. Garretson and S. Burton, "The Role of Spokescharacters as Advertisement and Package Cues in Integrated Marketing Communications," *Journal of Marketing,* October 2005, pp. 118–32.

61. For an excellent overview, see T. Meenaghan, "Understanding Sponsorship Effects," *Psychology & Marketing,* February 2001, pp. 95–122; see also B. Walliser, "An International Review of Sponsorship Research," *International Journal of Advertising* 22 (2003), pp. 5–40.

62. "North American Sponsorship Spending Seen Up in '08," *Reuters.com,* January 22, 2008, www.reuters.com.

63. R. Thomaselli, "Nextel Sees Payoff as NASCAR Sponsor," *Advertising Age,* May 31, 2004, p. 3.

64. R. Thomaselli, "Official Sponsors Score with World Cup," *Advertising Age,* July 26, 2010, p. C-3.

65. R. Madrigal, "The Influence of Social Alliances with Sports Teams on Intentions to Purchase Corporate Sponsors' Products," *Journal of Advertising,* Winter 2000, pp. 13–24.

66. N. Zmuda, "Children's Hospital in Hot Water Over Corporate Sponsorships," *AdAge.com,* March 12, 2008, http://adage.com.

67. S. R. McDaniel, "An Investigation of Match-Up Effects in Sport Sponsorship Advertising," *Psychology & Marketing,* March 1999, pp. 163–84; N. J. Rifon et al., "Congruence Effects in Sponsorships," *Journal of Advertising,* Spring 2004, pp. 29–42; T. Bettina Cornwell, S. W. Pruitt, and J. M. Clark, "The Relationship between

416   **Part Three**   Internal Influences

Major-League Sports' Official Sponsorship Announcements and the Stock Prices of Sponsoring Firms," *Journal of the Academy of Marketing Science* 33, no. 4 (2005), pp. 401–12; and N. D. Fleck and P. Quester, "Birds of a Feather Flock Together," *Psychology & Marketing,* November 2007, pp. 975–1000.

68. C. Pechmann et al., "What to Convey in Antismoking Advertisements for Adolescents," *Journal of Marketing,* April 2003, pp. 1–18; M. S. LaTour and J. F. Tanner Jr., "Randon," *Psychology & Marketing,* May 2003, 377–94; and J. P. Dillard and J. W. Anderson, "The Role of Fear in Persuasion," *Psychology & Marketing,* November 2004, pp. 909–26.

69. P. A. Keller and L. G. Block, "Increasing the Persuasiveness of Fear Appeals," *Journal of Consumer Research,* March 1996, pp. 448–60; M. S. LaTour and H. J. Rotfeld, "There Are Threats and (Maybe) Fear-Caused Arousal," *Journal of Advertising,* Fall 1997, pp. 45–59; and M. Laroche et al., "A Cross-Cultural Study of the Persuasive Effect of Fear Appeal Messages in Cigarette Advertising," *International Journal of Advertising* 3 (2001), pp. 297–317.

70. K. Passyn and M. Sujan, "Self-Accountability Emotions in Fear Appeals," *Journal of Consumer Research,* March 2006, pp. 583–89.

71. See M. S. LaTour, R. L. Snipes, and S. J. Bliss, "Don't Be Afraid to Use Fear Appeals," *Journal of Advertising Research,* March 1996, pp. 59–66.

72. D. L. Alden, A. Mukherjee, and W. D. Hoyer, "The Effects of Incongruity, Surprise and Positive Moderators and Perceived Humor in Television Advertising," *Journal of Advertising,* Summer 2000, pp. 1–14; K. Flaherty, M. G. Weinberger, and C. S. Gulas, "The Impact of Perceived Humor, Product Type, and Humor Style in Radio Advertising," *Journal of Current Issues and Research in Advertising,* Spring 2004, pp. 25–36; and J. Elpers, A. Mukherjee, and W. D. Hoyer, "Humor in Television Advertising," *Journal of Consumer Research,* December 2004, pp. 592–98.

73. T. W. Cline, M. B. Altsech, and J. J. Kellaris, "When Does Humor Enhance or Inhibit Ad Responses?" *Journal of Advertising,* Fall 2003, pp. 31–45.

74. M. Eisend, "A Meta-analysis of Humor in Advertising," *Journal of the Academy of Marketing Science* 37 (2009), pp. 191–203.

75. See, e.g., H. S. Krishnan and D. Chakravarti, "A Process Analysis of the Effects of Humorous Advertising Executions on Brand Claims Memory," *Journal of Consumer Psychology* 13, no. 3 (2003), pp. 230–45.

76. E. B. York, "Snickers Uses Humor to Satisfy Generations of Hunger," *Advertising Age,* March 29, 2010, p. 22.

77. H. Chung and X. Zhao, "Humour Effect on Memory and Attitude," *International Journal of Advertising* 22 (2003), pp. 117–44; and Y. Zhang and G. M. Zinkhan, "Responses to Humorous Ads," *Journal of Advertising,* Winter 2006, pp. 113–27.

78. D. L. Fugate, J. B. Gotlieb, and D. Bolton, "Humorous Services Advertising," *Journal of Professional Services Marketing* 21, no. 1 (2000), pp. 9–22; M. F. Toncar, "The Use of Humour in Television Advertising," *International Journal of Advertising* 20 (2001), pp. 521–39; K. Macarthur, "Subway Cans Schtick to Focus on Food in Its Creative," *Advertising Age,* March 1, 2004, p. 4.

79. D. Grewal et al., "Comparative versus Noncomparative Advertising," *Journal of Marketing,* October 1998, pp. 1–15; M. E. Hill and M. King, "Comparative vs. Noncomparative Advertising,"

Journal of Current Issues and Research in Advertising, Fall 2001, pp. 33–52; K. C. Manning et al., "Understanding the Mental Representations Created by Comparative Advertising," *Journal of Advertising,* Summer 2001, pp. 27–39; L. D. Compeau, D. Grewal, and R. Chandrashekaran, "Bits, Briefs, and Applications," *Journal of Consumer Affairs,* Winter 2002, pp. 284–94; and J. R. Priester et al., "Brand Congruity and Comparative Advertising," *Journal of Consumer Psychology* 14, no. 1/2 (2004), pp. 115–23.

80. A. Chattopadhyay, "When Does Comparative Advertising Influence Brand Attitude?" *Psychology & Marketing,* August 1998, pp. 461–75; M. J. Barone and P. W. Miniard, "How and When Factual Ad Claims Mislead Consumers," *Journal of Marketing Research,* February 1999, pp. 58–74; S. V. Auken and A. J. Adams, "Across- versus Within-Class Comparative Advertising," *Psychology & Marketing,* August 1999, pp. 429–50; A. B. Sorescu and B. D. Gelb, "Negative Comparative Advertising," *Journal of Advertising,* Winter 2000, pp. 25–40; S. P. Jain, B. Buchanan, and D. Maheswaran, "Comparative versus Non-comparative Advertising," *Journal of Consumer Psychology* 9, no. 4 (2000), pp. 201–11; A. V. Muthukrishnan, L. Warlop, and J. W. Alba, "The Piecemeal Approach to Comparative Advertising," *Marketing Letters* 12, no. 1 (2001), pp. 63–73; S. P. Jain and S. S. Posavac, "Valenced Comparisons," *Journal of Marketing Research,* February 2004, pp. 46–58; and M. J. Barone, K. M. Palan, and P. W. Miniard, "Brand Usage and Gender as Moderators of the Potential Deception Associated with Partial Comparative Advertising," *Journal of Advertising,* Spring 2004, pp. 19–28.

81. See, e.g., M. E. Hill et al., "The Conjoining Influences of Affect and Arousal on Attitude Formation," *Research in Consumer Behavior* 9 (2000), pp. 129–46; J. D. Morris et al., "The Power of Affect," *Journal of Advertising Research,* May–June 2002, pp. 7–17; M.-H. Huang, "Romantic Love and Sex," *Psychology & Marketing,* January 2004, pp. 53–73; and D. J. MacInnis and G. E. de Mello, "The Concept of Hope and Its Relevance to Product Evaluation and Choice," *Journal of Marketing,* January 2005, pp. 1–14.

82. R. K. Chandy et al., "What to Say When," *Journal of Marketing Research,* November 2001, pp. 399–414; and R. D. Jewell and H. R. Unnava, "Exploring Differences in Attitudes between Light and Heavy Brand Users," *Journal of Consumer Psychology* 14, no. 1/2 (2004), pp. 75–80.

83. J. S. Johar and M. J. Sirgy, "Value-Expressive versus Utilitarian Advertising Appeals," *Journal of Advertising,* September 1991, pp. 23–33; S. Shavitt, "Evidence for Predicting the Effectiveness of Value-Expressive versus Utilitarian Appeals," *Journal of Advertising,* June 1992, pp. 47–51; M. E. Slama and R. B. Singley, "Self-Monitoring and Value-Expressive vs. Utilitarian Ad Effectiveness," *Journal of Current Issues and Research in Advertising,* Fall 1996, pp. 39–49; L. Dube, A. Chattopadhyay, and A. Letarte, "Should Advertising Appeals Match the Basis of Consumers' Attitudes?" *Journal of Advertising Research,* November 1996, pp. 82–89; and J.-shen Chiou, "The Effectiveness of Different Advertising Message Appeals in the Eastern Emerging Society," *International Journal of Advertising* 21 (2002), pp. 217–36.

84. M. Dahlen and J. Bergendahl, "Informing and Transforming on the Web," *International Journal of Advertising* 20, no. 2 (2001), pp. 189–205.

85. A. E. Crowley and W. D. Hoyer, "An Integrative Framework for Understanding Two-Sided Persuasion," *Journal of Consumer Research,* March 1994, pp. 561–74; G. Bohner et al., "When Small Means Comfortable," *Journal of Consumer Psychology* 13, no. 4 (2003), pp. 454–63; and M. Eisend, "Understanding Two-Sided Persuasion," *Psychology & Marketing,* July 2007, pp. 615–640.

86. I. P. Levin, S. L. Schneider, and G. J. Gaeth, "All Frames Are Not Created Equal," *Organizational Behavior and Human Decision Processes,* November 1998, pp. 149–88.

87. Ibid.

88. P. A. Keller, I. M. Lipkus, and B. K. Rimer, "Affect, Framing, and Persuasion," *Journal of Marketing Research,* February 2003, pp. 54–64; J. Meyers-Levy and D. Maheswaran, "Exploring Message Framing Outcomes When Systematic, Heuristic, or Both Types of Processing Occur," *Journal of Consumer Psychology* 14, no. 1/2 (2004), pp. 159–67; and B. Shiv, J. A. E. Britton, and J. W. Payne, "Does Elaboration Increase or Decrease the Effectiveness of Negatively versus Positively Framed Messages?" *Journal of Consumer Research,* June 2004, pp. 199–208.

89. See, e.g., J. W. Peltier and J. A. Schribrowsky, "The Use of Need-Based Segmentation for Developing Segment-Specific Direct Marketing Strategies," *Journal of Direct Marketing,* Fall 1997, pp. 53–62; and R. Ahmad, "Benefit Segmentation," *International Journal of Marketing Research* 45 (2003), pp. 373–88.

90. H. E. Bloom, "Match the Concept and the Product," *Journal of Advertising Research,* October 1977, pp. 25–27.

13 Situational Influences

LEARNING OBJECTIVES

L01 Define situational influence

L02 Explain the four types of situations and their relevance to marketing strategy

L03 Summarize the five characteristics of situations and their influence on consumption

L04 Discuss ritual situations and their importance to consumers and marketers

L05 Describe the use of situational influence in developing marketing strategy

Did you realize that companies change their marketing tactics geographically depending on the weather and how it is changing? How weather is *changing* is the critical part here because it creates "situations" into which marketers can offer their products as solutions. For example, when temperatures are temporarily *colder than usual,* consumers will deviate from their normal purchase pattern. Sometimes this means buying more of a certain item such as chicken soup. Sometimes this means buying different products such as a heavier jacket.[1] Planalytics is a major global player in helping marketers track and react to changing weather situations. It is a geographically based system that looks at what we will later term "momentary conditions." Planalytics offers a Weather-Driven Demand (WDD) approach, which they describe, in part, as "a numerical representation of the consumer need for a product or service caused by perceived changes in the weather at a time/location intersection." This perception change by time/location intersection creates a situation that marketers attempt to take advantage of. As Planalytics's COO states:

> That's where the marketing gold that needs to be mined is. Marketing into a situation that's favorable to your product [causes] the numbers to go off the chart.

Examples of clients who use Planalytics to adjust their marketing efforts include:

- **Campbell Soup**—has created a "misery index," which is based on weather changes, such as within day, within week, year-over-year, and so on, with bonus points for snow or rain. When the misery index hits a certain mark, Campbell will deliver chicken soup ads to that market. It has over 30 such geographic markets that it tracks and targets in this way and is also in the process of creating a flu index.

- **Lands' End**—this global retailer uses weather information to plan and forecast inventories, tweak merchandising and promotional offerings, and so on. It also examines historical demand as a function of "unusual" weather patterns and discounts future estimates accordingly. So, for example, if there was an unusually hot spring season in the United Kingdom one year, with sales of certain items (e.g., light apparel such as shorts) being high, they will discount next year's estimates accordingly to avoid having overstocks.

New media options are available as well. Google can track "trending" weather-related phrases such as "hot chocolate" and launch appropriate "new search campaigns within hours." So, what's your weather situation?

As the model we have used to organize this text indicates, the purchase decision and consumption process always occur in the context of a specific situation. Therefore, before examining the decision process, we must first develop an understanding of situations. In this chapter, we examine the situations in which consumption occurs, the way situations influence consumption behaviors, key characteristics of situations, the nature of ritual situations, and situation-based marketing strategies.

THE NATURE OF SITUATIONAL INFLUENCE

Consumers do not respond to stimuli such as advertisements and products presented by marketers in isolation; instead, they respond to marketing influences and the situation simultaneously. To understand a consumer's behavior, we must know about the *consumer;* about the primary *stimulus* object, such as a product or advertisement that the consumer is responding to; and about the *situation* in which the response is occurring.[2]

We define **situational influence** as *all those factors particular to a time and place that do not follow from a knowledge of the stable attributes of the consumer and the stimulus and that have an effect on current behavior.*[3] Thus, with one exception, the situation stands apart from the consumer and the stimulus. The exception is in the case of *temporary* (as opposed to stable) characteristics of a consumer or stimulus that are specific to the situation and sometimes even caused by it. For example, a consumer may generally be upbeat (stable trait), but just prior to viewing a firm's ad sees a disturbing news flash that puts her in a bad mood. This bad mood is a transient state (situational factor) caused by the surrounding media context in which the focal ad appears. Other such temporary conditions include illness and time pressure. Consumer involvement also includes a situation-specific component. That is, some consumers are involved only when they have to make a purchase.

A key marketing finding is that consumers often react and behave very differently depending on the situation. We discussed some of these effects in earlier chapters. For example, an ad or in-store display that might otherwise attract consumer attention may not do so in a cluttered environment (Chapter 8). Or an ad that might be persuasive in a non-purchase situation may be much less persuasive in a purchase situation where consumers are in the market to buy (Chapter 11). The interplay between situation, marketing, and the individual is shown in Figure 13-1.

Consumer behavior occurs within four broad categories or types of situations: the communications situation, the purchase situation, the usage situation, and the disposition situation.

The Communications Situation

The situation in which consumers receive information has an impact on their behavior. Whether one is alone or in a group, in a good mood or bad, in a hurry or not influences the degree to which one sees and listens to marketing communications. Is it better to advertise on a happy or sad television program? A calm or exciting program? These are some of the questions managers must answer with respect to the **communications situation.**[4] Marketers often attempt to place their ads in appropriate media contexts to enhance their effectiveness. Some even go so far as to mandate that their ads be "pulled" when programming content negative to their company or industry will appear. Recent examples include Morgan Stanley and BP. *What are the ethical implications of such policies?*[5]

A marketer is able to deliver an effective message to consumers who are interested in the product and are in a receptive communications situation. However, finding high-interest

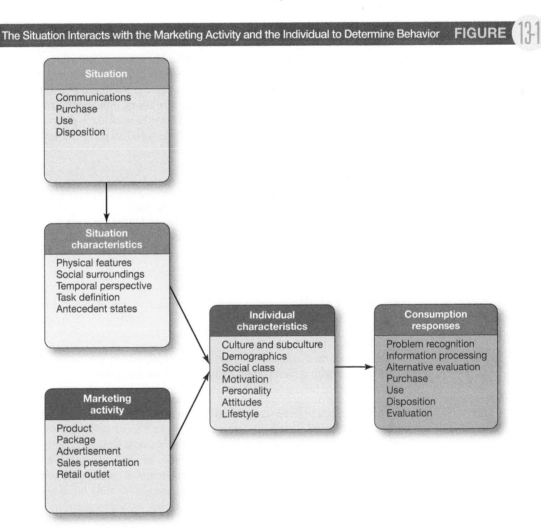

The Situation Interacts with the Marketing Activity and the Individual to Determine Behavior   FIGURE 13-1

potential buyers in receptive communications situations is a difficult challenge. For example, consider the difficulty a marketer would have in communicating to you in the following communications situations:

- Your favorite team just lost the most important game of the year.
- Final exams begin tomorrow.
- Your roommates watch only comedy programs.
- You have the flu.
- You are driving home on a cold night, and your car heater doesn't work.

The Purchase Situation

The situation in which a purchase is made can influence consumer behavior. Mothers shopping with children are more apt to be influenced by the product preferences of their children than when shopping without them. A shortage of time, such as trying to make a purchase between classes, can affect the store-choice decision, the number of brands considered, and the price the shopper is willing to pay. At an even more basic level, whether or not a consumer is in a "purchase mode" influences a whole host of behaviors from advertising responses to shopping. Consider, for example, how differently you might behave at Best Buy if you were there only to browse versus being there to replace a broken Blu-ray player.

Marketers must understand how **purchase situations** influence consumers in order to develop marketing strategies that enhance the purchase of their products. For example, how would you alter your decision to purchase a beverage in the following purchase situations?

- You are in a very bad mood.
- A good friend says, "That stuff is bad for you!"
- The store you visit does not carry your favorite brand.
- There is a long line at the checkout counter as you enter the store.
- You are with someone you want to impress.

The Usage Situation

What beverage would you prefer to consume in each of the following usage situations?

- Friday afternoon after your last final exam.
- With your parents for lunch.
- After dinner on a cold, stormy evening.
- At a dinner with a friend you have not seen in several years.
- When you are feeling sad or homesick.

Marketers need to understand the **usage situations** for which their products are, or may become, appropriate. Using this knowledge, marketers can communicate how their products create consumer satisfaction in each relevant usage situation. For example, a recent study found that consuming two 1.5-cup servings of oat-based cereal a day could lower cholesterol. How could General Mills take advantage of this finding to increase sales of its oat-based cereal Cheerios? A recent ad depicts a dad coming home late from work and having Cheerios for dinner. When asked why by his young daughter, he replies, "Because they taste just as good at night."

Research indicates that *expanded usage situation* strategies can produce major sales gains for established products.[6] Coach went away from the traditional two-occasion (everyday and dressy) approach to handbags and moved toward what it calls a "usage voids" approach. Now Coach offers a wide range of products, including weekend bags, coin purses, clutches, and wristlets in a variety of colors and fabrics. The goal is to get consumers more attuned to the various usage situations available in which to accessorize and then create bags to fit the situations.[7] Dunkin' Donuts found that over half of donut consumption was for breakfast, but roughly 34 percent was for nonbreakfast snacks. In response the company has:[8]

> . . . created simple yet imaginative make-at-home snack and dessert recipes, such as Cocoa Donut and Strawberry Grilled Cheese, to encourage consumers to think of and use the company's products in new ways. [They are also tapping the specialty occasions market with] limited-time offers, such as the heart-shaped Valentine's "Cupid's Choice."

Illustration 13–1 shows another example of a company trying to expand the usage situations for its brand.

The Disposition Situation

Consumers must frequently dispose of products or product packages after or before product use. As we will examine in detail in Chapter 18, decisions made by consumers regarding the **disposition situation** can create significant social problems as well as opportunities for marketers.

Some consumers consider ease of disposition an important product attribute. These people may purchase only items that can be easily recycled. Often disposition of an existing product must occur before or simultaneously with the acquisition of the new product. For example, most consumers must remove their existing bed before using a new one. Marketers need to understand how situational influences affect disposition decisions in order to develop more effective and ethical products and marketing programs. Government and environmental organizations need the same knowledge in order to encourage socially responsible disposition decisions.

How would your disposition decision differ in these situations?

- You have finished a soft drink in a can at a mall. There is a trashcan nearby, but there is no sign of a recycling container.
- You have finished reading the newspaper after class, and you note that you are running late for a basketball game.
- You and two friends have finished soft drinks. Both your friends toss the recyclable cans into a nearby garbage container.
- A local charity will accept old refrigerators if they are delivered to the charity. Your garbage service will haul one to the dump for $15. You just bought a new refrigerator. You don't know anyone (or you do know someone) with a pickup or van.

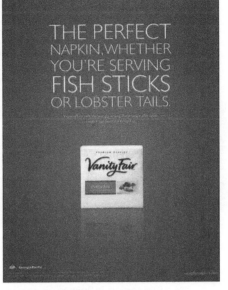

ILLUSTRATION 13–1

Many products become defined for particular usage situations. Firms that are able to expand the range of usage situations deemed appropriate for their brands can capture significant sales gains.

SITUATIONAL CHARACTERISTICS AND CONSUMPTION BEHAVIOR

The situations discussed above can be described on a number of dimensions that determine their influence on consumer behavior. The five key dimensions or characteristics are physical surroundings, social surroundings, temporal perspectives, task definition, and antecedent states.[9] These characteristics have been studied primarily in the United States. While the same characteristics of the situation exist across cultures, a marketer should not assume that the response to these characteristics would be the same. For example, a crowded store might cause a different emotional reaction among American consumers than among Indian consumers.[10]

Physical Surroundings

Physical surroundings include decor, sounds, aromas, lighting, weather, and configurations of merchandise or other materials surrounding the stimulus object. Physical surroundings are a widely used type of situational influence, particularly for retail applications.

External retail factors such as the architecture, arrangement, and assortment of retailers are an important influence on consumer shopping experiences. In addition, store interiors are often designed to create specific feelings in shoppers that can have an important cueing or reinforcing effect on purchase. All physical aspects of the store, including lighting, layout, presentation of merchandise, fixtures, floor coverings, colors, sounds, odors, and dress and behavior of sales personnel, combine to produce these feelings, which in turn influence purchase tendencies.[11] A retail clothing store specializing in extremely stylish, modern clothing would want its fixtures, furnishings, and colors to reflect an overall mood of style, flair, and newness (see Illustration 13–2). In addition, the store personnel should carry this theme in terms of their own appearance and apparel. Compare this with the interior of a so-called discount retailer, also shown in the illustration. It is important to note that one is not superior to the other. Each attempts to create an appropriate atmosphere for its target audience.

The sum of all the physical features of a retail environment is referred to as the **store atmosphere** or environment (see Chapter 17). Store atmosphere influences consumer judgments of store quality and image. It also has been shown to influence shoppers' moods and their willingness to visit and linger. **Atmospherics** is *the process managers use to manipulate the physical retail environment to create specific mood responses in shoppers.*[12] Atmospherics is also important online and is receiving increasing attention from marketers.[13]

Atmosphere is referred to as **servicescape** when describing a service business such as a hospital, bank, or restaurant.[14] Figure 13-2 classifies services according to the reason the customer is using the service and the length of time the service will be used. The consumption purpose is categorized along a continuum from strictly utilitarian, such as dry cleaning, to completely hedonic, such as a massage. The time can range from a few minutes to days or weeks. Physical characteristics and the feelings and image they create become increasingly important as hedonic motives and the time involved with the service increase. Thus, the physical characteristics of a vacation resort may be as important as or more important than the intangible services provided.

It is important that Figure 13-2 be interpreted correctly. It indicates that the physical environment at Starbucks is more important to the service experience than the physical features of dry cleaners are. *This does not mean that the physical aspects of dry*

| Typology of Service Environments | | | FIGURE 13-2 |

Time Spent in Facility	Consumption Purpose		
	Utilitarian -- *Hedonic*		
Short [minutes]	Dry cleaner Bank	Fast food Hair salon	Facial Coffee at Starbucks
Moderate [hour(s)]	Medical appointment Legal consultation	Business dinner Exercise class	**Theater Sporting event**
Extended [day(s)]	Hospital Trade show	**Conference hotel Training center**	**Cruise Resort**

cleaners are not important. Indeed, an organized, professional-appearing dry cleaning establishment is likely to produce more satisfied customers than one with the opposite characteristics. What the figure does indicate is that the relative importance of tangible physical features increases as one moves to extended, hedonic consumption experiences.

Having established the importance of the physical environment, we now examine some of its components.

Colors   As we saw in Chapter 8, certain colors and color characteristics create feelings of excitement and arousal that are related to attention. Bright colors are more arousing than dull colors. And *warm* colors, such as reds and yellows, are more arousing than *cool* colors, such as blues and grays.[15] Which color would be best for store interiors? The answer is, it depends. For the dominant interior color, cool colors (e.g., blue) should probably be used since they increase sales and customer satisfaction.[16] However, the attention-getting nature of warm colors should not be overlooked and can be used effectively as an accent color in areas where the retailer wants to attract attention and drive impulse purchases.[17] Cool colors also appear to be capable of reducing wait time perceptions by inducing feelings of relaxation.[18]

As we saw in Chapter 2, the meaning of colors varies across cultures. Therefore, this and all other aspects of the physical environment should be designed specifically for the cultures involved.

Aromas   There is increasing evidence that odors can affect consumer shopping.[19] One study found that a scented environment produced a greater intent to revisit the store, higher purchase intention for some items, and a reduced sense of time spent shopping.[20] Another study found that one aroma, but not another, increased slot machine usage in a Las Vegas casino.[21] A third study found that the presence of a certain aroma in a retail setting increased pleasure, arousal, time spent, and money spent at the retailer.[22] A fourth study found that a pleasantly scented environment enhanced brand recall and evaluations, particularly for unfamiliar brands. The pleasant scent increased the time spent evaluating the brands (attention), which, in turn, increased memory.[23]

Given these results, it is not surprising that a billion-dollar *environmental fragrancing* industry has developed around the use of ambient scents.[24] However, marketers still have

TABLE 13-1   The Impact of Background Music on Restaurant Patrons

Variables	Slow Music	Fast Music
Service time	29 min.	27 min.
Customer time at table	56 min.	45 min.
Customer groups leaving before seated	10.5%	12.0%
Amount of food purchased	$55.81	$55.12
Amount of bar purchases	$30.47	$21.62
Estimated gross margin	$55.82	$48.62

Source: R. E. Milliman, "The Influence of Background Music on the Behavior of Restaurant Patrons," in the *Journal of Consumer Research*, September 1986, p. 289. Copyright © 1986 by the University of Chicago. Used by permission.

a lot to learn about if, when, and how scents can be used effectively in a retail environment.[25] In addition, scent preferences are highly individualized; a pleasant scent to one individual may be repulsive to another. Moreover, some shoppers object to anything being deliberately added to the air they breathe, and others worry about allergic reactions.[26]

Music   Music influences consumers' moods, which influence a variety of consumption behaviors both in traditional retailer settings and in online settings.[27] Is slow-tempo or fast-tempo background music better for a restaurant? Table 13-1 indicates that slow music increased gross margin for one restaurant by almost 15 percent per customer group compared with fast music. However, before concluding that all restaurants should play slow music, examine the table carefully. Slow music appears to have relaxed and slowed down the customers, resulting in more time in the restaurant and substantially more purchases from the bar. Restaurants that rely on rapid customer turnover might be better off with fast-tempo music.

Other aspects of music besides tempo are also important. For example, research suggests that matching music to the musical preferences of the target audience is critical to positive retail outcomes such as satisfaction and enjoyment, browsing time, spending, perceived service quality, and positive word of mouth. In addition, research suggests that music which creates moderate levels of arousal (versus extremely low or high) yields the most positive retail outcomes.[28]

Because of the impact that music can have on shopping behavior, firms exist to develop music programs to meet the unique needs of specific retailers. An emerging trend is having music more in the foreground so it becomes part of the shopping experience and drives store image. AEI, a major supplier of foreground music, does intense research on the demographics and psychographics of each client store's customers. The age mix, buying patterns, and traffic flows of each part of the day are analyzed. AEI characterizes its approach as:

> [Creating] environments where sounds, video, lighting and architecture blend together to give a brand a voice, creating emotional attachments that encourage consumers to shop longer, increase spending and return often.[29]

Firms such as Abercrombie & Fitch, Banana Republic, Bath & Body Works, and Eddie Bauer use companies like AEI to create appropriate and consistent shopping environments throughout their chains.

Crowding   Crowding generally produces negative outcomes for both the retail outlet and the consumer.[30] As more people enter a store or as more of the space of the store is filled with merchandise, an increasing percentage of the shoppers will experience a feeling of being crowded, confined, or claustrophobic. Most consumers find these feelings to be unpleasant and will take steps to change them. The primary means of doing so is to spend less time in the store by buying less, making faster decisions, and using less of the available information. This in turn tends to produce less satisfactory purchases, an unpleasant shopping trip, and a reduced likelihood of returning to the store.

Marketers should design their outlets in ways that will help reduce consumers' perceptions of crowding. This is difficult because retail shopping tends to occur at specific times, such as holiday weekends. Retailers must balance the expense of having a larger store than required most of the time against the cost of having dissatisfied customers during key shopping periods. Using extra personnel, opening additional checkout lines, and implementing similar measures can enhance the flow of consumers through a store during peak periods and reduce the crowding sensation. In addition, recent research shows that music tempo can be important. Specifically, music with a slow tempo offsets the negative emotions experienced as a result of crowding. Since music tempo adjustments are less expensive than store expansion or new personnel, this is an important finding for retail strategy.[31]

Marketers need to be sensitive to cross-cultural differences since personal space and resulting crowding perceptions can vary from culture to culture. For example, one study found that when the activity is for fun, such as an amusement park or concert, Middle East consumers perceive less crowding and appreciate crowding more than North American consumers.[32]

Social Surroundings

Social surroundings are *the other individuals present in the particular situation.* People's actions are frequently influenced by those around them. What would you wear in each of the following situations?

- Studying alone for a final.
- Meeting at the library with a date to study for a final.
- Going to a nice restaurant with a date.
- Meeting a prospective employer for lunch.

Illustration 13–3 shows a company that is positioning its brand for casual rather than formal social settings.

Social influence is a significant force acting on our behavior, since individuals tend to comply with group expectations, particularly when the behavior is visible (see Chapter 7). Thus, shopping, a highly visible activity, and the use of many publicly consumed brands are subject to social influences.[33] This is particularly true of those who are highly susceptible to interpersonal influence, a stable personality trait. As just one example, a recent study finds that consumers are more likely to engage in variety-seeking behavior in public (versus private) consumption situations even if it means consuming products they like less. The reason is that consumers feel that others view them more positively (more fun, interesting, exciting) if their purchases show more variety. This tendency is stronger for those more susceptible to interpersonal influence.[34]

Marketers have recently begun to examine the role of social influence on embarrassment. **Embarrassment** is a negative emotion influenced by both the product and the situation. Certain products are more embarrassing than others (condoms, hearing aids, etc.) and embarrassment is driven by the presence of others in the purchase or usage situation. Since

472   **Part Four**   Consumer Decision Process

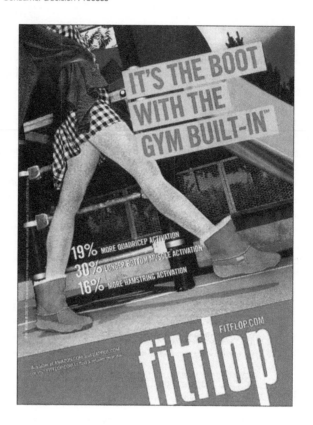

embarrassment can deter purchases, this is an important area for marketers. One finding is that familiarity with purchasing the product reduces embarrassment, so marketers might try advertisements that show the purchase of a potentially embarrassing product in which no awkwardness or embarrassment occurs. For extremely sensitive products (e.g., adult diapers), strategies might include home delivery options with discreet labeling to completely avoid the social component.[35]

Shopping can provide a social experience outside the home for making new acquaintances, meeting existing friends, or just being near other people (Consumer Insight 10-1 discusses the social shopping motive). Some people seek status and authority in shopping since the salesperson's job is to wait on the customer. This allows these individuals a measure of respect or prestige that may otherwise be lacking in their lives. Thus, consumers, on occasion, shop *for* social situations rather than, or in addition to, products. The presence of others *during* the shopping trip can also influence impulse buying, as discussed in Consumer Insight 13-1.

Frequently, marketing managers will not have any control over social characteristics of a situation. For example, when a television advertisement is sent into the home, the advertising manager cannot control whom the viewer is with at the time of reception. However, the manager can use the knowledge that some programs are generally viewed alone (weekday, daytime programs), some are viewed by the entire family (prime-time family comedies), and others are viewed by groups of friends (Super Bowl). The message presented can be structured to these viewing situations. Marketers can also use social consumption themes in their ads to enhance the likelihood that consumers will consider

CONSUMER INSIGHT 13-1

Does Shopping with Others Drive Impulse Buying?

Impulse buying can be defined as *a sudden and immediate unplanned purchase that occurs after experiencing a spontaneous urge to buy.* Clearly not all unplanned purchases are impulse purchases. Sometimes consumers are simply reminded by such factors as retail signage that they need the product in question (this is a reminder purchase; see Chapter 17). The sudden, spontaneous *urge to buy* is critical to impulse buying. Some people are more prone to impulse purchases, and in extreme situations, impulse buying can create negative consequences such as large credit card debt. One question is whether the presence of other people during a shopping trip can influence impulse buying. To answer this question, a recent study examined several scenarios, two of which are highlighted below.[36]

Scenario 1: Mary is a 21-year-old college student with a part-time job. It is two days before Mary gets her next paycheck and she only has $25 left for necessities. In addition to food, Mary needs to buy a pair of warm socks for an outdoor party this weekend. *After work she goes with a group of her best friends to the mall to purchase the socks.* As she is walking through a final department store, Mary sees a great-looking sweater on sale for $75.

Scenario 2: Mary is a 21-year-old college student with a part-time job. It is two days before Mary gets her next paycheck and she only has $25 left for necessities. In addition to food, Mary needs to buy a pair of warm socks for an outdoor party this weekend. *After work, her family meets her at the mall to shop and purchase the socks. Mary and her family are very close-knit.* As she is walking through a final department store, Mary sees a great-looking sweater on sale for $75.

Now that you've read the two scenarios, when do you think impulse buying (that is, buying the socks *and* the sweater on credit) is higher? If you said Scenario 1, you were correct. In fact, compared with shopping alone, shopping with close friends increased impulse buying, while shopping with close family members decreased impulse buying.

The role of others in impulse buying can be explained by social norms that we examined in depth in Chapter 7. It was found that consumers generally believe that friends think impulse buying is more acceptable than does family. Thus, close friends and family influence impulse buying in a manner consistent with social norms. Notice that in the scenarios, strength of the social tie was high. When the social ties to friends and family were weak (for example, co-workers from her part-time job instead of best friends), the influence of others on impulse buying disappeared.

Critical Thinking Questions

1. What insights can you find in this research for how retailers should advertise? What ethical implications are involved?

2. Relate this research to the different "self-concepts" discussed in Chapter 12.

3. What coping mechanisms could parents teach their children to help offset the influence of close friends on impulse buying?

the social component in their decisions. For example, a recent study found that brand personality (fun and sophistication) conveyed by a celebrity endorser in an ad only enhanced purchase intentions when a social context was evoked.[37]

Temporal Perspectives

Temporal perspectives are *situational characteristics that deal with the effect of time on consumer behavior.* Time as a situational factor can manifest itself in a number of ways.[38] The amount of time available for the purchase has a substantial impact on the consumer

474   Part Four   Consumer Decision Process

ILLUSTRATION 13–4

In the United States and other countries, dual-career and single-parent families have caused consumers to feel time starved. Internet shopping provides many such consumers both time savings and control over when they shop.

decision process. In general, the less time there is available (i.e., increased time pressure), the shorter will be the information search, the less available information will be used, and the more suboptimal purchases will be made.[39] In addition, research suggests that time pressure decreases perceptions of retailer service quality.[40]

Limited purchase time can also result in a smaller number of product alternatives being considered. The increased time pressure experienced by many dual-career couples and single parents tends to increase the incidence of brand loyalty, particularly for nationally branded products. The obvious implication is that these consumers feel safer with nationally branded or "known" products, particularly when they do not have the time to engage in extensive comparison shopping.

Time as a situational influence affects consumers' choice of stores and behaviors in those stores.[41] A number of retail firms have taken advantage of the temporal perspective factor. Perhaps the most successful of these is the 7-Eleven chain, which caters almost exclusively to individuals who either are in a hurry or want to make a purchase after regular shopping hours.

Internet shopping is growing rapidly in part as a result of the time pressures felt by many dual-career and single-parent households. Shopping on the Internet has two important time-related dimensions. First, it has the potential to reduce the amount of time required to make a specific purchase. Second, it provides the consumer with almost total control over *when* the purchase is made (see Chapter 17). These features are among the major reasons for the rapid growth in Internet outlets and sales (see Illustration 13–4).

Task Definition

Task definition is *the reason the consumption activity is occurring.* The major task dichotomy used by marketers is between purchases for self-use versus gift giving.

Gift Giving   Consumers use different shopping strategies and purchase criteria when shopping for gifts versus shopping for the same item for self-use.[42] Consumers give gifts for many reasons. Social expectations and ritualized consumption situations such as birthdays often require gift giving independent of the giver's actual desires.[43] Gifts are also given to elicit return favors in the form of either gifts or actions. And, of course, gifts are given as an expression of love and caring.[44]

The type of gift given and desired varies by occasion and gender.[45] One study found that wedding gifts tend to be *utilitarian,* while birthday gifts tend to be *fun.* Thus, both the general task definition (gift giving) and the specific task definition (gift-giving occasion) influence purchase behavior, as does the relationship between the giver and the recipient.

Gift giving produces anxieties on the part of both givers and receivers.[46] Gifts communicate symbolic meaning on several levels. The gift item itself generally has a known, or knowable, price that can be interpreted as a measure of the esteem the giver has for the receiver. The image and functionality of the gift implies the giver's impression of the image and personality of the receiver. It also reflects on the image and thoughtfulness of the giver.

The nature of a gift can signify the type of relationship the giver has or desires with the receiver.[47] A gift of stationery implies a very different desired relationship between two individuals than does a gift of cologne. Consider the following:

> The biggest moment of revelation, the moment I knew he was "serious" about me, was when he showed up with a gift for my daughter. Other men had shown the typical false affection for her in order to get on my good side, but he was only civil and polite to her, never gushy. One day, however, he showed up with a very nice skateboard for my daughter. . . . The gift marked a turning point in our relationship. I think for him it marked the time that he decided it would be OK to get serious about a woman with a child.[48]

As the example above indicates, the act of giving/receiving a gift can alter the relationship between the giver and receiver. In addition, items received as gifts often take on meaning associated with the relationship or the giver. For example a gift may be cherished and protected because it symbolizes an important friendship.[49]

Of course, gift giving is culture specific (see Chapter 2).[50] For example, in characterizing gift giving in Korea (collectivist) compared with the United States (individualistic), one expert summarized:

> Koreans reported more gift giving occasions, a wider exchange network, more frequent giving of practical gift items, especially cash gifts, strong face-saving and group conformity motivations, more social pressure to reciprocate, higher gift budget, and frequent workplace giving.[51]

Antecedent States

Features of the individual person that are not lasting characteristics, such as momentary moods or conditions, are called **antecedent states.** For example, most people experience states of depression or excitement from time to time that are not normally part of their individual makeup.

Moods   **Moods** are *transient feeling states that are generally not tied to a specific event or object.*[52] They tend to be less intense than emotions and may operate without the individual's awareness. Although moods may affect all aspects of a person's behavior, they generally do not completely interrupt ongoing behavior as an emotion might. Individuals use such terms as *happy, cheerful, peaceful, sad, blue,* and *depressed* to describe their moods.

Moods both affect and are affected by the consumption process.[53] Moods influence decision processes, the purchase and consumption of various products, and perceptions of service.[54] Positive moods appear to be associated with increased browsing and impulse purchasing. Negative moods also increase impulse and compulsive purchasing in some consumers. One explanation is that some shopping behaviors play both a mood maintenance (positive moods) and mood enhancement (negative moods) role.[55]

Mood can also play an important role in the communications situation. Such effects are often called *program context effects* and relate to the nature of the programming surrounding the focal ad (see Chapter 8). The television, radio, and magazine content viewed just prior to the focal ad can influence consumers' moods and arousal levels, which, in turn, influence their information-processing activities.[56] A basic finding is that ad and brand attitudes

are often influenced in a mood-congruent manner. Thus, a TV show that puts a consumer in a positive mood (elicits positive affective reactions) should improve ad and brand attitudes compared with one that puts the consumer in a negative mood. However, in cases where so-called negative programming is also liked by the viewer (a sad movie that a viewer loves), then program liking can still provide a positive boost in ad and brand attitudes.[57] Given such complexities, marketers must pretest their ads in contexts as close to their expected programming environment as possible.

Consumers actively manage their mood states (see Illustration 13–5).[58] That is, consumers often seek situations, activities, or objects that will alleviate negative moods or enhance positive ones. Products and services are one means consumers use to manage their mood states. Thus, a person feeling bored, sad, or down might view a situation comedy on television, go to a cheerful movie, visit a fun store, eat at an upbeat restaurant, or purchase a new Blu-ray disc, shirt, or other fun product.[59] Consumers may engage in such mood-regulating behavior both at a nonconscious level and also at a deliberate, conscious level:

> [T]here are certain products that I purchase specifically to make me feel better. For instance, occasionally, I enjoy smoking a cigar. Certainly the cigar serves no other purpose than to make me feel good.
>
> While other cosmetics, perfumes and nice clothes can make me feel good, they seldom have the same power to transform my temperament like a manicure and pedicure can.[60]

Marketers attempt to influence moods and to time marketing activities with positive mood-inducing events.[61] Many companies prefer to advertise during light television programs because viewers tend to be in a good mood while watching these shows. Restaurants, bars, shopping malls, and many other retail outlets are designed to induce positive moods in patrons. As discussed earlier, music is often played for this reason. Finally, marketers can position their products and services in terms of mood enhancement.

Momentary Conditions   Whereas moods reflect states of mind, *momentary conditions reflect temporary states of being,* such as being tired, being ill, having extra money, being broke, and so forth. However, for conditions, as for moods, to fit under the definition of antecedent states, they must be momentary and not constantly with the individual. Hence, an individual who is short of cash only momentarily will act differently from someone who is always short of cash.[62]

As with moods, individuals attempt to manage their momentary conditions, often through the purchase or consumption of products and services. For example, individuals feeling tired or sleepy during the day may drink a cup of coffee or a soft drink or eat a candy bar. Massages are consumed to relieve sore muscles. A variety of medications are sold to relieve physical discomfort associated with overexertion, colds, allergies, and so forth. Pawnshops provide cash for individuals temporarily needing funds, as do banks and other financial institutions. Thus, a great deal of marketing activity is directed toward momentary conditions. Illustration 13–6 is an ad for a product designed to relieve a momentary condition.

RITUAL SITUATIONS

Rituals are receiving increasing attention by marketing scholars and practitioners. A **ritual situation** can be described as a socially defined occasion that triggers a set of interrelated behaviors that occur in a structured format and that have symbolic meaning.[63] Ritual situations can range from completely private to completely public. A completely private ritual situation would be an individual's decision to drink a private toast or say a private prayer on the anniversary of an event with special meaning to the individual. A couple that celebrates their first date by returning to the same restaurant every year is involved in a more public ritual. Weddings tend to be even more public. Finally, national and global holidays present very public ritual situations.

Ritual situations are of major importance to marketers because they often involve prescribed consumption behaviors. Every major American holiday (ritual situation) has consumption rituals associated with it. For example, more than 60 percent of the toy industry's sales occur at Christmas.

While there is significant variation across individuals and households, there is enough shared behavior that marketers can develop products and promotions around the common ritual situations that arise each year. For example, candy marketers produce and promote

ILLUSTRATION 13–7

Ritual situations
generally have con-
sumption patterns
associated with
them. This brand is
tapping into ritual
situations.

Light the candles.
Brighten the celebration.

a wide array of candies for Valentine's Day
and Halloween. Illustration 13–7 shows
how one marketer is capitalizing on consumption rituals.

Marketers also attempt to change or create consumption patterns associated with
ritual situations.[64] Mother's Day is a $10
billion occasion in which card giving is
largely a ritual behavior created by marketers.[65] Halloween cards are now being
promoted as part of the Halloween ritual.[66]
And many firms seek to make their products
and services part of the consumption pattern associated with "coming of age." These
occasions are often marked with religious
ceremonies and after-ceremony parties.
Traditionally, these events have tended to
focus on religious aspects and responsibility
to family and community. For example:

In Latin America, the quinceañera, a celebration dating back to the Aztecs that commemorates
the spiritual and physical coming of age of a 15-year-old girl, is typically observed with a cer-
emony in the Catholic church and a backyard party for family members.[67]

The "after-ceremony" celebrations range from simple and inexpensive to elaborate and
costly. However, the trend is definitely toward more elaborate and costly parties with modern themes, expensive catering and entertainment, and interactive activities to entertain
hundreds of guests. For example:

One Hispanic family spent $30,000 to celebrate their daughter's quinceañera with "a horsedrawn,
pumpkin-shaped crystal carriage with liveried servants in powdered wigs, a silver tulle gown and a
gala at which 260 guests danced until dawn in the shadow of Sleeping Beauty's castle at Disneyland."[68]

Ritual situations can also result in injurious consumption. Binge or excessive drinking is a serious health and social problem on many college campuses, though its incidence appears to be on the decline. Recent research suggests that this can be understood
as a ritual behavior in that it is triggered by social occasions (e.g., birthdays), involves a
set of interrelated behaviors and routines (e.g., start drinking on game days at a specific
time), and results in special meaning and rewards for participants (e.g., fun, acceptance by
group). When approached from this perspective, more effective strategies for minimizing
such behaviors may result.

SITUATIONAL INFLUENCES AND MARKETING STRATEGY

In the previous sections, we described a variety of marketing strategies based on situational
influences. Here we focus more specifically on the process by which such strategies can be
developed.

It is important to note that individuals do not encounter situations randomly. Instead, most people "create" many of the situations they face. Thus, individuals who choose to engage in physically demanding sports such as jogging, tennis, or racquetball are indirectly choosing to expose themselves to the situation of "being tired" or "being thirsty." This allows marketers to develop products, advertising, and segmentation strategies based on the situations that individuals selecting various lifestyles are likely to encounter.

After identifying the different situations that might involve the consumption of a product, marketers must determine which products or brands are most likely to be purchased or consumed across those situations. One method of approaching this is to jointly scale situations and products. An example is shown in Figure 13-3. Here, *use situations* that ranged from "private consumption at home" to "consumption away from home where there is a concern for other people's reaction to you" were scaled in terms of their similarity and relationship to products appropriate for that situation.

For use situation I, "to clean my mouth upon rising in the morning," toothpaste and mouthwash are viewed as most appropriate (see Figure 13-3). However, use situation II, "before an important business meeting late in the afternoon," involves both consumption

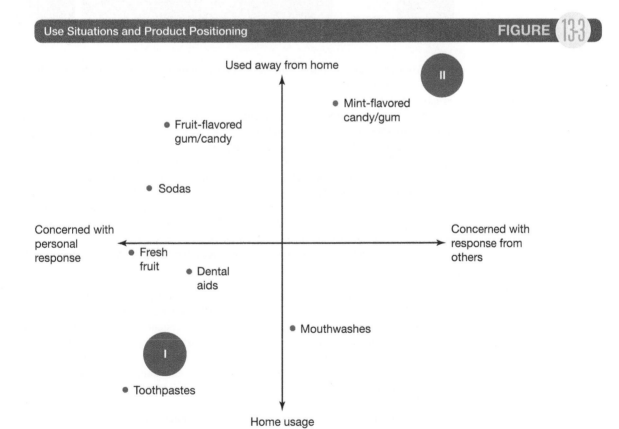

Use Situations and Product Positioning   FIGURE 13-3

Used away from home

II

• Mint-flavored candy/gum

• Fruit-flavored gum/candy

• Sodas

Concerned with personal response ← → Concerned with response from others

• Fresh fruit

• Dental aids

• Mouthwashes

I

• Toothpastes

Home usage

I = Use situation: "To clean my mouth upon rising in the morning."
II = Use situation: "Before an important business meeting late in the afternoon."

ILLUSTRATION 13–8

This ad shows products that move into new use situations for this retailer.

away from home and a concern for the response from others. As a result, mint-flavored gums or candies are preferred. *Where do you think a product like Listerine Breath Strips would be located on this map?*

Determining how products are *currently used* across situations can help the marketer develop appropriate advertising and positioning strategies. In our example, Wrigley's might advertise its Spearmint Gum as having breath-freshening capabilities that make it appropriate for use in social situations away from home. Or a marketer may try to change the situations for which a product is used. In Figure 13-3, mouthwash is not seen as appropriate for consumption away from home. What if a version of Scope was developed that one swallowed after use? Could it successfully be promoted for use away from home? Would it be able to compete against breath strips? Illustration 13–8 shows a company that is adding products to expand the number of usage situations.

Another approach for developing situation-based marketing strategies is to follow these five steps:[69]

1. Use observational studies, focus group discussions, depth interviews, and secondary data to discover the various usage situations that influence the consumption of the product.
2. Survey a larger sample of consumers to better understand and quantify how the product is used and the benefits sought in the usage situation by the market segment.
3. Construct a person–situation segmentation matrix. The rows are the major usage situations and the columns are groups of users with unique needs or desires. Each cell contains the key benefits sought. (Table 13-2 illustrates such a matrix for suntan lotion.) Then:
4. Evaluate each cell in terms of potential (sales volume, price level, cost to serve, competitor strength, and so forth).
5. Develop and implement a marketing strategy for those cells that offer sufficient profit potential given your capabilities.

Person–Situation Segments for Suntan Lotions

TABLE 13-2

Suntan Lotion Use Situation	Potential Users of Suntan Lotion				
	Young Children	Teenagers	Adult Women	Adult Men	General Situation Benefits
Beach/boat activities	Prevent sunburn/skin damage	Prevent sunburn while tanning	Prevent sunburn/ skin change/ dry skin	Prevent sunburn	Container floats
Home/pools sunbathing	Prevent sunburn/ skin damage	Tanning without sunburn	Tanning without skin damage or dry skin	Tanning without sunburn/ skin damage	Lotion won't stain clothes or furniture
Tanning booth		Tanning	Tanning with moisturizer	Tanning	Designed for sunlamps
Snow skiing		Prevent sunburn	Prevent sunburn/ skin damage/ dry skin	Prevent sunburn	Antifreeze formula
Person benefits	Protection	Tanning	Protection and tanning with soft skin	Protection and tanning	

Source: Adapted from P. Dickson, "Person–Situation: Segmentation's Missing Link," *Journal of Marketing*, Fall 1982, pp. 56–64. Published by the American Marketing Association. Reprinted with permission.

SUMMARY

LO1: Define situational influence

Situational influence is all those factors particular to a time and place that do not follow from a knowledge of the stable attributes of the consumer and the stimulus and that have an effect on current behavior.

LO2: Explain the four types of situations and their relevance to marketing strategy

Four categories of situations are communications, purchase, usage, and disposition situations. The situation in which consumers receive information is the communications situation. The situation in which a purchase is made is the purchase situation. The situation in which the product or service is used is the usage situation. The situation in which a product or product package is disposed of either after or before product use is the disposition situation. Each type of situation has marketing implications such as what programming to advertise within (communications situation), the effect of other people on an individual's shopping behavior in-store (buying situation), the ability to expand beyond traditional

uses for a given product (usage situation), and the factors contributing to recycling behavior (disposition situation).

LO3: Summarize the five characteristics of situations and their influence on consumption

Five characteristics of situations have been identified. *Physical surroundings* include geographical and institutional location, decor, sound, aromas, lighting, weather, and displays of merchandise or other material surrounding the product. Retailers are particularly concerned with the effects of physical surroundings. The sum of all the physical features of a retail environment is referred to as the *store atmosphere* or environment. *Atmospherics* is the process managers use to manipulate the physical retail environment to create specific mood responses in shoppers. Atmosphere is referred to as *servicescape* when describing a service business such as a hospital, bank, or restaurant.

Social surroundings deal with other persons present who could have an impact on the individual consumer's behavior. The characteristics of the other persons present, their roles, and their interpersonal interactions are potentially important social situational influences.

Temporal perspectives relate to the effect of time on consumer behavior, such as effects of time of day, time since last purchase, time since or until meals or payday, and time constraints imposed by commitments. Convenience stores have evolved and been successful by taking advantage of the temporal perspective factor.

Task definition reflects the purpose or reason for engaging in the consumption behavior. The task may reflect different buyer and user roles anticipated by the individual. For example, a person shopping for dishes to be given as a wedding present is in a different situation from a person buying dishes for personal use.

Antecedent states are features of the individual person that are not lasting or relatively enduring characteristics. *Moods* are temporary states of depression or high excitement, and so on, which all people experience. *Momentary conditions* are such things as being tired, ill, having a great deal of money (or none at all), and so forth.

LO4: Discuss ritual situations and their importance to consumers and marketers

A *ritual situation* can be described as a set of interrelated behaviors that occur in a structured format, that have symbolic meaning to consumers, and that occur in response to socially defined occasions. Ritual situations can range from completely private to completely public. They are of major importance to marketers because they often involve prescribed consumption behaviors.

LO5: Describe the use of situational influence in developing marketing strategy

Situational influences may have direct influences, but they also interact with product and individual characteristics to influence behavior. In some cases, the situation will have no influence whatsoever, because the individual's characteristics or choices are so intense that they override everything else. But the situation is always potentially important and therefore of concern to marketing managers.

KEY TERMS

Antecedent states 475
Atmospherics 468
Communications situation 464
Disposition situation 467
Embarrassment 471
Moods 475

Physical surroundings 467
Purchase situations 466
Ritual situation 477
Servicescape 468
Situational influence 464
Social surroundings 471

Store atmosphere 468
Task definition 474
Temporal perspectives 473
Usage situations 466

INTERNET EXERCISES

1. Visit several online retailers. How would you characterize this shopping situation relative to shopping in a physical store?

2. What type of online environment does BarnesandNoble.com have?

3. Visit www.planalytics.com, which was discussed in the chapter opener. View one or more of their client success videos and write a report on how, exactly, weather-based situational marketing is used by the company.

REVIEW QUESTIONS

1. What is meant by the term *situation*? Why is it important for a marketing manager to understand situational influences on purchasing behavior?

2. What are *physical surroundings* (as a situational variable)? Give an example of how they can influence the consumption process.

3. How does crowding affect shopping behavior?

4. What is *store atmosphere*?

5. What is *atmospherics*?

6. What is a *servicescape*?

7. What are *social surroundings* (as a situational variable)? Give an example of how they can influence the consumption process.

8. What is *temporal perspective* (as a situational variable)? Give an example of how it can influence the consumption process.

9. What is *task definition* (as a situational variable)? Give an example of how it can influence the consumption process.

10. Why do people give gifts?

11. How might the receipt of a gift affect the relationship between the giver and the receiver?

12. What are *antecedent conditions* (as a situational variable)? Give an example of how they can influence the consumption process.

13. What is a *mood*? How does it differ from an *emotion*? How do moods influence consumption behavior?

14. How do people manage their moods?

15. How do moods differ from *momentary conditions*?

16. What is meant by the statement, "Situational variables may interact with product or personal characteristics"?

17. Are individuals randomly exposed to situational influences? Why or why not?

18. What are *ritual situations*? Why are they important?

19. Describe a process for developing a situation-based marketing strategy.

DISCUSSION QUESTIONS

20. Discuss the potential importance of each type of situational influence in developing a marketing strategy to promote the purchase of (gifts to/shopping at):
    a. Audubon Society
    b. Subway
    c. iPhone
    d. Coca-Cola Zero
    e. 7-Eleven
    f. Eyewear

21. What product categories seem most susceptible to situational influences? Why?

22. Flowers are appropriate gifts for women for many situations but seem to be appropriate for men only when they are ill. Why is this so? How might 1-800-FLOWERS change this?

23. How could the store atmosphere at the following be improved?
    a. The main library on campus
    b. The bank lobby near campus
    c. A diner near campus
    d. A convenience store near campus
    e. The student advising office

24. Speculate on what a matrix like the one shown in Table 13-2 would look like for the following:
    a. Tablet computer
    b. Eyewear
    c. Ice cream
    d. Shoes
    e. Motor scooter
    f. Coffee

25. Does Table 13-1 have implications for outlets other than restaurants? If yes, which ones and why?

26. Do your shopping behavior and purchase criteria differ between purchases made for yourself and purchases made as gifts? How?

27. Describe a situation in which a mood (good or bad) caused you to make an unusual purchase.

28. Describe a relatively private ritual that you or someone you know has. What, if any, consumption pattern is associated with it?

29. Describe the consumption rituals your family has associated with the following ritual situations:
    a. Family birthdays
    b. Summer vacations
    c. Winter holiday
    d. Halloween
    e. Mother's Day
    f. Father's Day
    g. New Year's Eve

30. Respond to the questions in Consumer Insight 13-1.

APPLICATION ACTIVITIES

31. Interview five people who have recently purchased the following. Determine the role, if any, played by situational factors.
    a. Cell phone
    b. Jewelry
    c. Motorcycle
    d. A fast-food restaurant meal
    e. A cup of coffee
    f. Health insurance

32. Interview a salesperson for the following. Determine the role, if any, this individual feels situational variables play in his or her sales.
    a. Renter's insurance
    b. BMX bikes
    c. Fine chocolates
    d. Flowers

33. Conduct a study using a small (five or so) sample of your friends in which you attempt to isolate the situational factors that influence the type, brand, or amount of the following purchased or used.
    a. Health club
    b. Clothing
    c. Movie attendance
    d. Volunteer work
    e. TV dinners
    f. Car tires

34. Create a list of 10 to 20 use situations relevant to campus area restaurants. Then interview 10 students and have them indicate which of these situations they have encountered, and ask them to rank these situations in terms of how likely they are to occur. Discuss how a restaurant could use this information in trying to appeal to the student market.

35. Visit three stores selling the same product line. Describe how the atmosphere differs across the stores. Why do you think these differences exist?

36. Visit three local coffee shops. Describe how the servicescapes differ across the shops. Why do you think these differences exist?

37. What kind of online atmosphere does each of the following have? How would you improve it?
    a. Toyota.com
    b. Harley-Davidson.com
    c. Nike.com
    d. Charities.org
    e. Cabelas.com
    f. Cheerios.com

38. Copy or describe an advertisement that is clearly based on a situational appeal. Indicate:
    a. Which situational variable is involved
    b. Why the company would use this variable
    c. Your evaluation of the effectiveness of this approach

39. Create a graduation gift, an anniversary gift, and a self-use ad for the following. Explain the differences across the ads:
    a. Trip abroad
    b. Gourmet coffee maker
    c. Magazine subscription
    d. Set of dishes
    e. Blender
    f. Watch

40. Interview five students and determine instances where their mood affected their purchases. What do you conclude?

41. Interview five students and determine the consumption rituals they have with respect to the following. What do you conclude?
    a. New Year's Day
    b. Spring break
    c. Memorial Day
    d. Valentine's Day
    e. Mother's Day
    f. Father's Day

REFERENCES

1. This opener is based on H. Kimball, "Cold Weather Means Hot Demand for Soup, Boots," *newser*, January 11, 2010, www.newser.com, accessed June 15, 2011; N. Zmuda and E. B. York, "Marketers Make Most of Falling Mercury," *Advertising Age*, January 11, 2010, pp. 1, 20; and information from Planalytics' website, www.planalytics.com, accessed June 15, 2011.

2. See K. S. Lim and M. A. Razzaque, "Brand Loyalty and Situational Effects," *Journal of International Consumer Marketing* 4 (1997), pp. 95–115.

3. R. W. Belk, "Situational Variables and Consumer Behavior," *Journal of Consumer Research*, December 1975, p. 158.

4. See K. R. Lord, R. E. Burnkrant, and H. R. Unnava, "The Effects of Program-Induced Mood States on Memory for Commercial Information," *Journal of Current Issues and Research in Advertising,* Spring 2001, pp. 1–14; S. Shapiro, D. J. MacInnis, and C. Whan Park, "Understanding Program-Induced Mood Effects," *Journal of Advertising,* Winter 2002, pp. 15–26; P. De Pelsmacker, M. Geuens, and P. Anckaert, "Media Context and Advertising Effectiveness," *Journal of Advertising,* Summer 2002, pp. 49–61; S. Jun et al., "The Influence of Editorial Context on Consumer Response to Advertisements in a Specialty Magazine," *Journal of Current Issues and Research in Advertising,* Fall 2003, pp. 1–11; and C. Yoon, M. P. Lee, and S. Danziger, "The Effects of Optimal Time of Day on Persuasion Processes in Older Adults," *Psychology and Marketing,* May 2007, pp. 475–95.

5. L. Sanders and J. Halliday, "BP Institutes 'Ad-Pull' Policy for Print Publications," *AdAge.com,* May 24, 2005.

6. B. Wansink, "Making Old Brands New," *American Demographics,* December 1997, pp. 53–58.

7. E. Byron, "Case by Case," *The Wall Street Journal,* November 17, 2004, p. A1.

8. "Glazed Still Tops Among Donuts," *Baking Management,* May 23, 2011.

9. I. Sinha, "A Conceptual Model of Situation Type on Consumer Choice Behavior and Consideration Sets," in *Advances in Consumer Research,* vol. 21, ed. C. T. Allen and D. R. John (Provo, UT: Association for Consumer Research, 1994), pp. 477–82. See also E. Byron, "Case by Case."

10. See J. A. F. Nicholls et al., "Situational Influences on Shoppers," *Journal of International Consumer Marketing* 9, no. 2 (1996), pp. 21–39; and J. A. F. Nicholls, T. Li, and S. Roslow, "Oceans Apart," *Journal of International Consumer Marketing* 12, no. 1 (1999), pp. 57–72.

11. See E. Sherman, A. Mathur, and R. B. Smith, "Store Environment and Consumer Purchase Behavior," *Psychology & Marketing,* July 1997, pp. 361–78; and J. Baker et al., "The Influence of Multiple Design Cues on Perceived Merchandise Value and Patronage Intentions," *Journal of Marketing,* April 2002, pp. 120–41.

12. For an extensive review, see L. W. Turley and R. E. Milliman, "Atmospheric Effects on Shopping Behavior," *Journal of Business Research* 49 (2000), pp. 193–211. See also A. d'Astous, "Irritating Aspects of the Shopping Environment," and A. Sharma and T. F. Stafford, "The Effect of Retail Atmospherics on Customers' Perceptions of Salespeople and Customer Persuasion," both in *Journal of Business Research* 49 (2000), pp. 149–56 and 183–91, respectively.

13. P. Sautter, M. R. Hyman, and V. Lukosius, "E-Tail Atmospherics," *Journal of Electronic Commerce Research* 5, no. 1 (2004), pp. 14–24; and E. E. Manganari, G. J. Siomkos, and A. P Vrechopoulos, "Store Atmosphere in Web Retailing," *European Journal of Marketing* 43, no. 9/10 (2009), pp. 1140–53.

14. M. J. Bitner, "Servicescapes," *Journal of Marketing,* April 1992, pp. 57–71. See also K. D. Hoffman, S. W. Kelley, and B. C. Chung, "A CIT Investigation of Servicescape Failures and Associated Recovery Strategies," *Journal of Services Marketing* 17, no. 4/5 (2003), pp. 322–40.

15. G. J. Gorn, A. Chattopadhyay, T. Yi, and D. W. Dahl, "Effects of Color as an Executional Cue in Advertising," *Management Science,* October 1997, pp. 1387–99.

16. See J. A. Bellizzi and R. E. Hite, "Environmental Color, Consumer Feelings, and Purchase Likelihood," *Psychology & Marketing,* September 1992, pp. 347–63.

17. B. E. Kahn and L. McAlister, *Grocery Revolution* (Reading, MA: Addison-Wesley, 1997).

18. G. J. Gorn, A. Chattopadhyay, J. Sengupta, and S. Tripathi, "Waiting for the Web," *Journal of Marketing Research,* May 2004, pp. 215–25.

19. D. J. Mitchell, B. E. Kahn, and S. C. Knasko, "There's Something in the Air," *Journal of Consumer Research,* September 1995, pp. 229–38.

20. E. R. Spangenberg, A. E. Crowley, and P. W. Henderson, "Improving the Store Environment," *Journal of Marketing,* April 1996, pp. 67–80.

21. A. R. Hirsch, "Effects of Ambient Odors on Slot-Machine Usage in a Las Vegas Casino," *Psychology & Marketing,* October 1995, pp. 585–94.

22. M. Morrison et al., "In-Store Music and Aroma Influences on Shopper Behavior and Satisfaction," *Journal of Business Research* 64 (2011), pp. 558–64.

23. M. Morrin and S. Ratneshwar, "The Impact of Ambient Scent on Evaluation, Attention, and Memory for Familiar and Unfamiliar Brands," *Journal of Business Research* 49 (2000), pp. 157–65.

24. See, e.g., "Environmental Fragrancing," *Labnews.co.uk,* May 26, 2011, accessed June 15, 2011.

25. P. F. Bone and P. S. Ellen, "Scents in the Marketplace," *Journal of Retailing* 75, no. 2 (1999), pp. 243–62.

26. P. Sloan, "Smelling Trouble," *Advertising Age,* September 11, 1995, p. 1.

27. See S. Oakes, "The Influence of the Musicscape within Service Environments," *Journal of Services Marketing* 4, no. 7 (2000), pp. 539–56; M. Morrison et al., "In-Store Music and Aroma Influences on Shopper Behavior and Satisfaction"; and S. Morin, L. Dube, and J. C. Chebat, "The Role of Pleasant Music in Servicescapes," *Journal of Business Research* 83, no. 1 (2007), 115–30.

28. J. C. Sweeney and F. Wyber, "The Role of Cognitions and Emotions in the Music-Approach-Avoidance Behavior Relationship," *Journal of Services Marketing* 16, no. 1 (2002), pp. 51–69; and C. Caldwell and S. A. Hibbert, "The Influence of Music Tempo and Musical Preference on Restaurant Patrons' Behavior," *Psychology & Marketing,* November 2002, pp. 895–917.

29. B. Zimmers, "Business Deals Put AEI Music CEO in Good Mood," *Puget Sound Business Journal,* June 23, 2000, p. 44; see also C. A. Olson, "Shopping to the Music Made Easy," *Billboard,* July 31, 1999, pp. 73–74.

30. See K. A. Machleit, S. A. Eroglu, and S. P. Mantel, "Perceived Retail Crowding and Shopping Satisfaction," *Journal of Consumer Psychology* 9, no. 1 (2000), pp. 29–42. For an exception, see F. Pons, M. Laroche, and M. Mourali, "Consumer Reactions to Crowded Retail Settings," *Psychology & Marketing,* July 2006, pp. 555–72.

31. S. A. Eroglu, K. A. Machleit, and J. C. Chebat, "The Interaction of Retail Density and Music Tempo," *Psychology & Marketing,* July 2005, pp. 577–89.

32. F. Pons, M. Laroche, and M. Mourali, "Consumer Reactions to Crowded Retail Settings."

33. T. R. Graeth, "Consumption Situations and the Effects of Brand Image on Consumers' Brand Evaluations," *Psychology & Marketing,* January 1997, pp. 49–70. See also S. Ramanathan and A. L. McGill, "Consuming with Others," *Journal of Consumer Research,* December 2007, pp. 506–24.

Part Four Consumer Decision Process

34. R. K. Ratner and B. E. Kahn, "The Impact of Private versus Public Consumption on Variety-Seeking Behavior," *Journal of Consumer Research,* September 2002, pp. 246–57.

35. See, e.g., D. W. Dahl, R. V. Manchanda, and J. J. Argo, "Embarrassment in Consumer Purchase," *Journal of Consumer Research,* December 2001, pp. 473–81. See also D. Grace, "How Embarrassing!" *Journal of Service Research,* February 2007, pp. 271–84.

36. Consumer Insight 13-1 is based on S. E. Beatty and M. E. Ferrell, "Impulse Buying," *Journal of Retailing,* Summer 1998, pp. 161–91; and X. Luo, "How Does Shopping with Others Influence Impulsive Purchasing?" *Journal of Consumer Psychology* 15, no. 4 (2005), pp. 288–94.

37. R. Batra and P. M. Homer, "The Situational Impact of Brand Image Beliefs," *Journal of Consumer Psychology* 14, no. 3 (2004), pp. 318–30.

38. L. A. Brannon and T. C. Brock, "Limiting Time for Responding Enhances Behavior Corresponding to the Merits of Compliance Appeals," *Journal of Consumer Psychology* 10, no. 3 (2001), pp. 135–46; and R. Suri and K. B. Monroe, "The Effects of Time Constraints on Consumers' Judgments of Prices and Products," *Journal of Consumer Research,* June 2003, pp. 92–104.

39. S. M. Nowlis, "The Effect of Time Pressure on the Choice of Brands That Differ in Quality, Price, and Product Features," *Marketing Letters,* October 1995, pp. 287–96; R. Dhar and S. M. Nowlis, "The Effect of Time Pressure on Consumer Choice Deferral," *Journal of Consumer Research,* March 1999, pp. 369–84; and R. Pieters and L. Warlop, "Visual Attention during Brand Choice," *International Journal of Research in Marketing,* February 1999, pp. 1–16.

40. S. D. Strombeck and K. L. Wakefield, "Situational Influences on Service Quality Evaluations," *Journal of Services Marketing* 22, no. 5 (2008), pp. 409–19.

41. P. Van Kenhove, K. De Wulf, and W. Van Waterschoot, "The Impact of Task Definition on Store-Attribute Saliences and Store Choice," *Journal of Retailing* 75, no. 1 (1999), pp. 125–37; P. Van Kenhove and K. De Wulf, "Income and Time Pressure," *International Review of Retail, Distribution and Consumer Research,* April 2000, pp. 149–66.

42. See B. H. Schmitt and C. J. Shultz II, "Situational Effects on Brand Preferences for Image Products," *Psychology & Marketing,* August 1995, pp. 433–46.

43. T. M. Lowrey, C. C. Otnes, and J. A. Ruth, "Social Influences on Dyadic Giving over Time," *Journal of Consumer Research,* March 2004, pp. 547–58.

44. For a review and framework, see D. Larsen and J. J. Watson, "A Guide Map to the Terrain of Gift Value," *Psychology & Marketing,* August 2001, pp. 889–906; see also G. Saad and T. Gill, "An Evolutionary Psychology Perspective on Gift Giving among Young Adults," *Psychology & Marketing,* September 2003, pp. 765–84.

45. M. A. McGrath, "Gender Differences in Gift Exchanges," *Psychology & Marketing,* August 1995, pp. 371–93; K. M. Palan, C. S. Areni, and P. Kiecker, "Gender Role Incongruency and Memorable Gift Exchange Experiences," J. F. Durgee and T. Sego, "Gift-Giving as a Metaphor for Understanding New Products That Delight," both in *Advances in Consumer Research,* vol. 28, ed. M. C. Gilly and J. Meyers-Levy (Provo, UT: Association for Consumer Research, 2001), pp. 51–57 and 64–69, respectively.

46. D. B. Wooten, "Qualitative Steps toward an Expanded Model of Anxiety in Gift-Giving," *Journal of Consumer Research,* June 2000, pp. 84–95.

47. See, e.g., J. A. Ruth, C. C. Otnes, and F. F. Brunel, "Gift Receipt and the Reformulation of Interpersonal Relationships," *Journal of Consumer Research,* March 1999, pp. 385–402.

48. R. W. Belk and G. S. Coon, "Gift Giving as Agapic Love," *Journal of Consumer Research,* December 1993, pp. 404–5. See also J. A. Ruth, F. F. Brunel, and C. C. Otnes, "An Investigation of the Power of Emotions in Relationship Realignment," *Psychology & Marketing,* January 2004, pp. 29–52.

49. C. S. Areni, P. Kiecker, and K. M. Palan, "Is It Better to Give Than to Receive?" *Psychology & Marketing,* January 1998, pp. 81–109.

50. A. Joy, "Gift Giving in Hong Kong and the Continuum of Social Ties," *Journal of Consumer Research,* September 2001, pp. 239–55; and S. L. Lotz, S. Shim, and K. C. Gehrt, "A Study of Japanese Consumers' Cognitive Hierarchies in Formal and Informal Gift-Giving Situations," *Psychology & Marketing,* January 2003, pp. 59–85.

51. S.-Y. Park, "A Comparison of Korean and American Gift-Giving Behaviors," *Psychology & Marketing,* September 1998, pp. 577–93.

52. See R. P. Bagozzi, M. Gopinath, and P. U. Nyer, "The Role of Emotion in Marketing," *Journal of the Academy of Marketing Science,* Spring 1999, pp. 184–206; and H. T. Luomala and M. Laaksonen, "Contributions from Mood Research," *Psychology & Marketing,* March 2000, pp. 195–233.

53. M. B. Holbrook and M. P. Gardner, "Illustrating a Dynamic Model of the Mood-Updating Process in Consumer Behavior," *Psychology & Marketing,* March 2000, pp. 165–94.

54. J. P. Forgas and J. Ciarrochi, "On Being Happy and Possessive," *Psychology & Marketing,* March 2001, pp. 239–60; and R. Adaval, "Sometimes It Just Feels Right," *Journal of Consumer Research,* June 2001, pp. 1–17.

55. D. W. Rook and M. P. Gardner, "In the Mood," *Research in Consumer Behavior* 6 (1993), pp. 1–28; W. R. Swinyard, "The Effects of Mood, Involvement, and Quality of Store Experience on Shopping Intentions," *Journal of Consumer Research,* September 1993, pp. 271–80; and R. J. Faber and G. A. Christenson, "In the Mood to Buy," *Psychology & Marketing,* December 1996, pp. 803–19. See also N. Garg, B. Wansink, and J. J. Inman, "The Influence of Incidental Affect on Consumers' Food Intake," *Journal of Marketing,* January 2007, pp. 194–206 for an application of mood to food choice.

56. See Reference 4.

57. See, e.g., K. S. Coulter, "The Effects of Affective Responses to Media Context on Advertising Evaluations," *Journal of Advertising,* Winter 1998, pp. 41–51.

58. H. T. Luomala and M. Laaksonen, "A Qualitative Exploration of Mood-Regulatory Self-Gift Behaviors," *Journal of Economic Psychology* 20 (1999), pp. 147–82.

59. H. Mano, "The Influence of Pre-Existing Negative Affect on Store Purchase Intentions," *Journal of Retailing* 75, no. 2 (1999), pp. 149–73.

60. S. J. Gould, "An Interpretive Study of Purposeful, Mood Self-Regulating Consumption," *Psychology & Marketing,* July 1997, pp. 395–426.

61. See M. G. Meloy, "Mood-Driven Distortion of Product Information," *Journal of Consumer Research,* December 2000, pp. 345–58.

62. See P. A. Walsh and S. Spiggle, "Consumer Spending Patterns," in *Advances in Consumer Research,* vol. 21, ed. Allen and John, pp. 35–40; and N. Karlsson, T. Garling, and M. Selart, "Explanations of Prior Income Changes on Buying Decisions," *Journal of Economic Psychology* 20 (1999), pp. 449–63.

63. See B. Gainer, "Ritual and Relationships," *Journal of Business Research,* March 1995, pp. 253–60.

64. See C. C. Otnes and L. M. Scott, "Something Old, Something New," *Journal of Advertising,* Spring 1996, pp. 33–50.

65. "$10 Billion for Mom," *CNNmoney,* April 21, 2004, http:// money .cnn.com/.

66. A. Z. Cuneo, "Using Halloween to Scare Up Sales," *Advertising Age,* October 8, 2001, p. 4.

67. A. Chozick, "Fairy-Tale Fifteenths," *The Wall Street Journal,* October 15, 2004, p. B1.

68. Ibid.

69. For a similar approach, see R. Brodie, "Segmentation and Market Structure When Both Consumer and Situational Characteristics Are Explanatory," *Psychology & Marketing,* September 1992, pp. 395–408.

15 Information Search

LEARNING OBJECTIVES

LO1 Discuss internal and external information search and their role in different decision types

LO2 Summarize the types of information consumers search for

LO3 Describe the categories of decision alternatives relating to the evoked set

LO4 Discuss available information sources and the role of Internet and mobile search

LO5 Discuss the major cost-benefit factors driving the amount of external search

LO6 Summarize the marketing strategies based on information search patterns

The Internet has dramatically expanded the ability of consumers to search for information. It allows easy access to manufacturers' websites, to other consumers, and to third parties such as consumer groups and government agencies. It also greatly expands the ability of marketers to provide information to consumers, either directly through their corporate or brand sites or indirectly through ads placed on other sites. Internet strategies continue to evolve. However, most companies go well beyond simply providing company and product information in an electronic format. Consider the following:[1]

- BMW was perhaps the first automobile company to take its website to the next level. Not only does BMW provide detailed information about each make and model, they also allow consumers to build their own cars from the "ground up," choosing exterior and interior colors, packages, accessories, and so on. Information about options, features, and price are included along the way, as are realistic 360° visuals. According to one BMW representative, their website changes the way consumers search for and purchase their cars, with many coming into the dealership with their BMW already "picked out." Other features of

the site include BMW TV, links to BMW brand communities, and a news feed.

- Nike's website has various pages relating to its shoes and apparel. However, it goes well beyond a place to find out information about shoes. For example, Nike+ is an online interactive tool that interfaces with special Nike equipment to allow runners to get real-time feedback through an armband or iPod while running, to upload data and track goals, and to connect and compete with others. It is so popular that 90 percent of Nike+ runners say they would recommend it to a friend. The website has a runner's blog, forums, a news tab, and customized training programs. And this is only for running. Nike has similarly sophisticated sites for basketball, soccer, and so on.

Note how each site goes beyond basic product information by personalizing information to specific customer needs, and adding other information, activities, and applications of relevance to the consumer and their information needs. These firms want consumers to use their sites not only when explicitly seeking product-specific information but also on a regular basis for a variety of purposes as a means to build ongoing relationships.

This chapter examines the information search stage of the decision process that occurs after problem recognition. Within information search, we focus on (1) the amount and type of search, (2) categories of decision alternatives relating to the evoked set, (3) sources and channels of information including the Internet and mobile, (4) the cost-benefit factors driving external search, and (5) marketing strategies based on information search patterns.

THE NATURE OF INFORMATION SEARCH

Once a problem is recognized, relevant information from long-term memory is used to determine such things as (1) if a satisfactory solution is known, (2) what the characteristics of potential solutions are, and (3) what appropriate ways exist to compare solutions. This is **internal search.** If a resolution is not reached through internal search, then the search process is focused on external information relevant to solving the problem. This is **external search,** which can involve independent sources, personal sources, marketer-based information, and product experience.[2] It is important to note that even in extended decision making with extensive external search, the initial internal search generally produces a set of guides (e.g., must have attributes) or decision constraints (e.g., maximum price that can be paid) that limit and guide external search. Search has benefits such as finding a lower price or getting higher quality. However, search has costs that tend to limit the amount of search even for very important decisions. That is, information search involves mental as well as physical activities that consumers must perform that take time, energy, and money.

As discussed in Chapter 14, the amount of search depends on purchase involvement, which is a major determinant of the type of decision process consumers engage in. Purchase involvement, and the amount of external search, increase as consumers move from nominal decision making to extended decision making. Internal information tends to dominate in nominal decision making, where typically a consumer recalls a single satisfactory solution and purchases it without further search or evaluation. External search tends to dominate in extended decision making, where typically a consumer examines and evaluates numerous alternatives across numerous criteria using information from many sources. For limited decision making, external search can play a moderate role in some instances particularly when the consumer is aware of several possible alternative solutions to his or her problem and therefore must search and evaluate on a limited basis to make a choice.[3]

Search after problem recognition can also be limited by prior search and learning. That is, deliberate external search also occurs in the absence of problem recognition. **Ongoing search** is done both *to acquire information for possible later use and because the process itself is pleasurable.* For example, individuals highly involved with an activity, such as tennis, are apt to seek information about tennis-related products on an ongoing basis without a recognized problem with their existing tennis equipment (recall that enduring involvement is characteristic of opinion leaders). In addition, consumers acquire a substantial amount of relevant information on an ongoing basis without deliberate search—through low-involvement learning (see Chapter 9).

TYPES OF INFORMATION SOUGHT

A consumer decision requires information on the following:[4]

1. The appropriate evaluative criteria for the solution of a problem.
2. The existence of various alternative solutions.
3. The performance level or characteristic of each alternative solution on each evaluative criterion.

Information Search in Consumer Decisions

FIGURE 15-1

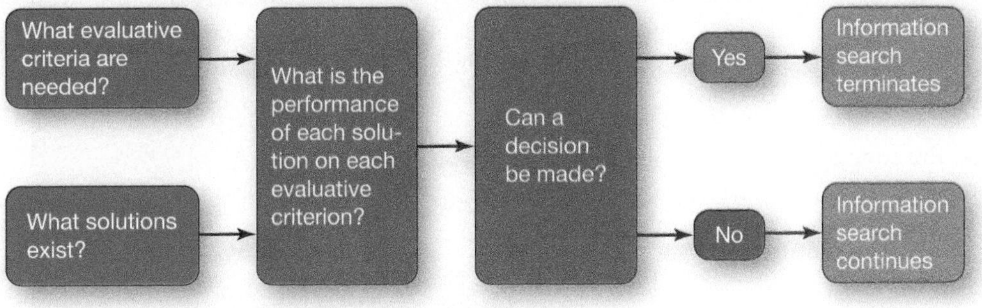

Information search, then, seeks each of these three types of information, as shown in Figure 15-1.

Evaluative Criteria

Suppose you are provided with money to purchase a laptop computer, perhaps as a graduation present. Assuming you have not been in the market for a computer recently, your first thought would probably be, "What features do I want in a computer?" You would then engage in internal search to determine the features or characteristics required to meet your needs. These desired characteristics are your *evaluative criteria*. If you have had limited experience with computers, you might also engage in external search to learn which characteristics a good computer should have. You could check with friends, read reviews in *PC Magazine* online, talk with sales personnel, visit computer websites, post questions on an online discussion board, or personally inspect several computers. Illustration 15–1 shows an example of how a company is trying to focus consumers toward an attribute on which it excels but which consumers may not automatically have in mind when selecting a brand.

A detailed discussion of evaluative criteria appears in Chapter 16.

Appropriate Alternatives

After and while searching for appropriate evaluative criteria, you would probably seek *appropriate alternatives*—in this case, brands, or possibly stores. In general, there are five groupings of alternatives. First is the set of all possible alternatives that could solve a consumer problem. Within this set there are four categories of decision alternatives. The **awareness set** is composed of those brands consumers are aware of. The **inert set** is composed of those brands consumers are aware of and view in a neutral manner. These are brands that might be seen as acceptable by consumers if their favorite alternative is not available. These are also brands for which consumers will be open to positive information although they will not be actively seeking it out. The **inept set** is composed of those brands consumers are aware of and view negatively. These brands are ones for which consumers will generally not process or accept positive information even if readily available.

The **evoked set** (also called the **consideration set**) is composed of *those brands or products one will evaluate for the solution of a particular consumer problem.*[5] Note that while evoked sets are frequently composed of brands from a single product category (brands of cereals or computers), this need not be the case since substitute products can

ILLUSTRATION 15–1

Consumers often search for information on appropriate evaluative criteria to use. This ad seeks to influence the criteria used and position the brand accordingly.

also play a role.[6] For example, one landscaping company found that consumers often view landscaping as a "home improvement decision." As a consequence, their landscaping services often compete with other home improvement products such as interior decorating instead of, or in addition to, other landscaping services.

In addition, the evoked set or consideration set often varies with the usage situation. For example, pancakes may only be in a consumer's consideration set for weekend breakfast situations since they are too inconvenient for busy weekday mornings. Companies will often try to expand the usage situations for their products in various ways as we saw in Chapter 13. In this example, premade frozen pancakes that are toaster-ready may be a way to get pancakes into the weekday breakfast consideration set.[7]

Finally, note that if consumers do not have an evoked set or they lack confidence that their evoked set is adequate, they will probably engage in external search to learn about additional alternatives. In addition, they may also learn about additional acceptable brands as an incidental aspect of moving through the decision process. Thus, an important outcome of information search is the development of a *complete* evoked set.

Figure 15-2 illustrates the general relationships among these classes of alternatives. A similar process operates with respect to retail outlet selection.[8]

One study examined the awareness and evoked sets across numerous product categories. Several results and strategic implications of this study are worth noting.

- The awareness set was always larger than the evoked set. That is, consumers know about more brands than they will seriously consider. And since awareness does not equal consideration and since consideration is necessary for a chance at being chosen, marketers

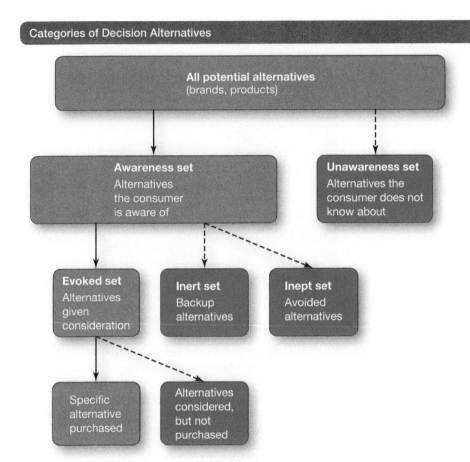

Categories of Decision Alternatives   FIGURE 15-2

are very concerned (once they have built sufficient awareness) about moving their brands into consumer evoked sets and must engage in persuasive messaging and other strategies to do so.

- The evoked set for some categories like mouthwash and toothpaste were basically one brand. This means that for categories, nominal decision making (choosing one brand repeatedly over time) is the norm. Later in the chapter we will discuss the use of disruption strategies for brands in this situation that are not in a consumer's evoked set.

- The evoked sets for some categories were somewhat large, but may be due to variety seeking. For example, the evoked set for fast food was five brands. However, one can imagine that consumers are loyal to brands of fast-food restaurants *within* type but they variety seek or otherwise switch across situations. So, McDonald's may be the hamburger alternative, KFC the chicken alternative, Pizza Hut the pizza alternative, Taco Bell the Mexican alternative, and so on.

Now let's apply Figure 15-2 to our laptop example. Again, you would start with an internal search. You might say to yourself, "Lenovo, Compaq, Toshiba, Apple, Dell, Sony, Fujitsu, and HP all make notebook computers. After my brother's experience, I'd never buy Toshiba. I've heard good things about Lenovo, Apple, and Compaq. I think I'll check them out." Thus, the eight brands you thought of as potential solutions are your awareness set, and Figure 15-3 shows how these break out into the other three categories of decision alternatives.

FIGURE   Example of Decision Alternatives for Laptop Computers

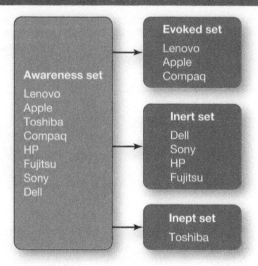

Alternative Characteristics

To choose among the brands in the evoked set, the consumer compares them on relevant evaluative criteria. This process requires the consumer *to gather information about each brand on each pertinent evaluative criterion.* In our example of a computer purchase, you might collect information on the price, memory, processor, weight, screen clarity, and software package for each brand you are considering. In addition, emotional considerations relating to comfort, styling, and ease of use may factor in as well.

SOURCES OF INFORMATION

Refer again to our laptop computer example. We suggested that you might recall what you know about computers, check with friends and an online discussion board, consult *Consumer Reports* and read reviews in *PC Magazine,* talk with sales personnel, or personally inspect several computers to collect relevant information. These represent the five primary sources of information available to consumers:

- *Memory* of past searches, personal experiences, and low-involvement learning.
- *Personal sources,* such as friends, family, and others.
- *Independent sources,* such as magazines, consumer groups, and government agencies.
- *Marketing sources,* such as sales personnel, websites, and advertising.
- *Experiential sources,* such as inspection or product trial.

These sources are shown in Figure 15-4. Each of these sources has an offline, online, and mobile component.[9] As just one example, offline marketing sources such as TV advertising and brochures correspond to online banner ads and corporate websites, and mobile ads.

Internal information is the primary source used by most consumers most of the time (nominal and limited decision making). However, note that information in long-term memory was *initially* obtained from external sources. Thus, a consumer may resolve a consumption problem using only or mainly stored information. At some point, however, the individual acquired that information from an external source, such as direct product experience, friends, or low-involvement learning.

Information Sources for a Purchase Decision   FIGURE **15-4**

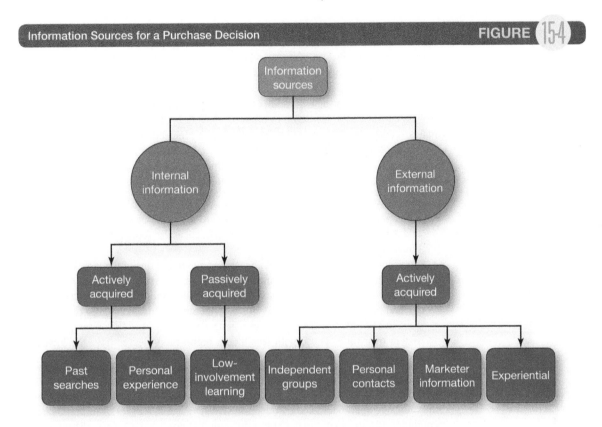

Marketing-originated messages are only one of five potential information sources, and they are frequently reported to be of limited *direct* value in consumer decisions.[10] However, marketing activities influence all five sources. Thus, the characteristics of the product, the distribution of the product, and the promotional messages about the product provide the underlying or basic information available in the market. An independent source such as *Consumer Reports* bases its evaluation on the functional characteristics of the product, as do personal sources such as friends. Marketers are continually looking for ways to get their information channeled through nonmarketing sources. As we discussed in Chapter 7, product sampling to influential bloggers (with appropriate disclosure) is just one means of getting the word out through nonmarketing channels.

In addition, although consumers may not use (or believe they use) advertising or other marketer-provided data as immediate input into many purchase decisions, there is no doubt that continual exposure to advertising frequently influences the perceived need for the product, the composition of the awareness and evoked sets, the evaluative criteria used, and beliefs about the performance levels of each brand.[11] As a consequence, the long-term *total* influence of advertising and other marketer-provided information on consumer decision making and sales can be substantial.

Internet Search

The Internet gives consumers unprecedented access to information. Global Internet usage continues to grow rapidly, and more than 2 billion people are online around the world. Asia (922 million), Europe (476 million), and North America (272 million) have the highest number of Internet users. Growth potential is strongest for regions such as Africa, Asia, and Latin America, where Internet usage as a percentage of the total population is still relatively low. Asia overshadows other regions of the world in terms of current users and potential growth, in view of its population size (3.9 billion), growing middle class, and increased access to low-cost technology.[12] *What are the marketing implications of such global trends for American businesses?*

Nearly 80 percent of U.S. adults have used the Internet, and growth of new users has slowed considerably. Early on, Internet users were predominantly young, educated, white males. Today, the demographic characteristics of Internet users look much more like that of the population in general, with several notable exceptions. Based on Pew Research statistics (for specifics go to www.pewinternet.org), the following demographic patterns characterize and differentiate today's Internet users:[13]

- *Gender*—Males and females are comparable in their rate of Internet use.
- *Ethnicity*—Hispanics and African Americans are lower users of the Internet than whites and Asian Americans. However, these differences are reduced or eliminated when language and/or education are considered.
- *Age*—Internet usage decreases with age, and age is still one of the largest Internet drivers. However, its importance is diminishing rapidly as tech-savvy boomers move into their 60s.
- *Income*—Internet usage increases with income, although increased affordability has pushed Internet usage among even lower-income groups to roughly two-thirds.
- *Education*—Internet usage increases with education. This factor seems the most persistent over time. Those with less than a high-school degree have the lowest Internet usage at 40 percent.

Perhaps not surprisingly, given this demographic information, 6 of the top 10 reasons why the remaining 23 percent of Americans don't use the Internet are related (directly and indirectly) to age, income, and education. These reasons in order of importance are (1) no computer, (2) too expensive, (3) too difficult, (4) don't have access, (5) too old to learn, and (6) don't know how.[14]

The Internet is a major and often preferred avenue through which consumers search for information.[15] Consider the following:[16]

- *Online information is expected.* Most Internet users *expect* to find information about a product or brand of interest to them on a company's website.
- *Online information boosts offline sales.* Internet users are more likely to purchase a company's product offline if its website provides product-related information.
- *Online sources are viewed as valuable.* Corporate and third-party websites match or beat traditional TV and print advertising as an information source in many categories.
- *Online sources reduce salesperson's role.* Internet users tend to require considerably less purchase assistance from a salesperson.

Not surprisingly, the most important search-related activity online is *using a search engine to find information.* And 7 of the top 20 activities on the Internet are tied to information search or purchase as follows:[17]

Use search engine to find information	87%
Look for health-related information	83
Look for information about a hobby or interest	83
Research a product/service before buying it	78
Buy a product	66
Buy or make a travel reservation	66
Use an online classified ad or site	53

Source: Pew Internet & American Life Project, www.pewinternet.org.

It is important to note, however, that traditional media can be effective at guiding consumers' information search activities to company websites, as shown in Illustration 15–2.

Search engines such as Google, Yahoo!, and MSN are an important search tool for consumers. Online search prior to purchase is the norm for most Internet users. In fact, search engines are the number one online shopping tool, followed by coupon sites, retailer e-mails, online reviews, and shopping comparison sites. Notice that all the tools listed are sources of some form of information and thus play a role in the information search and acquisition process. The influence of online search cannot be overestimated since:[18]

- Ninety-four percent of online purchases are preceded by online search.
- Seventy-four percent of offline purchases are likely to be preceded by online search.
- Consumers who "presearch" and are exposed to online ads spend 41 percent more in-store.

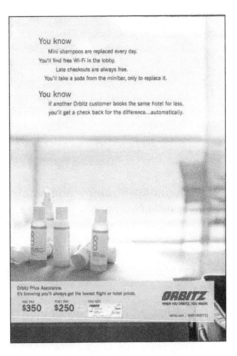

ILLUSTRATION 15–2

The Internet is an important source of information as well as a place to purchase products and services. Marketers often use traditional mass media ads to encourage consumers to visit their websites.

The nature of search terms used by consumers is critical for marketers to understand so that they can build these into their search marketing strategies. One study categorized search terms into *brand only* (retailer's brand), *generic* (general product-related terms), and *brand-item* (brand plus generic). As shown in Figure 15-5, most of the search leading up to the purchase was generic—that is, general product-related terms that did not include any of the retailers being tracked in the study. As you might expect, generic search dominated early in the search process (3 to 12 weeks out), while branded search dominated just prior to purchase.[19] *What strategic implications do these results hold for online marketers?*

Economic considerations are a major motivator of online search.[20] For example, car buyers who used the Internet were able to make decisions faster and get a better buy—on average by $741.[21] And coupon sites, which are increasingly popular, help consumers get better deals with ease. However, *information overload* (see Chapter 8) is a challenge on the Internet. General search engines are useful. However, more specialized services and tools continue to evolve to aid consumers more specifically in their search and decision making. Comparison shopping sites are a popular version of these services. Comparison sites often focus on price, but can be designed to filter brands based on a broader set of evaluative criteria set by the consumer (see Illustration 15–3). These services use **bots,** or software "robots," that do the shopping/searching for users and are therefore often referred to as *shopping bots*.[22] Examples include BizRate.com, mySimon.com, and NexTag.com.

In addition to marketer-based information, the Internet contains personal sources of information in bulletin boards and chat rooms as well as in the brand review features of many shopping services.[23] One study finds that consumer reviews are utilized heavily (72 percent) by consumers during online search for performance information.[24] As discussed in Chapter 7, WOM and personal sources are influential because of consumer trust in these sources.

520   **Part Four**   Consumer Decision Process

Marketing Strategy and Information Search on the Internet As the online population increasingly mirrors the general population, segmentation and target marketing are increasingly critical to online success. Consider the following:

> Where higher education marketing is different is the complexity of the audiences. A college . . . in particular has to please—if you are talking about the institutional Web site—alumni, donors, current students, prospective students, parents (and) the media. It's daunting sometimes.

Furman University decided that its general website was inadequate for admissions. So the university created a separate website to target high school students interested in the institution. The site is designed to target this tech-savvy group specifically, with virtual tours, message boards, and online student journals (with no editing by administration!).[25]

Obviously, universities are not the only ones who must deal with diverse consumer needs and characteristics. For example, consumers of various ethnicities in the United States

FIGURE 15-5   The Nature of Search Using Online Search Engines

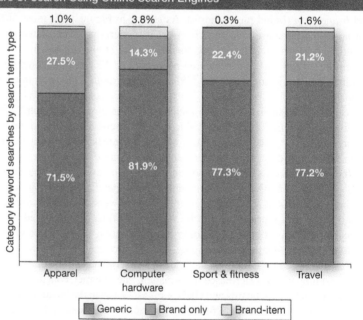

Source: "The Nature of Search Using Online Search Engines," *Search Before the Purchase* (New York: DoubleClick, February 2005), p. 2. Copyright: DoubleClick, Inc., 2005.

often prefer and primarily use ethnic (versus mainstream) websites.[26] Global marketers must adapt as well. A recent study finds that Japanese websites use less individualistic approaches than do U.S. websites.[27]

More specifically, with respect to the Internet's role in information search and decision making, marketers have at least three major strategic issues to deal with:

1. How can they drive their information to consumers?
2. How can they drive consumers to their information?
3. How (if at all) can online selling be utilized or integrated with existing channels?

The first two issues are addressed in this section. The third is covered in Chapter 17. The first two issues are highly interrelated in that many of the strategies companies use to drive information to consumers (e.g., banner ads) are also designed, ultimately, to drive consumers to additional sources of information about the company (e.g., the company's website).

Driving a firm's information to consumers is important since consumers are not always actively searching. One way is through web advertising, including *banner ads.* Internet marketing spending (including display, search, and behavioral placement) continues to grow rapidly. It is expected to grow to $55 billion by 2014, which would represent a substantial proportion of all media spending, which is currently estimated at around $150 billion.[28] Broadband is changing the nature of online advertising, allowing for more use of streaming media. For example, in response to data showing that many new car buyers visit the web prior to visiting a dealer, Honda placed its national TV ads for the Odyssey minivan on numerous websites. Viewers could click off the video or view it and ask for additional information. This goes beyond the traditional banner ad approach, and yet both drive the brand and information to the consumer.[29]

E-mail is also an important tool for pushing information to consumers. Many consumers see e-mail as a replacement for direct mail. However, spam (unsolicited e-mails) is not well received by consumers. Thus, *permission-based e-mail* (PBE), in which the consumer "opts in" to receive e-mail is the norm for most reputable marketers. Even with PBE, marketers need to be careful—too many e-mails that lack relevance may still be viewed as spam.[30]

As we saw earlier, social media such as Facebook and Twitter can be used to drive a firm's information to consumers in a number of ways. Facebook allows for the delivery of ads to its members. Twitter has an ad option called promoted tweets, where a promotion code shows up on the tweet and then the tweet comes up in search results (see Chapter 7).[31]

Driving consumers to a firm's information is a daunting and important task given the explosion in the amount and sources of information on the web. Companies have websites to which they want consumers to go and return frequently.[32] Various strategies are possible. As we saw in Illustration 15–2, offline media are one avenue for calling attention to a website. In fact, given that many younger consumers watch TV and surf the web simultaneously, research is demonstrating "upticks" in search volume on search engines such as Google *in real time,* based on traditional TV ads that attract consumer interest. That is, consumers see a TV ad for a product of interest, then use Google to search for more information. This behavioral outcome of traditional advertising online is an important step in driving consumers to a company's information and to the next stage in the decision process.[33]

Banner ads are another way to drive traffic to websites. While *click-through rates* (percentage who click through to the corporate website) are generally low, marketers are looking beyond immediate click-through to measures that include brand awareness, brand attitudes, and purchase intentions. The idea is that boosting awareness and attitudes will drive *long-term* website visits and purchases.

Website visits that occur as a result of *exposure* to an online ad but that do not occur at the time of exposure have been termed *view-throughs.* It is estimated that "half or more of the ad-related visits in a campaign are attributed to the view-through effect as opposed to direct clicks." And, beyond view-through, as online ads become more interactive, other metrics are possible. MINI Cooper used an interactive banner that allowed viewers to see various owner profiles. Useful metrics here would be the interaction rate (percentage that interacted in some way with the ad, such as paging through the owner profiles) and time spent with the ad.[34]

As you might expect, appropriate or targeted ad placement is helpful in increasing online ad performance across various outcomes including click-through rates. For example, Dolby ran interactive banners relating to thunder and the outdoors. The campaign did well overall, but did markedly better (e.g., 60 percent higher click-through rate) when placed on the National Geographic site, because of the higher relevance of these themes to the site's viewers.[35]

Social networking sites are also getting into the act. MySpace offers targeted advertising based on member profiles and indicates that ad performance increases by as much as 300 percent by using their targeted approach.[36] Facebook has similar ad-targeting features and can also target based on the "Fan" status of a member, whereby ads are only delivered to Facebook members who have "liked" a given brand.[37] Given that relevance is a key driver of attention, interest, and engagement as measured by processing and click-throughs (Chapter 8), such personalized targeting can be extremely effective. Levi's is using interactive videos placed in social media in China to tap the self-expression needs of urban youth. The interactive videos allow users to tailor the experience through different destinations and plots, and are designed ultimately to "drive users" to key Levi product information and images.[38]

Behavioral targeting is another form of targeting that is based not on what people say but what they actually do online. Specifically, **behavioral targeting** *involves tracking consumer click patterns on a website and using that information to decide on banner ad placement.*[39] Pepsi used behavioral targeting to promote Aquafina to consumers interested in healthy lifestyles. Online behavioral tracking helped them determine which consumers were the "healthy lifestyles" consumers, and then ads for Aquafina were delivered to those consumers across over 4,000 websites. The result was a 300 percent greater click-through rate for the targeted Aquafina campaign compared to their previous nontargeted campaigns. Again, the perceived relevance of the message to the target audience is a key factor to the success of behavioral targeting.[40] Concerns over privacy and transparency are driving efforts at industry self-regulation that could or already do include "no-tracking lists" and privacy browsing features.

As we saw earlier, online consumers are heavy users of search engines. Not surprisingly, spending on search-related marketing efforts (including ads and search optimization activities discussed shortly) is the largest single category of Internet marketing, and represents 60 percent of all Internet marketing spending.[41] Since search results are ordered and consumers often don't *drill down* beyond the first page of listings, keyword selection and other techniques relating to search engine optimization are critical for the firm in terms of getting its website the highest priority listing for the most appropriate search terms. **Search engine optimization (SEO)** *involves techniques designed to ensure that a company's web pages "are accessible to search engines and focused in ways that help improve the chances they will be found."*[42]

SEO strategies are critical to Internet search success. One estimate is that the top five spots on a Google search can be worth $50 to $100 million per year depending on the industry and company. A recent report found that searching for the generic keyword "home repair" did not get Home Depot in the top ten listings. Rather, it came in at number

16 (and on page 2) behind such brands as Lowe's, This Old House, and BobVila.com. The problem, according to one expert, is that Home Depot failed to place key "category-defining keywords [such as "home repair"] in the URLs."[43] This is in line with our earlier discussion of the critical nature of generic terms in the consumer Internet search process. SEO relates to what is termed "organic" or natural search results. Paid or "sponsored" listings are also available through programs such as Google's Adword program, in which companies pay for "sponsored" listings for specific search terms.

Website design is also critical. While we will discuss this issue more in Chapter 17, it is clear that driving *ongoing and repeat* traffic to a website requires such factors as relevant and frequently updated content. Techniques can include product-related news features, user-related discussion forums, updates on new products and features, and so on. RSS (really simple syndication) feeds that pull information on an ongoing basis from various online sources can be used to keep sites relevant and current. Marketers can also offer opt-in e-mail updates, which can trigger site visits.[44]

Mobile Search

Mobile search and marketing appears to be the next major growth arena for firms. Roughly 84 percent of U.S. adults have a mobile phone (a small but growing segment of mobile phone users also has a tablet device such as the iPad, which is also included as a mobile device).[45] Not surprising, U.S. mobile advertising spending (including display, search, and messaging-based) is expected to be somewhere between $1.5 and $3 billion by 2013.[46] While this is just a fraction of the nearly $150 billion spent overall on measured media, it is expected to continue to grow, particularly as the functionality of smartphones takes off and users become more comfortable operating and using phones as an information, decision, and buying tool. A recent study of mobile phone users by Experian found five segments as follows:[47]

- *Mobirati* (19 percent)—are younger, grew up with cell phones, phone central to life. Trend high on interest in services to use phone to buy in store, accepting ads if get value in return, using information to decide social activities like where to eat.
- *Mobile Professionals* (17 percent)—are both younger and older, use phone for business and personal life. Phone features are critical, and phone is an information tool. Trend high on wanting features beyond just calling, and on using phone in many ways to get information they need.
- *Social Connectors* (22 percent)—are younger, communication is key, mobile device helps them connect socially. Trend high on feeling that text messages are just as meaningful as a "real" conversation, and feeling that their phone connects them to their social world.
- *Pragmatic Adopters* (22 percent)—are older, cell phones came later in their lives. Learning to use beyond just calling. More functional, but still quite important because they are one of the highest-income segments.
- *Basic Planners* (20 percent)—are older, not into mobility or technology. Use cell phone for basic calling. Trend high on using cell phone only for emergencies and only for basic calling.

Clearly these segments and their characteristics are important to marketers in relation to information search and product purchasing. In particular, the Mobirati and Mobile Professionals are key users of search and buying features of cell phones and to some degree are open to mobile "push" marketing in the form of advertisements. Pragmatic Adopters seem to be worth pursuing, because of their willingness to learn new features and adopt new functionality beyond basic calling, and also because they have high incomes.

One area of particular importance to marketers is local mobile search. **Local mobile search** is defined as *searches for information from a mobile device pertaining to the current (or future planned) geographic location of a consumer.* Google provides a useful illustration of this type of search, and marketing efforts related to it. Punch the key words "Italian restaurant" into Google on your mobile phone and what you will get will be heavily skewed to "local" search results. That is, Google knows your location based on your phone's location and will deliver results that not only list Italian restaurants close to you, but also provide a map of how to get there, the phone number for each restaurant, and so on. You could also select alternate locations as when you are planning to go on a vacation and want to search for restaurants ahead of time. Google can also deliver relevant mobile banner ads to you through its AdWords location-based targeting program.[48]

You may have noticed from the mobile segment descriptions that some consumers are much more likely to use their cell phones for local mobile search. Pew Research finds that two of the top eight local search categories include search for (1) local restaurants and businesses, and (2) search for local coupons and discounts. Clearly, "apps" for local information are a key strategic point that we will also return to later. Table 15-1 provides the demographics of cell phone users who search for local information on their mobile devices and who have apps for local searches.

Marketing Strategy and Mobile Search

Mobile browsers and apps appear to be a critical part of local mobile search strategies. Examine Figure 15-6. Notice how local mobile search is changing how consumers find stores and brands, and also how they search for information. Consumers have historically searched for information that was available "within" a store while they were at the store and searched for information "outside" of the store either prior to or after their store search. No longer is that the case with many mobile users who search for information "outside" the store while shopping in the store. This gives retailers and in-store sales personnel somewhat less control over the shopping experience and puts the consumer more in the driver's seat. Clearly, however, retailers must figure out how to be a part of this emerging new search pattern and design or participate in apps and programs that resonate with consumers. Walmart was reluctant to share prices with price-matching apps at first, but it has relented.

Many useful search and shopping apps exist. Consider RetrevoQ, which provides mobile local search via an app or Twitter:

> RetrevoQ uses texts and tweets to dispense [information]. Shoppers can text 41411 or tweet @retrevoq including the make and model of the electronics product they're considering, and RetrevoQ will respond with advice on whether it's a good buy, a fair price, the price range available online for that product and a link to reviews at Retrevo.com, a consumer-electronics shopping and review site.

Such functionality, ease, and possible search benefits make it clear why this and other apps are becoming increasingly popular with shoppers. Why go from store to store to make sure you are getting the lowest price, when Shopsavvy will conduct the search for you from your mobile phone while you are in the store.[49] Figure 15-6 provides additional directions for thinking about the kinds of local mobile apps that consumers may want.

Consumer Insight 15-1 examines additional strategic considerations in the mobile marketing arena.

Push and Pull Strategies in Mobile Marketing

Mobile marketing strategies can be viewed similarly to those on the Internet—that is, driving information to consumers (push strategies) and driving consumers to information (pull strategies).[50]

Mobile Push. Driving information to consumers on mobile devices can involve a variety of strategies. One strategy that will continue to grow as more consumers use mobile Internet is ads placed on mobile web pages. As with computer-based approaches, mobile ads can be targeted to be most relevant to the specific mobile content being viewed. Another strategy is permission-based or opt-in text messaging promotions. Text messaging is growing in popularity across all age groups and is one of the most popular activities on cell phones. According to SmartReply, a media consulting group, the best text message programs involve:

- Building an "opt-in" database—this can be done through traditional and e-mail marketing in which consumers are asked to text in or register at a specific website.
- Developing the text-message "ad"—should include (a) a hook relating to why they are being contacted; (b) a call to action, such as entering a code to get a discount; and (c) an "opt-out" option.
- Rolling out the campaign—involves delivering the text promotion to those on the opt-in list.

Adidas used a variation of this approach as sponsor for the NBA All-Star week. It had game information, store events, athlete appearances, and shoe releases as part of its promotions. Consumers opted in and then could access all the promotional materials at any time during the week by texting "originals."

Mobile Pull. Driving consumers to information on mobile devices can also involve a number of strategies. One is to use traditional media to build awareness about a mobile site or promotional event. AT&T held a mobile contest on U.S. college campuses for a free Dave Matthews Band concert to the school that could generate the most "invitations" sent through text messaging for the band to play at their school. To generate awareness and drive students to its mobile space, AT&T blanketed college campuses with posters telling students to "Text DMB to 959" or "visit ATTBLUEROOM.COM to enter." As we have seen mobile search is another important option. Mobile Internet use is increasing rapidly and the functionality and geo-targeting capabilities of providers such as Google and Yahoo allow marketers to drive traffic to not only traditional websites and mobile content, but also to local restaurants and retailers.

Critical Thinking Questions

1. With cell phones even less easily controlled and monitored than home computers, what ethical and regulatory issues are raised regarding mobile marketing to children?

2. Beyond the approaches discussed above, what other mobile marketing approaches are emerging? Are they effective? Explain.

3. What challenges do marketers face as they have to create campaigns that span mobile, Internet, and traditional media?

AMOUNT OF EXTERNAL INFORMATION SEARCH

Marketers are particularly interested in external information search, as this provides them with direct access to the consumer. How much external information search do consumers actually undertake? Nominal and limited decision making (e.g., convenience goods such as soft drinks) involve little or no external search by definition. Therefore, this section focuses on major purchases such as appliances, professional services, and automobiles where we might expect substantial amounts of direct external search prior to purchases.

TABLE 15-1   Local Mobile Search and App Demographics

	Get Local Information on Mobile Device	Have Local Information App
Total	56%	13%
Age		
18–29	77	20
30–49	69	17
50–64	39	7
65+	13	3
Race/Ethnicity		
White, non-Hispanic	53	12
Black, non-Hispanic	58	14
Hispanic	62	21
Household Income		
LT $30,000	52	12
$30,000–$49,999	54	17
$50,000–$74,999	57	11
$75,000+	70	19
Education		
Less than High School	37	13
High School	51	10
Some College	62	13
College+	63	17
Have Children Under 18 at Home		
Yes	71	17
No	49	12
Community		
Urban	57	14
Suburban	59	14
Rural	49	10
Time in Community		
Five years or less	67	N/A
Six to 20 years	59	N/A
Twenty-one years+	34	N/A

Note: Numbers represent the percentage of consumers who have mobile devices (cell phones and tablets) and who engage in local mobile search and have a local search app.

N/A is not available.

Source: *How Mobile Devices Are Changing Community Information Environments* (Washington, DC: Pew Internet & American Life Project, March 14, 2011), p. 8.

However, across various measures (stores visited, brands considered, sources utilized, total overall search) one observation emerges: *external information search is skewed toward limited search, with the greatest proportion of consumers performing little external search immediately prior to purchase.* Consider the following results:

- Surveys of *shopping behavior* have shown a significant percentage of all durable purchases are made after the consumer has visited only one store.[51]
- Although the *number of alternative brands or models considered* tends to increase as the price of the product increases, various studies show small consideration sets as follows

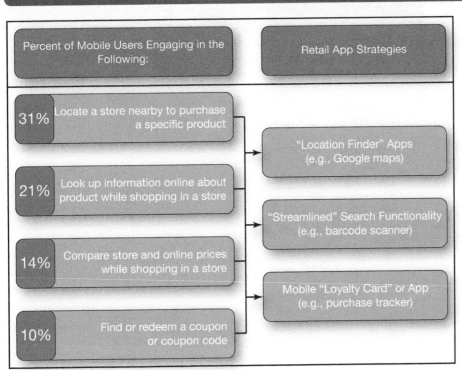

FIGURE 15-6

Mobile Local Search and Marketing Strategy

(1) nearly half of watch purchasers considered only one brand *and* one model, (2) twenty-seven percent of major appliance buyers considered only one brand,[52] and (3) while Internet use increased automobile search, Internet searchers still only examined three models.[53]

- In terms of *total overall search,* the following classification scheme can be used: (1) nonsearchers—little or no search, (2) limited information searchers—low to moderate search, and (3) extended information searchers—high search. Eight separate studies spanning almost 50 years (1955 to 2003), products and services (appliances, automobiles, and professional services), and two countries (America and Australia) show remarkable consistency in terms of the total external information search undertaken. Namely, extended searchers only account for between seven and 20 percent of buyers.[54]

The following section tries to explain why, even for high-involvement products and services, external search immediately prior to purchases is often low.

COSTS VERSUS BENEFITS OF EXTERNAL SEARCH

Buyers appear to weigh the benefits of search against the costs they incur. Search benefits include such aspects as lower price, higher quality, greater comfort with purchase, and so on. Search costs include time, money, hassle, the opportunity costs of other more enjoyable foregone activities, and so on. All else equal, greater perceived benefits increase search, while greater perceived costs reduce search. When buyers perceive that the next brand (or store, or bit of information) will cost them more than it will benefit them, they stop

TABLE 15-2   Factors Affecting External Search Immediately Prior to Purchase

Influencing Factor	Increasing the Influencing Factor Causes External Search To:
I. Market Characteristics	
A. Number of alternatives	Increase
B. Price range	Increase
C. Store concentration	Increase
D. Information availability	Increase
1. Advertising	
2. Point-of-purchase	
3. Websites	
4. Sales personnel	
5. Packaging	
6. Experienced customers	
7. Independent sources	
II. Product characteristics	
A. Price	Increase
B. Differentiation	Increase
C. Positive products	Increase
III. Consumer characteristics	
A. Learning and experience	Decrease
B. Shopping orientation	Mixed
C. Social status	Increase
D. Age and household life cycle	Mixed
E. Product involvement	Mixed
F. Perceived risk	Increase
IV. Situation characteristics	
A. Time availability	Increase
B. Purchase for self	Decrease
C. Pleasant surroundings	Increase
D. Social surroundings	Mixed
E. Physical/mental energy	Increase

searching. On the benefits side, given ongoing search and incidental learning, as discussed earlier, the amount of accumulated knowledge can be substantial for many consumers and thus lower the benefits of search *just prior to purchase*. On the costs side, the Internet can greatly lower search costs. When it does, it increases search and leads to better consumer decisions and a more enjoyable shopping experience.[55]

In this section, we examine four basic types of factors that influence the expected benefits and perceived costs of search both online and offline: *market characteristics, product characteristics, consumer characteristics,* and *situation characteristics* (see Table 15-2).[56]

Market Characteristics

Market characteristics (or more accurately, consumer perceptions of them) include the number of alternatives, price range, store distribution, and information availability.[57] Obviously, the greater the *number of alternatives* (products, stores, brands) available to resolve a particular problem, the more external search there is likely to be. At the extreme, there is no need to search for information in the face of a complete monopoly such as utilities or driver's licenses. However, too many brands or too many noncomparable models across stores can frustrate consumer search efforts and lead to lower search or search within one store. Some marketers strategically develop a large number of models so that key accounts can have exclusive models and avoid direct price competition with other retailers on those exact models.[58] *What ethical concerns are raised by this practice?*

The *perceived range of prices* among equivalent brands in a product class is a major factor in stimulating external search. For example, shopping 36 retail stores in Tucson for five popular-branded toys produced a total low cost of $51.27 and a total high cost of $105.95. Clearly, efficient shopping for those products in that market would provide a significant financial gain. Pricing strategies such as price matching can affect consumer price perceptions. A recent study suggests that consumers interpret such policies as signaling lower prices, which, under high search costs, yields less search.[59] It appears that the percentage savings available from shopping may be as important as the dollar amount. The chance to save $50 when purchasing a $200 item appears to motivate more search than is the case when purchasing a $5,000 item.[60] This relates to the perceptual relativity discussed in Chapter 8.

Store distribution—the number, location, and distances between retail stores in the market—affects the number of store visits a consumer will make before purchase. Because store visits take time, energy, and in many cases, money, a close proximity of stores will often increase this aspect of external search.[61]

In general, *information availability,* including format, is directly related to information use.[62] However, too much information can cause information overload and the use of less information. In addition, readily available information tends to produce learning over time, which may reduce the need for additional external information immediately prior to a purchase.[63]

Product Characteristics

Perceived product *differentiation*—feature and quality variation across brands—is associated with increased external search.

In addition, consumers appear to enjoy shopping for *positive products*—those whose acquisition results in positive reinforcement (e.g., flowers, sports equipment). In contrast, shopping for *negative products*—those whose primary benefit is negative reinforcement, or the removal of an unpleasant condition (e.g., grocery shopping, auto repairs)—is viewed as less pleasant. All else equal, consumers engage in more external search for positive products.[64]

Consumer Characteristics

A variety of consumer characteristics affect perceptions of expected benefits, search costs, and the need to carry out a particular level of external information search.[65] As described earlier, the first step a consumer normally takes in response to a problem or opportunity is a search of memory for an appropriate solution. If the consumer finds a solution that he or she is confident is satisfactory, external search is unlikely.[66] However, overconfidence can lead to inadequate search and poor choices. It can also make it harder for companies to reposition their brands when consumers wrongly assume they "know" about the brand.[67]

A satisfying *experience* with a particular brand is a positively reinforcing process. It increases the probability of a repeat purchase of that brand and decreases the likelihood of external search.[68] However, at least some familiarity with a product class is necessary for external search to occur. For example, external search prior to purchasing a new automobile is high for consumers who have a high level of *general knowledge about cars* and low for those who have a substantial level of knowledge about existing brands.[69] Thus, consumers facing a completely unfamiliar product category may lack sufficient general knowledge to conduct an external search.

Consumers tend to form general approaches or patterns of external search. These general approaches are termed *shopping orientations*.[70] For example, some individuals engage in extensive ongoing information search because they are market mavens, as described in Chapter 7. This orientation would generally reduce the need to search *just prior to a purchase* as adequate existing knowledge would exist. Other orientations would have different effects.

External search tends to increase with various measures of *social status* (education, occupation, and income), though middle-income individuals search more than those at higher or lower levels. *Age* of the shopper is inversely related to information search. External search appears to decrease as the age of the shopper increases. This may be explained in part by increased learning and product familiarity gained with age. New households and individuals moving into new stages of the *household life cycle* have a greater need for external information than established households.

Consumers who are *highly involved with a product category* generally seek information relevant to the product category on an ongoing basis.[71] This ongoing search and the knowledge base it produces may reduce their need for external search immediately before a purchase, although variety-seeking needs can override this effect.[72]

The *perceived risk* associated with unsatisfactory product performance, either instrumental or symbolic, increases information search prior to purchase.[73] Higher perceived risk is associated with increased search and greater reliance on personal sources of information and personal experiences. Perceived risk can be situational, such as the higher risk felt when buying wine for a dinner party versus for personal consumption at home. Risk can also be perceived as high when a consumer has little prior purchase experience in the product category, in which case information search may help reduce perceived risk.[74] We discuss perceived risk further in Chapter 17.

Situation Characteristics

As indicated in Chapter 13, situational variables can have a major impact on search behavior. For example, recall that one of the primary reactions of consumers to crowded store conditions is to minimize external information search. *Temporal perspective* is probably the most important situational variable with respect to search behavior. As the time available to solve a particular consumer problem decreases, so does the amount of external information search.[75]

Gift-giving situations (*task definition*) tend to increase perceived risk, which, as we have seen, increases external search. Likewise, multiple-item purchase tasks such as buying a bike and a bike rack or several items for a meal produce increased levels of information search.[76] Shoppers with limited physical or emotional energy (*antecedent state*) will search for less information than others. Pleasant *physical surroundings* increase the tendency to search for information, at least *within* that outlet. *Social surroundings* can increase or decrease search, depending on the nature of the social setting (see Chapter 13 for a more complete discussion).

MARKETING STRATEGIES BASED ON INFORMATION SEARCH PATTERNS

Sound marketing strategies take into account the nature of information search engaged in by the target market prior to purchase. Two dimensions of search are particularly appropriate: The type of decision influences the level of search, and the nature of the evoked set influences the direction of the search. Table 15-3 illustrates a strategy matrix based on these two dimensions. This matrix suggests the six marketing strategies discussed in the following sections. As you will see, although there is considerable overlap between the strategies, each has a unique thrust.

Marketing Strategies Based on Information Search Patterns   TABLE 15-3

	Target Market Decision-Making Pattern		
Position	Nominal Decision Making (no search)	Limited Decision Making (limited search)	Extended Decision Making (extensive search)
Brand in evoked set	Maintenance strategy	Capture strategy	Preference strategy
Brand not in evoked set	Disrupt strategy	Intercept strategy	Acceptance strategy

Maintenance Strategy

If the brand is purchased habitually by the target market, the marketer's strategy is to maintain that behavior. This requires consistent attention to product quality, distribution (avoiding out-of-stock situations), and a reinforcement advertising strategy. In addition, the marketer must defend against the disruptive tactics of competitors. Thus, it needs to maintain product development and improvements and to counter short-term competitive strategies, such as coupons, point-of-purchase displays, or rebates.

Morton salt and Del Monte canned vegetables have large repeat purchaser segments that they have successfully maintained. Budweiser, Marlboro, and Crest have large brand-loyal purchaser segments. They have successfully defended their market positions against assaults by major competitors in recent years. In contrast, Liggett & Myers lost 80 percent of its market share when it failed to engage in maintenance advertising.[77] Quality control problems caused Schlitz to lose substantial market share.

Illustration 15–4 shows the use of a maintenance strategy against the challenge of competitors. Note that the ad stresses the improvements to the product.

Disrupt Strategy

If the brand is not part of the evoked set and the target market engages in nominal decision making, the marketer's first task is to *disrupt* the existing decision pattern. This is a difficult task since the consumer does not seek external information or even consider alternative brands before a purchase. Low-involvement learning over time could generate a positive product position for the brand, but this alone would be unlikely to shift behavior.

In the long run, a major product improvement accompanied by attention-attracting advertising could shift the target market into a more extensive form of decision making. In the short run, attention-attracting advertising aimed specifically at breaking habitual decision making can be successful. This advertising might be targeted via online and social media

ILLUSTRATION 15–4

Firms with a significant group of loyal or repeat purchasers must continually improve their products and communicate their advantages to their consumers.

as well with a strong but simple benefits-based approach. Free samples, coupons, rebates, and tie-in sales are common approaches to disrupting nominal decision making. Thus, participation in local mobile coupon app programs could be helpful. Likewise, striking package designs and point-of-purchase displays may disrupt a habitual purchase sequence.[78] Comparative advertising is also often used for this purpose.

Illustration 15–5 is an example of a disrupt strategy. The ad tries to convince consumers to change to the advertised brand based on several key benefits.

Capture Strategy

Limited decision making generally involves a few brands that are evaluated on only a few criteria, such as price or availability. Much of the information search occurs at the point-of-purchase or in readily available media prior to purchase. If the brand is one given this type of consideration by the target market, the marketer's objective is to capture as large a share of the purchases as practical.

ILLUSTRATION 15–5

Firms trying to disrupt the habitual purchase or consumption patterns of consumers who do not even consider their brand need attention-attracting ads and a strong benefit or other inducement to try the brand.

ILLUSTRATION 15–6

The ad shown here reflects an intercept strategy in that it gives consumers an immediate incentive to purchase its brand.

Because these consumers engage in limited search, the marketer needs to know where they search and what information they are looking for. In general, the marketer will want to supply information, often on price and availability, on its website, mobile apps, in local media including efforts related to local mobile search, and at the point of purchase through displays and adequate shelf space. The marketer will also be concerned with maintaining consistent product quality and adequate distribution.

Intercept Strategy

If the target market engages in limited decision making and the brand is not part of the evoked set, the objective will be to intercept the consumer during the search for information on the brands in the evoked set or during general search for related information. Again, the emphasis will be on local media with cooperative advertising and at the point of purchase with displays, shelf space, package design, and so forth. Coupons can also be effective. The marketer will have to place considerable emphasis on attracting the consumers' attention, because they will not be seeking information on the brand. The behavioral targeting strategy used by Snapple on iVillage's website is a great example of an online intercept strategy. As one ad executive stated:

> The big trick with this product was changing [the audience's perception] of Snapple-a-Day from an on-the-go, quirky product to something that has real health benefits for women and that has to be more of a planned purchase.[79]

The promotion shown in Illustration 15–6 would be effective as part of a capture or intercept strategy.

In addition to the strategies mentioned above, low-involvement learning, product improvements, and free samples can be used to move the brand into the target market's evoked set.

Preference Strategy

Extended decision making with the brand in the evoked set requires a preference strategy. Because extended decision making generally involves several brands, many attributes, and a number of information sources, a simple capture strategy may not be adequate. Instead, the marketer needs to structure an information campaign that will result in the brand being preferred by members of the target market.

The first step is a strong position on those attributes important to the target market.[80] This is discussed in considerable detail in Chapter 16. Next, information must be provided in

ILLUSTRATION 15–7

This promotion assumes an extended search process. It provides substantial data on numerous product features.

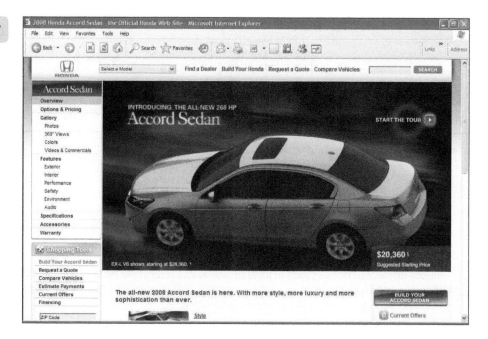

all the appropriate sources. This may require extensive advertising to groups or influential online participants (e.g., bloggers) who will recommend it to others (e.g., druggists for over-the-counter drugs, veterinarians, and county agents for agricultural products). Independent groups should be encouraged to test the brand, and sales personnel should be provided detailed information on the brand's attributes. In addition, it may be wise to provide the sales personnel with extra motivation (e.g., extra commissions paid by the manufacturer) to recommend the product. Point-of-purchase displays and pamphlets should also be available. A well-designed website is essential.

Illustration 15–7 shows part of an effective preference strategy. It assumes an involved search, provides detailed information relative to multiple product attributes, shopping venues, and so on.

Acceptance Strategy

Acceptance strategy is similar to preference strategy. However, it is complicated by the fact that the target market is not seeking information about the brand. Therefore, in addition to the activities involved in the preference strategy described above, the marketer must attract the consumers' attention or otherwise motivate them to learn about the brand. This can be difficult, but various automakers over the years have gone as far as to pay customers to test drive their cars (Chrysler) or loan their cars to opinion leaders (Ford) in an effort to move their brand into consumer consideration sets by encouraging trial and/or positive WOM.

The Internet can play an important role in an acceptance strategy. Since keyword searches prior to a purchase tend to be generic, this opens up important opportunities for companies that are not in the evoked set to engage in search engine optimization strategies to give their brand exposure to the consumer during the decision process—hopefully, to the point of moving the brand into consumers' evoked sets. Obviously, a well-designed website is a critical part of this strategy.

Long-term advertising designed to enhance low-involvement learning is another useful technique for gaining acceptance. Extensive advertising with strong emphasis on attracting attention can also be effective. The primary objective of these two approaches is not to sell the brand; rather, the objective is to move the brand into the evoked set. Then, when a purchase situation arises, the consumer will seek additional information on this brand.

SUMMARY

LO1: Discuss internal and external information search and their role in different decision types

Following problem recognition, consumers typically engage in some form and amount of search. *Internal search* is accessing relevant information from long-term memory to be used to determine if a satisfactory solution is known, what the characteristics of potential solutions are, what are appropriate ways to compare solutions, and so forth. If a resolution is not reached through internal search, then the search process is focused on external information relevant to solving the problem. This is *external search*, which can involve independent sources, personal sources, marketer-based information, and product experience. Internal information tends to dominate in nominal decision making, whereas external search tends to dominate in extended decision making. For limited decision making, external search can play a moderate role in some instances.

LO2: Summarize the types of information consumers search for

Information may be sought on (1) the appropriate *evaluative criteria* for the solution of the problem, (2) the existence of various *alternative solutions,* and (3) the *performance* of each alternative solution on each evaluative criterion.

LO3: Describe the categories of decision alternatives relating to the evoked set

From the set of all possible alternatives that could solve a consumer problem, there are the following categories of decision alternatives. There are alternatives that consumers are aware of (*awareness set*), alternatives that consumers are aware of and view in a neutral manner (*inert set*), alternatives that consumers are aware of and view negatively (*inept set*), and alternatives that consumers are aware of and view positively (*evoked set*). The evoked set (also called the consideration set) represents the alternatives that the consumer seeks additional information on during the remaining

internal and external search process. Therefore, marketers are first concerned with making sure their brand is in the awareness set. But, since awareness does not equal consideration and since consideration is necessary for a chance at being chosen, marketers are also very concerned about moving their brands into consumer evoked sets and must engage in persuasive messaging and other strategies to do so.

LO4: Discuss available information sources and the role of Internet and mobile search

Consumer internal information (information stored in memory) may have been actively acquired in previous searches and personal experiences, or it may have been passively acquired through low-involvement learning. In addition to their own *memory,* consumers can seek information from four major types of external sources: (1) *personal sources,* such as friends and family; (2) *independent sources,* such as consumer groups, paid professionals, and government agencies; (3) *marketing sources,* such as sales personnel and advertising; and (4) *experiential sources,* such as direct product inspection or trial. Each of these sources of information can be accessed through the Internet or mobile devices. Internet and mobile search options are dramatically changing the way in which consumers search for information prior to a purchase and provide marketers with many unique opportunities and challenges.

LO5: Discuss the major cost-benefit factors driving the amount of external search

Explicit external information search *after* problem recognition is often limited. It is often suggested that consumers generally should engage in relatively extensive external search prior to purchasing an item in order to reap higher benefits of the purchase such as higher brand quality or lower price. However, this view ignores the fact that information search is not free. It takes time, energy, and money and can often require giving up more desirable activities. Therefore, consumers should engage in external search only to the extent that the expected benefits, such as a lower price or a more satisfactory purchase, outweigh the expected costs. Numerous aspects affect the perceived costs and/or benefits of search. They can be *market characteristics* (e.g., number of brands), *product characteristics* (e.g., price), *consumer characteristics* (e.g., prior search and learning), and *situational characteristics* (e.g., time availability).

LO6: Summarize the marketing strategies based on information search patterns

Sound marketing strategy takes into account the nature of information search engaged in by the target market. The level of search and the brand's position in or out of the evoked set are two key dimensions. Based on these two dimensions, six potential information strategies are suggested: (1) *maintenance,* (2) *disrupt,* (3) *capture,* (4) *intercept,* (5) *preference,* and (6) *acceptance.*

KEY TERMS

Awareness set 513
Behavioral targeting 522
Bots 519
Consideration set 513
Evoked set 513

External search 512
Inept set 513
Inert set 513
Internal search 512
Local mobile search 524

Ongoing search 512
Search engine optimization (SEO) 522

INTERNET EXERCISES

1. The demographic composition of Internet users in the United States is changing over time as are the activities that users engage in. Go to the Pew Internet and American Life Project website (www.pewinternet .org). Go to the section on trends and report on how demographics and activities have changed substantially from those described in the text.

2. Go to www.searchenginewatch.com under their *search engine marketing 101* section. Examine the various resources in this section, including strategies for search engine optimization (SEO). Prepare a brief report on the various techniques involved in SEO.

3. Find and describe a magazine ad that is particularly effective at causing readers to consult a website. Why is it effective?

4. Use an Internet shopping service such as mysimon .com to determine the "best buy" for a product that interests you. Evaluate this process. How could it be improved? If you were actually going to make the purchase, would you buy this one or would you purchase elsewhere? Why?

5. Visit Amazon.com, epinions.com, or a similar site. Examine the product reviews provided by other customers. How useful do you think these are? What could make them more useful?

6. Click on two banner ads for similar products. Describe where you encountered the banner ads, and evaluate each banner ad and the target site. Do you feel like behavioral targeting was being used? Explain.

DDB LIFE STYLE STUDY™ DATA ANALYSES

1. Using the DDB data (Tables 1B through 7B), describe the major determinants of the following search-related behaviors and beliefs. What are the marketing implications?
   a. Consult consumer reports before making major purchases.
   b. Information in advertising helps me make better decisions.

2. Some consumers feel more *technology savvy* than others. Examine the DDB data in Tables 1B through 7B to determine what characterizes one who is likely to feel tech savvy.

3. Using Table 3B, specifically examine the relationship between consumer perceptions of being tech savvy and the two search-related variables in Question 1. What are the relationships and implications?

REVIEW QUESTIONS

1. When does *information search* occur? What is the difference between internal and external information search?

2. What kind of information is sought in an external search for information?

3. What are *evaluative criteria* and how do they relate to information search?

4. How does a consumer's *awareness set* influence information search?

5. What roles do the *evoked set, inert set,* and *inept set* play in a consumer's information search?

6. What are the primary sources of information available to consumers?

7. What is *behavioral targeting*?

8. What is *search engine optimization*?

9. What is *local mobile search*?

10. How do nonsearchers, limited information searchers, and extended information searchers differ in their search for information?

11. What factors might influence the search effort of consumers who are essentially one-stop shoppers? How do these factors differ in terms of how they influence limited information searchers and extended information searchers?

12. What factors have to be considered in the total cost of the information search? How might these factors be different for different consumers?

13. Explain how different *market characteristics* affect information search.

14. How do different *consumer characteristics* influence a consumer's information search effort?

15. How do *product characteristics* influence a consumer's information search effort?

16. How do *situational characteristics* influence a consumer's information search effort?

17. Describe the information search characteristics that should lead to each of the following strategies:
    a. Maintenance
    b. Disrupt
    c. Capture
    d. Intercept
    e. Preference
    f. Acceptance

18. Describe each of the strategies listed in Question 17.

DISCUSSION QUESTIONS

19. Pick a product/brand that you believe would require each strategy in Table 15-3 (six products in total). Justify your selection. Develop a specific marketing strategy for each (six strategies in total).

20. Which product classes are most likely to have evoked sets of one? Relate this to the type of decision process.

21. Use a shopping service such as Nex Tag to help you choose a brand of digital camera. In what way does it help you form your evoked or consideration set? Is information overload a problem? Explain.

22. Do you have a local mobile search app? If so, what is your evaluation of it? If no, why not?

23. What information sources do you think students on your campus use when acquiring the items listed below? Consider the various sources listed in Figure 15-4 in developing your answer. Do you think there will be individual differences? Why?
    a. Movies
    b. Restaurants
    c. Apartment
    d. Computer
    e. Fitness equipment
    f. A charity contribution
    g. Dress clothes
    h. Cell phones

24. What factors contribute to the size of the awareness set, evoked set, inert set, and inept set?

25. Discuss factors that may contribute to external information search and factors that act to reduce external search for information before purchase or adoption of the following:
    a. Car insurance
    b. International travel
    c. Exercise club
    d. Formal wear
    e. Eye wear
    f. Counseling services

26. Is it ever in the best interest of a marketer to encourage potential customers to carry out an extended prepurchase search? Why or why not?

27. What implications for marketing strategy does Figure 15-2 suggest?

28. What implications for online marketing strategy does Figure 15-5 suggest?

29. What role, if any, should the government play in ensuring that consumers have easy access to relevant product information? How should it accomplish this?

30. Respond to the questions in Consumer Insight 15-1.

31. Describe a recent purchase in which you engaged in extensive search and one in which you did little prepurchase search. What factors caused the difference?

32. What is your awareness set, evoked set, inert set, and inept set for the following? In what ways, if any, do you think your sets will differ from the average member of your class? Why?
    a. Automobiles
    b. Energy drinks
    c. Car insurance providers
    d. Jewelry stores
    e. Book stores
    f. Laptop computers
    g. Restaurants

APPLICATION ACTIVITIES

33. Develop an appropriate questionnaire and complete Question 23 using information from five students not in your class. Prepare a report discussing the marketing implications of your findings.

34. For the same products listed in Question 32, ask five students to list all the brands they are aware of in each product category. Then have them indicate which ones they might buy (evoked set), which ones they are indifferent toward (inert set), and which brands they strongly dislike and would not purchase (inept set). What are the marketing implications of your results?

35. Develop a short questionnaire designed to measure the information search consumers engage in prior to purchasing an expensive recreational or entertainment item or service. Your questionnaire should include measures of types of information sought, as well as sources that provide this information. Also include measures of the relevant consumer characteristics that might influence information search, as well as some measure of past experience with the products. Then interview two recent purchasers of each product, using the questionnaire you have developed. Analyze each consumer's response and classify each consumer in terms of information search. What are the marketing implications of your results?

36. For each strategy in Table 15-3, find one brand that appears to be following that strategy. Describe in detail how it is implementing the strategy.

37. Develop a questionnaire to determine which products college students view as positive and which they view as negative. Measure the shopping effort associated with each type. Explain your overall results and any individual differences you find.

REFERENCES

1. The Chapter 15 opener is based on information found on the various corporate websites.

2. G. Punji and R. Brookes, "Decision Constraints and Consideration-Set Formation in Consumer Durables," *Psychology & Marketing,* August 2001, pp. 843–63.

3. An outstanding discussion of the trade-off consumers make between memory-based decisions (internal search) and external search is in J. R. Bettman, M. F. Luce, and J. W. Payne, "Constructive Consumer Choice Processes," *Journal of Consumer Research,* December 1998, pp. 187–217.

4. See, e.g., R. Smith and B. Deppa, "Two Dimensions of Attribute Importance," *Journal of Consumer Marketing* 26, no. 1 (2009), pp. 28–38.

5. S. S. Posavac, D. M. Sanbonmatsu, and E. A. Ho, "The Effects of the Selective Consideration of Alternatives on Consumer Choice and Attitude-Decision Consistency," *Journal of Consumer Psychology* 12, no. 3 (2002), pp. 203–13; T. Erdem and J. Swait, "Brand Credibility, Brand Consideration, and Choice," *Journal of Consumer Research,* June 2004, pp. 191–98; M. Paulssen and R. P. Bagozzi, "A Self-Regulatory Model of Consideration Set

Formation," *Psychology & Marketing,* October 2005, pp. 785–812; and J. R. Hauser et al., "Disjunctions of Conjunctions, Cognitive Simplicity, and Consideration Sets," *Journal of Marketing Research,* June 2010, pp. 485–96.

6. E. M. Felcher, P. Malaviya, and A. L. McGill, "The Role of Taxonomic and Goal-Derived Product Categorization in, within, and across Category Judgments," *Psychology & Marketing,* August 2001, pp. 865–87.

7. P. Aurier, S. Jean, and J. L. Zaichkowsky, "Consideration Set Size and Familiarity with Usage Context," *Advances in Consumer Research,* vol. 27, ed. S. J. Hoch and R. J. Meyer (Provo, UT: Association for Consumer Research, 2000), pp. 307–13; and K. K. Desai and W. D. Hoyer, "Descriptive Characteristics of Memory-Based Consideration Sets," *Journal of Consumer Research,* December 2000, pp. 309–23.

8. R. R. Brand and J. J. Cronin, "Consumer-Specific Determinants of the Size of Retail Choice Sets," *Journal of Services Marketing* 11, no. 1 (1997), pp. 19–38.

9. L. R. Klein and G. T. Ford, "Consumer Search for Information in the Digital Age," *Journal of Interactive Marketing,* Summer 2003, pp. 29–49; B. T. Ratchford, M.-Soo Lee, and D. Talukdar, "The Impact of the Internet on Information Search for Automobiles," *Journal of Marketing Research,* May 2003, pp. 193–209; H. Li, T. Daugherty, and F. Biocca, "The Role of Virtual Experience in Consumer Learning," *Journal of Consumer Psychology* 13, no. 4 (2003), pp. 395–407; A. E. Schlosser, "Experience Products in the Virtual World," *Journal of Consumer Research,* September 2003, pp. 184–98; and D. A. Griffith and Q. Chen, "The Influence of Virtual Direct Experience (VDE) on On-line Ad Message Effectiveness," *Journal of Advertising,* Spring 2004, pp. 55–68.

10. For a review and conflicting evidence, see A. A. Wright and J. G. Lynch Jr., "Communications Effects of Advertising versus Direct Experience When Both Search and Experience Attributes Are Present," *Journal of Consumer Research,* March 1995, pp. 108–18.

11. See C. F. Mela, S. Gupta, and D. R. Lehmann, "The Long-Term Impact of Promotion and Advertising on Consumer Brand Choice," *Journal of Marketing Research,* May 1997, pp. 248–61; and M. J. Sirgy et al., "Does Television Viewership Play a Role in the Perception of Quality of Life?" *Journal of Advertising,* Spring 1998, pp. 125–42.

12. *World Internet Usage Statistics News and World Population Stats* (Bogota, Colombia: Miniwatts Marketing Group, March 2011).

13. *Demographics of Internet Users* (Washington, DC: Pew Internet & American Life Project, December 2010).

14. *Generations 2010* (Washington, DC: Pew Internet & American Life Project, December 2010).

15. S. Hays, "Has Online Advertising Finally Grown Up?" *Advertising Age,* April 1, 2002, p. C1.

16. *Counting on the Internet,* Pew Internet & American Life Project, December 29, 2002, www.pewinternet.org; Klein and Ford, "Consumer Search for Information in the Digital Age"; Ratchford, Lee, and Talukdar, "The Impact of the Internet on Information Search for Automobiles"; *DoubleClick's Touch-points II,* Double Click research report, March 2004, www.doubleclick.com; *Double-Click's Touch-points III,* DoubleClick research report, July 2005, www.doubleclick.com; and B. T. Ratchford, D. Talukdar, and M. Lee, "The Impact of the Internet on Consumers' Use of

Information Sources for Automobiles," *Journal of Consumer Research,* June 2007, pp. 111–19.

17. *Internet Activities,* Pew Internet & American Life Project, www.pewinternet.org, accessed June 18, 2011.

18. "Yahoo! and comScore Study Finds Online Consumers Who Pre-Shop on the Web Spend More In-Store," *comScore Press Release,* July 30, 2007, www.comscore.com, accessed June 19, 2011; *State of the U.S. Online Retail Economy through Q1 2009* (Reston, VA: comScore, 2009); D. M. Arbesman, "Online Shopper Intelligence Study Released," *compete pulse,* February 22, 2010, http://blog.complete.com, accessed June 15, 2011; and "Study Shows Online Shoppers Are Doing Their Homework," *e-commerce news,* February 26, 2010, http://ecommercejunkie.com, accessed June 15, 2011.

19. *Search before the Purchase,* DoubleClick research report, February 2005, www.doubleclick.com.

20. J. L. Joines, C. W. Scherer, and D. A. Scheufele, "Exploring Motivations for Consumer Web Use and Their Implications for E-commerce," *Journal of Consumer Marketing* 20, no. 2 (2003), pp. 90–108.

21. Ratchford, Lee, and Talukdar, "The Impact of the Internet on Information Search for Automobiles."

22. L. Gentry and R. Calantone, "A Comparison of Three Models to Explain Shop-Bot Use on the Web," *Psychology & Marketing,* November 2002, pp. 945–56; and Y. Xu and H. Kim, "Order Effect and Vendor Inspection in Online Comparison Shopping," *Journal of Retailing* 84, no. 4 (2008), pp. 477–86.

23. B. Bickart and R. M. Schindler, "Internet Forums as Influential Sources of Consumer Information," *Journal of Interactive Marketing,* Summer 2001, pp. 31–40; and P. Chatterjee, "Online Reviews," *Advances in Consumer Research,* vol. 28, ed. M. C. Gilly and J. Meyers-Levy (Provo, UT: Association for Consumer Research, 2001), pp. 129–33.

24. J. Loechner, "Online Research a Significant Part of Consumer Buying," *MediaPost,* February 22, 2011, www.mediapost.com, accessed June 15, 2011.

25. A. Parmar, "Student e-union," *Marketing News,* April 1, 2004, pp. 14–15.

26. "Ethnic Groups Online," *eMarketer,* June 20, 2005.

27. N. Singh and H. Matsuo, "Measuring Cultural Adaptation on the Web," in *Advances in Consumer Research,* vol. 30, ed. P. A. Keller and D. W. Rook (Provo, UT: Association for Consumer Research, 2003), pp. 271–72.

28. "Want Consumer Engagement?" *Launchfire,* October 5, 2009, www.launchfire.com, accessed June 15, 2011.

29. J. Halliday, "Half Hit Web before Showrooms," *Advertising Age,* October 4, 2004, p. 76.

30. E-mail material based on *DoubleClick's 2004 Consumer E-mail Study,* DoubleClick, October 2004, www.doubleclick.com.

31. *Who Tweets?* (Washington, DC: Pew Internet, 2009); J. Van Grove, "Sponsored Tweets Launches," mashable.com, August 3, 2009, accessed May 23, 2011; and "How Does Twitter Make Money," Buzzle.com, accessed May 23, 2011.

32. J. S. Ilfeld and R. S. Winer, "Generating Web Traffic," *Journal of Advertising Research,* October 2002, pp. 49–61.

33. D. Zigmond and H. Stipp, "Assessing a New Advertising Effect," *Journal of Advertising Research,* June 2010, pp. 162–68.

34. *Best Practices for Optimizing Web Advertising Effectiveness,* DoubleClick, May 2006, www.doubleclick.com.

35. Ibid.

36. C. McCarthy, "MySpace Gets 'Hyper' with Targeted Ads," *CNET News.com,* November 5, 2007, http://news.cnet.com/; and J. Kirk, "MySpace User Ad Targeting Will Be Optional," *The Industry Standard,* April 29, 2008, www.thestandard.com.

37. J. Smith, "10 Powerful Ways to Target Facebook Ads Every Performance Advertiser Should Know," *Inside Facebook,* July 27, 2009, www.insidefacebook.com, accessed June 19, 2011.

38. N. Madden, "Levi's Partners with Tudou for Interactive Video Campaign," *Advertising Age,* December 22, 2010.

39. W. Dou, R. Linn, and S. Yang, "How Smart Are 'Smart Banners'?" *Journal of Advertising Research* 41, no. 4 (2001), pp. 31–43.

40. E. Steel, "How Marketers Hone Their Aim Online," *The Wall Street Journal,* June 19, 2007.

41. "Search Marketing Fact Pack 2008," *Advertising Age,* November 8, 2008.

42. D. Sullivan, "Intro to Search Engine Optimization," *Search EngineWatch.com,* October 14, 2002.

43. B. S. Bulik, "Meet the Brands Hiding on Google," *Advertising Age,* April 27, 2010.

44. See, e.g., T. P. Novak, D. L. Hoffman, and Y.-F. Yung, "Measuring the Customer Experience in Online Environments," *Marketing Science,* Winter 2000, pp. 22–42; and J. R. Coyle and E. Thorson, "The Effects of Progressive Levels of Interactivity and Vividness in Web Marketing Sites," *Journal of Advertising,* Fall 2001, pp. 65–77.

45. *How Mobile Devices Are Changing Community Information Environments* (Washington, DC: Pew Internet & American Life Project, March 14, 2011).

46. Estimates from *eMarketer.* This and related information available at www.emarketer.com/reports.

47. Segment information from *2010 American Mobile Consumer Report* (Cost Mesa, CA: Experian, Information Systems, Inc., March 5, 2010); H. Leggatt, "Experian Segments Mobile Users by Behavior/Attitudes," *BizReport,* March 8, 2010, www.bizreport.com, accessed June 18, 2011; and J. Loechner, "Holiday Layaway," *MediaPost,* August 17, 2010, www.mediapost.com, accessed June 15, 2011. See also M. Pihlstrom and G. J. Brush, "Comparing the Perceived Value of Information and Entertainment Mobile Services," *Psychology & Marketing,* August 2008, pp. 732–55.

48. R. Aronauer, "Going Mobile to Market," *Sales & Marketing Management,* June 2007; and "Search Marketing Fact Pack 2008."

49. N. Zmuda, "Yes, There's an App for That Too," *Advertising Age,* March 1, 2010, p. 8.

50. Consumer Insight 15-1 is based on M. Kamvar and S. Baluja, "A Large Scale Study of Wireless Search Behavior," in *Proceedings of SIGCHI Conference on Human Factors in Computing Systems,* ed. R. Ginter et al. (Montreal: Conference on Human Factors in Computing Systems, 2006), pp. 701–709; "Search Marketing," in *Advertising Age Fact Pack 2007* (New York: Crain Communications, November 5, 2007); *Best Practices: A Blueprint for Building a Retail Mobile Marketing Program* (Irvine, CA: SmartReply, 2007); "Case Studies," *MobileMarketing Magazine,* November 19, 2007, p. 22; and "Special Report: Interactive Marketing," promomagazine.com, accessed April 15, 2008.

51. R. A. Westbrook and C. Farnell, "Patterns of Information Source Usage among Durable Goods Buyers," *Journal of Marketing Research,* August 1979, pp. 303–12; and J. E. Urbany, P. R. Dickson, and W. L. Wilkie, "Buyer Uncertainty and Information Search," *Journal of Consumer Research,* September 1989, pp. 208–15.

52. Urbany, Dickson, and Wilkie, "Buyer Uncertainty and Information Search"; and *Warranties Rule Consumer Follow-Up* (Washington DC: Federal Trade Commission, 1984), p. 26.

53. Ratchford, Lee, and Talukdar, "The Impact of the Internet on Information Search for Automobiles."

54. G. Katona and E. Mueller, "A Study of Purchase Decisions," in *Consumer Behavior: The Dynamics of Consumer Reaction,* ed. L. Clark (New York: New York University Press, 1955), pp. 30–87; J. Newman and R. Staelin, "Prepurchase Information Seeking for New Cars and Major Household Appliances," *Journal of Marketing Research,* August 1972, pp. 249–57; J. Claxton, J. Fry, and B. Portis, "A Taxonomy of Prepurchase Information Gathering Patterns," *Journal of Consumer Research,* December 1974, pp. 35–42; G. C. Kiel and R. A. Layton, "Dimensions of Consumer Information Seeking Behavior," *Journal of Marketing Research,* May 1981, pp. 233–39; J. B. Freiden and R. E. Goldsmith, "Prepurchase Information-Seeking for Professional Services," *Journal of Services Marketing,* Winter 1989, pp. 45–55; Urbany, Dickson, and Wilkie, "Buyer Uncertainty and Information Search"; G. N. Souter and M. M. McNeil, *Journal of Professional Services Marketing* 11, no. 2 (1995), pp. 45–60; and Klein and Ford, "Consumer Search for Information in the Digital Age."

55. J. G. Lynch Jr. and D. Ariely, "Wine Online," *Marketing Science,* Winter 2000, pp. 83–103; D. Ariely, "Controlling the Information Flow," *Journal of Consumer Research,* September 2000, pp. 233–48; and Ratchford, Lee, and Talukdar, "The Impact of the Internet on Information Search for Automobiles."

56. For a similar model of online search, see S. Kulviwat, C. Guo, and N. Engchanil, "Determinants of Online Search," *Internet Research* 14, no. 3 (2004), pp. 245–53; and A. L. Jepsen, "Factors Affecting Consumer Use of the Internet for Information Search," *Journal of Interactive Marketing,* Summer 2007, pp. 21–34.

57. D. R. Lichtenstein, N. M. Ridgway, and R. G. Netemeyer, "Price Perceptions and Consumer Shopping Behavior," *Journal of Marketing Research,* May 1993, pp. 234–45.

58. M. N. Bergen, S. Dutta, and S. M. Shugan, "Branded Variants," *Journal of Marketing Research,* February 1996, pp. 9–19.

59. J. Srivastava and N. Lurie, "A Consumer Perspective on Price-Matching Refund Policies," *Journal of Consumer Research,* September 2001, pp. 296–307.

60. D. Grewal and H. Marmorstein, "Market Price Variation, Perceived Price Variation, and Consumers' Price Search Decisions for Durable Goods," *Journal of Consumer Research,* December 1994, pp. 453–60.

61. See B. G. C. Dellaert, "Investigating Consumers' Tendency to Combine Multiple Shopping Purposes and Destinations," *Journal of Marketing Research,* May 1998, pp. 177–89.

62. See C. Moorman, "Market-Level Effects of Information," *Journal of Marketing Research,* February 1998, pp. 82–98; and A. D. Miyazaki, D. E. Sprott, and K. C. Manning, "Unit Prices on Retail Shelf Labels," *Journal of Retailing* 76, no. 1 (2000), pp. 93–112.

63. See C. M. Fisher and C. J. Anderson, "The Relationship between Consumer Attitudes and Frequency of Advertising in Newspapers for Hospitals," *Journal of Hospital Marketing* 7, no. 2 (1993), pp. 139–56.

64. S. Widrick and E. Fram, "Identifying Negative Products," *Journal of Consumer Marketing,* no. 2 (1983), pp. 59–66.

65. See D. D'Rozario and S. P. Douglas, "Effect of Assimilation on Prepurchase Information-Search Tendencies," *Journal of Consumer Psychology* 8, no. 2 (1999), pp. 187–209; and C. Merrill, "Where the Cars Are Caliente," *American Demographics,* January 2000, pp. 56–59.

66. J. Lee and J. Cho, "Consumers' Use of Information Intermediaries and the Impact on Their Information Search Behavior in the Financial Market," *The Journal of Consumer Affairs* 39, no.1 (2005), pp. 95–120.

67. J. W. Alba and J. W. Hutchinson, "Knowledge Calibration," *Journal of Consumer Research,* September 2000, pp. 123–49.

68. C. M. Heilman, D. Bowman, and G. P. Wright, "The Evolution of Brand Preferences and Choice Behaviors of Consumers New to a Market," *Journal of Marketing Research,* May 2000, pp. 139–55. See also D. Mazursky, "The Effects of Invalidating Information on Consumers' Subsequent Search Patterns," *Journal of Economic Psychology,* April 1998, pp. 261–77.

69. See J. A. Barrick and B. C. Spilker, "The Relations between Knowledge, Search Strategy, and Performance in Unaided and Aided Information Search," *Organizational Behavior and Human Decision Processes* 90 (2003), pp. 1–18.

70. See T. Williams, M. Slama, and J. Rogers, "Behavioral Characteristics of the Recreational Shopper," *Journal of Academy of Marketing Science,* Summer 1985, pp. 307–16; J. R. Lumpkin, J. M. Hawes, and W. R. Darden, "Shopping Patterns of the Rural Consumer," *Journal of Business Research,* February 1986, pp. 63–81; and W. W. Moe, "Buying, Searching, or Browsing," *Journal of Consumer Psychology* 13, no. 1/2 (2003), pp. 29–39.

71. See U. M. Dholakia, "Involvement-Response Models of Joint Effects," *Advances in Consumer Research,* vol. 25, ed. Alba and Hutchinson, pp. 499–506.

72. T. H. Dodd, B. E. Pinkleton, and A. W. Gustafson, *Psychology & Marketing,* May 1996, pp. 291–304. See also J. R. McColl-Kennedy and R. E. Fetter Jr., "An Empirical Examination of the Involvement to External Search Relationship," *Journal of Services Marketing* 15, no. 2 (2001), pp. 82–98.

73. G. R. Dowling and R. Staelin, "A Model of Perceived Risk and Intended Risk-Handling Activity," *Journal of Consumer Research,* June 1994, pp. 119–34. See also J. B. Smith and J. M. Bristor, "Uncertainty Orientation," *Psychology & Marketing,* November 1994, pp. 587–607.

74. A. Chaudhuri, "Product Class Effects on Perceived Risk," *International Journal of Research in Marketing,* May 1998, pp. 157–68; and K. Mitra, M. C. Reiss, and L. M. Capella, "An Examination of Perceived Risk, Informational Search, and Behavioral Intentions," *Journal of Services Marketing* 13, no. 3 (1999), pp. 208–28.

75. See, e.g., M. W. H. Weenig and M. Maarleveld, "The Impact of Time Constraint on Information Search Strategies in Complex Choice Tasks," *Journal of Economic Psychology* 23 (2002), pp. 689–702. For an exception, see C. J. Hill, "The Nature of Problem Recognition and Search in the Extended Health Care Decision," *Journal of Services Marketing* 15, no. 6 (2001), pp. 454–79.

76. A. G. Abdul-Muhmin, "Contingent Decision Behavior," *Journal of Consumer Psychology* 8, no. 1 (1999), pp. 91–111.

77. "L&M Lights Up Again," *Marketing and Media Decisions,* February 1984, p. 69.

78. L. L. Garber, "The Package Appearance in Choice," in *Advances in Consumer Research,* vol. 22, ed. F. R. Kardes and M. Sujan (Provo, UT: Association for Consumer Research, 1995), pp. 653–60.

79. Oser, "Snapple Effort Finds Women as They Browse."

80. See, e.g., Erdem and Swait, "Brand Credibility, Brand Consideration, and Choice."

16

Alternative Evaluation and Selection

LEARNING OBJECTIVES

LO1 Discuss how actual consumer choice often differs from rational choice theory

LO2 Summarize the types of choice processes consumers engage in

LO3 Explain evaluative criteria and their measurement

LO4 Describe the role of evaluative criteria in consumer judgment and marketing strategy

LO5 Summarize the five decision rules for attribute-based choice and their strategic relevance

Online shopping services can help consumers with information search. These services, sometimes called recommendation agents or bots, can also aid in evaluating and choosing alternatives. Some shopping services simply list available brands or look for the lowest price. For example, if a consumer reasons that all flights from New York to Denver are the same and they simply want the lowest price, they could use a shopping service that does price comparisons. Once they have a list of prices from the various carriers, their decision is simple—pick the lowest-priced offering.[1]

Other decisions are more complex, and online shopping services exist to help consumers with that complexity. For example, PriceGrabber allows consumers to filter available alternatives based on various features or evaluative criteria, thus helping consumers form their evoked set. Consumers decide what their acceptable levels are on various features and PriceGrabber only presents the set of brands that meet those criteria. In Chapter 15 we referred to this set as the evoked or consideration set. The only remaining decision task for consumers at this point is to evaluate the brands in the consideration set and to make a final choice.

Some online shopping services go even further in aiding consumer choice. For example, Shopper.com filters available alternatives based on various criteria, and also does side-by-side comparisons of any subset of alternatives the consumer selects on a feature-by-feature basis. Such "alignment" of brands on key features can make consumer decisions easier, reduce decision time, and increase decision quality. Shopper.com also tries to simplify consumer decisions by listing the key "pros" and "cons" of a given brand. And it provides user reviews and ratings, which, as we saw in Chapter 15, are heavily used as a trusted source by online shoppers.

Even with all this web shopping functionality, consumers are typically left with numerous acceptable alternatives to choose from. For consumers who are knowledgeable in the category, such choices are relatively easy since they know how to match key features to their needs. Novice consumers often find such choices much more difficult, and the quality of their decisions suffers as a consequence.

As the opening examples suggest, consumers make decisions in a variety of ways and the decisions they make range from simple to complex. The decision stage after problem recognition and information search is alternative evaluation and selection. Alternative selection is also referred to as consumer choice and in reality consumers are often evaluating alternatives for choice even during the search process. Consumer evaluation and choice of alternatives is the focus of this chapter.

CONSUMER CHOICE AND TYPES OF CHOICE PROCESS

L01

Marketers sometimes assume that the process underlying consumer choice follows *rational choice theory*. Rational choice theory implicitly or explicitly assumes a number of things about consumer choice that often are not true. These assumptions are discussed next.

- *Assumption 1:* Consumers seek one optimal solution to a problem and choose on that basis.

  However, increasingly, marketers are coming to understand that these conditions don't always describe consumer choice. First, consumers don't always have the goal of finding the "optimal brand" for them. Instead, there are alternative metagoals, where a **metagoal** refers to *the general nature of the outcome being sought.* In addition to selecting the optimal alternative, metagoals include minimizing decision effort or maximizing the extent to which a decision is justifiable to others.[2] Consider nominal decision making from Chapter 14. Consumers who are low in purchase involvement may engage in little or no external search because they can recall from memory a brand that is at least satisfactory. In this case, consumers will usually choose this brand with no further search or decision effort, even though it may not be the optimal brand for them. This is because, given low purchase involvement, other goals come into play such as minimizing search and decision effort.

- *Assumption 2:* Consumers have the skill and motivation to find the optimal solution.

  However, marketers are increasingly aware that consumers often don't have the ability or the motivation to engage in the highly demanding task of finding the optimal solution. For example, consumers are subject to **bounded rationality**—*a limited capacity for processing information.*[3] Moreover, as suggested in Chapter 14, most decisions do not generate enough purchase involvement to motivate consumers to seek the optimal solution through extended decision making. As the opening example suggests, many websites in the United States are attempting to help consumers deal with the information overload that accompanies too many choices.

  In the United Kingdom, choice overload was the motivation behind a site called Just Buy This One, which recommends only one brand within a product category and price range with three reasons why it's the best choice. According to a company executive:

  > We knew that 25% of people are overwhelmed by the choice on price comparison sites and we decided to create something utterly simple and extremely useful. Online shopping used to be the simple solution, but it's gotten too crowded.[4]

- *Assumption 3:* The optimal solution does not change as a function of situational factors such as time pressure, task definition, or competitive context.

However, marketers are increasingly aware that preferences can and do shift as a function of the situation (Chapter 13). For example, limited decision making is more likely when we are tired or hurried. In addition, when new brands are added to the competitive set, it can alter consumer choices, as we discuss later in the chapter.

Thus, as you read this chapter, it is important to keep in mind that consumer decisions (a) are often not rational in the sense of finding the optimal solution, (b) are not optimal due to the cognitive and time limits of consumers, and (c) are malleable in that they change based on the situation. In addition, it is important to keep in mind that consumer decisions are much more circular, emotional, and incomplete than our formal examination here might suggest.

Types of Consumer Choice Processes

LO2

Let's begin by examining the three general types of decision processes that consumers can engage in. You will notice that some are not even based on a comparison of brands and their features, which is often a major (and sometimes incorrect) assumption made by marketing managers. The three choice processes are affective choice, attitude-based choice, and attribute-based choice. While we describe them separately for simplicity, it is important to keep in mind that these are not mutually exclusive and combinations may be used in a single decision. First, let's look at three decision scenarios involving a digital camera:

Scenario 1 (Affective Choice): As a consumer shops at a local store, one camera catches her eye: she examines it, looking at the lines and overall look. She thinks the camera looks sleek, modern, and cool. She examines another camera, but she thinks it looks too serious and boring. After a few more minutes of contemplation about what a great impression she would make using the first camera to take pictures at parties and weddings, she decides to buy the first camera.

Scenario 2 (Attitude-based Choice): The consumer remembers that her friend's Olympus Stylus worked well and looked "good"; her parents had a Kodak Easyshare that also worked well but was rather large and bulky; and her old Fujifilm FinePix had not performed as well as she had expected. At her local electronics store she sees that the Olympus and Kodak models are about the same price and decides to buy the Olympus Stylus.

Scenario 3 (Attribute-based Choice): After consulting the Internet to determine what features she is most interested in, the consumer then goes to her local electronics store and compares the various brands on the features most important to her—namely, camera size, zoom, automatic features, and storage size. She mentally ranks each model on these attributes and her general impression of each model's quality. On the basis of these evaluations, she chooses the Olympus Stylus.

These three scenarios relate to different choice processes. The first scenario represents affective choice.[5] **Affective choice** tends to be more holistic in nature. The brand is not decomposed into distinct components, each of which is evaluated separately from the whole. The evaluation of such products is generally focused on the way they will make the user feel as they are used. The evaluation itself is often based exclusively or primarily on the immediate emotional response to the product or service.[6] Decisions based on affect use the "How do I feel about it" heuristic or decision rule.[7] Consumers imagine or picture using the product or service and evaluate the feeling that this use will produce.[8]

ILLUSTRATION 16–1

The ad on the left appeals to a consummatory motive by showing that the product or consumption is rewarding in and of itself. The ad on the right appeals to an instrumental motive by showing that the product is a means to an end.

Consumer use of the affective choice process is affected by underlying purchase motives. Affective choice is most likely when the underlying motive is consummatory rather than instrumental. **Consummatory motives** *underlie behaviors that are intrinsically rewarding to the individual involved.* **Instrumental motives** *activate behaviors designed to achieve a second goal.* For example, the consumer in Scenario 1 is clearly motivated primarily by the emotional rewards involved in having and using a camera that makes her look trendy and fashionable (consummatory motive), whereas other consumers may be motivated by having a camera that takes high-quality pictures that can be enjoyed later (instrumental motive).[9] Illustration 16–1 shows ads appealing to each of these motives.

Marketers continue to learn more about affect-based decisions.[10] It is clear that such decisions require different strategies than the more cognitive decisions generally considered in marketing. For those decisions that are likely to be affective in nature (largely triggered by consummatory motives), marketers should design products and services that will provide the appropriate emotional responses.[11] They also should help consumers visualize how they will feel during and after the consumption experience.[12] This is particularly important for new brands or products and services. Consumers who have experience with a product or brand have a basis for imagining the affective response it will produce. Those who do not may incorrectly predict the feelings the experience will produce. For example, individuals imagining a white-water rafting trip may conclude that it would produce feelings of terror rather than exhilaration. Illustration 16–2 shows an ad that helps consumers envision the positive experiences and accompanying feelings they would have if they owned the product.

The second scenario represents attitude-based choice. **Attitude-based choice** *involves the use of general attitudes, summary impressions, intuitions, or heuristics; no attribute-by-attribute comparisons are made at the time of choice.*[13] It is important to note that many decisions, even for important products, appear to be attitude based. Recall from Chapters 14 and 15 that most individuals collect very little product information from external sources immediately before a purchase. They are most likely making attitude-based decisions.

Motivation, information availability, and situational factors interact to determine the likelihood that attitude-based choices are made. As one would suspect, the lower the motivation to make an optimal decision, the more likely an attitude-based choice will be made. This relates to purchase involvement and nominal and limited decision making in Chapter 14, which are likely to be heavily skewed toward attitude-based choice. When information is difficult to find or access, or when consumers face time pressures, attitude-based choices are more likely. Notice how time pressures increase the perceived cost of search and make attitude-based choices from memory appear much more attractive.

The third scenario represents attribute-based choice. **Attribute-based choice** *requires the knowledge of specific attributes at the time the choice is made, and it involves attribute-by-attribute comparisons across brands.* This is a much more effortful and time-consuming process than the global comparisons made when affective and attitude-based choice is involved. It also tends to produce a more nearly optimal decision. Again, motivation, information availability, and situational factors interact to determine the likelihood that attitude-based choices are made.

ILLUSTRATION 16–2

This ad encourages an affect-based choice by encouraging consumers to imagine the pleasure they will derive from owning the product.

Consumers with high purchase involvement or motivation are more likely to make attribute-based choices that most resemble the extended decision-making approach we discussed in Chapter 14. More accessible brand and attribute information increases the likelihood that attribute-based choices are made. This can be used by marketers of brands that have important attribute-based advantages but that lack strong reputations or images in the target market. The approach would be to provide attribute-based comparisons in an easy-to-process format, such as a brand-by-attribute matrix. Such a matrix could be presented in ads, on packages, in point-of-purchase displays, on the brand's website, and so on. An appropriate comparison format and structure is critical to make the firm's brand the focal point of comparison.[14] This could be done by listing the company's brand first, perhaps in bold or colored type.

The ads in Illustration 16–3 show the differences between attribute-based and attitude-based choice strategies. The ad on the left focuses on specific features of the brand and would be consistent with an attribute-based choice. The ad on the right focuses on the brand and an overall impression of the product and its users and would be consistent with an attitude-based choice.

It is important to note that these three processes are not always used in isolation. For example, affective or emotional criteria can be considered along with functional criteria. Sometimes consumers are more driven by emotions and end up choosing functionally inferior brands.[15] Such trade-offs between hedonic and utilitarian attributes are important for marketers to consider in developing products and promotional campaigns. In addition, sometimes affective and attitude-based processes can be used by consumers to establish or narrow their consideration sets. This type of *phased* decision making is common, and understanding the role of affect and attitudes in the formation of the evoked set is critical for marketers.

ILLUSTRATION 16–3

The ad on the left encourages attribute-based choice with primacy given to its key product features. Ads such as that on the right assume or encourage attitude-based choice, by focusing on brand, overall performance, and image rather than specific product features.

L03

Given the nature, complexity, and importance of attribute-based choice to both consumers and marketers, the focus of the remainder of the chapter is on issues related to attribute-based choice. Figure 16-1 provides an overview of the stages of the attribute-based choice process.

EVALUATIVE CRITERIA

Attribute-based choices rely heavily on a comparison of brands on one or more attributes. These attributes are called evaluative criteria since they are the dimensions on which the brands are evaluated. **Evaluative criteria** are *the various dimensions, features, or benefits a consumer looks for in response to a specific problem.* While functional attributes are common, evaluative criteria can also be emotions (the pleasure associated with eating chocolate cake) and the reactions of important reference group members (for socially consumed products). Before purchasing a computer, you might be concerned with cost, speed, memory, operating system, display, and warranty. These would be your evaluative criteria. Someone else could approach the same purchase with an entirely different set of evaluative criteria.

Evaluative criteria are perceived and utilized by consumers in a number of ways, including extremes (lower price or more miles per gallon is better), limits (it must not cost more than $100; it must get more than 25 miles per gallon), or ranges (any price between $85 and $99 is acceptable).[16] For new product categories, consumers must often first determine which levels of various criteria are desirable. For example, a consumer

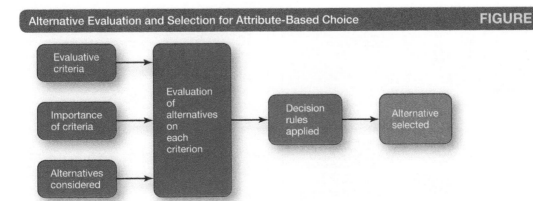

FIGURE 16-1

Alternative Evaluation and Selection for Attribute-Based Choice

who buys a barbecue grill for the first time and has limited experience with grills may have to determine if he prefers gas to charcoal, domed or traditional shape, and so forth. After purchase and use, these preference levels become more firmly established and stable.[17]

Nature of Evaluative Criteria

Evaluative criteria are typically associated with desired benefits. Thus, consumers want fluoride (evaluative criteria) in their toothpaste to reduce cavities (benefit). It is often more persuasive for marketers to communicate brand benefits rather than (or in addition to) evaluative criteria, since it is the benefits that consumers specifically desire. The ad in Illustration 16–4 focuses primarily on product benefits rather than technical features.

Evaluative criteria can differ in type, number, and importance. The *type of evaluative criteria* a consumer uses in a decision varies from *tangible* cost and performance features to *intangible* factors such as style, taste, prestige, feelings generated, and brand image.[18] Illustration 16–5 shows how two similar products stress different types of evaluative criteria. The ad on the left stresses tangible attributes and technical performance. The ad on the right focuses more on intangible attributes and feelings.

For fairly simple products such as toothpaste, soap, or facial tissue, consumers use relatively few evaluative criteria. On the other hand, the purchase of an automobile, smartphone, or house may involve numerous criteria. Individual characteristics such as product familiarity and age, and situational characteristics such as time pressure also affect the number of evaluative criteria considered.[19] For example, time pressure tends to reduce the number of attributes examined.[20]

The *importance* that consumers assign to each evaluative criterion is of great interest to marketers. Three consumers could use the

ILLUSTRATION 16–4

Consumers are generally interested in product features only in relation to the benefits those features provide. This ad emphasizes core benefits rather than the technical characteristics that generate those benefits.

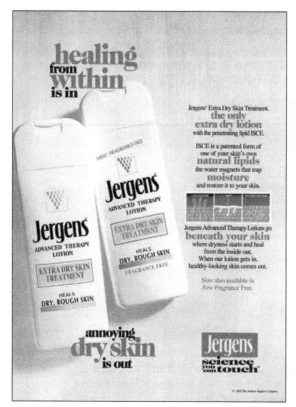

<table>
</table>

ILLUSTRATION 16–5	same six evaluative criteria shown in the following table when considering a laptop computer. However, if the importance rank they assigned each criterion varied as shown, they would likely purchase different brands.

These ads are for the same product category but assume differing evaluative processes by consumers.

	Importance Rank for		
Criterion	Consumer A	Consumer B	Consumer C
Price	1	6	3
Processor	5	1	4
Display quality	3	3	1
Memory	6	2	5
Weight	4	4	2
After-sale support	2	5	6

Consumer A is concerned primarily with cost and support services. Consumer B wants computing speed and power (as represented by processor and memory). Consumer C is concerned primarily with ease of use (as represented by display and weight). If each of these three consumers represented a larger group of consumers, we would have three distinct market segments based on the importance assigned to the same criteria.

Evaluative criteria and their importance affect which brands consumers select. They also influence if and when a problem will be recognized. For example, consumers who attach more importance to automobile styling relative to cost buy new cars *more frequently* than do those with the opposite importance rankings.[21] Thus, marketers want to understand which criteria consumers use to evaluate their brands so they can develop and communicate appropriate brand features to the target market. Also, marketers sometimes want to change the evaluative criteria that consumers utilize in ways that benefit their brands.[22] Thus measuring evaluative criteria is an important marketing activity.

Measurement of Evaluative Criteria

Before a marketing manager or a public policy decision maker can develop a sound strategy to affect consumer decisions, he or she must determine

- Which evaluative criteria are used by the consumer.
- How the consumer perceives the various alternatives on each criterion.
- The relative importance of each criterion.

Therefore, it is often difficult to determine which criteria consumers are using in a particular brand-choice decision, particularly if emotions or feelings are involved. This is even more of a problem when trying to determine the relative importance they attach to each evaluative criterion.

Determination of Which Evaluative Criteria Are Used   To determine which criteria are used by consumers in a specific product decision, the marketing researcher can use either direct or indirect methods of measurement.

Direct methods include asking consumers what criteria they use in a particular purchase or, in a focus group setting, noting what consumers say about products and their attributes. However, consumers sometimes will not or cannot verbalize their evaluative criteria for a product, particularly if emotions or feelings are involved. For example, Hanes Corporation suffered substantial losses ($30 million) on its L'erin cosmetics line when, *in response to consumer interviews,* it positioned it as a functional rather than a romantic or emotional product. Eventually, the brand was successfully repositioned as glamorous and exotic, although consumers did not *express* these as desired attributes.[23]

Thus, *indirect* measurement techniques such as **projective techniques** (Appendix A, Table A-1), which allow the respondent to indicate the criteria someone else might use are often helpful. The "someone else" will likely be a *projection* of the respondent, of course—thus, the marketer can indirectly determine the evaluative criteria that would be used.

Perceptual mapping is another useful indirect technique for determining evaluative criteria. First, consumers judge the similarity of alternative brands. This generally involves having the consumer look at possible pairs of brands and indicate which pair is most similar, which is second most similar, and so forth until all pairs are ranked. These similarity judgments are processed via a computer to derive a perceptual map of the brands. No evaluative criteria are specified by the consumer. The consumer simply ranks the similarity between all pairs of alternatives, and a perceptual configuration is derived in which the consumer's still unnamed evaluative criteria are the dimensions of the configuration.

For example, consider the perceptual map of beers shown in Figure 16-2. This configuration was derived from a consumer's evaluation of the relative similarity of these brands of beer. The horizontal axis is characterized by physical characteristics such as taste, calories, and fullness. The vertical axis is characterized by price, quality, and status. Naming each axis, and thus each evaluative criterion, is done using judgment. This procedure allows marketers to understand consumers' perceptions and the evaluative criteria they use to differentiate brands.

FIGURE 16-2   Perceptual Mapping of Beer Brand Perceptions

Determination of Consumers' Judgments of Brand Performance on Specific Evaluative Criteria

A variety of methods are available for measuring consumers' judgments of brand performance on specific attributes. These include *rank ordering scales, semantic differential scales,* and *Likert scales* (see Appendix A and Appendix Table A-3). The semantic differential scale is probably the most widely used technique.

None of these techniques are very effective at measuring emotional responses to products or brands. Projective techniques can provide some insights. SAM, the graphical approach designed to tap more directly into the pleasure-arousal-dominance dimensions of emotions (see Chapter 11), is also a useful option.

Determination of the Relative Importance of Evaluative Criteria

The importance assigned to evaluative criteria can be measured either by direct or by indirect methods. No matter which technique is used, the usage situation should be specified since attribute importance often changes with the situation. The *constant sum scale* is the most common method of direct measurement (see Chapter 11).

The most popular indirect measurement approach is **conjoint analysis.** In conjoint analysis, the consumer is presented with a set of products or product descriptions in which the evaluative criteria vary. For example, the consumer may be presented with the description of 24 different laptop computers that vary on four criteria. Two might be

Intel Core Duo 2.4 GHz	Intel Core Duo 2.0 GHz
Energy Star compliant (yes)	Energy Star compliant (no)
5.1 pounds	4 pounds
$1,250	$850

The consumer ranks all 24 such descriptions in terms of his or her preference for those combinations of features. Using these preference ranks, sophisticated computer programs derive the relative importance consumers assign to each level of each attribute tested (see Appendix A and Appendix Figure A-1 for details).

Conjoint analysis was used by Sunbeam in reformulating its food processor line for various segments. Sunbeam tested 12 different attributes: price, motor power, number of blades, bowl shape, and so forth. Various segments emerged *based on the relative importance of these attributes.* In order of importance, the key attributes for two segments were as follows. These results helped Sunbeam develop models specifically for each of these segments and to better meet their needs on important evaluative criteria.

Cheap/Large Segment	Multispeed/Multiuse Segment
$49.99 price	$99.99 price
4-quart bowl	2-quart bowl
Two speeds	Seven speeds
Seven blades	Functions as blender and mixer
Heavy-duty motor	Cylindrical bowl
Cylindrical bowl	Pouring spout

INDIVIDUAL JUDGMENT AND EVALUATIVE CRITERIA

LO4

If you were buying a laptop computer, you would probably make direct comparisons across brands on features such as price, weight, and display clarity. These comparative judgments might not be completely accurate. For example, the display that is the easiest to read in a five-minute trial might not be the easiest to read over a two-hour work session. For other attributes, such as quality, you might not be able to make direct comparisons. Instead, you might rely on brand name or price to indicate quality. In addition, consumer perceptions of the importance of product features are influenced by various external factors. The accuracy of direct judgments, the use of one attribute to indicate performance on another (surrogate indicator), and variations in attribute importance are critical issues for marketers.

Accuracy of Individual Judgments

The average consumer is not adequately trained to judge the performance of competing brands on complex evaluative criteria such as quality or durability. For more straightforward criteria, however, most consumers can and do make such judgments. Prices generally can be judged and compared directly. However, even this can be complex. Is a six-pack of 12-ounce cans of Coca-Cola selling for $2.49 a better buy than two liters priced at $1.59 each? Consumer groups have pushed for unit pricing (pricing by common measurements such as cost per ounce) to make such comparisons simpler. The federal truth-in-lending law was passed to facilitate direct price comparisons among alternative lenders.

ILLUSTRATION 16–6

Marketers sometimes use price, warranty, brand, or country of origin as surrogate indicators of quality.

GRANA PADANO

The Premier Cheese of Italy.

The ability of an individual to distinguish between similar stimuli is called **sensory discrimination** (see Chapter 8). This could involve such variables as the sound of stereo systems, the taste of food products, or the clarity of display screens. The minimum amount that one brand can differ from another with the difference still being noticed is referred to as the *just noticeable difference (j.n.d.)*. As we saw in Chapter 8, this ability is not well developed in most consumers. In general, research indicates that *individuals typically do not notice relatively small differences between brands or changes in brand attributes.* In addition, the complexity of many products and services as well as the fact that some aspects of performance can be judged only after extensive use makes accurate brand comparisons difficult.[24]

The inability of consumers to accurately evaluate many products can result in inappropriate purchases (buying a lower-quality product at a higher price than necessary).[25] This is a major concern of regulatory agencies and consumer groups as well as for marketers of high-value brands.

Use of Surrogate Indicators

Consumers frequently use an observable attribute of a product to indicate the performance of the product on a less observable attribute.[26] For example, a consumer might infer that since a product has a relatively high price it must also be high quality. *An attribute used to stand for or indicate another attribute* is known as a **surrogate indicator.** As discussed in Chapter 8, consumers often use such factors as price, advertising intensity, warranties, brand, and country of origin as surrogate indicators of quality—what we termed quality signals. Illustration 16–6 shows a company attempting to take advantage of a surrogate indicator of quality.

In general, surrogate indicators operate more strongly when consumers lack the expertise to make informed judgments on their own, when consumer motivation or interest in the decision is low, and when other quality-related information is lacking. Unfortunately, the relationship between surrogate indicators and functional measures of quality is often modest at best.[27] Obviously, when consumers rely on surrogates that have little relationship to actual quality, they are likely to make suboptimal decisions.

Surrogate indicators are based on consumers' beliefs that two features such as price level and quality level generally go together. Consumers also form beliefs that certain variables do not go together—such as *lightweight* and *strong; rich taste* and *low calories;* and *high fiber* and *high protein.*[28] Marketers attempting to promote the presence of two or more variables that many consumers believe to be mutually exclusive have a high risk of failure unless very convincing messages are used. Thus, it is important for marketers to fully understand consumers' beliefs about the feasible relationships of attributes related to their products.

The Relative Importance and Influence of Evaluative Criteria

The importance of evaluative criteria varies among individuals and also within the same individual over time. That is, although consumers often have a general sense of how important various criteria are, this can be influenced by a number of factors. These include:

- *Usage situation.* The situation in which a product or service is used (Chapter 13) can have important influences on the criteria used to make a choice. For example, speed of service and convenient location may be very important in selecting a restaurant over a lunch break but relatively unimportant when selecting a restaurant for a special occasion.[29]
- *Competitive context.* Generally speaking, the lower the variance across competing brands on a given evaluative criterion, the less influence it is likely to have in the decision process.[30] For example, you might think that the weight of a notebook computer is important. However, if all the brands you are considering weigh between 4 and 5 pounds, this attribute may suddenly become less of a factor in your decision.
- *Advertising effects.* Advertising can affect the importance of evaluative criteria in a number of ways. For example, an ad that increases attention and elaborative processing of an attribute can increase its perceived importance and/or influence in the decision.[31] As we saw in Chapters 8 and 9, contrast, prominence, and imagery are just a few of the tactics that can be used to enhance attention and elaboration.

Evaluative Criteria, Individual Judgments, and Marketing Strategy

Obviously, marketers must understand the evaluative criteria consumers use relative to their products and develop products that excel on those features. All aspects of the marketing communications mix must then communicate this excellence.

Marketers must also recognize and react to the ability of individuals to judge evaluative criteria, as well as to their tendency to use surrogate indicators. For example, most new consumer products are initially tested against competitors in blind tests. A **blind test** is one in which *the consumer is not aware of the product's brand name.* Such tests enable the marketer to evaluate the functional characteristics of the product and to determine if an advantage over a particular competitor has been obtained without the contaminating, or halo, effects of the brand name or the firm's reputation. *Can you see any drawbacks to only using blind tests in evaluating the market potential of products?*

Marketers also make direct use of surrogate indicators. Hyundai's 10-year, 100,000-mile warranty was a milestone in the industry when the company introduced it over a decade ago. The goal was to overcome low-quality perceptions related to another surrogate—namely, country of origin. That is, consumers in the United States were unsure of the quality of Korean-made automobiles at the time, and the warranty was designed to overcome this.

For image products such as fine wines, import beers, and so forth, higher prices tend to signal higher quality. Therefore, although for most products, higher prices lead to lower quantity demanded, for such image-based products, higher prices generally drive higher demand due to the quality that is inferred based on the higher price.

Brand names are also a strong surrogate for quality. Elmer's glue emphasized the well-established reputation of its brand in promoting its new super glue: Ads for Elmer's

Wonder Bond said, "Stick with a name you can trust." Firms with a limited reputation can sometimes form *brand alliances* with a reputable firm and gain from the quality associated with the known brand. Thus, a new brand of ice cream that used a branded ingredient such as M&M's would gain from M&M's quality image.[32] Country-of-origin themes such as "Made in America," "Italian Styling," or "German Engineering" are also common.

Marketers must also understand the factors that influence consumer perceptions of the importance of evaluative criteria. Understanding that attributes may be important but wield little influence on decisions because of similarity across competitors is a critical insight. It speaks to the need for marketers to examine critical *points of differentiation* on which the brand can be positioned. Advertising themes that emphasize specific usage occasions for which the brand is particularly appropriate can be effective, as can strategies such as imagery that draw attention to attributes on which the firm's brand excels.

DECISION RULES FOR ATTRIBUTE-BASED CHOICES

As we describe some of the choice rules consumers use to select among alternatives, remember that these rules are representations of imprecise and often nonconscious or low-effort mental processes. The following example is a good representation of a consumer using a complex choice rule (compensatory with one attribute weighted heavily):

> I really liked the Ford [minivan] a lot, but it had the back tailgate that lifted up instead of the doors that opened. I suspect that if that had been available we might have gone with the Ford instead because it was real close between the Ford and the GM. The lift gate in the back was the main difference, and we went with the General Motors because we liked the doors opening the way they did. I loved the way the Ford was designed on the inside. I loved the way it drove. I loved the way it felt and everything, but you are there manipulating all these kids and groceries and things and you have got to lift this thing, and it was very awkward. It was hard to lift, and if you are holding something you have got to steer all the kids back, or whack them in the head. So that was a big thing. You know it was a lot cheaper than the GM. It was between $1,000 and $2,000 less than General Motors, and because money was a factor, we did go ahead and actually at one point talk money with a [Ford] dealer. But we couldn't get the price difference down to where I was willing to deal with that tailgate is what it comes down to.[33]

Despite the fact that the choice rules we describe are not precise representations of consumer decisions, they do enhance our understanding of how consumers make decisions and provide guidance for marketing strategy.

Suppose you have six laptop computers in your evoked set and that you have assessed them on six evaluative criteria: price, weight, processor, battery life, after-sale support, and display quality. Further, suppose that each brand excels on one attribute but falls short on one or more of the remaining attributes, as shown in Table 16-1.

Which brand would you select? The answer would depend on the decision rule you utilize. Consumers commonly use five decision rules: conjunctive, disjunctive, elimination-by-aspects, lexicographic, and compensatory. More than one rule may be used in any given decision. The most common instance of this is using a relatively simple rule to reduce the number of alternatives considered and then to apply a more complex rule to choose among the remaining options.[34] An example would be eliminating from consideration all those apartments that are too far from campus or that rent for more than $700 per month (conjunctive decision rule). The choice from among the remaining apartments might involve carefully trading off among features such as convenience of location, price, presence of

Performance Levels on the Evaluative Criteria for Six Laptop Computers						TABLE 
	Consumer Perceptions*					
Evaluative Criteria	**Acer**	**HP**	**Compaq**	**Dell**	**Lenovo**	**Toshiba**
Price	5	3	3	4	2	1
Weight	3	4	5	4	3	4
Processor	5	5	5	2	5	5
Battery life	1	3	1	3	1	5
After-sale support	3	3	4	3	5	3
Display quality	3	3	3	5	3	3

*1 = Very poor; 5 = Very good.

a pool, and size of rooms (compensatory rule). Note that as the opening example demonstrated, some online shopping services such as PriceGrabber complete the first phase in this process by filtering out all brands that don't meet the consumer's criteria.

The first four rules we describe are *noncompensatory* rules. This means that a high level of one attribute cannot offset a low level of another. In the apartment example, the consumer would not consider an apartment that was right next to campus if it cost more than $700 per month. An excellent location could not compensate for an inappropriate price. In contrast, the last rule we describe is a *compensatory* rule in which consumers average across attribute levels. This allows a high level of one value to offset a low value of another.

Finally, note that the conjunctive and disjunctive decision rules may produce a set of acceptable alternatives, whereas the remaining rules generally produce a single "best" alternative.

Conjunctive Decision Rule

The **conjunctive decision rule** establishes minimum required performance standards for each evaluative criterion and selects the first or all brands that meet or exceed these minimum standards. Thus, in making the decision on the computer, you would say, "I'll consider all (or I'll buy the first) brands that are acceptable on the attributes I think are important." For example, assume that the following represent your minimum standards:

Price	3
Weight	4
Processor	3
Battery life	1
After-sale support	2
Display quality	3

Any brand of computer falling below any of these minimum standards (cutoff points) would be eliminated from further consideration. Referring to Table 16-1, we can see that four computers are eliminated—Lenovo, Acer, Dell, and Toshiba. These are the computers that failed to meet all the minimum standards. Under these circumstances, the two remaining brands may be equally satisfying. Or you might use another decision rule to select a single brand from these two alternatives.

ILLUSTRATION 16–7

This ad tries to assure consumers its brand has every feature they might need. This is consistent with consumers' using a conjunctive decision rule.

Because individuals have limited ability to process information, the conjunctive rule is frequently used to reduce the size of the information-processing task to some manageable level. This is often done in the purchase of such products as homes, computers, and bicycles; in the rental of apartments; or in the selection of vacation options. A conjunctive rule is used to eliminate alternatives that are out of a consumer's price range, are outside the location preferred, or do not offer other desired features. After eliminating those alternatives not providing these features, the consumer may use another decision rule to make a brand choice among those remaining alternatives that satisfy these minimum standards.

The conjunctive decision rule is commonly used in many low-involvement purchases as well. In such a purchase, the consumer generally evaluates a set of brands one at a time and selects the first brand that meets all the minimum requirements.

If the conjunctive decision rule is used by a target market, it is critical to meet or surpass the consumers' minimum requirement on each criterion. For low-involvement purchases, consumers often purchase the first brand that does so. For such products, extensive distribution and dominant shelf space are important. It is also necessary to understand how consumers "break ties" if the first satisfactory option is not chosen. The ad in Illustration 16–7 tries to assure consumers that its brand has every feature they might need.

Disjunctive Decision Rule

The **disjunctive decision rule** *establishes a minimum level of performance for each important attribute* (often a fairly high level that sets the performance standard very high and makes it hard for a brand to attain). All brands that meet or exceed the performance level for *any* key attribute are considered acceptable. Using this rule, you would say, "I'll consider all (or buy the first) brands that perform really well on any attribute I consider important." Assume that you are using a disjunctive decision rule and the attribute cutoff points shown below:

Price	5
Weight	5
Processor	Not critical
Battery life	Not critical
After-sale support	Not critical
Display quality	5

You would find Acer (price), Compaq (weight), and Dell (display quality) to warrant further consideration (see Table 16-1). As with the conjunctive decision rule, you might purchase the first brand you find acceptable, use another decision rule to choose among the three, or add additional criteria to your list.

When the disjunctive decision rule is used by a target market, it is critical to meet or surpass the consumers' requirements on at least one of the key criteria. This should be emphasized in advertising messages and on the product package. Because consumers often purchase the first brand that meets or exceeds one of the requirements, extensive distribution and dominant shelf space are important. Again, it is also necessary to understand how consumers break ties if the first satisfactory option is not chosen. Illustration 16–8 stresses one important attribute and would be appropriate for consumers who placed a high importance on this attribute and used a disjunctive decision rule.

Elimination-by-Aspects Decision Rule

The **elimination-by-aspects decision rule** requires the consumer to rank the evaluative criteria in terms of their importance and to establish a cutoff point for each criterion. All brands are first considered on the most important criterion. Those that do not meet or exceed the cutoff point are dropped (eliminated) from further consideration. If more than one brand remains in the set after this first elimination phase, the process is repeated on those brands for the second most important criterion. This continues until only one brand remains. Thus, the consumer's logic is, "I want to buy the brand that has a high level of an important attribute that other brands do not have."

Consider the rank order and cutoff points shown below. What would you choose using the elimination-by-aspects rule?

	Rank	Cutoff Point
Price	1	3
Weight	2	4
Display quality	3	4
Processor	4	3
After-sale support	5	3
Battery life	6	3

Price would eliminate Lenovo and Toshiba (see Table 16-1). Of those remaining, Compaq, HP, and Dell meet or exceed the weight hurdle (Acer is eliminated). Notice that Toshiba also meets the minimum weight requirement but would not be considered because it had been eliminated in the initial consideration of price. Only Dell meets or exceeds the third requirement, display quality.

560   Part Four   Consumer Decision Process

Using the elimination-by-aspects rule, you end up with a choice that has all the desired features of all the other alternatives, plus one more.

For a target market using the elimination-by-aspects rule, it is critical to meet or surpass the consumers' requirements on one more (in order) of the criteria used than the competition. This competitive superiority should be emphasized in advertising messages and on the product package. Firms can also attempt to alter the relative importance that consumers assign to the evaluative criteria. The ad in Illustration 16–9 is consistent with this rule. It indicates that the brand has desirable features other competitors do not have.

Lexicographic Decision Rule

The **lexicographic decision rule** *requires the consumer to rank the criteria in order of importance.* The consumer then selects the brand that performs *best* on the most important attribute. If two or more brands tie on this attribute, they are evaluated on the second most important attribute. This continues through the attributes until one brand outperforms the others. The consumer's thinking is something like this: "I want to get the brand that does best on the attribute of most importance to me. If there is a tie, I'll break it by choosing the one that does best on my second most important criterion."

The lexicographic decision rule is similar to the elimination-by-aspects rule. The difference is that the lexicographic rule seeks maximum performance at each stage, whereas the elimination-by-aspects seeks satisfactory performance at each stage. Thus, using the lexicographic rule and the data from the elimination-by-aspects example above would result in

ILLUSTRATION 16–9

Elimination-by-aspects choices seek a brand that has a high level of an attribute that other brands do not have.

the selection of Acer, because it has the best performance on the most important attribute. Had Acer been rated a 4 on price, it would be tied with Dell. Then, Dell would be chosen based on its superior weight rating.

When this rule is being used by a target market, the firm should try to be superior to the competition on *the* key attribute. This competitive superiority should be emphasized in advertising. It is essential that the product at least equal the performance of all other competitors on the most important criterion. Outstanding performance on lesser criteria will not matter if a competitor is superior on the most important attribute. If a competitive advantage is not possible on the most important feature, attention should be shifted to the second most important (assuming equal performance on the most important one). If it is not possible to meet or beat the competition on the key attribute, the firm must attempt to make another attribute more important.

The ad shown in Illustration 16–10 emphasizes one key feature, presumably the most important to the company's target market. To the extent that its customers use a lexicographic rule, this ad should be effective in driving choice of this brand.

Compensatory Decision Rule

The four previous rules are *noncompensatory* decision rules, because very good performance on one evaluative criterion cannot compensate for poor performance on another evaluative criterion. On occasion, consumers may wish to average out some very good

features with some less attractive features of a product in determining overall brand preference. That appears to be the case with the new minipackage craze being used by companies such as Frito-Lay, Nabisco, and Keebler. Some consumers have complained that the prices are high on a per-serving basis. Frito-Lay and others are counting on the fact that the convenience and calorie-control elements of their new 100-calorie packets will offset price in the minds of their target consumer. That is, they assume the target market will use a compensatory decision rule for this product. It appears this is the case, as explained by one customer who balked at the notion of buying in bulk and then measuring out 100-calorie servings into baggies:

> If you want to mess with those baggies, that's fine. But for those of us in the real world, we'll take the 100 cal packs. Sure, we might pay a few more pennies per ounce, but we also can't sneak any extra in while refilling.[35]

The **compensatory decision rule** states that *the brand that rates highest on the sum of the consumer's judgments of the relevant evaluative criteria will be chosen.* This can be illustrated as

$$R_b = \sum_{i=1}^{n} W_i B_{ib}$$

Where

R_b = overall rating of brand b

W_i = importance or weight attached to evaluative criterion i

B_{ib} = evaluation of brand b on evaluative criterion i

n = number of evaluative criteria considered relevant

This is the same as the multiattribute attitude model described in Chapter 11. If you used the relative importance scores shown below, which brand would you choose using the compensatory rule?

	Importance Score
Price	30
Weight	25
Processor	10
Battery life	05
After-sale support	10
Display quality	20
Total	100

Using this rule, you would choose Dell, since it has the highest preference (see Table 16-1). The calculations for Dell are as follows:

$$R_{Dell} = 30(4) + 25(4) + 10(2) + 5(3) + 10(3) + 20(5)$$
$$= 120 + 100 + 20 + 15 + 30 + 100$$
$$= 385$$

Products and services targeting consumers likely to use a compensatory rule can offset low performance on some features with relatively high performance on others. However, it is important to have a performance level at or near the competition's on the more important features because they receive more weight in the decision than do other attributes. Recall the description of the minivan purchase from the beginning of this section. This customer preferred most of the features of the Ford but bought the GM because Ford was very weak on one key attribute. However, the consumer did express a willingness to change the decision had the price differential been greater. Thus, for compensatory decisions, the total mix of the relevant attributes must be considered to be superior to those of the competition.

The compensatory rule tends to be the most time consuming and mentally taxing. Also, consumers often find it difficult to consider more than a few attributes at a time in the trade-off process. In addition, as competitors enter the market, they can change the attractiveness of existing alternatives. This situational effect is discussed in Consumer Insight 16-1.

Summary of Decision Rules

As shown below, each decision rule yields a somewhat different choice. Therefore, marketers must understand which decision rules are being used by target consumers in order to position a product within this decision framework.

Decision Rule	Brand Choice
Conjunctive	HP, Compaq
Disjunctive	Dell, Compaq, Acer
Elimination-by-aspects	Dell
Lexicographic	Acer
Compensatory	Dell

Situational Influences on Consumer Choice

Rational choice theory suggests that consumer choices and preferences should be independent of the context. As a simple example, it is assumed that consumers will evaluate a $5 discount the same way regardless of context. However, this is not the case. Consumers tend to perceive the value of the $5 discount as higher when it is on a product originally priced at $10 and lower on a product originally priced at $100. The reason goes back to Chapter 8 and relative preferences. Consumers appear to evaluate the $5 savings *in the context of* or *relative to* the original price of the product.

In a similar way, consumers are affected by the competitive context in which they make choices, or what we referred to in Chapter 13 as the purchase situation. There are numerous context effects on consumer choice. Here we discuss the compromise effect.[36] We begin with Choice Set 1 (left graph) in which there are two apartments (A and B) evaluated on two attributes (distance from campus in miles and quality on a 1–100 scale where 100 is best). As the graph on the left shows, option A is farther from campus (a negative) but higher quality (a positive), while option B is nearer to campus (a positive) but lower quality (a negative). Choosing between these apartments involves a *compensatory choice process* in

which distance and quality must be traded off against each other. As configured here, the apartments split the market equally. That is, 50 percent of the students chose option A (presumably weighting quality more heavily) and 50 percent chose option B (presumably weighting distance more heavily).

Now consider Choice Set 2 (right graph). In this context, there is a third apartment that consumers are aware of but that is not currently available. It is closer than A or B in terms of distance (a positive) but poorer than A or B in terms of quality (a negative). Rational choice theory assumes that if an option such as C is included, consumers should still prefer the brands the same way as they did previously. Particularly since option C is not even available, rational choice theory would suggest that options A and B would hold steady at 50 percent of the market each. However, this is not what happens. Instead, adding option C, even though not available for rent, increases B's share up to 66 percent!

This is called the compromise effect, because, adding option C made option B the compromise solution. It is a compromise between the two extremes of A (farthest away, best quality) and C (nearest, worst quality). Consumers prefer compromise options and find them easy to justify (a metagoal). The compromise effect

---

Research clearly indicates that people do use these decision rules.[37] Low-involvement purchases generally involve relatively simple decision rules (conjunctive, disjunctive, elimination-by-aspects, or lexicographic), because consumers will attempt to minimize the mental cost of such decisions.[38] High-involvement decisions and purchases involving considerable perceived risk tend to increase evaluation efforts and often may involve not only more complex rules (compensatory) but stages of decision making, with different attributes being evaluated using different rules at each stage.[39] Of course, individual, product, and situational characteristics also influence the type of decision rule used.[40]

A marketing manager must first determine which rule or combination of rules the target consumers will most likely use in a particular purchase situation and then develop the appropriate marketing strategy.

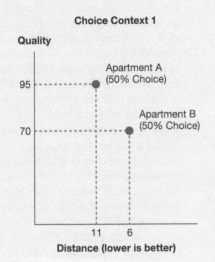

Choice Context 1

Quality

95 ┄┄┄┄┄┄● Apartment A
(50% Choice)

70 ┄┄┄┄┄┄┄┄● Apartment B
(50% Choice)

11   6

Distance (lower is better)

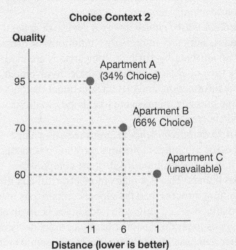

Choice Context 2

Quality

95 ┄┄┄┄┄● Apartment A
(34% Choice)

70 ┄┄┄┄┄┄┄┄● Apartment B
(66% Choice)

60 ┄┄┄┄┄┄┄┄┄┄● Apartment C
(unavailable)

11   6   1

Distance (lower is better)

seems strongest when the compromise brand is the more familiar brand in the set.

The compromise effect has important implications for marketers. Real estate agents who want to sell a particular property might first show their clients an unavailable property that makes their available property seem like the compromise option to increase the chances their client will purchase it. For retailers, since consumers often search and evaluate alternatives online and then go to a physical store to purchase the selected brand, an "online only" option (option C) could be created to make

their in-store options seem like compromise options to increase their choice share.

Critical Thinking Questions

1. Why does the compromise effect contradict rational choice theory?

2. Beyond being easy to justify, can you think of other reasons why consumers prefer compromise options?

3. Do you see any ethical issues related to strategies designed to position brands as compromise alternatives? Explain.

SUMMARY

LO1: Discuss how actual consumer choice often differs from rational choice theory

Rational choice theory assumes that (1) consumers seek one optimal solution to a problem and choose on that basis, (2) consumers have the skill and motivation to find the optimal solution, and (3) the optimal choice does not change as a function of the situation. However, all these assumptions have been shown to be incorrect for at least some consumer decisions.

Reasons include that consumers have alternative *meta-goals*, consumers are subject to *bounded rationality*, and situations actually influence consumer perceptions of the optimal choice.

LO2: Summarize the types of choice processes consumers engage in

Affective choice tends to be more holistic in nature. The brand is not decomposed into distinct components, each of which is evaluated separately from the whole. Decisions based on affect use the "How do I feel about it" heuristic or decision rule and tend to occur in response to *consummatory motives.*

Attitude-based choice involves the use of general attitudes, summary impressions, intuitions, or heuristics; no attribute-by-attribute comparisons are made at the time of choice. Lower purchase involvement, scarce information, and certain situational factors such as time pressure increase the likelihood of attitude-based choice.

Attribute-based choice requires the knowledge of specific attributes at the time the choice is made, and it involves attribute-by-attribute comparisons across brands. This is a much more effortful and time-consuming process than the global comparisons made when affective and attitude-based choice is involved. It also tends to produce a more nearly optimal decision. Higher purchase involvement, easily accessible brand-attribute information, and situational factors such as lower time pressure increase the likelihood of attribute-based choice.

LO3: Explain evaluative criteria and their measurement

Evaluative criteria are the various features or benefits a consumer looks for in response to a specific problem. They are the performance levels or characteristics consumers use to compare different brands in view of their particular consumption problem.

The measurement of (1) which evaluative criteria are used by the consumer, (2) how the consumer perceives the various alternatives on each criterion, and (3) the relative importance of each criterion is a critical first step in utilizing evaluative criteria to develop marketing strategy. The measurement task is not easy although a number of techniques are available, including *perceptual mapping,* the *constant-sum scale,* and *conjoint analysis.*

LO4: Describe the role of evaluative criteria in consumer judgment and marketing strategy

The ability of an individual to distinguish between similar stimuli is called *sensory discrimination.* Some evaluative criteria such as price, size, and color can be judged easily and accurately by consumers. Other criteria, such as quality, durability, and health benefits, are much more difficult to judge. In general, research indicates that *individuals typically do not notice relatively small differences between brands or changes in brand attributes.* In addition, the complexity of many products and services as well as the fact that some aspects of performance can be judged only after extensive use makes accurate brand comparisons difficult. In such cases, consumers often use price, brand name, or some other variable as a *surrogate indicator* of quality. Marketers can use surrogate cues as a means to affect consumer choice in situations where consumers find it difficult to make accurate assessments of alternatives. Marketers can also attempt to influence the relative importance of attributes in such a way as to favor their brands through advertising as well as position in regards to specific usage occasions.

LO5: Summarize the five decision rules for attribute-based choice and their strategic relevance

When consumers judge alternative brands on several evaluative criteria, they must have some method to select one brand from the various choices. Decision rules serve this function. A decision rule specifies how a consumer compares two or more brands. Five commonly used decision rules are *disjunctive, conjunctive, lexicographic, elimination-by-aspects,* and *compensatory.* The decision rules work best with functional products and cognitive decisions. Marketing managers must be aware of the decision rule(s) used by the target market, because different decision rules require different marketing strategies.

KEY TERMS

Affective choice 545
Attitude-based choice 546
Attribute-based choice 547
Blind test 555
Bounded rationality 544
Compensatory decision rule 562
Conjoint analysis 552

Conjunctive decision rule 557
Consummatory motives 546
Disjunctive decision rule 558
Elimination-by-aspects decision
  rule 559
Evaluative criteria 548
Instrumental motives 546

Lexicographic decision rule 560
Metagoal 544
Perceptual mapping 551
Projective techniques 551
Sensory discrimination 554
Surrogate indicator 554

INTERNET EXERCISES

1. Use Dell's recommendation feature to select a laptop computer (hint: go to www.dell.com, select "small and medium business," then click on "laptop"). What decision rule or combination of rules does this decision aid reflect? What type of consumer would be most likely to utilize this adviser function?

2. Visit Orbitz.com. What decision rule and evaluative criteria seem to dominate? Why do you think this is?

3. Visit three websites for brands in the same product category. Using the brand information provided and the manner in which it is provided, determine what decision rule each brand appears to assume its market uses. If there are differences, how would you explain them?

DDB LIFE STYLE STUDY™ DATA ANALYSES

1. Based on the DDB Tables 1B through 7B, what characterizes an individual who would say, "In making big decisions, I go with my heart rather than my head"? How does this relate to affective decision making? What are the marketing implications of this?

REVIEW QUESTIONS

1. What is *rational choice* theory?
2. What is meant by *bounded rationality*?
3. What is a *metagoal*?
4. What are three common metagoals for consumer decisions?
5. What is *affective choice*, and when is it most likely to occur?
6. What is the difference between *consummatory motives* and *instrumental motives*?
7. How does *attribute-based choice* differ from *attitude-based choice*? When is each most likely?
8. What are *evaluative criteria*, and on what characteristics can they vary?
9. How can you determine which evaluative criteria consumers use?
10. What methods are available for measuring consumers' judgments of brand performance on specific attributes?
11. How can the importance assigned to evaluative criteria be assessed?
12. What is *sensory discrimination*, and what role does it play in the evaluation of products? What is meant by a *just noticeable difference*?
13. What are *surrogate indicators*? How are they used in the consumer evaluation process?
14. What factors influence the *importance* of evaluative criteria?
15. What is the *conjunctive decision rule*?
16. What is the *disjunctive decision rule*?
17. What is the *elimination-by-aspects decision rule*?
18. What is the *lexicographic decision rule*?
19. What is the *compensatory decision rule*?
20. How can knowledge of consumers' evaluative criteria and criteria importance be used in developing marketing strategy?
21. How can knowledge of the decision rules consumers might use in a certain purchase assist a firm in developing marketing strategy?

DISCUSSION QUESTIONS

22. Respond to the questions in Consumer Insight 16-1.
23. Would you use an attribute-based or an attitude-based decision approach to purchasing (or renting or giving to) the following? Which, if any, situational factors would change your approach?

a. Adopting a pet from a shelter
b. A movie
c. A digital reader
d. A BBQ grill
e. A personal trainer
f. Athletic shoes
g. A new shampoo
h. An apartment
i. A smartphone
j. Habitat for Humanity

24. Repeat Question 23, but speculate on how your instructor would answer. In what ways might his or her answer differ from yours? Why?

25. For which, if any, of the options in Question 23 would you make an affective decision? What role would situational factors play?

26. What metagoals might you have, and what would be their relative importance to you, in purchasing (or renting or giving to) the options in Question 23?

27. List the evaluative criteria and the importance of each that you would use in purchasing (or renting or giving to) the options in Question 23.

Would situational factors change the criteria? The importance weights? Why?

28. Repeat Question 27, but speculate on how your instructor would answer. In what ways might his or her answer differ from yours? Why?

29. Describe a purchase decision for which you used affective choice, one for which you used attitude-based choice, and one for which you used attribute-based choice. Why did the type of decision process you used vary?

30. Identify five products for which surrogate indicators may be used as evaluative criteria in a brand choice decision. Why are the indictors used, and how might a firm enhance their use (i.e., strengthen their importance)?

31. The table below represents a particular consumer's evaluative criteria, criteria importance, acceptable level of performance, and judgments of performance with respect to several brands of mopeds. Discuss the brand choice this consumer would make when using the lexicographic, compensatory, and conjunctive decision rules.

Evaluative Criteria	Criteria Importance	Minimum Acceptable Performance	Alternative Brands					
			Motron	Vespa	Cimatti	Garelli	Puch	Motobecane
Price	30	4	2	4	2	4	2	4
Horsepower	15	3	4	2	5	5	4	5
Weight	5	2	3	3	3	3	3	3
Gas economy	35	3	4	4	3	2	4	5
Color selection	10	3	4	4	3	2	5	2
Frame	5	2	4	2	3	3	3	3

Note: 1 = Very poor; 2 = Poor; 3 = Fair; 4 = Good; and 5 = Very good.

32. Describe the decision rule(s) you used or would use in buying, renting, or giving to the options listed for Question 23. Would you use different rules in different situations? Which ones? Why? Would any of these involve an affective choice?

33. Describe your last two major and your last two minor purchases. What role did emotions

or feelings play? How did they differ? What evaluative criteria and decision rules did you use for each? Why?

34. Discuss surrogate indicators that could be used to evaluate the perceived quality of the products or activities listed in Question 23.

APPLICATION ACTIVITIES

35. Present 10 students with the choice set from the left panel of Consumer Insight 16-1 and present a different set of 10 students with the choice set from the right panel. Do you observe the compromise

effect (choice share of option B goes up with the addition of the nonavailable option C)? Have the students who chose the compromise alternative explain their choice—what reasons do they provide?

36. Conduct an extensive interview with two students who recently made a major purchase. Have them describe the process they went through. Report your results. If each represented a market segment, what are the strategy implications?

37. Develop a list of evaluative criteria that students might use in evaluating alternative apartments they might rent. After listing these criteria, go to the local newspaper or student newspaper, select several apartments, and list them in a table similar to the one in Question 31. Then have five other students evaluate this information and have each indicate the apartment they would rent if given only those alternatives. Next, ask them to express the importance they attach to each evaluative criterion, using a 100-point constant sum scale. Finally, provide them with a series of statements that describe different decision rules and ask them to indicate the one that best describes the way they made their choice. Calculate the choice they should have made given their importance ratings and stated decision rules. Have them explain any inconsistent choices. Report your results.

38. Develop a short questionnaire to elicit the evaluative criteria consumers might use in selecting the following. Also, have each respondent indicate the relative importance he or she attaches to each of the evaluative criteria. Then, working with several other students, combine your information and develop a segmentation strategy based on consumer evaluative criteria and criteria importance. Finally, develop an advertisement for each market segment to indicate that their needs would be served by your brand.
    a. Wristwatch
    b. Running shoes
    c. Movie
    d. Fast-food restaurant
    e. Credit card
    f. Charity
    g. Home theater system
    h. Health club

39. Set up a taste test experiment to determine if volunteer taste testers can perceive a just noticeable difference between three different brands of the following. To set up the experiment, store each test brand in a separate but identical container and label the containers L, M, and N. Provide volunteer taste testers with an adequate opportunity to evaluate each brand before asking them to state their identification of the actual brands represented as L, M, and N. Evaluate the results and discuss the marketing implications of these results.
    a. Colas
    b. Diet colas
    c. Lemon-lime drinks
    d. Carbonated waters
    e. Chips
    f. Orange juices

40. For a product considered high in social status, develop a questionnaire that measures the evaluative criteria of that product, using both a *direct* and an *indirect* method of measurement. Compare the results and discuss their similarities and differences and which evaluative criteria are most likely to be used in brand choice.

41. Find and copy or describe an ad that uses a surrogate indicator. Is it effective? Why? Why do you think the firm uses this approach?

42. Find and copy or describe an ad that attempts to change the importance consumers assign to product class evaluative criteria. Is it effective? Why? Why do you think the firm uses this approach?

43. Find and copy or describe two ads that are based on affective choice. Why do you think the firm uses this approach? Are the ads effective? Why?

44. Interview a salesperson for one of the following products. Ascertain the evaluative criteria, importance weights, decision rules, and surrogate indicators that he or she believes consumers use when purchasing this product. What marketing implications are suggested if their beliefs are accurate for large segments?
    a. Luxury cars
    b. Kitchen furniture
    c. Air purification systems
    d. Cosmetics
    e. Ski clothes
    f. Fine art

REFERENCES

1. This opener is based on W. Wang and I. Benbasat, "Recommendations for Electronic Commerce," *Journal of Management Information Systems*, Spring 2007, pp. 217–46;

G. N. Punj and R. Moore, "Smart Versus Knowledgeable Online Recommendation Agents," *Journal of Interactive Marketing*, Autumn 2007, pp. 46–60; L. Aksoy et al. "Should Recommendation

Agents Think Like People?" *Journal of Service Research,* May 2006, pp. 297–315; A. Herrmann et al., "Consumer Decision Making and Variety of Offerings," *Psychology & Marketing* 26, no. 4 (2009), pp. 333–58; C. Qui, Y. H. Lee, and C. W. M. Yeung, "Suppressing Feelings," *Journal of Consumer Psychology* 19 (2009), pp. 427–39; and J. Loechner, "Online Research a Significant Part of Consumer Buying," *MediaPost,* February 22, 2011, www.mediapost.com, accessed June 15, 2011.

2. See, for example, J. R. Bettman, M. F. Luce, and J. W. Payne, "Constructive Consumer Choice Processes," *Journal of Consumer Research,* December 1998, pp. 187–217; C. L. Brown and G. S. Carpenter, "Why Is the Trivial Important?" *Journal of Consumer Research,* March 2000, pp. 372–85; J. Swait and W. Adamowicz, "The Influence of Task Complexity on Consumer Choice," *Journal of Consumer Research,* June 2001, pp. 135–48; and M. Heitmann, D. R. Lehmann, and A. Herrmann, "Choice Goal Attainment and Decision and Consumption Satisfaction," *Journal of Marketing Research,* May 2007, pp. 234–50. See also O. Amir and D. Ariely, "Decisions by Rules," *Journal of Marketing Research,* February 2007, pp. 142–52.

3. For a discussion and related research see G. A. Haynes, "Testing Boundaries of the Choice Overload Phenomenon," *Psychology and Marketing,* March 2009, pp. 204–12.

4. E. Hall, "Overwhelmed U.K. Online Shoppers Can Justbuythisone," *Advertising Age,* December 16, 2010.

5. B. Mittal, "A Study of the Concept of Affective Choice Mode for Consumer Decisions," in *Advances in Consumer Research,* vol. 21, ed. C. T. Allen and D. R. John (Provo, UT: Association for Consumer Research, 1994), p. 256.

6. J. F. Durgee and G. C. O'Connor, "Why Some Products 'Just Feel Right,'" in *Advances in Consumer Research,* vol. 22, ed. F. R. Kardes and M. Sujan (Provo, UT: Association for Consumer Research, 1995), p. 652.

7. See M. T. Pham et al., "Affect Monitoring and the Primacy of Feelings in Judgment," *Journal of Consumer Research,* September 2001, pp. 167–87. See also P. R. Darke, A. Chattopadhyay, and L. Ashworth, "The Importance and Functional Significance of Affective Cues in Consumer Choice," *Journal of Consumer Research,* December 2006, pp. 322–28.

8. M. T. Pham, "Representativeness, Relevance, and the Use of Feelings in Decision Making," *Journal of Consumer Research,* September 1998, pp. 144–59. For a more elaborate model of affective appraisal and its influence on subsequent judgment, see C. W. M. Yeung and R. S. Wyer Jr., "Affect, Appraisal, and Consumer Judgment," *Journal of Consumer Research,* September 2004, pp. 412–24.

9. See also R. Dhar and K. Wertenbroch, "Consumer Choice between Hedonic and Utilitarian Goods," *Journal of Marketing Research,* February 2000, pp. 60–71.

10. See B. Shiv and A. Fedorikhin, "Heart and Mind in Conflict," *Journal of Consumer Research,* December 1999, pp. 278–91.

11. J. A. Ruth, "Promoting a Brand's Emotional Benefits," *Journal of Consumer Psychology* 11, no. 2 (2001), pp. 99–113; and J. C. Sweeney and G. N. Soutar, "Consumer Perceived Value," *Journal of Retailing* 77 (2001), pp. 203–20.

12. See P. Krishnamurthy and M. Sujan, "Retrospection versus Anticipation," *Journal of Consumer Research,* June 1999, pp. 55–69.

See also B. Shiv and J. Huber, "The Impact of Anticipating Satisfaction on Consumer Choice," *Journal of Consumer Research,* September 2000, pp. 202–16; and C. P. S. Fong and R. S. Wyer Jr., "Cultural, Social, and Emotional Determinants of Decisions under Uncertainty," *Organizational Behavior and Human Decision Processes* 90 (2003), pp. 304–22.

13. This section is based on S. P. Mantell and F. R. Kardes, "The Role of Direction of Comparison, Attribute-Based Processing, and Attitude-Based Processing in Consumer Preference," *Journal of Consumer Research,* March 1999, pp. 335–52. For a discussion of the specific role of advertising-based attitudes, see W. E. Baker, "The Diagnosticity of Advertising Generated Brand Attitudes in Brand Choice Contexts," *Journal of Consumer Psychology* 11, no. 2 (2001), pp. 129–39.

14. See R. Dhar, S. M. Nowlis, and S. J. Sherman, "Comparison Effects on Preference Construction," *Journal of Consumer Research,* December 1999, pp. 293–306.

15. C. Qui, Y. H. Lee, and C. W. M. Yeung, "Suppressing Feelings," *Journal of Consumer Psychology,* 19, 2009, 427–39.

16. G. Kalyanaram and J. D. C. Little, "An Empirical Analysis of Latitude of Price Acceptance in Consumer Package Goods," *Journal of Consumer Research,* December 1994, pp. 408–18.

17. See S. Hoeffler and D. Ariely, "Constructing Stable Preferences," *Journal of Consumer Psychology* 8, no. 2 (1999), pp. 113–39; and A. V. Muthukrishnan and F. R. Kardes, "Persistent Preferences for Product Attributes," *Journal of Consumer Research,* June 2001, pp. 89–102.

18. P. H. Bloch, "Seeking the Ideal Form," *Journal of Marketing,* July 1995, pp. 16–29; and Dhar and Wertenbroch, "Consumer Choice between Hedonic and Utilitarian Goods." See also D. Horsky, P. Nelson, and S. S. Posavac, "Stating Preference for the Ethereal but Choosing the Concrete," *Journal of Consumer Psychology* 14, no. 1/2 (2004), pp. 132–40.

19. D. J. Mitchell, B. E. Kahn, and S. C. Knasko, "There's Something in the Air," *Journal of Consumer Research,* September 1995, pp. 229–38; D. R. Lichtenstein, R. G. Netemeyer, and S. Burton, "Assessing the Domain Specificity of Deal Proneness," *Journal of Consumer Research,* December 1995, pp. 314–26; D. R. Lichtenstein, S. Burton, and R. G. Netemeyer, "An Examination of Deal Proneness across Sales Promotion Types," *Journal of Retailing* 2 (1997), pp. 283–97; and V. Ramaswamy and S. S. Srinivasan, "Coupon Characteristics and Redemption Intentions," *Psychology & Marketing,* January 1998, pp. 50–80.

20. See, e.g., R. Pieters and L. Warlop, "Visual Attention during Brand Choice," *International Journal of Research in Marketing* 16 (1999), pp. 1–16 .

21. B. L. Bagus, "The Consumer Durable Replacement Buyer," *Journal of Marketing,* January 1991, pp. 42–51.

22. A. Kirmani and P. Wright, "Procedural Learning, Consumer Decision Making, and Marketing Choice," *Marketing Letters* 4, no. 1 (1993), pp. 39–48; G. S. Carpenter, R. Glazer, and K. Nakamoto, "Meaningful Brands from Meaningless Differentiation," *Journal of Marketing Research,* August 1994, pp. 339–50; and S. M. Broniarczyk and A. D. Gershoff, "Meaningless Differentiation Revisited," in *Advances in Consumer Research,* vol. 24, ed. M. Bruck and D. J. MacInnis (Provo, UT: Association for Consumer Research, 1997), pp. 223–28.

23. B. Abrams, "Hanes Finds L'eggs Methods Don't Work with Cosmetics," *The Wall Street Journal,* February 3, 1983, p. 33.

24. See S. H. Ang, G. J. Gorn, and C. B. Weinberg, "The Evaluation of Time-Dependent Attributes," *Psychology & Marketing,* January 1996, pp. 19–35.

25. P. M. Parker, "Sweet Lemons," *Journal of Marketing Research,* August 1995, pp. 291–307; S. Shapiro and M. T. Spence, "Factors Affecting Encoding, Retrieval, and Alignment of Sensory Attributes in a Memory-Based Brand Choice Task," *Journal of Consumer Research,* March 2002, pp. 603–17; and B.-K. Lee and W.-N. Lee, "The Effect of Information Overload on Consumer Choice Quality in an On-Line Environment," *Psychology & Marketing,* March 2004, pp. 159–83.

26. See A. Kirmani and A. R. Rao, "No Pain, No Gain," *Journal of Marketing,* April 2000, pp. 66–79.

27. See, e.g., V. P. Norris, "The Economic Effects of Advertising," *Current Issues and Research in Advertising,* 1984, pp. 39–134; S. Burton and D. R. Lichtenstein, "Assessing the Relationship between Perceived and Objective Price-Quality," in *Advances in Consumer Research,* vol. 27, ed. M. E. Goldberg, G. Gorn, and R. W. Pollay (Provo, UT: Association for Consumer Research, 1990), pp. 715–22; and D. J. Faulds, O. Grunewald, and D. Johnson, "A Cross-National Investigation of the Relationship between the Price and Quality of Consumer Products," *Journal of Global Marketing* 8, no. 1 (1994), pp. 7–25.

28. K. M. Elliott and D. W. Roach, "Are Consumers Evaluating Your Products the Way You Think and Hope They Are?" *Journal of Consumer Marketing,* Spring 1991, pp. 5–14; and J. Baumgartner, "On the Utility of Consumers' Theories in Judgments of Covariation," *Journal of Consumer Research,* March 1995, pp. 634–43.

29. See S. Ratneshwar et al., "Benefit Salience and Consumers' Selective Attention to Product Features," *International Journal of Research in Marketing* 14 (1997), pp. 245–59; R. Dhar and I. Simonson, "Making Complementary Choices in Consumption Episodes," *Journal of Marketing Research,* February 1999, pp. 29–44; and J. K. H. Lee and J. H. Steckel, "Consumer Strategies for Purchasing Assortments within a Single Product Class," *Journal of Retailing* 75, no. 3 (1999), pp. 387–403.

30. See, e.g., P. W. J. Verlegh, H. N. J. Schifferstein, and D. R. Wittink, "Range and Number-of-Levels Effects in Derived and Stated Measures of Attribute Importance," *Marketing Letters* 13, no. 1 (2002), pp. 41–52.

31. M. P. Gardner, "Advertising Effects on Attributes Recalled and Criteria Used for Brand Evaluations," *Journal of Consumer Research,* December 1983, pp. 310–18; S. B. MacKenzie, "The Role of Attention in Mediating the Effect of Advertising on Attribute Importance," *Journal of Consumer Research,* September 1986, pp. 174–95; and G. D. Olsen, "Creating the Contrast," *Journal of Advertising,* Winter 1995, pp. 29–44.

32. A. R. Rao, L. Qu, and R. W. Ruekert, "Signaling Unobservable Product Quality through a Brand Ally," *Journal of Marketing Research,* May 1999, pp. 258–68; and C. Janiszewski and S. M. J. van Osselaer, "A Connectionist Model of Brand-Quality Associations," *Journal of Marketing Research,* August 2000, pp. 331–50.

33. C. J. Thompson, "Interpreting Consumers," *Journal Marketing Research,* November 1997, p. 443. Published by the American Marketing Association; reprinted with permission.

34. See G. Haubl and V. Trifts, "Consumer Decision Making in Online Shopping Environments," *Marketing Science,* Winter 2000, pp. 2–21.

35. S. Thompson, "Food Marketers Count on Snacks," *Advertising Age,* April 24, 2006, p. 4.

36. This insight is based on I. Simonson, "Choice Based on Reasons," *Journal of Consumer Research,* September 1989, pp. 158–74; S. Sheng, A. M. Parker, K. Nakamoto, "Understanding the Mechanism and Determinants of Compromise Effects," *Psychology & Marketing,* July 2005, 591–608; and F. Sinn et al., "Compromising the Compromise Effect," *Marketing Letters,* December 2007, pp. 223–36.

37. M. L. Ursic and J. G. Helgeson, "The Impact of Choice and Task Complexity on Consumer Decision Making," *Journal of Business Research,* August 1990, pp. 69–86; P. L. A. Dabholkar, "Incorporating Choice into an Attitudinal Framework," *Journal of Consumer Research,* June 1994, pp. 100–18; and T. Elrod, R. D. Johnson, and J. White, "A New Integrated Model of Non-compensatory and Compensatory Decision Strategies," *Organizational Behavior and Human Decision Processes* 95 (20 04), pp. 1–19.

38. See E. Coupey, "Restructuring," *Journal of Consumer Research,* June 1994, pp. 83–99.

39. See D. L. Alden, D. M. Stayman, and W. D. Hoyer, "Evaluation Strategies of American and Thai Consumers," *Psychology & Marketing,* March 1994, pp. 145–61; and J. E. Russo and F. Lecleric, "An Eye-Fixation Analysis of Choice Processes for Consumer Nondurables," *Journal of Consumer Research,* September 1994, pp. 274–90.

40. See J. G. Helgeson and M. L. Ursic, "Information Load, Cost/ Benefit Assessment and Decision Strategy Variability," *Journal of the Academy of Marketing Science,* Winter 1993, pp. 13–20; W. J. McDonald, "The Roles of Demographics, Purchase Histories, and Shopper Decision-Making Styles in Predicting Consumer Catalog Loyalty," *Journal of Direct Marketing,* Summer 1993, pp. 55–65; M. S. Yadav, "How Buyers Evaluate Product Bundles," *Journal of Consumer Research,* September 1994, pp. 342–53; A. V. Muthukrishnan, "Decision Ambiguity and Incumbent Brand Advantage," *Journal of Consumer Research,* June 1995, pp. 98–109; and D. E. Hansen and J. G. Helgeson, "Consumer Response to Decision Conflict from Negatively Correlated Attributes," *Journal of Consumer Psychology* 10, no. 3 (2001), pp. 150–69.

18 Postpurchase Processes, Customer Satisfaction, and Customer Commitment

LEARNING OBJECTIVES

LO1 Describe the various postpurchase processes engaged in by consumers

LO2 Define and discuss postpurchase dissonance

LO3 Discuss the issues surrounding product use and nonuse and their importance to marketers

LO4 Summarize disposition options and their relevance to marketers and public policy

LO5 Explain the determinants and outcomes of satisfaction and dissatisfaction

LO6 Describe the relationship between satisfaction, repeat purchase, and customer commitment

Customer relationship management (CRM) programs are increasingly common in American firms. The objective of such programs is to increase the satisfaction, commitment, and retention of key customers. *BusinessWeek* publishes an annual ranking of the Top 25 Service Organizations. These companies invest heavily in programs, processes, technology, and training to allow for the delivery of superior customer value. A few of the companies at the top of *BusinessWeek's* list and their profiles are presented below.[1]

- Four Seasons Hotels. They rely on their customer service personnel heavily and understand that CRM is more than just a database management program. Each hotel employs a "guest historian" who is in charge of tracking guest preferences. And part of their employee training involves the employees actually staying at the hotel as a guest to give them the customer perspective.

- Amica Insurance. This company is dedicated to loyalty. Amica could assume their customers have made their purchase and will remain loyal, and loyalty rates for Amica are amazingly high. However, they don't take this for granted. One example is that when serious weather like a tornado strikes, they call customers whom they haven't heard from!

- L.L.Bean has always been a high-quality product cataloger. Its unconditional product guarantee is famous around the world. However, as shoppers have moved online, L.L.Bean has had to adjust. It has juiced its website to include customer ratings, "live help," and "call me." Call me gets an L.L.Bean rep to call the customer within minutes to provide additional product information.

- USAA Insurance. Service representatives are highly rewarded, with recent bonuses of around 20 percent. The company also instituted a call center tool that tracks frontline suggestions for customer-friendly innovations. And it is innovating in mobile apps to allow consumers to file claims from their phones at the scene of the accident, and to send photos and attach voice messages of the accident description to their file.

As you can see, the best companies appear to blend technology and people in a way that is appropriate for their industry and their target customer. Firms that struggle often make the mistake of thinking that CRM is as simple as buying a computer program. These companies often fail to create great service organizations, and they damage loyalty by failing to satisfy core customer needs.

FIGURE 18-1 Postpurchase Consumer Behavior

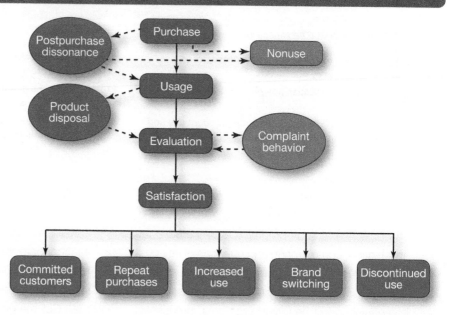

Purchase is followed by a number of processes including use, evaluation, and in some cases satisfaction, and consumer responses related to satisfaction including repurchase, positive word of mouth, and loyalty. Evaluation can also lead to dissatisfaction, which is sometimes associated with complaining, as well as erosion of loyalty, brand switching, and negative word of mouth. Appropriate responses to product and service failure is critical, including putting in processes—such as call centers and the social media options discussed in Chapter 7—to track potential problems. Once a problem is recognized, appropriate action is important as a way to try to reverse or eliminate the negative outcomes of dissatisfaction. Effective CRM programs and high-quality service, as discussed in the opener, are often important aspects of marketing strategy designed to either deliver high satisfaction or deal effectively with dissatisfaction when it occurs.

L01 Figure 18-1 shows the relationships among these various processes, which is the focus of this chapter. It also indicates that immediately following a purchase, and often prior to usage, consumers may feel doubt or anxiety known as postpurchase dissonance.

POSTPURCHASE DISSONANCE

L02 I still like it [a dining room set] a whole lot better than what we used to have. But I think if we had taken longer we would have gotten more precisely what we wanted. I mean we got a great deal. You couldn't get that for that price, so I am happy with the money part of it, but some days I wish we had spent more and gotten something a bit different.[2]

This is a common consumer reaction after making a difficult, relatively permanent decision. Doubt or anxiety of this type is referred to as **postpurchase dissonance**.[3] Some, but not all, consumer purchase decisions are followed by postpurchase dissonance. The probability and magnitude of such dissonance is a function of:

- *The degree of commitment or irrevocability of the decision.* The easier it is to alter the decision, the less likely the consumer is to experience dissonance.
- *The importance of the decision to the consumer.* The more important the decision, the more likely dissonance will result.
- *The difficulty of choosing among the alternatives.* The more difficult it is to select from among the alternatives, the more likely the experience and magnitude of dissonance. Decision difficulty is a function of the number of alternatives considered, the number of relevant attributes associated with each alternative, and the extent to which each alternative offers attributes not available with the other alternatives.
- *The individual's tendency to experience anxiety.* Some individuals have a higher tendency to experience anxiety than do others. The higher the tendency to experience anxiety, the more likely the individual will experience postpurchase dissonance.

Dissonance does not generally occur for low-involvement nominal and limited decision making. These decisions are relatively easy and unimportant. Dissonance is most common in high-involvement extended decision making, where trade-offs among desirable attributes create conflict (as in the price-quality trade-off made in the dining room decision above). Such trade-offs create negative emotions and decision delay.[4] Thus, when such trade-offs exist, salespeople and ads could attempt to refocus consumer attention on the positive aspects of the decision or provide incentives to make a purchase even in the face of the difficult trade-off.

After the purchase, consumers may use one or more of the following approaches to reevaluate or alter the decision to reduce dissonance:

- Increase the desirability of the brand purchased.
- Decrease the desirability of rejected alternatives.
- Decrease the importance of the purchase decision.
- Reverse the purchase decision (return the product before use).

Advertising and follow-up sales efforts can have a huge effect on postpurchase dissonance because consumers, in their reevaluation process, often search for and are receptive to, information that confirms the wisdom of their purchase. Direct mailers, follow-up calls, and e-mails can all be effective. Johnston & Murphy sends follow-up e-mails thanking customers for their recent purchase, pointing them to its website, and soliciting feedback. Such communications can go a long way in reducing dissonance and increasing satisfaction. Illustration 18–1 provides an additional example of the reinforcement potential of advertising in the postpurchase process.

A concept very similar to postpurchase dissonance is **consumption guilt.** Consumption guilt occurs when *negative emotions or guilt feelings are aroused by the use of a product or a service.* A person driving a large car may experience some negative feelings due to concern over resource utilization and pollution. The example below illustrates consumption guilt quite clearly:

> I have to count calories much more than I did before. I still buy a sundae once in a while but the joy of eating ice cream will probably forever be connected with guilt over eating something so unhealthy. When I think about it, I realize that most products make me feel good and bad at the same time.[5]

Marketers of products whose target markets might experience consumption guilt need to focus on validating the consumption of the product. They need to find ways to give the consumer permission or a rationale for indulging in that consumption act.[6]

ILLUSTRATION 18–1

Advertisements for high-involvement purchase items can serve to confirm the wisdom of a purchase as well as influence new purchasers.

PRODUCT USE AND NONUSE

Product Use

L03 Most consumer purchases involve nominal or limited decision making and therefore arouse little or no postpurchase dissonance. Instead, the purchaser or some other member of the household uses the product without first worrying about the wisdom of the purchase. And as Figure 18-1 shows, even when postpurchase dissonance occurs, it is still generally followed by product use.

Marketers need to understand how consumers use their products for a variety of reasons. Understanding both the functional and symbolic ways in which a product is used can lead to more effective product designs and marketing campaigns. For example, the existence of the sneakerhead consumption subculture (Chapter 7) has influenced many aspects of sneaker design and marketing, including the creation of expensive, limited-edition designs that are targeted specifically to the sneakerhead collector.

Use innovativeness refers to *a consumer using a product in a new way*.[7] Marketers who discover new uses for their products can greatly expand sales.

- Arm & Hammer discovered that consumers were using its baking soda for a variety of noncooking uses, such as deodorizing refrigerators. It now advertises such uses and has developed product packaging, such as its Fridge Fresh Air Filters, specific to such uses. It also has a section on its website where consumers can submit their own "solutions" to common household problems using Arm & Hammer baking soda.

- WD-40, a lubricant, is renowned for the wide array of applications that consumers suggest for it, including as an additive to fish bait and for removing gum from a carpet.
- Bounce had a contest where consumers submitted stories that were merged into an online booklet that can be found on its website. Company lawyers cleared the stories and deleted any that could be harmful to consumers or the environment.

Just as the Internet can be used as a way to observe and track consumer problems, it can also be used as a means for tracking innovative product uses. And web-based submission options on a brand's website make direct collection of such ideas easier than ever.[8]

Marketers can frequently take advantage of the fact that the use of one product may require, be enhanced, or suggest the use of other products (see Illustration 18–2). Consider houseplants and fertilizer; bikes and helmets; dresses and shoes. Retailers can promote such items jointly, display them together, or train their sales personnel to make relevant complementary sales.

ILLUSTRATION 18–2

Marketers can leverage the fact that certain products are used together by developing product mixes consisting of complementary products.

Stringent product liability laws and aggressive civil suits also are forcing marketing managers to examine how consumers use their products. These laws have made firms responsible for harm caused by products *not only when the product is used as specified by the manufacturer but in any reasonably foreseeable use of the product.* Thus, the manufacturer must design products with both the primary purpose *and* other potential uses in mind. This requires substantial research into how consumers actually use products.

When marketers discover confusion about the proper way to use a product, it is often to their advantage to teach consumers how to use it and engage in marketing communications that increase the chances of proper use. After all, how many consumers blame themselves when a product failure occurs as a result of their own failure to follow usage instructions?[9] At other times, a firm can gain a competitive advantage by redesigning the product so that it is easier to use properly.

Product Nonuse

As Figure 18-1 indicates, not all purchases are followed by use. **Product nonuse** occurs when a consumer actively acquires a product that is not used or used only sparingly relative to potential use.[10]

For many products and most services, the decisions to purchase and to consume are made simultaneously. A person who orders a meal in a restaurant is also deciding to eat the meal at that time. However, a decision to purchase food at a supermarket requires a second decision to prepare and consume the food. The second decision occurs at a different point in time and in a different environment from the first. Thus, nonuse can occur because the situation or the purchaser changes between the purchase and the potential usage occasion. For example, a point-of-purchase display featuring a new food item shown as part of an appealing entrée might cause a consumer to imagine an appropriate usage situation and to

ILLUSTRATION 18–3

Advertisements can encourage purchases, consumption of previously purchased items, or both.

purchase the product. However, without the stimulus of the display, the consumer may not remember the intended use or may just never get around to it. Nonuse situations such as the following are common:[11]

> Wok. "I wanted to try and cook stirfry, but I didn't take time out to use it."
>
> Skirt. "My ingenious idea was that I'd lose a few pounds and fit into the size 4 rather than gain a few and fit into the size 6. Obviously, I never lost the weight, so the skirt was snug."
>
> Gym membership. "Couldn't get in the groove to lift."

In such cases, the consumer has wasted money, and the marketer is unlikely to get repeat sales or positive referrals. Many such purchases are difficult for the marketer to correct after the purchase. In other cases, consumers would have used the product if reminded or motivated at the proper time. In the last example above, good records would indicate that this member was not using the gym. A personal letter, e-mail, or telephone invitation to come in might be enough to get this person started.

Some products are known to be kept on hand by consumers; that is, they stock up on certain items. In this case, a major goal of advertising should be to encourage people to consume the product at the next appropriate occasion and perhaps even suggest situations that would be appropriate. Since consumers have the product available, the task is not to encourage purchase but to motivate near-term consumption, as in Illustration 18–3.

The division between the initial purchase decision and the decision to consume is particularly strong with catalog and online purchases. In effect, two decisions are involved in these purchases—the initial decision to order the product, and a second decision to keep or return the item when it is received. Not only is it likely that several days will have passed between the two decisions, but substantially different information is available at the "keep or return" decision point. In particular, consumers can physically touch, try on, or otherwise experience the item.

Obviously, online and catalog retailers want to maximize the percentage of items kept rather than returned. Intuitively, one might think that a strict return policy would accomplish this. However, such a policy might also reduce the number of initial orders. In fact, a liberal return policy appears to maximize initial orders and may also minimize returns. Such a policy reduces perceived risk and signals higher quality (surrogate indicator), which increases initial orders. Consumers also tend to perceive items ordered under liberal return policies as having higher quality after receiving them, which reduces returns.[12] In addition to return policies, online tools that can better represent products so that a maximal fit to consumer needs is attained can help. Scanner-based, full-body measurement technology that also makes recommendations about sizes, styles, and brands (Chapter 17) should dramatically increase how well clothing fits even if it is ordered online without first trying it on. This should reduce returns and company costs and increase customer satisfaction.

DISPOSITION

Disposition of the product or the product's container may occur before, during, or after product use. Or for products that are completely consumed, such as an ice cream cone, no disposition may be involved.

The United States produces several hundred million tons of refuse a year.[13] Packaging is an important component. Millions of pounds of product packages are disposed of every day. These containers are thrown away as garbage or litter, used in some capacity by the consumer, or recycled. Creating packages that utilize a minimal amount of resources is important for economic reasons as well as being a matter of social responsibility. Many firms are responding to this issue, as the examples below illustrate:

- Crate & Barrel stopped using white bleached board in its famous black and white boxes and switched to more renewable fiber that contains postconsumer recyclable material.
- Casio redesigned its consumer and channel-based packaging so as to reduce the total amount of materials used.

Beyond packaging is the physical product that continues to exist even though it may no longer meet a consumer's needs either in an instrumental (no longer works) or a symbolic (no longer the latest trend) way. Either situation requires disposition. For some consumers, recycling is more prominent than others (see Chapter 3 on green marketing), and companies and government organizations are working to encourage recycling and make it more convenient. Still, only about a third of solid waste (trash) is recycled.[14]

Exploding demand and short product life spans for high-tech gadgets such as cell phones, personal computers, and various other personal electronics devices is creating growing concerns over **e-waste.** Both instrumental and symbolic considerations can drive e-waste. Consumer and corporate solutions are necessary and evolving, although one recent estimate is that only 1 in 4 computers is recycled![15] Examples of efforts to reduce e-waste include:

- TechForward offers a guaranteed buy-back plan for electronics products.[16]
- Sony has developed a recycling plan whereby it will offset, pound for pound, that amount of materials recycled for new products produced. Sony is partnering with a recycling company and banking on the project's paying for itself as a result of the value of such ingredients as copper typically found in e-waste. Big issues are consumer awareness and convenience.[17]

- Companies such as HP and Office Depot are engaged in ongoing efforts related to print cartridges. HP provides a self-addressed, postage-paid envelope in which you can return used ink cartridges to its recycling center. Office Depot offers discounts through their customer rewards program for those who return used cartridges.

Figure 18-2 illustrates the various alternatives for disposing of a product or package. Unfortunately, while "throw it away" is only one of many disposition alternatives, it is by far the most widely used by many consumers. Environmental groups work hard to change these behaviors, as do some firms and other organizations (see Illustration 18–4). Other firms, however, continue to use unnecessary or hard-to-recycle packaging and product components.

Product Disposition and Marketing Strategy

Why should a marketing manager be concerned about the disposition of a used product? Perhaps the best reason is the cumulative effect that these decisions have on the quality of the environment and the lives of current and future generations. However, there are also short-term economic reasons for concern. Disposition decisions affect the purchase decisions of both the individual making the disposition and other individuals in the market for that product category.

There are five major ways in which disposition decisions can affect a firm's marketing strategy. First, for most durable goods, consumers are reluctant to purchase a new item until they have "gotten their money's worth" from the old one. These consumers mentally depreciate the value of a durable item over time. If the item is not fully mentally depreciated, they are reluctant to write it off by disposing of it to acquire a new one. Allowing old items to be traded in is one way to overcome this reluctance.[18]

Second, disposition sometimes must occur before acquisition of a replacement because of space or financial limitations. For example, because of a lack of storage space, a family living in an apartment may find it necessary to dispose of an existing bedroom set before acquiring a new one. Or someone may need to sell his current bicycle to raise supplemental funds to pay for a new bicycle. Thus, it is to the manufacturer's and retailer's advantage to assist the consumer in the disposition process.

Third, frequent decisions by consumers to sell, trade, or give away used products may result in a large used-product market that can reduce the market for new products. A **consumer-to-consumer sale** occurs when *one consumer sells a product directly to another with or without the assistance of a commercial intermediary.* Garage sales, swap meets, flea markets, classified ads, and online outlets such as eBay exist as a result of consumer demand to buy and sell used items. In addition, consumers may give or sell their used items to resellers. Thrift stores, featuring used clothing, appliances, and furniture, run by both commercial and nonprofit groups, are an important part of the economy.

A fourth reason for concern with product disposition is that the United States is not completely a throwaway society. Many Americans continue to be very concerned with

Disposition Alternatives   FIGURE 18-2

waste and how their purchase decisions affect waste.[19] Such individuals might be willing to purchase, for example, a new vacuum cleaner if they were confident that the old one would be rebuilt and resold. However, they might be reluctant to throw their old vacuums away or to go to the effort of reselling the machines themselves. Thus, manufacturers and retailers could take steps to ensure that products are reused.

The fifth reason is that environmentally sound disposition decisions benefit society as a whole and thus the firms that are part of that society. Firms' owners and employees live and work in the same society and environment as many of their consumers. Their environment and lives are affected by the disposition decisions of consumers. Therefore, it is in their best interest to develop products, packages, and programs that encourage proper disposition decisions.

PURCHASE EVALUATION AND CUSTOMER SATISFACTION

As we saw in Figure 18-1, a consumer's evaluation of a purchase can be influenced by the purchase process itself, postpurchase dissonance, product use, and product/package disposition. Further, the outlet or the product or both may be involved in the evaluation. Consumers may evaluate each aspect of the purchase, ranging from information availability to price to retail service to product performance. In addition, satisfaction with one component, such as the product itself, may be influenced by the level of satisfaction with other components, such as the salesperson.[20] For many products, this is a dynamic process, with the factors that drive satisfaction evolving over time.[21] However, keep in mind that nominal decisions and many limited decisions are actively evaluated only if some factor, such as an obvious product malfunction, directs attention to the purchase.[22]

The Evaluation Process

A particular alternative such as a product, brand, or retail outlet is selected because it is thought to be a better overall choice than other alternatives considered in the purchase process. Whether that particular item is selected because of its presumed superior functional performance or because of some other reason, such as a generalized liking of the item or outlet, the consumer has a level of expected performance for it. The expected level of performance can range from quite low (this brand or outlet isn't very good, but it's the only one available and I'm in a hurry) to quite high.[23] As you might suspect, expectations and perceived performance are not independent. Up to a point, consumers tend to perceive performance to be in line with their expectations.[24]

While and after using the product, service, or outlet, the consumer will perceive some level of performance. This perceived performance level could be noticeably above the expected level, noticeably below the expected level, or at the expected level. As Table 18-1 indicates, satisfaction with the purchase is primarily a function of the initial performance expectations and perceived performance relative to those expectations.[25]

Two general expectation levels are presented in Table 18-1. The first is when consumers expect the brand to perform below some minimum level and requires a bit of explanation. Choice of such brands and outlets is not typical since they would normally be in a consumer's inept set (see Chapter 15). However, three situations will drive choice in this case. These are (1) where available alternatives don't exist (the iPhone was only available on AT&T until recently), (2) in an emergency situation (your tire goes flat and the repair service only carries a brand you find undesirable), or (3) when family decisions result in a

Expectations, Performance, and Satisfaction		TABLE 18-1
	Expectation Level	
Perceived Performance Relative to Expectation	**Below Minimum Desired Performance**	**Above Minimum Desired Performance**
Better	Satisfaction*	Satisfaction/Commitment
Same	Nonsatisfaction	Satisfaction
Worse	Dissatisfaction	Dissatisfaction

*Assuming the perceived performance surpasses the minimum desired level.

suboptimal choice for some family members (the child is thrilled with Chuck E. Cheese, the parents are not).

Table 18-1 shows that an outlet or brand whose performance confirms a low-performance expectation generally will result in neither satisfaction nor dissatisfaction but rather with what can be termed *nonsatisfaction*. That is, the consumer is not likely to feel disappointment or engage in complaint behavior. However, this purchase will not reduce the likelihood that the consumer will search for a better alternative the next time the problem arises.

A brand whose perceived performance falls below expectations generally produces dissatisfaction. If the discrepancy between performance and expectation is sufficiently large, or if initial expectations were low, the consumer may restart the entire decision process. Most likely, he or she will place an item performing below expectations in the inept set and no longer consider it. In addition, the consumer may complain or initiate negative word-of-mouth communications.

When perceptions of product performance match expectations that are at or above the minimum desired performance level, satisfaction generally results. Likewise, performance above the minimum desired level that exceeds a lower expectation tends to produce satisfaction. Satisfaction reduces the level of decision making the next time the problem is recognized; that is, a satisfactory purchase is rewarding and encourages one to repeat the same behavior in the future (nominal decision making). Satisfied customers are also likely to engage in positive word-of-mouth communications about the brand, which can lead to the acquisition of new customers.

Product performance that exceeds expected performance will generally result in satisfaction and sometimes in commitment. Commitment, discussed in depth in the next section, means that the consumer is enthusiastic about a particular brand and is somewhat immune to actions by competitors.

The need to develop realistic consumer expectations poses a difficult problem for the marketing manager. For a brand or outlet to be selected, the consumer must view it as superior on the relevant combination of attributes. Therefore, the marketing manager naturally wants to emphasize its positive aspects. If such an emphasis creates expectations in the consumer that the item cannot fulfill, a negative evaluation may occur. Negative evaluations can produce brand switching, unfavorable word-of-mouth communications, and complaint behavior. Thus, the marketing manager must balance enthusiasm for the product with a realistic view of the product's attributes.

Determinants of Satisfaction and Dissatisfaction   Because performance expectations and actual performance are major factors in the evaluation process, we need to understand the dimensions of product and service performance. A major study of the reasons customers switch service providers found competitor actions to be a relatively minor cause. Most customers did not switch from a satisfactory provider to a better provider. Instead, they switched because of perceived problems with their current service provider. The nature of these problems and the percentage listing each as a reason they changed providers follow (the percentages sum to more than 100 because many customers listed several reasons that caused them to switch):[26]

- *Core service failure* (44 percent). Mistakes (booking an aisle rather than the requested window seat), billing errors, and service catastrophes that harm the customer (the dry cleaner ruined my wedding dress).
- *Service encounter failures* (34 percent). Service employees were uncaring, impolite, unresponsive, or unknowledgeable.
- *Pricing* (30 percent). High prices, price increases, unfair pricing practices, and deceptive pricing.
- *Inconvenience* (21 percent). Inconvenient location, hours of operation, waiting time for service or appointments.
- *Responses to service failures* (17 percent). Reluctant responses, failure to respond, and negative responses (it's your fault).
- *Attraction by competitors* (10 percent). More personable, more reliable, higher quality, and better value.
- *Ethical problems* (7 percent). Dishonest behavior, intimidating behavior, unsafe or unhealthy practices, or conflicts of interest.
- *Involuntary switching* (6 percent). Service provider or customer moves, or a third-party payer such as an insurance company requires a change.

Other studies have found that waiting time has a major impact on evaluations of service. Consumers have particularly negative reactions to delays over which they believe the service provider has control and during which they have little to occupy their time.[27] *What are the marketing strategy implications of these results?*

Failure on a given product or service characteristic often has a stronger effect on consumers than success on that same characteristic, something referred to as the *negativity bias.*[28] Thus, depending on the attributes and decision rule involved (see Chapter 16), this could mean first meeting expectations across all relevant features before maximizing performance on a few.

Firms are using technology as a way to deliver more convenient service both online and in the store. Price check scanners in the store or mobile local price apps can make the in-store experience more satisfying. And website functionality, such as avatars and text and video chat with customer representatives, can be critical to customer satisfaction online. When technology fails or is complicated to use, consumers typically experience dissatisfaction. In the case of online checkout, such factors can result in lost sales as consumers abandon their shopping carts (see Chapter 17).

For many products, there are two dimensions to performance: instrumental, and expressive or symbolic. **Instrumental performance** relates to *the physical functioning of the product.* **Symbolic performance** relates to *aesthetic or image-enhancement performance.* For example, the durability of a sport coat is an aspect of instrumental performance, whereas styling represents symbolic performance. Complete satisfaction requires adequate performance on both dimensions. However, for at least some product categories, such as clothing, "Dissatisfaction is caused by a failure of instrumental performance, while complete satisfaction also requires the symbolic functions to perform at or above the expected levels."[29]

In addition to symbolic and instrumental performance, products also provide affective performance. **Affective performance** is *the emotional response that owning or using the* *product or outlet provides.*[30] It may arise from the instrumental or symbolic performance or from the product itself; for example, a suit that produces admiring glances or compliments may produce a positive affective response. Or the affective performance may be the primary product benefit, such as for an emotional movie or novel.

Research regarding online satisfiers and dissatisfiers finds the following four dimensions to be important:[31]

- *Website Design and Interaction:* Includes factors such as information quality, navigation, price, merchandise availability, purchase process, and order tracking.
- *Security and Privacy:* Includes factors related to security such as fraud and identity theft and privacy related to unwanted marketing efforts.
- *Fulfillment and Reliability:* Includes factors such as timely delivery, order accuracy, billing accuracy, and the quality of the merchandise.
- *Customer Service:* Includes factors relating to service level, such as customer support, ability and ease of communication, as well as factors relating to returns, such as clear and fair return policies.

A study of German consumers finds similar drivers of satisfaction with online retailers.[32] Finally, research suggests that in multi-channel contexts involving the Internet, the issue of integration is critical in that content, processes, image, and so on should be consistent to the extent possible and appropriate across different channels within a company or brand.[33]

DISSATISFACTION RESPONSES

Figure 18-3 illustrates the major options available to a dissatisfied consumer. The first decision is whether or not to take any external action. By taking no action, the consumer decides to live with the unsatisfactory situation. This decision is a function of the importance of the purchase to the consumer, the ease of taking action, the consumer's existing

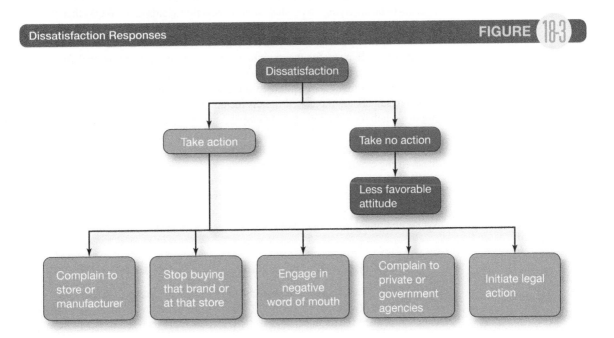

Dissatisfaction Responses   FIGURE 18-3

level of overall satisfaction with the brand or outlet, and the characteristics of the consumer involved. It is important to note that even when no external action is taken, the consumer is likely to have a less favorable attitude toward the store or brand.[34]

Consumers who take action in response to dissatisfaction generally pursue one or more of five alternatives. As Figure 18-3 indicates, the most favorable of these alternatives from a company's standpoint is for consumers to complain to them. This at least gives the company a chance to resolve the problem. Many times, however, consumers do not complain to the company, but instead take actions such as switching brands or engaging in negative word of mouth (WOM).

Consumers are satisfied with the vast majority of their purchases. Still, because of the large number of purchases they make each year, most individuals experience dissatisfaction with some of their purchases. For example, one study asked 540 consumers if they could recall a case in which one or more of the grocery products they normally purchase were defective. They recalled 1,307 separate unsatisfactory purchases.

These purchases produced the following actions (the study did not measure negative word-of-mouth actions such as warning friends):

- 25 percent of these unsatisfactory purchases resulted in brand switching.
- 19 percent caused the shopper to stop buying the products.
- 13 percent led to an in-store inspection of future purchases.
- 3 percent produced complaints to the manufacturer.
- 5 percent produced complaints to the retailer.
- 35 percent resulted in the item's being returned.

In a similar study of durable goods, 54 percent of the dissatisfied customers said they would not purchase the brand again (brand switching), and 45 percent warned their friends (negative WOM) about the product.[35]

As we discussed in Chapter 7, WOM is a critical factor in consumer behavior. Consumers trust WOM more than many other sources and, therefore, tend to rely on it heavily when making decisions. Unfortunately for companies, when it comes to WOM, there appears to be an asymmetry—that is, dissatisfaction yields more WOM than does satisfaction. One estimate puts the ratio at 2 to 1, with consumers telling twice as many people about a negative product or service experience than a positive one.[36]

One of the reasons for the asymmetry in WOM is the motivational force behind the emotions surrounding dissatisfaction, which can range from disappointment to frustration to rage. The results clearly point to the fact that the stronger the negative emotion, the more consumers are motivated to hurt the company in some way. That is, rather than trying to explain their problem to the company in hopes of fixing the situation, angry customers want to "get even." Learning how to avoid situations that would provoke such negative emotions is critical, as is training customer service employees to identify and deal with these strong emotions when they occur.[37]

Obviously, marketers should strive to minimize dissatisfaction *and* to effectively resolve dissatisfaction when it occurs. However, marketers also need to strive to maximize the chances that consumers will complain to their firm rather than engage in negative WOM and brand switching. We discuss these issues next.

Marketing Strategy and Dissatisfied Consumers

Firms need to satisfy consumer expectations by (1) creating reasonable expectations through promotional efforts and (2) maintaining consistent quality so the reasonable expectations are fulfilled. Since dissatisfied consumers tend to engage in negative WOM and since WOM is such a powerful decision influence, one dissatisfied consumer can cause a ripple or multiplier effect in terms of discouraging future sales.[38] Both offline and online WOM are important to consider.

> I feel mad. I put it in my Christmas letter to 62 people across the country. I mean, I told everybody don't buy one of these things because the transmission is bad.[39]

The above example is a marketer's nightmare. Yet the rise of social media has created challenges in this arena that make the above example seem like a minor nuisance. One such incident involved Dave Carroll and United Airlines:[40]

> Dave Carroll is a musician and was travelling with his $3,500 710 Taylor acoustic guitar. From his seat he saw baggage handlers throwing his guitar without regard to its safety. When he reached his destination, he found that the guitar was ruined. United did not take responsibility even though Carroll complained to the company numerous times in numerous ways. So, being a musician, Dave made a music video about this experience and posted it on YouTube. This video has had over 10 million views and within days of being posted, United's stock fell 10 percent!

When a consumer is dissatisfied, the most favorable consequence is for the person to communicate this dissatisfaction to the firm but to no one else. In the above example, Dave Carroll made numerous attempts that United did not heed. This is unfortunate, since such complaining can alert the firm to problems, enable it to make amends where necessary, and minimize negative word-of-mouth communications. Many firms have discovered that customers whose complaints are resolved to their satisfaction are sometimes even more satisfied than are those who did not experience a problem in the first place, particularly if the problem is minor and not repeated.[41]

Unlike Dave Carroll, consumers often do not complain for a variety of reasons.[42] These include:

- **Demographics:** Lack of resources such as income and education.
- **Personality:** Traits such as introversion and agreeableness.
- **Company:** Makes complaining process difficult and uncomfortable.

A lack of consumer complaining is always a problem, but when firms contribute to it, they do so at the risk of damaging their reputation and their bottom line. Consider United's stock price drop worth $180 million.

Handling negative consumer comments and complaints generated via online social media can be particularly challenging. AT&T is one company that has gotten serious about dealing with bad press online based on issues with its network, particularly as it was the only option for iPhone users until just recently. Consider the following:[43]

> On a normal day, AT&T has 10,000 mentions on social networks, but during stressful moments . . . they rise precipitously. The marketer is out to calm those twit storms by staffing up its social-media customer-care corps. The team began with five people dedicated to responding to customer dissatisfaction on Twitter and YouTube and has since moved to Facebook and grown to 19 people. To date, 47% of people reached on social media respond to the social team, which results in 32,000 service tickets per month.

Such efforts by AT&T and others are designed to (a) recognize customer problems and utilize their input in the new era of social media, (b) act on the consumer input, and (c) influence the "narrative" by contributing to the conversation (see Consumer Insight 14-1 for more detail on such strategies).

Acting on complaints in a timely and effective manner is a key to customer satisfaction.[44] Most consumers who complain want a tangible result. Further, the results desired vary by customer type and the nature of the problem, requiring customized response capabilities.[45] Failure to deal effectively with this expectation can produce increased dissatisfaction. Therefore, firms need to resolve the cause of consumer complaints, not just give the consumers the opportunity to complain.[46]

In fact, for many firms, retaining customers by encouraging and responding effectively to complaints is more economical than attracting new customers through advertising or other promotional activities. It has been estimated that it costs only one-fifth as much to retain an old customer as to obtain a new one.[47] Training *frontline employees* who deal directly with customers to use appropriate communication styles and empowering them to resolve problems as they arise is one way firms can increase customer satisfaction and retention.[48]

Unfortunately, many corporations are not organized to effectively resolve and learn from consumer complaints. This area represents a major opportunity for many businesses.[49] Consider the following:[50]

> When Sprint's new CEO Gary Forsee joined the company last March, he wanted to know why hundreds of millions of dollars were being spent on bringing in new wireless customers, while existing unsatisfied customers went out the back door. Mr. Forsee, a 30-year veteran of telephone companies including AT&T and BellSouth, wanted Sprint to put customer service in its place, right next to customer acquisition. So, Sprint changed—a lot. In fact, Sprint business units were completely reorganized around a new focus: the customer experience. No longer are customers acquired and then "thrown over the wall" to customer service. Marketing, customer service and sales are no longer three different silos, but reside in a combined unit working together.

Sprint's companywide approach yielded dividends, with customer turnover down since the reorganization. Illustration 18–5 shows another company that is aligning its processes to proactively deal with customer issues and the customer experience in an online context.

CUSTOMER SATISFACTION, REPEAT PURCHASES, AND CUSTOMER COMMITMENT

Satisfaction is an important driver of customer loyalty, and many organizations are investing in programs to enhance customer satisfaction, as shown by the following excerpt about New York–Presbyterian Hospital (NYP):

NYP has looked very carefully at best practices for improving patient satisfaction across the country. To improve the patient experience, NYP implemented the Commitment to Care philosophy. Commitment to Care is a set of service expectations for all staff to follow in their work and interaction with patients, families and colleagues. The expectations are based on feedback that comes directly from patients and address their key priorities and needs. It was created to give employees clarity about what is expected of them and a clear set of standards by which to evaluate and recognize staff for issues related to service. Metrics [on key service dimensions] are an important tool for both the hospital and for our patients.[51]

Given increasingly sophisticated and value-conscious consumers and multiple brands that perform at satisfactory levels, producing satisfied customers is necessary but not sufficient for many marketers. Instead, the objective is to produce committed or brand-loyal customers.

Figure 18-4 illustrates the composition of the buyers of a particular brand at any point in time. Of the total buyers, some percentage will be satisfied with the purchase. As we have seen, marketers are spending considerable effort to make this percentage as high as possible. The reason is that, while many satisfied customers will switch brands,[52] satisfied customers are much more likely to become or remain repeat purchasers than are dissatisfied customers, particularly when satisfaction perceptions are strong and held with confidence.[53] **Repeat purchasers** continue to buy the same brand though they do not have an emotional attachment to it. They may do so out of habit, or because they don't see viable options to their current choice.

As we saw earlier, some dissatisfied customers may also become or remain repeat purchasers. These individuals perceive the **switching costs**—*the costs of finding, evaluating, and adopting another solution*—to be too high.[54] However, they may engage in negative word of mouth and are vulnerable to competitors' actions.

Repeat purchasers are desirable, but *mere* repeat purchasers are vulnerable to competitor actions. That is, they are buying the brand out of habit or because it is readily available

Creating Committed Customers is Increasingly the Focus of Marketing Strategy   **FIGURE**

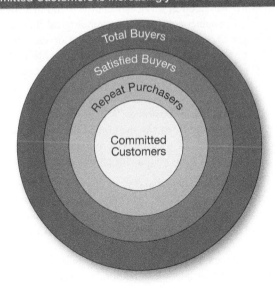

where they shop, or because it has the lowest price, or for similar superficial reasons. These customers have no commitment to the brand. They are not brand loyal. **Brand loyalty** is defined as

a biased (i.e., nonrandom) behavioral response (i.e., purchase/recommend) expressed over time by a decision-making unit with respect to one or more alternative brands out of a set of such brands that is a function of psychological (decision-making, evaluative) processes.[55]

Service and store loyalty are generally defined in the same or a similar manner.[56] Thus, a consumer loyal to a brand (store or service), or a **committed customer,** has an emotional attachment to the brand or firm. The customer likes the brand in a manner somewhat similar to friendship. Consumers use expressions such as "I trust this brand," "I like this outlet," and "I believe in this firm" to describe their commitment, as in the following customer quote:

I tried it myself one time and eventually adopted a taste for it. Now I drink it all the time. I have it every morning after I come in from my run. I drink it after I clean the house. I always have a glass of it in my hand. That's me. I am very loyal to Gatorade. I would say that I am very loyal to that. I know they have other brands of that now, I see coupons all the time, but I have never even picked up a bottle of them. Never even tried them. Because I like Gatorade a lot. I really do.[57]

In a higher-involvement context, NYP Hospital, discussed earlier, goes well beyond having, measuring, and reporting on key metrics to high-touch efforts that deliver personalized and humane service to its patients and treat patients and family with compassion and respect. Such efforts go well beyond mere satisfaction toward building a committed, loyal customer base.

Brand loyalty can arise through a number of processes including:

- **Brand Identification:** When a consumer believes the brand reflects and reinforces some aspect of his or her self-concept. This type of commitment is most common for symbolic products such as beer and automobiles. It is also likely in service situations that involve extended interpersonal encounters.[58]
- **Brand Comfort:** Research in services has also found that loyalty can arise from *consumer comfort.* Consumer comfort is "a psychological state wherein a customer's anxiety concerning a service has been eased, and he or she enjoys peace of mind and is calm and worry free concerning service encounters with [a specific] provider."[59] Service employees likely play a strong role in developing comfort given the high-contact nature of many services.
- **Brand Delight:** Brand loyalty may also arise through performance so far above expected that it delights the customer.[60] Such superior performance can be related to the product, the firm itself, or, as mentioned earlier, the manner in which the firm responds to a complaint or a customer problem. Delight has been demonstrated for high-involvement services as well as for more mundane customer website visits.[61]

Given the above, it is obvious that it is more difficult to develop brand-loyal consumers for some product categories than for others. Indeed, for low-involvement product categories with few opportunities for truly distinct performance or customer service, most firms should focus on creating satisfied repeat purchasers rather than loyal or committed customers.[62]

Committed customers are unlikely to consider additional information when making a purchase. They are also resistant to competitors' marketing efforts—for example, coupons.

Even when loyal customers do buy a different brand to take advantage of a promotional deal, they generally return to their original brand for their next purchase.[63] Committed customers are more receptive to line extensions and other new products offered by the same firm. They are also more likely to forgive an occasional product or service failure.[64]

Finally, committed customers are likely to be a source of positive word-of-mouth communications. This is extremely valuable to a firm. Positive word-of-mouth communications from a committed customer increase the probability of the recipient's both becoming a customer and sharing the positive comments with other people.[65] Consumer Insight 18-1 shows how some marketers are utilizing a word-of-mouth measure to capture customer satisfaction and loyalty and predict future growth.

It is no surprise, therefore, that many marketers attempt to create satisfied customers and then try to convert them to committed customers. Committed customers are much more profitable to the firm than mere repeat purchasers, who in turn are more profitable than occasional buyers.[66]

Repeat Purchasers, Committed Customers, and Profits

Churn is a term used to refer to *turnover in a firm's customer base.* If a firm has a base of 100 customers and 20 leave each year and 20 new ones become customers, it has a churn rate of 20 percent. Churn at Amica, one of the companies profiled in the opener, is at an amazingly low 2 percent per year! Reducing churn is a major objective of many firms today. Why? It typically costs more to obtain a new customer than to retain an existing one, and new customers generally are not as profitable as longer-term customers. Consider the profits generated by one credit card firm's customers over time:[67]

Year	Profits
Acquisition cost	($51)
Year 1	$30
Year 2	$42
Year 3	$44
Year 4	$49
Year 5	$55

Acquisition costs include such expenses as advertising, establishing the account, mailing the card, and so forth. First-year profits are low because many new customers are acquired as a result of a promotional deal of some type. In addition, their initial usage rate tends to be low and they don't use all the features. This is a common pattern for both consumer and industrial products. Auto service profits per customer increased from $25 the first year to $88 in the fifth year, and an industrial laundry found they went from $144 to $258.

Figure 18-5 shows the sources of the growth of profit per customer over time. *Price premium* refers to the fact that repeat and particularly committed customers tend to buy the brand consistently rather than waiting for a sale or continually negotiating price. *Referrals* refers to profits generated by new customers acquired as a result of recommendations from existing customers. *Lower costs* occur because both the firm and the customer learn how to interact more efficiently over time. Finally, customers tend to use a wider array of a firm's products and services over time.[68]

Although committed customers are most valuable to a firm, reducing churn can have a major impact on profit even if the retained customers are primarily repeat purchasers.

CONSUMER INSIGHT 18-1

Do You Know Your Net Promoter Score?

Companies are always looking for better ways to measure true attitudinal loyalty. A recent approach that has garnered considerable interest is called the Net Promoter Score (NPS). It might surprise you to find that NPS does not measure attitudinal loyalty through satisfaction scores or through some direct loyalty measure.[69] Instead, it is an *indirect* measure based on word of mouth (WOM). The technique is based on the following question:

"How likely is it that you would recommend (company X) to a friend or colleague?"

0-----1-----2-----3-----4-----5-----6-----7-----8-----9-----10

Not at All   Neutral   Extremely
Likely   Likely

Three categories of consumers are created based on their answers to this question as follows:

Promoters—score 9 or 10
Passively Satisfied—score 7 or 8
Detractors—score 0 to 6

NPS is then calculated by subtracting the proportion of a firm's customers who are detractors from the proportion who are promoters. Passively satisfied customers are seen as essentially neutral in a way that makes them unlikely to engage in any proactive behavior regarding the company, either positive or negative. So a company with 60 percent promoters, 30 percent passively satisfied, and 10 percent detractors would have an NPS of (60% promoters − 10% detractors) or NPS = 50. Thus, the **Net Promoter Score** *measures the percentage of a firm's promoter customer base left after subtracting out the firm's detractors.*

Several points about NPS are worth noting.

1. Higher NPS scores, in many industries, are strongly related to positive firm growth. That is, if a firm's NPS score is going up (growth in promoters relative to detractors), then future growth in revenues is likely. This makes sense when you consider how powerful and trusted WOM is as a source of consumer information and as a basis for consumer choice.

2. NPS, although based on a WOM question, appears to tap into attitudinal loyalty since recom-

mending to a friend or colleague involves social risk and requires proactive behavior on the part of the firm. Such risk taking and effort on behalf of a brand would seem most likely for a consumer who is highly *committed* to that brand.

3. NPS is very simple compared to many satisfaction and loyalty questionnaires that can involve dozens of questions.

NPS is not perfect (doesn't work well in all industries) and is not the only measure out there (other measures exist that are highly correlated with a firm's financial performance). However, the simplicity of NPS and its strong relationship with growth have made it popular with companies such as GE, Intuit, and American Express. The simplicity of NPS can also be a weakness when used inappropriately, and care in its use is important. NPS is a barometer of what's going on with the company. Measuring NPS is useless unless it aids change management at all levels of the organization to align firm and employee actions with customer feedback. As one expert notes:

> If we're going to act, we need more than a number. [Consumer] comments are essential, with driver analysis the next step. What do [consumers] comment about? What leads to being a promoter? To a detractor? And what will get passives off the fence?

Therefore, companies who use NPS often recommend supplementing the "recommend" question with questions that get at underlying reasons for the score. One company follows the "recommend" question with an open-ended question that asks "What is your primary reason for your rating [on the recommend question]?" Such an approach is still quite simple and yet provides the basis for marketing strategies to convert passively satisfied and detractor customers into promoters.

Critical Thinking Questions

1. Why do you think NPS is strongly related to firm growth?

2. Do you think NPS is also related to firm profits?

3. When might NPS not be a good predictor of firm growth?

Chapter Eighteen   Postpurchase Processes, Customer Satisfaction, and Customer Commitment   631

Sources of Increased Customer Profitability over Time   FIGURE 18-5

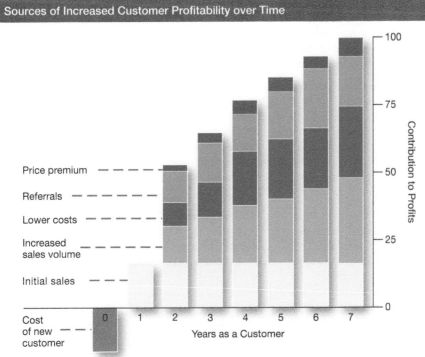

Source: "Sources of Increased Customer Profitability over Time © 1999 TIME." Inc. Reprinted by permission.

Reducing the number of customers who leave a firm in a year increases the average life of the firm's customer base.[70] As we saw earlier, the longer a customer is with a firm, the more profits the firm derives from that customer. Thus, a stable customer base tends to be highly profitable per customer. Reducing the number of customers who leave various types of firms each year by 5 percent has been found to increase the average profits per customer as follows:[71]

Firm Type	Percent Increase in Average Profits per Customer
Auto service	30%
Branch banks	85
Credit card	75
Credit insurance	25
Insurance brokerage	50
Industrial laundry	45

The motivation for marketers to retain customers is obvious. Phil Bressler, the co-owner of five Domino's Pizza outlets in Maryland, found that a regular customer was worth more than $5,000 over the 10-year life of the franchise agreement. He makes sure that every employee in every store is constantly aware of that number. Poor service or a bad attitude may cost the outlet several thousands of dollars, not just the $10 or $15 that might be lost on the single transaction![72]

However, retaining some customers is more profitable than others. For example, at a typical commercial bank, the top 20 percent of customers generate six times more revenue than they cost. In contrast, the bottom 20 percent generate three to four times more costs than they do revenue. Firms increasingly understand the need to either strip out value-added services, raise prices to the point where unprofitable customers become profitable (or leave because they don't perceive enough value for the price), or gently encourage unprofitable customers to leave. Consider the following:

- One electric utility serves its top 350 business clients with six customer service representatives. The next 700 are served by six more, and the remaining 30,000 are served by two. The 300,000 residential customers must deal with an automated 800 number.
- One financial institution codes its credit card customers with colors that appear when their accounts appear on a service rep's screen. Green (profitable) customers are granted waivers and otherwise given white-glove treatment. Red (unprofitable) customers have no bargaining power. Yellow (marginal profit) customers are given a moderate level of accommodation.

ING even goes so far as to "fire" customers that don't match its profile of a "low touch, low margin" financial services provider. High-touch customers, that is, those who need a lot of personal attention, are not part of ING's target market and these customers cost more to serve than ING charges. That's because ING's pricing is based on their targeted "low touch" customer.[73]

Firing customers is tricky business. It can keep costs down and profits up, but can also alienate former customers, create negative emotions (abandonment, anger, rage), and thus negative WOM.[74] Therefore, marketers are trying to understand the best ways to "fire" customers. Clearly a gentle, humane, and fair approach can help. For example, some companies go so far as to offer suggestions about where the customer might find a better "fit" with his or her needs.

Repeat Purchasers, Committed Customers, and Marketing Strategy

An important step in developing a marketing strategy for a particular segment is to specify the objectives being pursued. Several distinct possibilities exist:

1. Attract new users to the product category.
2. Capture competitors' current customers.
3. Encourage current customers to use more.
4. Encourage current customers to become repeat purchasers.
5. Encourage current customers to become committed customers.

Each of the objectives listed above will require different strategies and marketing mixes. The first two objectives require the marketer to convince potential customers that the marketer's brand will provide superior value to not using the product or to using another brand. Advertisements promising superior benefits, coupons, free trials, and similar strategies are common approaches. While some firms are content to consider the sale the last step, smart firms now realize the critical importance of retaining customers after the initial sale. This is true even for infrequently purchased items—rather than repeat sales, the marketer wants positive, or at least neutral, word-of-mouth communications.

The last three objectives, listed earlier, focus on marketing to the firm's current customers. All require customer satisfaction as a necessary precondition. As Figure 18-6 indicates, this requires that the firm deliver the value expected by the customer. Techniques for

Customer Satisfaction Outcomes   FIGURE 18-6

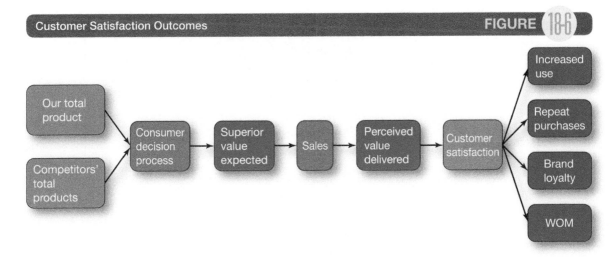

creating satisfied customers were described earlier. Marketing efforts focused on a firm's current customers are generally termed *relationship marketing.*

Relationship Marketing   *An attempt to develop an ongoing, expanding exchange relationship with a firm's customers* is called **relationship marketing.**[75] In many ways, it seeks to mimic the relationships that existed between neighborhood stores and their customers many years ago. In those relationships, the store owner knew the customers not only as customers but also as friends and neighbors. The owner could anticipate their needs and provide help and advice when needed. Relationship marketing attempts to accomplish the same results, but because of the large scale of most operations, the firm must use databases, customized mass communications, and advanced employee training and motivation.[76]

Consider the following example:

> Lees Supermarkets, a family-owned and -operated company, started a Shoppers Club that records the purchases of members. Frequent or heavy shoppers are offered special incentives and deals. These offers can be customized on the basis of past purchasing patterns. In addition, last Thanksgiving, 600 regular, high-volume members were rewarded with free turkeys. Such an unexpected reward can produce delight and loyalty among key customers.[77]

Relationship marketing has five key elements:[78]

1.   Developing a core service or product around which to build a customer relationship.
2.   Customizing the relationship to the individual customer.
3.   Augmenting the core service or product with extra benefits.
4.   Pricing in a manner to encourage loyalty.
5.   Marketing to employees so that they will perform well for customers.

This list of elements makes it clear that relationship marketing is centered on understanding consumer needs at the individual consumer level.[79] Not all customers are equally receptive to relationship marketing efforts. Perceptions that such relationships with the firm will be inconvenient, not yield adequate benefits, and concerns over privacy are several factors that reduce consumer propensity to engage with relationship marketing efforts.[80]

ILLUSTRATION 18–6

Successful customer loyalty programs are based on understanding the needs of key customers and providing benefits of value to them.

A substantial amount of effort is currently being focused on **customer loyalty programs.** In addition to frequent-flier programs offered by most major airlines, programs designed to generate repeat purchases include the following:

• Marriott has Marriott Rewards. Members earn points for staying at Marriott hotels and are classified into Silver, Gold, or Platinum, based on number of stays per year. This classification system and its large customer database help Marriott customize its amenities and promotions based on each customer's individual profile.

• Sports franchises use card-based reward programs where members earn points for attending events and can redeem those points for team memorabilia, food, and drinks. Teams can also use the member data to create personalized communications and offerings, including season-ticket packages to their most attractive members.[81]

However, it is important to distinguish between programs that simply generate repeat purchases and those that generate committed and loyal customers.[82] Committed customers have a reasonably strong emotional attachment to the product or firm. Generating committed customers requires that the firm consistently meet or exceed customer expectations. Further, customers must believe that the firm is treating them fairly and is, to some extent at least, concerned about their well-being. Thus, *generating committed customers requires a customer-focused attitude in the firm.* It also requires that this attitude be translated into actions that meet customers' needs.[83]

Loyalty programs can be effective in generating committed customers if they understand and fulfill key customer needs, as shown in Illustration 18–6.

Research continues to investigate online loyalty. While differences in type of site and purpose of visit (buying versus browsing) are likely to exist, evidence supports Figure 18-6 in suggesting that perceived value and satisfaction are important determinants of online loyalty just as they are for products, services, and traditional retail outlets.[84] In addition, research has identified factors unique to online settings that drive e-loyalty. For example, one study finds security and privacy to be critical.[85] Other research identifies customization and personalization, interactivity, convenience, and online community as factors that drive *e-loyalty,* WOM, and willingness to pay.[86]

SUMMARY

LO1: Describe the various postpurchase processes engaged in by consumers

Purchase is followed by a number of processes, including use, evaluation, and in some cases satisfaction, and consumer responses related to satisfaction, including repurchase, positive word of mouth, and loyalty. Evaluation can also lead to dissatisfaction, which is sometimes associated with complaining, as well as erosion of loyalty, brand switching, and negative word of mouth.

LO2: Define and discuss postpurchase dissonance

Following some purchases, consumers experience doubts or anxiety about the wisdom of the purchase. This is known as *postpurchase dissonance*. It is most likely to occur (1) among individuals with a tendency to experience anxiety, (2) after an irrevocable purchase, (3) when the purchase was important to the consumer, and (4) when it involved a difficult choice between two or more alternatives.

LO3: Discuss the issues surrounding product use and nonuse and their importance to marketers

Whether or not the consumer experiences dissonance, most purchases are followed by product use. This use may be by the purchaser or by some other member of the purchasing unit. Monitoring product usage can indicate new uses for existing products, needed product modifications, appropriate advertising themes, and opportunities for new products. Product liability laws have made it increasingly important for marketing managers to be aware of all potential uses of their products.

Product nonuse is also a concern. Both marketers and consumers suffer when consumers buy products that they do not use or use less than they intended.

Thus, marketers frequently attempt to influence the decision to use the product as well as the decision to purchase the product.

LO4: Summarize disposition options and their relevance to marketers and public policy

Disposition of the product or its package may occur before, during, or after product use. Understanding disposition behavior is important to marketing managers because of the ecological concerns of many consumers (and resulting green marketing efforts, see Chapter 3), the costs and scarcity of raw materials, and the activities of federal and state legislatures and regulatory agencies. *E-waste* is an emerging area of concern related to disposition.

LO5: Explain the determinants and outcomes of satisfaction and dissatisfaction

Consumer perceptions regarding satisfaction and dissatisfaction are a function of a comparison process between consumer expectations of performance and their perceptions of actual performance. When expectations are met or exceeded, satisfaction is likely to result, and in some cases commitment or loyalty is developed. When expectations are not met, dissatisfaction is the likely result. Service is a major determinant of customer satisfaction even when the core purchase involves a physical product. Service and product failures, failure to adequately address product and service problems, and bad pricing are key factors that lead to dissatisfaction.

Dissatisfaction can lead to many undesirable responses from the perspective of the firm, including erosion of loyalty, negative word of mouth, and switching brands. One positive response for the firm is customer complaining, although customers often are reluctant to complain and companies are often not well prepared to act on those complaints when they do occur.

LO6: Describe the relationship between satisfaction, repeat purchase, and customer commitment

Satisfaction results in a number of positive outcomes, including repeat purchases, positive word of mouth, and, in some cases, loyalty. Not all satisfied customers are loyal. Simply meeting expectations (passive satisfaction in the language of Consumer Insight 18-1) is typically not enough to generate the psychological commitment that is associated with loyalty. *Repeat purchasers* are also not necessarily loyal customers. Repeat purchasing can occur out of habit (it's what I always buy) or

necessity (it is the only option out there) and not out of a commitment to the brand. Repeat purchasers who are not *committed customers* are vulnerable to competitor attempts to steal them away. Thus, *brand loyalty* or customer commitment, defined as a willingness to repurchase coupled with a psychological commitment to the brand, is critical to marketers. As online retailing continues to grow, marketers are examining ways in which e-satisfaction and e-loyalty can be bolstered. *Relationship marketing* and loyalty programs are strategic efforts on the part of the firm that can be used to bolster satisfaction, repeat purchases, and in some cases, loyalty.

KEY TERMS

Affective performance 622
Brand loyalty 628
Churn 629
Committed customer 628
Consumer-to-consumer sale 618
Consumption guilt 613

Customer loyalty programs 634
E-waste 617
Instrumental performance 622
Net Promoter Score 630
Postpurchase dissonance 612
Product nonuse 615

Relationship marketing 633
Repeat purchasers 627
Switching costs 627
Symbolic performance 622
Use innovativeness 614

INTERNET EXERCISES

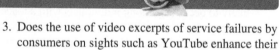

1. Monitor several social media sites for a brand for a week. Prepare a report on how a marketer could learn about the following by doing this.
   a. Customer satisfaction levels and customer commitment
   b. Product use
   c. Customer evaluation processes
2. Find a company site that helps the company in terms of relationship marketing. Describe and evaluate this effort.

3. Does the use of video excerpts of service failures by consumers on sights such as YouTube enhance their influence? Find an example and justify.
4. Find a product, company, or brand site that helps the consumer use a product properly or effectively. Describe and evaluate this effort.

DDB LIFE STYLE STUDY™ DATA ANALYSES

1. What characterizes individuals who feel they have acquired too much debt (DDB Tables 1B through 7B)? What are the marketing implications of this? What are the regulatory implications of this?

2. Using DDB Tables 1B through 7B, what characterizes people who become committed enough to favorite brands to resist other brands when they are on sale? What are the marketing implications of this?

REVIEW QUESTIONS

1. What are the major postpurchase processes engaged in by consumers?

2. How does the type of decision process affect the postpurchase processes?

3. What is *postpurchase dissonance*?

4. What characteristics of a purchase situation are likely to contribute to postpurchase dissonance?

5. In what ways can a consumer reduce postpurchase dissonance?

6. What is *consumption guilt*?

7. What is *use innovativeness*?

8. What is an *off-label use*, and why is it important to companies?

9. Why are surveys not always the most effective way to get at innovative product uses?

10. What is meant by *product nonuse*, and why is it a concern of marketers?

11. What is meant by the disposition of products and product packaging, and why does it interest governmental regulatory agencies and marketers?

12. What is *e-waste*, and why is it a growing concern?

13. What factors influence consumer satisfaction? In what way do they influence consumer satisfaction?

14. What is the difference between *instrumental* and *symbolic performance*, and how does each contribute to consumer satisfaction?

15. What is *affective performance*?

16. What courses of action can a consumer take in response to dissatisfaction? Which are used most often?

17. What determines satisfaction for online retailers?

18. What would marketers like consumers to do when dissatisfied? How can marketers encourage this?

19. What is *churn*? How does it affect profits?

20. What are the sources of increased profits from longer-term customers?

21. What is the relationship between customer satisfaction, repeat purchases, and committed customers?

22. What is the difference between *repeat purchasers* and *committed customers*?

23. What are *switching costs*?

24. Why are marketers interested in having committed customers?

25. What is the *Net Promoter Score*?

26. What is *relationship marketing*? What strategies are involved?

27. What are *loyalty programs*? What do most of them actually do?

28. What factors influence e-loyalty?

DISCUSSION QUESTIONS

29. How should retailers deal with consumers immediately after purchase to reduce postpurchase dissonance? What specific action would you recommend, and what effect would you intend it to have on the recent purchaser of (gift of) the following?
    a. PBS donation
    b. A condominium
    c. Dance lessons
    d. A hybrid automobile
    e. Microwave oven
    f. Tropical fish

30. What type of database should your university maintain on its students? In general, what ethical concerns surround the use of such databases by institutions and companies?

31. How should manufacturers deal with consumers immediately after purchase to reduce postpurchase dissonance? What specific action would you recommend, and what effect would you intend it to have on the recent purchaser of the following?
    a. Cell phone
    b. Expensive watch

c. Tablet computer

d. Corrective eye surgery

32. How do some companies capitalize on the concept of use innovativeness?

33. Discuss how you could determine how consumers actually use the following. How could this information be used to develop marketing strategy?

a. Microwave

b. Wristwatches

c. Online banking services

d. Movies on demand

e. Hair color

f. Hotel reward points

34. How would you go about measuring consumer satisfaction among purchasers of the following? What questions would you ask, what additional information would you collect, and why? How could this information be used for evaluating and planning marketing programs?

a. Cell phone service

b. Walmart.com

c. Car insurance

d. Six Flags theme parks

e. Health care services

f. Exercise bike

35. What level of product dissatisfaction should a marketer be content with in attempting to serve a particular target market? What characteristics contribute to dissatisfaction, regardless of the marketer's efforts?

36. Describe the last time you were dissatisfied with a purchase. What action did you take? Why?

37. Are you a *mere* repeat purchaser of any brand, service, or outlet? Why are you not a committed customer? What, if anything, would make you a committed customer?

38. Respond to the questions in Consumer Insight 18-1.

39. What are some of the possible negative consequences of "firing" customers?

40. Are you a committed customer to any brand, service, or outlet? Why?

41. Design a customer loyalty program for the following.

a. High-end hotel chain

b. Grocery store chain

c. Cosmetics line

d. Catering service

APPLICATION ACTIVITIES

42. Develop a brief questionnaire to determine product nonuse among college students and the reasons for it. With four other classmates, interview 50 students. What do you conclude?

43. Develop a questionnaire designed to measure consumer satisfaction of a clothing purchase of $100 or more. Include in your questionnaire items that measure the product's instrumental, symbolic, and affective dimensions of performance, as well as what the consumer wanted on these dimensions. Then interview several consumers to obtain information on actual performance, expected performance, and satisfaction. Using this information, determine if consumers received what they expected (i.e., evaluation of performance) and relate any difference to consumer expressions of satisfaction. What are the marketing implications of your results?

44. Develop a survey to measure student dissatisfaction with service purchases.

For purchases they were dissatisfied with, determine what action they took to resolve this dissatisfaction and what the end result of their efforts were. What are the marketing implications of your findings?

45. Develop a questionnaire to measure repeat purchase behavior and brand loyalty. Measure the repeat purchase behavior and brand loyalty of 10 students with respect to the following. Determine why the brand-loyal students are brand loyal.

a. Batteries

b. Spaghetti sauce

c. Coffee

d. Lightbulbs

e. Clothing stores

f. Online stores

46. With the cooperation of a durables retailer, assist the retailer in sending a postpurchase letter of thanks to every other customer immediately after purchase. Then, approximately two weeks after

purchase, contact the same customers (both those who received the letter and those who did not) and measure their purchase satisfaction. Evaluate the results.

47. Interview a grocery store manager, a department store manager, and a restaurant manager. Determine the types of products their customers are most likely to complain about and the nature of those complaints.

48. Measure 10 students' disposition behaviors with respect to the following. Determine why they use the alternatives they do.

   a. Laptop computer

   b. Cell phones

   c. Mattress

   d. Televisions

   e. Plastic items

49. Interview 20 students to determine which, if any, customer loyalty programs they belong to, what they like and dislike about them, and the impact they have on their attitudes and behaviors. What opportunities do your results suggest?

REFERENCES

1. The chapter opener is based on J. McGregor, "Customer Service Champs," *BusinessWeek*, March 5, 2007, pp. 52–64; J. McGregor, "Customer Service Champs," *BusinessWeek*, February 18, 2010; and M. Arndt, "L.L.Bean Follows Its Customers to the Web," *BusinessWeek*, February 18, 2010.

2. G. J. Thompson, "Interpreting Consumers," *Journal of Marketing Research*, November 1997, p. 444. Published by the American Marketing Association; reprinted with permission.

3. See J. C. Sweeney, D. Hausknecht, and G. N. Soutar, "Cognitive Dissonance after Purchase," *Psychology & Marketing*, May 2000, pp. 369–85.

4. M. F. Luce, "Choosing to Avoid," *Journal of Consumer Research*, March 1998, pp. 409–33.

5. S. J. Gould, "An Interpretative Study of Purposeful, Mood Self-Regulating Consumption," *Psychology & Marketing*, July 1997, pp. 395–426.

6. See, e.g., R. Kivetz and I. Simonson, "Self-Control for the Righteous," *Journal of Consumer Research*, September 2002, pp. 199–217; and J. Xu and N. Schwarz, "Do We Really Need a Reason to Indulge?" *Journal of Marketing Research*, February 2009, pp. 25–36.

7. See S. Ram and H.-S. Jung, "Innovativeness in Product Usage," and N. M. Ridgway and L. L. Price, "Exploration in Product Usage," both in *Psychology & Marketing*, January 1994, pp. 57–69 and 70–84, respectively; and K. Park and C. L. Dyer, "Consumer Use Innovative Behavior," in *Advances in Consumer Research*, vol. 22, ed. F. R. Kardes and M. Sujan (Provo, UT: Association for Consumer Research, 1995), pp. 566–72.

8. M. B. Kemp, *CMOs Must Connect the Dots of the Online Brand* (Cambridge, MA: Forrester Research, Inc., July 27, 2010).

9. V. A. Taylor and A. B. Bower, "Improving Product Instruction Compliance," *Psychology & Marketing*, March 2004, pp. 229–45; and D. Bowman, C. M. Heilman, and P. B. Seetharaman, "Determinants of Product-Use Compliance Behavior," *Journal of Marketing Research*, August 2004, pp. 324–38.

10. A. B. Bower and D. E. Sprott, "The Case of the Dusty Stair-Climber," in *Advances in Consumer Research*, vol. 22, ed. Kardes

and Sujan, pp. 582–87. See also B. Wansink and R. Deshpande, *Marketing Letters* 5, no. 1 (1994), pp. 91–100.

11. Bower and Sprott, "The Case of the Dusty Stair-Climber," p. 585.

12. S. L. Wood, *Journal of Marketing Research*, May 2001, pp. 157–69.

13. For detailed statistics, visit the U.S. Environmental Protection Agency website, www.epa.gov.

14. L. Williams, "Current United States Recycling Statistics," *Green Living*, www.greenliving.lovetoknow.com, accessed June 30, 2011.

15. K. Y. Larkin, "Computer Recycling Statistics," *Green Living*, at www.greenliving.lovetoknow.com, accessed June 30, 2011.

16. "Cashing in on Old Gadgets," CNN.com, accessed January 17, 2008.

17. K. Hall, "Sony Likes the Yield from Its Junk," *BusinessWeek*, September 17, 2007, p. 40.

18. E. M. Okada, "Trade-ins, Mental Accounting, and Product Replacement Decisions," *Journal of Consumer Research*, March 2001, pp. 433–66.

19. A. Biswas, "The Recycling Cycle," *Journal of Public Policy & Marketing*, Spring 2000, pp. 93–105.

20. See B. G. Goff, J. S. Boles, D. N. Bellenger, and C. Stojack, "The Influence of Salesperson Selling Behaviors on Customer Satisfaction with Products," *Journal of Retailing* 2 (1997), pp. 171–83.

21. V. Mittal, P. Kumar, and M. Tsiros, "Attribute-Level Performance, Satisfaction, and Behavioral Intentions over Time," *Journal of Marketing*, April 1999, pp. 88–101; and R. J. Slotegraff and J. J. Inman, "Longitudinal Shifts in the Drivers of Satisfaction with Product Quality," *Journal of Marketing Research*, August 2004, pp. 269–80.

22. See, e.g., A. S. Mattila, "The Impact of Cognitive Inertia on Post-consumption Evaluation Processes," *Journal of the Academy of Marketing Science* 31, no. 3 (2003), pp. 287–99.

23. See, e.g., K. E. Clow, D. L. Kurtz, J. Ozment, and B. S. Ong, "The Antecedents of Consumer Expectations of Services," *Journal of Services Marketing* 4 (1997), pp. 230–48.

24. See J. Ozment and E. A. Morash, "The Augmented Service Offering for Perceived and Actual Service Quality," *Journal of the Academy of Marketing Science,* Fall 1994, pp. 352–63; and G. B. Voss, A. Parasuraman, and D. Grewal, "The Roles of Price, Performance, and Expectations in Determining Satisfaction in Service Exchanges," *Journal of Marketing,* October 1998, pp. 48–61.

25. See, e.g., C. P. Bebko, "Service Intangibility and Its Impact on Customer Expectations," *Journal of Services Marketing* 14, no. 1 (2000), pp. 9–26; B. Bickart and N. Schwartz, "Service Experiences and Satisfaction Judgments," *Journal of Consumer Psychology* 11, no. 1 (2001), pp. 29–41; D. M. Szymanski and D. H. Henard, "Customer Satisfaction," *Journal of the Academy of Marketing Science,* Winter 2001, pp. 16–35; J. C. Sweeney and G. N. Soutar, "Consumer Perceived Value," *Journal of Retailing* 77 (2001), pp. 203–20; P. K. Kopalle and D. R. Lehmann, "Strategic Management of Expectations," *Journal of Marketing Research,* August 2001, pp. 386–94; J. Wirtz and A. Mattila, "Exploring the Role of Alternative Perceived Performance Measures and Needs-Congruency in the Customer Satisfaction Process," *Journal of Consumer Psychology* 11, no. 3 (2001), pp. 181–92; E. Garbarino and M. S. Johnson, "Effects of Consumer Goals on Attribute Weighting, Overall Satisfaction, and Product Usage," *Psychology & Marketing,* September 2001, pp. 929–49; and M. Heitmann, D. R. Lehmann, and A. Herrmann, "Choice Goal Attainment and Decision and Consumption Satisfaction," *Journal of Marketing Research,* May 2007, pp. 234–50.

26. S. M. Keaveney, "Customer Switching Behavior in Service Industries," *Journal of Marketing,* April 1995, pp. 71–82. See also D. Grace and A. O'Cass, "Attributions of Service Switching," *Journal of Services Marketing* 14, no. 4 (2001), pp. 300–21; V. Mittal, J. M. Katrichis, and P. Kumar, "Attribute Performance and Customer Satisfaction over Time," *Journal of Services Marketing* 15, no. 5 (2001), pp. 343–56; C. de Matos, J. Henrique, C. Rossi, "Service Recovery Paradox," *Journal of Service Research,* August 2007, pp. 66–77; and S. Anderson, L. K. Pearo, and S. K. Widener, "Drivers of Service Satisfaction," *Journal of Service Research,* May 2008, pp. 365–81.

27. See, e.g., S. Taylor, "The Effects of Filled Waiting Time and Service Provider Control over the Delay on Evaluations of Service," *Journal of the Academy of Marketing Science,* Winter 1995, pp. 38–48; and M. K. Hui, M. V. Thakor, and R. Gill, "The Effect of Delay Type and Service Stage on Consumers' Reactions to Waiting," *Journal of Consumer Research,* March 1998, pp. 469–79.

28. V. Mittal, W. T. Ross, Jr., and P. M. Baldsare, "The Asymmetric Impact of Negative and Positive Attribute-Level Performance on Overall Satisfaction and Repurchase Levels," *Journal of Marketing,* January 1998, pp. 33–47. See also G. J. Gaeth et al., "Consumers' Attitude Change across Sequences of Successful and Unsuccessful Product Usage," *Marketing Letters,* no. 1 (1997), pp. 41–53.

29. I. E. Swan and L. J. Combs, "Product Performance and Consumer Satisfaction: A New Concept," *Journal of Marketing,* April 1976, pp. 25–33.

30. See H. Mano and R. L. Oliver, "Assessing the Dimensionality and Structure of the Consumption Experience," *Journal of Consumer Research,* December 1993, pp. 451–66; and L. W. Turley and D. L. Bolton, "Measuring the Affective Evaluations of Retail Service Environments," *Journal of Professional Services Marketing* 19, no. 1 (1999), pp. 31–44. See also S. M. Nowlis, N. Mandel, and D. B. McCabe, "The Effect of a Delay between Choice and Consumption on Consumption Enjoyment," *Journal of Consumer Research,* December 2004, pp. 502–10; and R. D. Raggio, and J. Folse, "Gratitude Works," *Journal of the Academy of Marketing Science* 37 (2009), pp. 455–69.

31. B. B. Holloway and S. E. Beatty, "Satisfiers and Dissatisfiers in the Online Environment," *Journal of Service Research* 10, no. 4 (2008), pp. 347–64.

32. H. Evanschitzky et al., "E-satisfaction," *Journal of Retailing* 80 (2004), pp. 239–47.

33. R. Sousa and C. A. Voss, "Service Quality in Multichannel Services Employing Virtual Channels," *Journal of Service Research,* May 2006, pp. 356–71.

34. See., e.g., J. Singh, "A Typology of Consumer Dissatisfaction Response Styles," *Journal of Retailing,* Spring 1990, pp. 57–97; J. Singh, "Voice, Exit, and Negative Word-of-Mouth Behaviors," *Journal of the Academy of Marketing Science,* Winter 1990, pp. 1–15; K. Gronhaug and O. Kvitastein, "Purchases and Complaints," *Psychology & Marketing,* Spring 1991, pp. 21–35; and S. W. Kelley and M. A. Davis, "Antecedents to Customer Expectations for Service Recovery," *Journal of the Academy of Marketing Science,* Winter 1994, pp. 52–61; M. A. Jones, D. L. Mothersbaugh, and S. E. Beatty, "Switching Barriers and Repurchase Intentions in Services," *Journal of Retailing* 76, no. 2 (2000), pp. 259–74; M. A. Jones and J. Suh, "Transaction-Specific Satisfaction and Overall Satisfaction," *Journal of Services Marketing* 14, no. 2 (2000), pp. 147–59; J. Lee, J. Lee, and L. Feick, "The Impact of Switching Costs on the Customer Satisfaction-Loyalty Link," *Journal of Services Marketing* 15, no. 1 (2001), pp. 35–48; and I. Roos, B. Edvardsson, and A. Gustafsson, "Customer Switching Patterns in Competitive and Noncompetitive Service Industries," *Journal of Service Research,* February 2004, pp. 256–71.

35. See also S. P. Brown and R. F. Beltramini, "Consumer Complaining and Word-of-Mouth Activities," in *Advances in Consumer Research,* vol. 16, ed. T. K. Srull (Provo, UT: Association for Consumer Research, 1989), pp. 9–11; and J. E. Swan and R. L. Oliver, "Postpurchase Communications by Consumers," *Journal of Retailing,* Winter 1989, pp. 516–33.

36. J. Goodman and S. Newman, "Understanding Customer Behavior and Complaints," *Quality Progress,* January 2003, pp. 51–55. For additional research and statistics, visit www.tarp.com.

37. See, e.g., A. K. Smith and R. N. Bolton, "The Effect of Consumers' Emotional Responses to Service Failures on Their Recovery Effort Evaluations and Satisfaction Judgments," *Journal of the Academy of Marketing Science,* Winter 2002, pp. 5–23; N. N. Bechwati and M. Morrin, "Outraged Consumers," *Journal of Consumer Psychology* 13, no. 4 (2003), pp. 440–53; and R. Bougie, R. Pieters, and M. Zeelenberg, "Angry Customers Don't Come Back, They Get Back," *Journal of the Academy of Marketing Science,* Fall 2003, pp. 377–93.

38. I. M. Wetzer, M. Zeelenberg, and R. Pieters, "'Never Eat in That Restaurant, I Did!'" *Psychology & Marketing,* August 2007, pp. 661–80.

39. Thompson, "Interpreting Consumers."

40. See, e.g., C. Ayres, "Revenge Is Best Served Cold—on YouTube," *The Times,* July 22, 2009; and R. Sawhney, "Broken Guitar Has United Playing the Blues to the Tune of $180 Million," *Fast Company,* July 28, 2009.

41. See R. A. Spreng, G. D. Harrell, and R. D. Mackoy, "Service Recovery," *Journal of Services Marketing* 9, no. 1 (1995), pp. 15–23; and L. Dube and M. F. Maute, "Defensive Strategies for Managing Satisfaction and Loyalty in the Service Industry," *Psychology & Marketing,* December 1998, pp. 775–91. For an alternative view, see T. W. Andreassen, "From Disgust to Delight," *Journal of Service Research,* August 2001, pp. 39–49; G. Maxham II and R. G. Netemeyer, "A Longitudinal Study of Complaining Customers' Evaluations of Multiple Service Failures and Recovery Efforts," *Journal of Marketing,* October 2002, pp. 57–71; and S. Weun, S. E. Beatty, and M. A. Jones, "The Impact of Service Failure Severity on Service Recovery Evaluations and Post-Recovery Relationships," *Journal of Services Marketing* 18, no. 2 (2004), pp. 133–46.

42. A literature review and model is in N. Stephens and K. P. Gwinner, "Why Don't Some People Complain?" *Journal of the Academy of Marketing Science,* Summer 1998, pp. 172–89. See also A. L. Dolinsky et al., "The Role of Psychographic Characteristics as Determinants of Complaint Behavior," *Journal of Hospital Marketing* 2 (1998), pp. 27–51; E. G. Harris and J. C. Mowen, "The Influence of Cardinal-, Central-, and Surface-Level Personality Traits on Consumers' Bargaining and Complaining Behavior," *Psychology & Marketing,* November 2001, pp. 1115–85; C. Kim et al., "The Effect of Attitude and Perception on Consumer Complaint Intentions," *Journal of Consumer Marketing* 20, no. 4 (2003), pp. 352–71; J. C. Chebat, M. Davidow, and I. Codjovi, "Silent Voices," *Journal of Service Research,* May 2005, pp. 328–42; K. Bodey and D. Grace, "Contrasting 'Complainers' with 'Non-complainers' on Attitude Toward Complaining, Propensity to Complain, and Key Personality Characteristics," *Psychology & Marketing,* July 2007, pp. 579–94; and C. Orsingher, S. Valentini, and M. de Angelis, "A Meta-Analysis of Satisfaction with Complaint Handling in Services," *Journal of the Academy of Marketing Science* 38 (2010), pp. 169–86.

43. K. Patel, "How AT&T Plans to Lift Its Image Via Social Media," *Advertising Age,* June 21, 2010.

44. J. Strauss and D. J. Hill, "Consumer Complaints by E-Mail," *Journal of Interactive Marketing,* Winter 2001, pp. 63–73. See also A. S. Mattila and J. Wirtz, "Consumer Complaining to Firms," *Journal of Services Marketing* 18, no. 2 (2004), pp. 147–55.

45. See A. K. Smith, R. N. Bolton, and J. Wagner, "A Model of Customer Satisfaction with Service Encounters Involving Failure and Recovery," *Journal of Marketing Research,* August 1999, pp. 356–72; A. Palmer, R. Beggs, and C. Keown-McMullan, "Equity and Repurchase Intention Following Service Failure," *Journal of Services Marketing* 14, no. 6 (2000), pp. 513–28; A. S. Mattila, "The Effectiveness of Service Recovery in a Multi-Industry Setting," *Journal of Services Marketing* 15, no. 7 (2001), pp. 583–96; J. G. Maxham III and R. G. Netemeyer, "Modeling Customer Perceptions of Complaint Handling over Time," *Journal of Retailing* 78 (2002), pp. 239–52; M. Davidow, "Organizational Responses to

Customer Complaints," *Journal of Service Research,* February 2003, pp. 225–50; and C. Homburg and A. Furst, "How Organizational Complaint Handling Drives Customer Loyalty," *Journal of Marketing,* July 2005, pp. 95–114.

46. See C. Goodwin and I. Ross, "Consumer Evaluations of Response to Complaints," *Journal of Consumer Marketing,* Spring 1990, pp. 39–47; J. G. Blodgett, D. J. Hill, and S. S. Tax, "The Effects of Distributive, Procedural, and Interactional Justice on Postcomplaint Behavior," *Journal of Retailing* 2 (1997), pp. 185–210; and C. M. Voorhees, M. K. Brady, and D. M. Horowitz, "A Voice from the Silent Masses," *Journal of the Academy of Marketing Science* 34, no. 4 (2006), pp. 514–27.

47. P. Sellers, "What Customers Really Want," *Fortune,* June 4, 1990, pp. 58–62.

48. B. A. Sparks, G. L. Bradley, and V. J. Callan, "The Impact of Staff Empowerment and Communication Style on Customer Evaluations," *Psychology & Marketing,* August 1997, pp. 475–93.

49. See F. F. Reichheld, "Learning from Customer Defections," *Harvard Business Review,* March 1996, pp. 56–69. See also H. Estelami, "The Profit Impact of Consumer Complaint Solicitation across Market Conditions," *Journal of Professional Services Marketing* 20, no. 1 (1999), pp. 165–95; and N. A. Morgan, E. W. Anderson, and V. Mittal, "Understanding Firms' Customer Satisfaction Information Usage," *Journal of Marketing,* July 2005, pp. 131–51.

50. B. S. Bulik, "Brands Spotlight Customer Experience," *Advertising Age,* April 19, 2004, pp. 1, 14.

51. R. Liebowitz, "Putting Patients First," *Healthcare Executive,* July–August 2008, pp. 42–44.

52. T. O. Jones and W. E. Sasser Jr., "Why Satisfied Customers Defect," *Harvard Business Review,* November 1995, pp. 88–95; P. P. Leszczyc and H. J. P. Timmermans, "Store-Switching Behavior," *Marketing Letters,* no. 2 (1997), pp. 193–204; B. Mittal and W. M. Lassar, "Why Do Customers Switch?" *Journal of Services Marketing,* no. 3 (1998), pp. 177–94; and C. Homburg and A. Giering, "Personal Characteristics as Moderators of the Relationship between Customer Satisfaction and Loyalty," *Psychology & Marketing,* January 2001, pp. 43–66.

53. See V. Mittal and W. Kamakura, "Satisfaction, Repurchase Intent, and Repurchase Behavior," *Journal of Marketing Research,* February 2001, pp. 131–42; and M. Chandrashekaran et al., "Satisfaction Strength and Customer Loyalty," *Journal of Marketing Research,* February 2007, pp. 153–63.

54. For a discussion of switching costs and repurchase intentions, see Jones, Mothersbaugh, and Beatty, "Switching Barriers and Repurchase Intentions in Services"; P. G. Patterson and T. Smith, "A Cross-Cultural Study of Switching Barriers and Propensity to Stay with Service Providers," *Journal of Retailing* 79 (2003), pp. 107–20; T. A. Burnham, J. K. Frels, and V. Mahajan, "Consumer Switching Costs," *Journal of the Academy of Marketing Science,* Spring 2003, pp. 109–26; and M. A. Jones et al., "The Positive and Negative Effects of Switching Costs on Relational Outcomes," *Journal of Service Research,* May 2007, pp. 335–55.

55. J. Jacoby and D. B. Kyner, "Brand Loyalty versus Repeat Purchasing Behavior," *Journal of Marketing Research,* February 1973, pp. 1–9. See also S. Rundle-Thiele and M. M. Mackay,

"Assessing the Performance of Brand Loyalty Measures," *Journal of Services Marketing* 15, no. 7 (2001), pp. 529–46; A. Chaudhuri and M. B. Holbrook, "The Chain of Effects from Brand Trust and Brand Affect to Brand Performance," *Journal of Marketing,* April 2001, pp. 81–93; C. F. Curasi and K. N. Kennedy, "From Prisoners to Apostles," *Journal of Services Marketing* 16, no. 4 (2002), pp. 322–41; and V. Liljander and I. Roos, "Customer-Relationship Levels," *Journal of Services Marketing* 16, no. 7 (2002), pp. 593–614.

56. See, e.g., R. G. Javalgi and C. R. Moberg, "Service Loyalty," *Journal of Services Marketing* 3 (1997), pp. 165–79.

57. S. Fournier, "Consumers and Their Brands," *Journal of Consumer Research,* March 1998, p. 355.

58. See E. Garbarino and M. S. Johnson, "The Different Roles of Satisfaction, Trust, and Commitment in Customer Relationships," *Journal of Marketing,* April 1999, pp. 70–87; J. Singh and D. Sirdeshmukh, "Agency and Trust Mechanisms in Consumer Satisfaction and Loyalty Judgments," *Journal of the Academy of Marketing Science,* Winter 2000, pp. 150–67; D. Sirdeshmukh, J. Singh, and B. Sabol, "Consumer Trust, Value, and Loyalty in Relational Exchanges," *Journal of Marketing,* January 2002, pp. 15–37; and C. B. Battacharya and S. Sen, "Consumer–Company Identification," *Journal of Marketing,* April 2003, pp. 76–88.

59. D. F. Spake et al., "Consumer Comfort in Service Relationships," *Journal of Service Research,* May 2003, pp. 316–32.

60. R. L. Olvier, R. T. Rust, and S. Varki, "Customer Delight," *Journal of Retailing* 3 (1997), pp. 311–36; and R. T. Rust and R. L. Oliver, "Should We Delight the Customer?" *Journal of the Academy of Marketing Science,* Winter 2000, pp. 86–94.

61. A. Finn, "Reassessing the Foundations of Customer Delight," *Journal of Service Research,* November 2005, pp. 103–16.

62. R. L. Oliver, "Whence Consumer Loyalty," *Journal of Marketing,* Special Issue 1999, pp. 33–44.

63. See J. Deighton, C. M. Henderson, and S. A. Neslin, "The Effects of Advertising on Brand Switching and Repeat Purchasing," *Journal of Marketing Research,* February 1994, pp. 28–43.

64. See D. Bejou and A. Palmer, "Service Failure and Loyalty," *Journal of Services Marketing* 1 (1998), pp. 7–22; and R. L. Hess Jr., S. Ganesan, and N. M. Klein, "Service Failure and Recovery," *Journal of the Academy of Marketing Science,* Spring 2003, pp. 127–45.

65. M. Johnson, G. M. Zinkham, and G. S. Ayala, "The Impact of Outcome, Competency, and Affect on Service Referral," *Journal of Services Marketing* 5 (1998), pp. 397–415.

66. E. W. Anderson, C. Fornell, R. T. Rust, "Customer Satisfaction, Productivity, and Profitability," *Marketing Science* 2 (1997), pp. 129–45.

67. F. F. Reichheld and W. E. Sasser, Jr., "Zero Defections," *Harvard Business Review,* September 1990, pp. 105–11; and R. Jacob, "Why Some Customers Are More Equal Than Others," *Fortune,* September 19, 1994, pp. 215–24. See also V. A. Zeithaml, "Service Quality, Profitablity, and the Economic Worth of Customers," *Journal of the Academy of Marketing Science,* Winter 2000, pp. 67–85.

68. For additional research examining these various outcomes, see T. Hennig-Thurau, K. P. Gwinner, and D. D. Gremler,

"Understanding Relationship Marketing Outcomes," *Journal of Service Research,* February 2002, pp. 230–47; P. C. Verhoef, P. H. Franses, and J. C. Hoekstra, "The Effect of Relational Constructs on Customer Referrals and Number of Services Purchased from a Multiservice Provider," *Journal of the Academy of Marketing Science* 30, no. 3 (2002), pp. 202–16; H. S. Bansal, P. G. Irving, and S. F. Taylor, "A Three-Component Model of Customer Commitment to Service Providers," *Journal of the Academy of Marketing Science* 32, no. 3 (2004), pp. 234–50; C. Homburg, N. Koschate, and W. D. Hoyer, "Do Satisfied Customers Really Pay More?" *Journal of Marketing,* April 2005, pp. 84–96; and K. Seiders, G. B. Voss, D. Grewal, and A. L. Godfrey, "Do Satisfied Customers Buy More?" *Journal of Marketing,* October 2005, pp. 26–43.

69. This insight based on F. F. Reichheld, "The One Number You Need to Grow," *Harvard Business Review,* December 2003, pp. 46–54; M. Anstead, "What's Missing When It Comes to Net Promoter," *Credit Union Journal,* March 30, 2009, p. 8; M. Creamer, "Do You Know Your Score?" *Advertising Age,* July 23, 2006, pp. 1, 24; T. L. Keiningham et al., "A Longitudinal Examination of Net Promoter and Firm Revenue Growth," *Journal of Marketing,* July 2007, pp. 39–51; A. Gigliotto et al., "NPS Not the Only Way," *Marketing News,* September 15, 2007, pp. 48–52; and C. Pasquale, "Closing the Customer Feedback Loop," *Harvard Business Review,* December 2009, pp. 43–47.

70. See S. Li, "Survival Analysis," *Marketing Research,* Fall 1995, pp. 17–23.

71. Reichheld and Sasser, "Zero Defections," p. 110.

72. See also S. Lingle, "How Much Is a Customer Worth?" *Bank Marketing,* August 1995, pp. 13–16.

73. E. Esfahani, "How to . . .. Get Tough with Bad Customers," *Business 2.0,* October 2004, p. 52.

74. See, e.g., T. Wagner, T. Hennig-Thurau, and T. Rudolph, "Does Customer Demotion Jeopardize Loyalty?" *Journal of Marketing,* May 2009, pp. 69–85.

75. See G. S. Day, "Managing Market Relationships," *Journal of the Academy of Marketing Science,* Winter 2000, pp. 24–30.

76. See the special issue on relationship marketing, *Journal of the Academy of Marketing Science,* Fall 1995; and G. E. Gengler and P. P. Leszczyc, "Using Customer Satisfaction Research for Relationship Marketing," *Journal of Direct Marketing,* Winter 1997, pp. 23–29.

77. L. Freeman, "Marketing the Market," *Marketing News,* March 2, 1998, p. 1. Other examples are in G. B. Voss and Z. G. Voss, "Implementing a Relationship Marketing Program," *Journal of Services Marketing* 11 (1997), pp. 278–98; B. G. Yovovich, "Scanners Reshape the Grocery Business," *Marketing News,* February 16, 1998, p. 1; and G. Brewer, "The Customer Stops Here," *Sales & Marketing Management,* March 1998, pp. 31–36.

78. L. L. Berry, "Relationship Marketing of Services," *Journal of the Academy of Marketing Science,* Fall 1995, pp. 236–45.

79. See N. Bendapudi and L. L. Berry, "Customers' Motivations for Maintaining Relationships with Service Providers," *Journal of Retailing* 1 (1997), pp. 15–37.

Chapter Eighteen   Postpurchase Processes, Customer Satisfaction, and Customer Commitment   643

80. C. Ashley et al., "Why Consumers Won't Relate," *Journal of Business Research,* July 2011, pp. 749–56.

81. J. Raymond, "Home Field Advantage," *American Demographics,* April 2001, pp. 34–36.

82. See G. Levin, "Marketers Flock to Loyalty Offers," *Advertising Age,* May 24, 1993, p. 13; C. Miller, "Rewards for the Best Customers," *Marketing News,* July 5, 1993, p. 1; J. Fulkerson, "It's in the Cards," *American Demographics,* July 1996, pp. 38–43; and J. Passingham, "Grocery Retailing and the Loyalty Card," *Journal of the Market Research Society,* January 1998, pp. 55–63. See also L. O'Brien and C. Jones, "Do Rewards Really Create Loyalty?" *Harvard Business Review,* May 1995, pp. 75–82; R. N. Bolton, P. K. Kannan, and M. D. Bramlett, "Implications of Loyalty Programs Membership and Service Experiences for Customer Retention and Value," *Journal of the Academy of Marketing Science,* Winter 2000, pp. 95–108; and A. W. Magi, "Share of Wallet in Retailing," *Journal of Retailing* 79 (2003), pp. 97–106.

83. See F. Rice, "The New Rules of Superlative Services," and P. Sellers "Keeping the Buyers," both in *Fortune,* Autumn–Winter 1993, pp. 50–53 and 56–58, respectively; and G. A. Conrad, G. Brown, and H. A. Harmon, "Customer Satisfaction and Corporate Culture," *Psychology & Marketing,* October 1997, pp. 663–74.

84. J. Holland and S. M. Baker, "Customer Participation in Creating Site Brand Loyalty," *Journal of Interactive Marketing,* Autumn 2001, pp. 34–45; R. E. Anderson and S. S. Srinivasan, "E-Satisfaction and E-Loyalty," *Psychology & Marketing,* February 2003, pp. 123–38; L. C. Harris and M. M. H. Goode, "The Four Levels of Loyalty and the Pivotal Role of Trust," *Journal of Retailing* 80 (2004), pp. 139–58.

85. J. Gummerus et al., "Customer Loyalty to Content-based Web Sites," *Journal of Services Marketing* 18, no. 3 (2004), pp. 175–86.

86. S. S. Srinivasan, R. Anderson, and K. Ponnavolu, "Customer Loyalty in E-commerce," *Journal of Retailing* 78 (2002), pp. 41–50.

Subject Index